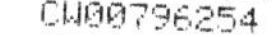

WHERE TO LIVE IN AUCKLAND

Published in New Zealand by Barbican Publishing Limited
PO Box 91572, Auckland
Phone: 64 9 376 4849
Fax: 64 9 376 4879
Email: info@wheretoliveinauckland.co.nz
Website: www.wheretolivebooks.com

ISBN 0-473-11366-X

Sources:

Recorded property sales
(years ending March 2005, 2006) – Quotable Value New Zealand

Population statistics
(2001 Census data) – Statistics New Zealand

Mosaic neigbourhood classification system 2002
supplied by PMP MICROMARKETING

Publisher	Stephen Hart
Associate publisher	James Hodgson
Editor	Sharon Newey
Contributing writers	Alice Leonard
	Billy Leonard
	Robyn Welsh
Photographers	Simon Young
	Marcel Tromp
	Max Hart
Additional Research	Belinda Hart
Design	Liesl Strauss
	Sid Roy
Imaging	Image Centre
Printing	PMP Print

Acknowledgments: Our sincere thanks and gratitude to the many industry sources, local authorities and individuals interviewed for this book. Special thanks to Quotable Value New Zealand, PMP MICROMARKETING and Statistics New Zealand for their invaluable contributions.

Thanks especially to The National Bank of New Zealand for their support.

Cover image: Perspective Apartments, Skyhome, Freemans Bay. Photographed by Tony Nyberg 021 137 0942. Marketed by Carla Pedersen 021 417 139.

Welcome to our neighbourhood

Orewa
Browns Bay
Albany
Mairangi Bay
Milford
Glenfield
Takapuna
Birkenhead
Auckland
Ponsonby
Parnell
Newton
St Heliers
Newmarket
Henderson
Mt Albert
Epsom
Remuera
Mt Roskill
Howick
Panmure
New Lynn
Onehunga
Penrose
Pakuranga
Otahuhu
Papatoetoe
Manukau
Manurewa
Papakura
Waiuku

INTRODUCTION

THE NEIGHBOURHOODS

Heraldhomes
Heraldhomes

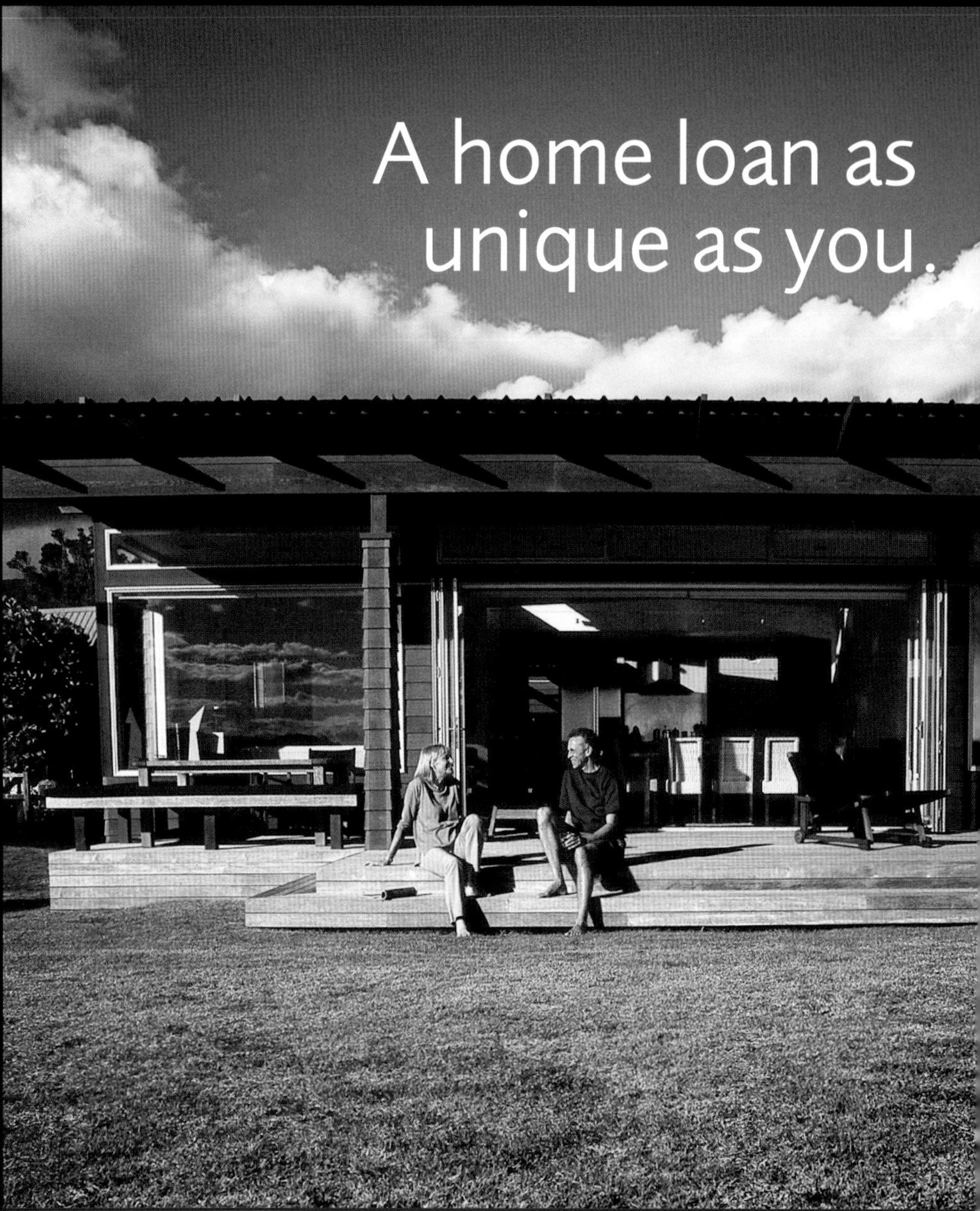
A home loan as
unique as you.

Buying and moving house is one of the most stressful times in your life, and buying property is one of the biggest investments you will make. To start you on your way, here is our guide to financing a home, looking for one and how you go about making it your own.

The content in this section is not provided by The National Bank. It was independently researched and written by *Where to Live in Auckland*. We believe that everyone wil find something of value in this guide, but inevitably it does not take into account your own individual personal circumstances. We recommend that you take professional advice before acting on the information.

Finance First

Buying a house is all about how much you can afford, or are willing to spend on a property. Most of us calmly and rationally set ourselves a budget - then end up spending more than we thought we would. Knowing how much you can or want to spend underpins all of the decisions you make about buying. It will determine how big the house can be, where it will be and in what condition. In some inner-city suburbs, however, unrenovated houses can sell for as much as their spruced-up neighbours, bought by people happy to have a blank canvas on which to create their own masterpiece of renovation.

Your pot of money will normally consist of a deposit - money you have saved up - and a mortgage. Under certain conditions, most banks will lend up to 90% of a house's registered value (banks will only lend a much lower portion on most apartments, however). If you are borrowing a high proportion of the purchase price, the bank may insist on mortgage protection insurance in the event of you losing your income for some reason - injury, death or redundancy.

Your bank will ask you to complete a budget summary showing income and expenses, to determine how much money they think you can comfortably afford to repay.

Banks can also provide you with a pre-purchase finance approval that will enable you to make offers on houses that are free of any finance condition clause, or let you bid comfortably at auction knowing how much you have to play with. Your ability to meet repayments is only one factor. The bank needs to be happy that the property being offered for security is satisfactory, so depending on the proportion of your loan, they may need a pre-purchase valuation. Pre-approval will speed up the processing of the actual mortgage once you have bought.

Visiting the Bank

In years gone by, there wasn't much choice about which lending institution to ask for a mortgage - it was the one where you did your day-to-day banking. That's no longer the case. You can shop around, and banks are always advertising special rates or conditions in the hope of netting new mortgage customers. Chances are, if you have your mortgage with one bank, you will take your day-to-day banking with you. Some banks insist on it anyway.

So as well as checking out the home loans your own bank has to offer, research the rest too. Compare not only interest rates and types of loans available but also charges for processing a home loan and other conditions. For example, can you make lump sum payments on a fixed interest loan without incurring penalties? Also consider which bank you feel best about - which one has given you good service and good advice.

Types of Loans

Consider which type of loan suits your ability to pay, and your lifestyle.

Table: this is the more common type of loan which spreads regular payments over the term of the loan, which only change when the prevailing interest rate changes. Initially, a bigger portion is made up of interest and a smaller portion of the principal, but that reverses over time. The benefit of this type of loan is that it lets you budget on a set amount each fortnight or month.

Reducing: this type of loan starts off high but reduces with each payment. Each repayment includes the same amount of principal. If you can cope with the higher initial payments, it's rewarding to see your principal steadily reducing. The benefit is that over the term of the loan, you will have paid less in interest than with a table mortgage.

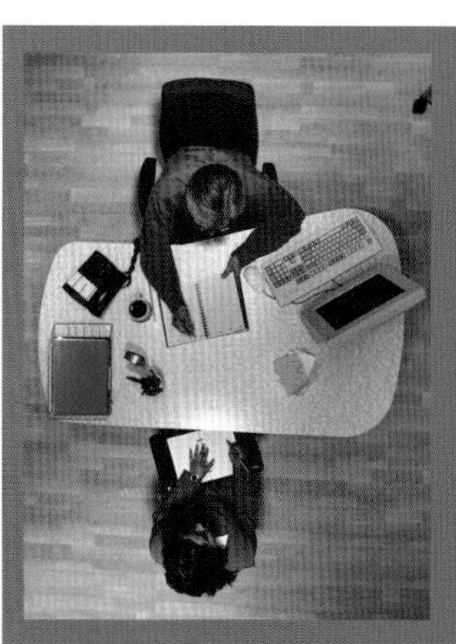

One-off cost

When doing your budget, don't forget the one-off costs of buying a house. These might include:

- legal fees
- a valuation
- a builder's, engineer's or architect's report
- moving costs (not just the truck, but also reconnections for phone, Sky TV etc)
- insurance (house and possibly mortgage protection)
- bank administration fees
- urgent maintenance

Does the house need any urgent renovations or repairs before you move in? Talk to the bank about extra finance for these.

Interest only: some lending institutions will allow you to pay just the interest and none of the principal, but usually only for a short time and under certain circumstances.

Mixed: many banks offer essentially tailor-made loans that suit your particular circumstances, made up of a mix of different types of loan and interest. Check with your bank about this option.

The Types of Interest Rates

Floating interest: this is the more commonly used, and allows you to benefit from any reductions in the floating interest rate. Conversely, your payments will increase if the rate goes up. Floating interest rates have been relatively low and steady recently.

Fixed: this is when the interest rate is fixed for a certain term (anything from six months to several years) and is not affected by fluctuations in the floating rate. Depending on the economy, these may be offered at slightly below or slightly above the floating rate. You gain the benefit if the floating rate stays above the fixed rate or, better still, rises (although if the floating rate or current fixed rates are much higher when your term finishes, you will need to cope with the sudden increase in your payments). In more volatile times, however, you risk the floating rate dropping below your once-attractive fixed rate. Lump sum payments usually can't be made on fixed interest loans without incurring penalties.

Mixed: a combination may be best so that you can benefit from the advantages of both floating and fixed. Any lump sum payments can be made on your floating mortgage. Once the term of the fixed-interest loan is up, you can either negotiate another fixed term or put it in with the floating interest loan.

The term of the loan will affect the payments. The longer the term, the lower the payments will be but at the end of the term you would have ended up paying more interest.

You can also choose the frequency of payments, the options usually being fortnightly or monthly, whichever suits your income and payment structure.

Going Shopping - the Area

Once you have done your mortgage homework, you can start looking for your perfect house. Read about the areas you have identified as having potential in the following chapters. Are they likely to include the type of house you prefer? Will you have like-minded people as your neighbours? Does the area have the amenities you need - shops, schools, parks? Does it match your budget? Check the commuting distance to work or public transport routes. What sort of setting would you like - quiet cul-de-sac, busy urban, established, new?

Drive around the areas, maybe refining your choices into certain streets.

The House

What type of house do you want or need?

The style (villa, bungalow, 1970s family home, ex-state, contemporary etc) will determine not only the general characteristics but also maintenance levels and costs. Are you prepared to renovate, or do you just want to arrive and unpack?

If you're buying the house with someone else, discuss everything in detail. Is storage for the windsurfer more important than a dishwasher? Work it out. Buying a house is stressful enough, without having it threaten your relationship.

You may like to make up a score card and use one for each house, so you don't have to rely on memory when you have been to numerous open homes.

Split your list of requirements into two - the must-haves and the would-likes. Think about the following variables and rate them according to your preferences:

- How many bedrooms? Do you also need a study or home office, or will a desk in the corner of the family room do?
- Do you need a guest room?
- How many bathrooms? Would an extra toilet be handy?
- A separate laundry? Or will a cupboard or back of the garage do?
- How many living areas? Formal and casual, or will the one do?
- Formal dining?
- Do you prefer open-plan living?
- Off-street parking? A garage? Double? Internal access?
- Aspect: do you want living areas to be north-facing for the sun?
- Is outdoor living important? Should it flow well from internal living areas?
- How big a garden do you need, if any? Big enough for a kids' cricket game, or is a small courtyard fine? Does it need to be fully fenced for the dog or toddlers?
- What sort of mod-cons do you want? Dishwasher? Filtered water tap? Gas fireplace? Gas heating? Underfloor bathroom heating?
- What level of security? Alarm? Video intercom?
- How much storage do you need, or are you going to be brave and have a big clean-out between moves?

The Hidden Things

Many faults can't be seen with a cruise through the open home. If you are not going to use a builder to inspect the property, watch for:

- level floors and sound piling
- rot in the weatherboards and timber joinery
- insulation
- water pressure - turn on the taps and flush the toilet

- noisy neighbours
- dampness (smell and/or mildew)
- leaks

In light of the leaking building syndrome, a building inspection on any plaster-clad house would be extremely sensible.

Armed with your wish list, start looking at the houses advertised - check the *New Zealand Herald's HeraldHomes* section and Sunday property pages, *Property Extra* and *Property Press*. Peruse local real estate agency windows. Check out websites - most real estate agencies put all listings on the internet. Ring agents and visit open homes to see what type of houses are available. Start to consolidate your ideas. Be prepared for any eventuality - you may fall in love with the first house you see, or it may take months to find the perfect home. Make sure you visit the property at least twice before you buy it, preferably at different times of the day.

Buying Methods

Selling by negotiation is the traditional way of marketing a house, where an asking price is advertised. In a competitive market when demand outstrips supply, auctions and tenders are more common. In a volatile market, it may be difficult to assess a house's worth so an auction or tender allows the upper limit to be left wide open.

Some houses are marketed by negotiation but without an asking price. After one or two open homes, the agent may give an indication of value - this may be a price range or it may just be the bottom limit.

For a buyer, these "no-price marketing" methods make it harder to know if you can afford a particular house. You have to do more homework, look at comparative recent sales in the area (ask the agent for a list of these) and visit lots of open homes. A house's CV (capital valuation) may be of some help. Even if it is out of date, you may be able to compare the CVs of recent sales with the actual sale price or ask real estate agents how much houses in the area are selling for in comparison to CV. Then you can apply that formula to the CVs of houses you are interested in.

If you are interested in a house being sold privately, make sure your lawyer thoroughly checks any contracts before you sign. If you don't feel comfortable negotiating directly with the homeowner, ask a friend to help.

Sale by Negotiation

Agents have standard contracts for making offers on a house. You may want your lawyer to check it over and help you with the wording of any conditional clauses you might add. Remember that the real estate agent is working for the vendor, so it is best to get independent advice.

A conditional contract is one which gives you a set time, say one or two weeks, to sort out various things. Common conditions may be:

- finance (so you can organise a mortgage) - make sure you stipulate that the finance is satisfactory to you, not just the bank
- a valuation (which will probably be part of the mortgage requirement anyway)
- a title search, checking for easements, covenants or restrictions
- a Land Information Memorandum (LIM) from council. The LIM is used to highlight anything that exists on the property that may not be permitted. If there's a garage or a deck that's higher than one metre from the ground on the property but no

permits showing for these on the LIM, alarm bells should ring. Once you have bought the property, the onus shifts on to you to remedy these problems

- a satisfactory builder's or engineer's report
- sale of the buyer's own house

The vendor may add a "cash-out" clause to any conditional offer, which means that if they receive an attractive back-up offer, they give the first buyer a set time (usually about three days) to satisfy the conditions.

If not all of the conditions are satisfied, it doesn't mean you should walk away from the deal. If you are still keen on the house but, say, the deck has no permit, you may renegotiate a drop in the sale price in compensation or add a clause that the vendor has to remedy the situation before settlement.

The offer will specify the chattels to be left in the house (curtains, dishwasher, etc) and a settlement or completion date, which is when you pay over all the money in exchange for the key. A common time frame is six weeks, although it can be shorter or much, much longer (called a delayed settlement). If you need to sell your existing house, a delayed settlement may be more attractive to the vendor than an offer conditional on you selling, but will still give you the time to take action.

Once your offer is drawn up, it is presented to the seller (or vendor in real estate speak) and they will usually counter-offer. More counter-offers may follow and the negotiations will either be successful or fail.

Auctions

Auctions normally follow a fairly high-profile advertising campaign that lasts three or four weeks. You may not have all of this time, however, to make up your mind, as some houses sell before auction. A buyer wants to guarantee they are going to get the house of their dreams, so will offer an amount that's too good to refuse.

On the other hand, beware of the agent who tells you something is going to sell before auction in order to prise an offer out of you - this may mean that they have identified you as the only real bidder in the running, but still want you to believe you are in a competitive situation. Or agents may use pre-auction offers to assess the sort of money people are prepared to pay to help guide the vendors on a reserve price, but then still take the property to auction.

If you are serious about a house that is being sold by auction (or tender), make sure you let the agent know. Don't be coy, or you may find out the property has already been sold and you've missed out on the chance.

To buy at auction you need to be sure of your finance. An auction sale is cash and unconditional and you must front up a cheque for 10% of the sale price straight after the bidding. This means doing any homework on the property beforehand, which can involve some costs - for example, if you want a LIM or a valuer's report. Real estate agents selling auction properties will often prepare a pack of information for you, including such things as a copy of the title and maybe even a LIM. They'll provide a copy of the sale contract with the usual details such as the settlement date, etc, for you and/or your lawyer to peruse.

The actual auction is an emotion-charged and fast-paced affair. You might want to go to another auction beforehand, just to watch what happens. Try to be calm. Go along with your top bid in mind and be prepared to stick to it. Be confident and firm - it will help psyche out the other bidders. If you don't feel confident at all, an agent can bid on your behalf.

The vendors would have set a reserve, which is the minimum price they want for the property. A property cannot be sold "under the hammer" until the bidding has reached that reserve. Once the bidding has reached the reserve, the auctioneer will say something like "this property is now on the market", which lets you know that from now on, the top bid wins and that the buyer is committed.

If the bidding doesn't reach the reserve, the property is "passed in" and normally negotiations will ensue between the vendor and the top bidder.

Tenders

A tender is like an auction but without the public bidding. Essentially, you fill out an offer document that states a price. On the day the tender closes, all of the tender offers are opened and the most acceptable (if any) chosen.

For a vendor, a tender gives the benefit of privacy - the sale price isn't shouted out in an auction room. They also don't have to accept any of the tenders. If they are not happy with the price or conditions, they will ask the agent to negotiate with one or more of the potential buyers to see if an agreement can be reached. They normally have five days to do this.

One buyer may be so keen, they will offer a good deal more than the others, so the vendor gets a premium price. This is a common characteristic of tenders.

It's trickier for a buyer, because you have no idea what level your competitors are at. The idea is to do your homework, study the market, get advice from a valuer and give it your best shot if you are serious about buying. Unlike other methods of selling, you probably won't get a chance to make another offer and you need to ask yourself how you would feel if you missed out by a thousand dollars.

One advantage is that you are able to ask that certain conditions be added to the tender offer, much like a negotiated sale - but remember that a cleaner offer is always more attractive to the vendor. Most tenders are "closed" or "blind", where buyers cannot be told what the other bids are.

Buying Land

Usable land is scarce in the more established parts of Auckland. A good percentage of subdividable sections have already been cut up and infill housing is now a feature of many suburbs.

When buying land, there are certain things to check. Make sure there is a clear title to the property. If it has only just been subdivided, the paperwork may still be going through council, so any offer should be conditional to clear title.

Check that there are no covenants or caveats on the land, or if there are, that you are happy with them. If it's someone's back yard you are buying, they may have lodged a caveat on the title stipulating that you can't build within so many metres of their boundary, or that your new house must be designed in such a way as to not encroach on their privacy. In a new subdivision, there may be covenants restricting the types of building materials or the style of house you may use, in order to keep the neighbourhood up to a certain standard.

Many developers will offer land and design packages, where you have a choice of sections and a choice of house designs. They then build for you and will often offer their own finance packages. Although these sorts of deals are standard, always have your own lawyer check the contract. You might want to add a penalty clause for completion, for example, if the developer doesn't build the house in the time they say they will, they incur financial penalties.

Your Lawyer

Whenever property is bought or sold, the ownership has to be legally transferred - known as conveyancing. This is normally carried out by a solicitor, either your regular one or there are specialist property and conveyancing groups set up, often offering set fees.

Conveyancing includes things like searching and approving the title, checking the sale agreement, making sure the mortgage documents are in order and properly signed, explaining the documents to you and registering them.

The cost of conveyancing will vary depending on the complexity of each deal, and may range from $600 to $1200.

Settlement Day

Before settlement day, you are entitled to a pre-settlement inspection of the property. This is to check that the property is in the condition agreed upon and that nothing has happened to it between signing the contract and moving in - like any sort of damage, or removal of stated chattels.

It's best to do this as close to settlement as possible, preferable once the previous owners have moved out, although this may be tricky. This allows you to see the condition of the property much more clearly.

If you do notice a problem, inform your lawyer, who will inform the vendor's lawyer. Your lawyer may decide to withhold some of the money until the problem is remedied.

Once the funds have gone through to the vendor (often electronically these days), you get the key and move in. Break open the champagne and congratulate yourself on your new home.

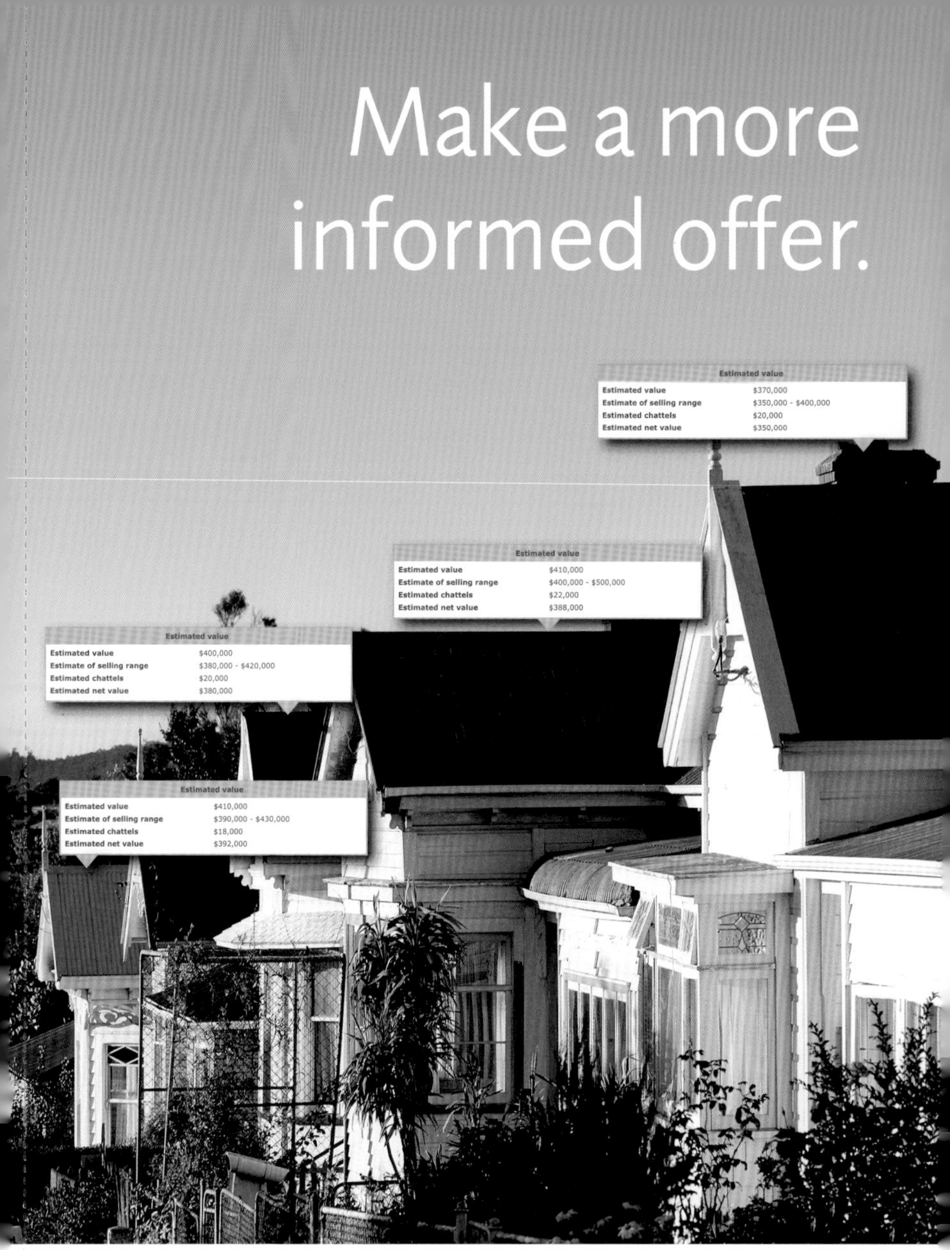

Get a free QV E-Valuer report with a pre-approved home loan from The National Bank and feel confident about your property choices. See over for details.

It can take time to find the right home – which is why we can offer **a free, no obligation, six-month home loan pre-approval** before you apply. It gives you the confidence of knowing how much you can afford right from the start, and the time to find your dream home.

And when you have found it, we want you to feel confident when making an offer on it. This is where a QV E-Valuer report can help; giving you an instant estimate of what a house is worth based on what nearby comparable properties have sold for.

What is an E-Valuer report?

A QV E-Valuer report provides an estimate of the current market value for your selected property. It also displays up to ten comparable sales on a map. For further details of QV's reports please visit www.qv.co.nz

Get your pre-approved home loan and free QV E-Valuer report today.

To arrange your pre-approved home loan and to get your **free** QV E-Valuer report, simply tear out this page and present it at any branch of The National Bank or to one of our Mobile Mortgage Managers who can visit you whenever you like. Just call us on **0800 185 185**.

The National Bank
The thoroughbred among banks

OFFER EXPIRES 30 JUNE 2008. OUR LENDING CRITERIA AND A HOME LOAN APPLICATION FEE OF UP TO $500 APPLY. FOR BORROWING OVER 80% OF A PROPERTY'S VALUE, A LOW EQUITY PREMIUM ON A GRADUATED SCALE WILL APPLY. CONDITIONS APPLY TO HOME LOAN PRE-APPROVALS. QV E-VALUER REPORTS ARE ONLY AVAILABLE FOR RESIDENTIAL PURPOSES AND ARE NOT AVAILABLE IN ALL CIRCUMSTANCES.
THE NATIONAL BANK OF NEW ZEALAND, PART OF ANZ NATIONAL BANK LIMITED.

Bank Use Only

Process home loan pre-approval and provide customer with E-Valuer voucher.

Send this to: E-Valuer, Branch 869, Auckland.

RM number: ____________ Customer Name: ____________

Voucher Number: ____________

Bank Staff Name: ____________

WTLIA 2007

Gez Johns examines the popularity of property as an investment medium, and finds that whilst its appeal lies in the fact you can see and touch it, it's what you can't see that defines its profitability.

Maybe it's an ancestral thing, but in the UK and across most of Western Europe, if you own and rent out even a second property, not to mention a third, fourth or fifth, then you're a landlord; a home-provider – more often than not viewed suspiciously by those you house as a direct descendent of the feudal aristocracy, and begrudgingly respected as such. Here, on the other side of the globe though, it would appear we care little for such medieval fantasy. Own a second property in New Zealand or Australia, and first and foremost you're an investor, whose first duty of care is to protect the income-producing ability of your asset.

Nevertheless as the popularity of property as an investment vehicle has increased, so too has the scrutiny under which it has fallen. Intense Government regulation today dictates that those who overlook the non-financial responsibilities of being a landlord do so at their peril. Good landlording is therefore every bit as important as making good investment decisions ... but more on this later.

With so many investment options available to us, and with New Zealand hardly boasting the world's most attractive mortgage rates, why property? Undoubtedly the primary reason we take property so seriously here is that, without the safety mat of a state pension, it represents the most understandable and accessible means of providing for the future. To many, property represents much less of a lottery than the sharemarket simply because you can, if you want, see your asset every day. Perhaps it's also a modern twist on the long-held quarter-acre dream.

Although many will invest in rental properties as part of a well-researched financial strategy, others have done so out of fear – a knee-jerk reaction to the warnings of the nation's self-proclaimed property experts; that those who don't invest in property now will be left with nothing. This was certainly a key driver behind the latest property boom, which unlike previous periods of sharp house price growth, stretched beyond Auckland to become a national phenomenon.

While the property market has now cooled, for the past couple of years the incessant rise in prices from Kaitaia to Invercargill became the sole focus of the nation's headline writers. For Aucklanders, owning a second property anywhere became as de rigueur as walking a small dog down Ponsonby Rd or tailgating down the north-western motorway.

Such increased competition for housing stock has, however, led new investors to parts of the country they may never have considered, let alone visited, with one-mill North Island towns such as Tokoroa competing with the newly-monikered Costa Del Invercargill as the most unlikely of hotspots. But for all this geographical diversity, property investment opportunities still remain closer to home; they're just not quite as obvious as they used to be.

After – and indeed during – every period of growth, we're told that this is the end of the road for the property market: that prices will crash and the market implode. Yet despite the hype there is no firm evidence to back this up. Indeed, with a worst-case scenario of property values dipping temporarily by 5 - 10%, bargain hunting is simply not that easy. Worse news still for investors is the fact that market rents have steadfastly refused to budge significantly during the past few years, despite the increase in sales prices, thereby reducing the return on investment.

So why does property remain the first choice investment vehicle for so many? The answer, as the huge number of Australian buyers still snapping up apartments off the plans, will tell you, is that on a global scale Auckland's prices still compare very favourably

Yields and Taxes: The Hidden Advantages

At their most basic level, investments of all types are rated on the yield that they offer: essentially the return on investment before tax. To calculate the yield of any prospective property purchase, simply divide the yearly total value of the rental income by the purchase price and multiply by 100. However, a good tip here is not to simply multiply the weekly rent by 52, since periods of vacancy between tenancies are inevitable, particularly in a city with such a transient population as Auckland's.

For example, the average price for a three-bedroom house in Mt Roskill today is around $395,000, with a median weekly rental of $365. Catering for three weeks of vacancy, the yield right now for this sort of property would be less than 5% ($365 x 49 / $395,000). This perhaps doesn't sound too promising, particularly with interest rates sitting comfortably above this.

However, as a new investor, what you should really be interested in is the net return, which takes into account all incomings, outgoings and numerous tax advantages, and will allow you to work out whether or not the property will be "cashflow positive" after tax – in other words, if it will return more income than you pay out on it.

At the heart of these tax savings is how you structure the ownership of your property The most heavily favoured option today is to detach yourself from personal ownership and place investment properties in what is known as an LAQC, or Loss Attributing Qualifying Company.

As a means of asset and income protection the full explanation as to how these work is unsurprisingly complicated, however the potted version goes something like this: An LAQC will allow losses from the rental property to be allocated to its individual shareholders (ie, you) to offset against personal income thus minimising the amount of tax you would have to pay.

There are obviously many specific rules and regulations involved in setting up a structure such as this, therefore it is vital to consult an accountant who specialises in asset planning.

Just as much a friend to investors is depreciation In the words of leading financial expert and author, Margaret Lomas: "In New Zealand you may make a range of depreciation claims on your tax return which serve to create a loss which is on-paper only. These on-paper claims give you back some of the tax you have paid on your income, often more than you need to close the gap between income and expenses on your property."

To maximise the depreciation you can claim it is vital to carry out what is known as a fu chattels apportionment, which breaks down the individual worth of each component of a property, from the letterbox to the bedroom carpet. According to IRD guidelines, these different assets depreciate from a ta perspective at different rates, thus affording the canny investor the opportunity to see ta as a friend, rather than an enemy.

While gaining intimate knowledge of New Zealand's depreciation schedule before ever thinking about buying an investment propert might seem to equate to learning to run before you can walk, forewarned is forearmed. To go about investing profitably, you need to hav carried out plenty of research and have your ownership structure tailored to your particular situation in advance. This knowledge can mean the difference between owning an income-producing asset and losing a lot of money.

Where, Oh Where?

So, having armed yourself with enough background knowledge of the "hows" and "whys", what about the "wheres"?

One common misconception surrounding property investment is that cashflow and capital gain are mutually exclusive. That is to say that properties bought for their ability to produce income in the short term will not serve a second, more long-term purpose. Of course, real estate in prime Auckland locations such as Herne Bay or Parnell is more likely to appreciate in perceived value than housing stock in the lower socio-economic areas during boom periods. However, to borrow a nautical analogy befitting of the City of Sails, a rising tide lifts all boats.

Statistics released by the National Property Data Centre reveal that in the 10 year period between 1994-2004, the South Auckland suburbs of Otara, Mangere and Otahuhu witnessed respective capital growth rates of 116%, 101% and 86%.

On the supposition that you're approaching the concept of property investment primarily as a means of achieving financial security, then perhaps the most important fact to remember is that you are not buying a house that you yourself would be happy to live in, rather one that is best suited to the needs or expectations of your target tenant.

As a first-time investor, chances are you will want to be investing in a property that is cashflow positive, as opposed to one that will require you to top up the mortgage significantly from your personal income. Unless you find a property with a twist, such as home and incomes or purpose-built student accommodation, this would inevitably lead you to the less salubrious parts of town, where prices are more affordable and returns are higher. The associated baggage that comes with that is, however, much heavier – tenants who may not pay and who may not be as house-proud as you. Which brings us back full circle to the importance of being an earnest landlord.

The Landlord, the Judge and the Tenant

If owning and renting out a property in certain Auckland suburbs, while theoretically appealing, is still pushing you a little too far beyond your comfort zone, then it could be time to call in the professionals. For a negotiable fee of less than 10% of the weekly rent, you can sign your feudal role over to a modern-day squire: the property manager. A professional property manager will take responsibility for the day-to-day running of the property, its profitability, its maintenance, and most importantly, its tenants.

However, if the idea of being a hands-on landlord is what attracted you to property as an investment vehicle in the first place, then you are going to need to familiarise yourself very quickly with the RTA: the Residential Tenancies Act. The RTA, a copy of which is available from Tenancy Services at www.dbh.govt.nz, outlines the responsibilities of both landlord and tenant ... of which there are more than you might imagine. Failure to adhere to these can lead rapidly to the landlord's worst nightmare: The Tenancy Tribunal. "If you've seen the TV show, Judge Judy, it runs a bit like that," explains leading Auckland property manager Pat Allen. "Adjudicators are a little less aggressive than her ... but not as humorous."

Although this may all sound a little scary, it doesn't have to be. Making friends with your tenants is ill-advised, as is letting to friends and family, since emotional attachment will more often than not distract you from the reason why you've invested in the first place: to make money.

Nevertheless, ensuring your tenants are confident in your, or your property manager's, ability as a landlord, through responding promptly to requests for maintenance or accommodating a few individual quirks, will help you retain your tenants for longer and at market rate rent. This, in turn, will keep supplying your investments with the lifeblood they need to provide for your future.

New Zealanders and their houses are a special partnership. In other countries, renting is the norm, or your house is merely a place to lay your head. For New Zealanders, buying a house is an emotive issue.

The Kiwi attachment to his or her quarter-acre paradise is well documented. It's where we spend a lot of our time, it's where we raise our children. Pride in our homes is a particularly Kiwi characteristic - but then we are often blessed with large houses, set within generous gardens and close to all sorts of outdoor spaces and amenities.

The do-it-yourself phenomenon is also rooted deep in our psyche. Part of it stems from the Number 8 wire, make-do mentality and part of it from the fact that we can - our timber houses are easy to chop and change. In generations gone by, if you were a male confessing to not being able to hammer in a nail, you would be hounded from the neighbourhood.

These days, Kiwis are still keen on renovating, but for different reasons. And it's all about location, location, location.

Concentrating much more where we want to live, we are not as concerned about the particulars of the house - because you can change it, but you can't change where it is. Buyers are not fazed about throwing renovation funds at a house to make it suit their needs, as long as the location is right and the section has the potential - like the right aspect for sun and enough space to fit a garage or extension. They know that if they stay put for a few years, they will recoup their investment.

Perhaps it's a particularly Auckland thing, too. The story goes that if you live in Christchurch, the question is which school you went to. If you live in Wellington, it's what movies you have seen lately. But if you live in Auckland, it's where do you live?

Auckland is easily New Zealand's biggest city, sprawling over 63,000ha - and it's growing all the time. Its population of nearly 1.32 million in the greater Auckland area is about one-third of the whole country. Forecasts put it at 1.65 million by the year 2021.

Despite being the nation's economic powerhouse, Auckland and its inhabitants seem to inspire extremes of emotion in other New Zealanders, being either admired or reviled. Aucklanders can also be heard complaining about the city's failings - it's a rat-race, it rains too much and the traffic is appalling.

We're also woefully ignorant of our own city. Ask a North Shore-ite where Glendene is and they'll confuse it with Glen Innes on the opposite side of town. Get a Mt Eden dweller to locate Clover Park and they might suggest Australia. But in such a sprawling city in which each area is so well serviced with amenities, venturing out of your own neighbourhood just isn't necessary.

So how is it that Auckland continues to grow faster than ever? The truth is that Auckland's sub-tropical climate, its attractive clean harbours, the number and variety of its beaches and native bush areas, its ethnic diversity, nightlife, cafés, universities, sporting facilities and large job market all make it a great place to live. Love it or not, the city is big, brassy and the closest New Zealand gets to an international cosmopolitan centre.

Auckland is located on the narrow isthmus of the Tamaki Peninsula, between the Waitemata and Manukau Harbours. In this city you're never far from the water - there's a mere 9km of land separating the Pacific Ocean from the Tasman Sea. Huge surf may be pounding the sparkly black sand of Auckland's west coast, while on the same morning gentle waves are lapping the golden sand of the east coast beaches.

Another name for Auckland is the City of Sails. It is said that Aucklanders own more boats per head of population than in any other city in the world. It's certainly true that lots of recreational activity centres around boating and beaches.

The dramatic remodelling of the Viaduct Harbour, and the subsequent creation of a harbourside community of apartments and cafés has made the area a popular drawcard for tourists and locals alike. The Viaduct's apartments have helped add glamour to the city's apartment living.

Buying and selling property is another popular Auckland activity; on average Aucklanders sell their home once every seven years. The importance of Auckland's coastline is also reflected in real estate; in many suburbs, proximity to the beach is the deciding value factor.

The importance of water, boating and property converges in particular on the Hauraki Gulf islands. Property prices on islands where you can buy permanent or weekend homes, like Waiheke Island and Great Barrier Island, have skyrocketed along with their popularity.

It's thought that Maori first settled in the richly fertile Auckland region about 650 years ago. Today, one in seven Aucklanders identify themselves as Maori. Auckland is also a Polynesian centre; one-third of all Polynesian people over the entire Pacific region choose to live in Auckland and some of our local body councillors have even mooted renaming the area as the "Gateway to the Pacific".

Ngati Whatua are considered to be Auckland's first tribe. During the 1820s Maori were involved in fierce inter-tribal conflict, and by 1840 the colonising British had either beaten or bought them out. Captain William Hobson, New Zealand's first governor, chose Auckland as a name to honour his patron and former commander, Lord Auckland (at that time, the Viceroy of India). Many Auckland place names carry the influence of Hobson's patron - Lord Auckland's family name was Eden, for example.

On May 30, 1959, the four-lane Harbour Bridge was opened, connecting Auckland's downtown business centre with the city's northern shore - and true North Shore suburbia was born. Ten years later the bridge was expanded to eight lanes, using Japanese engineering commonly referred to as the "Nippon clip-on". The motorway system has been growing ever since. Auckland's sprawl and relatively limited public transport system means that it's hard to get by without a car. The city's car-culture has been likened to a small-scale Los Angeles.

In 1997 the Sky Tower, New Zealand's tallest building, was completed. Its top viewing platform is 300m above sea level, making it the highest outdoor public viewing platform in the southern hemisphere. In 2001 the city's skyline was dramatically altered again when the lone pine tree on the summit of One Tree Hill was removed following a chainsaw attack by a Maori activist.

Auckland has abundant parks, and during weekends many Aucklanders use them for sport or recreation. The Domain is home to the Auckland War Memorial Museum, opened in 1929 to commemorate World War I casualties from the Auckland area.

"A better lifestyle", or "a great place to bring up a family", are typical reasons offered by expats or immigrants arriving to live in Auckland. It's therefore no surprise that proximity to the coast, to the West Coast bush, to work, or to urban attractions like Newmarket's shops, or Ponsonby's cafés, are major considerations when choosing where to live in Auckland.

A Potted History of Housing

Auckland is ever-changing and varied, architecturally speaking. In its 160-year history, it has collected a range of house styles from early worker's cottages, villas, bungalows, state houses, brick-and-tile homes and units to today's terrace and freestanding townhouses, apartments, and plaster and masonry homes.

By 1881, the highest population densities in the whole of New Zealand were on the upper slopes of Freemans Bay and Grafton Gully and the neighbouring areas of Ponsonby and Newton. By 1896, Auckland's population of 50,000 mostly lived in an area 6.5km long and 2.5km wide, made up of the boroughs of Auckland, Parnell, Newmarket, Newton and Grafton. There were also settlements at Avondale, Mt Eden, Epsom and Ellerslie and the maritime suburbs of Northcote, Birkenhead and Devonport.

Access to plentiful timber made it easy to build worker's cottages, which changed rapidly to accommodate family needs. Cottages, however, with their bad sanitation and crowding into urban pockets, affronted Victorian sensibilities enough to spur the creation of the villa.

Today, villas may be sought-after and trendy, but back then they were never viewed very favourably. Villas were seen as architecturally inept and built like packing cases. The classic villa hallway was condemned as a conduit of cold air in the winter and dust in the summer. Burnley Tce in Mt Eden is a landmark example of mass-produced villas in New Zealand.

The housing styles of Auckland continued to evolve from international influences, including the Californian bungalow and various Spanish Mission-style stucco and Art Deco houses. These latter two types were not wholly accepted in a colony that hankered for more classic British styles of housing.

The most recent change in Auckland's housing is the appearance of many apartments, from humble city units to large luxury apartments in our richer suburbs.

Real Estate Trends

After a few years of sky-rocketing prices, New Zealand's property boom appears to be well and truly over for the time being. And while the trend across the country is for slower growth, according to government valuers, Quotable Value, residential property values in Auckland have slowed more sharply than the rest (7.6% in the year to May 2006, when the national average was 12.4%). Still, the rest of the country has some way to catching up in terms of price: the average Auckland sale price was $517,455 compared with the national average of $327,779.

Auckland's property market has always been cyclical and even in a downturn, the city's property values tend to plateau rather than drop markedly.

Real estate sales people are having to be patient – and persuasive – with vendors who are still firmly fixated on sky-rocketing sales prices.

Quotable Value reports that "realistic" vendors are selling within four to 12 weeks, but that marketing periods are now stretching out in some areas, as buyers are being more discerning than they were able to be in the days when it was "grab it while you can, because tomorrow it might be $10,000 dearer".

Says Quotable Value: "In general the market has lost some of its buyer urgency, but there are no signs of oversupply in the market."

President of the Real Estate Institute of NZ, Howard Morley, says he expects the market to remain very flat until at least mid 2007, "unless we see a decreasing interest rate or a major downturn overseas".

Mortgage interest rate rises in early 2006 led to sharp intakes of breath in already overstretched households. Combined with a flattening off of rents, the interest rate rises also discouraged property investment dilettantes, leaving that game to those who are in it for the long haul.

There is a lot of talk about Aucklanders who don't own a home despairing of ever doing so, especially when the cost of travel is soaring and making it less feasible to buy on the cheaper outskirts of Auckland and commute in every day. REINZ president Howard Morley reckons it's always been difficult to break into home ownership: "It was hard for my daughter to buy her first home, yes, but it was hard when I bought my first home and it was hard for my parents before that."

The thought of how difficult it would be to get back into the Auckland housing market may be convincing people to stick with their uncomfortable mortgage repayments rather than selling up and renting.

Immigration hit a low in the year to October 2005, with a net gain of 6000 people, but by April 2006 it had bounced back to over 10,000 for the year. Although this is still below the average net migration gain of 10,500 during the past 10 years, and well below the record 12-month gain of 43,000 people in May 2003, it's not low enough to have a big impact on residential housing.

Transport – Getting Around The City

Between 7am and 9am every week day, 540,000 cars pour out of driveways and garages and onto Auckland's roads. Despite being the slowest time of day (average speed is below 34km/h), this is "rush" hour. The evening rush "hour" starts at the 3pm school run and lasts three hours.

As the city has spread further and further, Aucklanders have become more and more dependent on their vehicles. By 2001, we were making most of our trips – even very short trips – by car.

More than half of the morning journeys are to work and a third are to school: with all of these people traveling to the same place at the same

time every day, public transport would seem to be the natural response, right? Well, we're getting there - use of public transport increased by 15% between 2001 and 2005.

Until recently the train service was virtually non-existent and "bus service" was an oxymoron. Fortunately our transport heroes, the ARTA (Auckland Regional Transport Authority), have been doing great things with untangling the mess and putting together a $5 billion, 10-year plan which, with sufficient investment, will make public transport a viable and even attractive alternative for car commuters.

The authority calculates its plans would almost pay for themselves: increasing public transport patronage from 52 million passenger trips a year now to 100 million trips by 2016 would save having to build 130km of arterial roads and motorway lanes.

Soaring petrol prices have also helped change commuter behaviour. So, too, have initiatives like "walking school buses", which see 3000-plus kids getting to and from school under their own steam in groups of a dozen or so, with adults at the front and back to keep them safe.

Investment in rail has improved trains, tracks and stations and roughly doubled rail patronage, leading to more frequent services. In 2005, late night and Sunday train services were re-introduced, having been cut more than 40 years ago.

But we still have a long way to go. When stage one of New Zealand's biggest shopping mall opened in mid-2006 at Sylvia Park, the motor-vehicle mayhem took even Aucklanders by surprise. Traffic stood practically motionless on kilometres of motorway, and police temporarily closed the Mt Wellington off-ramps. The developer had, as required, set aside $5 million to build a new train station at Sylvia Park but it wasn't part of the first stage. Hmmm...

Whether the emphasis is on building roads or nurturing public transport, it all costs money – and regional and national government each say the other should pay more. The Auckland Regional Council has capped annual rates rises at 5% which, unless national government stumps up with the cash, also puts a cap on investment in buses and trains.

ARC member Joel Cayford has called for legislation that would allow regional bodies to levy developers for a share of the cost of getting public transport services to their subdivisions.

What seems almost certain, though, is that drivers will be paying road tolls before long. One proposal is to charge $6 to cross the Harbour Bridge into the city between 6am and 10am on weekdays. No prizes for guessing how popular that would be with Shore-ites, especially when traversing other "charging points" in the east, south and west of Auckland would cost just $3.

Others are up in arms about a proposed parking levy of up to $10 a day (on top of existing parking fees) within the Auckland-Newmarket, Manukau, Henderson and Takapuna CBDs.

Leaky Building Syndrome

Leaky building syndrome isn't in the headlines every couple of days any longer, but it remains a significant issue in the lives of up to 40,000 affected NZ homeowners.

In mid-2006, many of those owners were brutally disappointed by the outcome of a nine-month review of the struggling Weathertight Homes Resolution Service. The review saw $7.1 million allocated over two years for loans to those homeowners who had been declined by banks for loans to cover repairs.

One home rebuilding specialist said the amount wouldn't even "touch the sides". Others pointed out that that amount could all be spent on a single apartment complex.

The average cost of full recladding and repair of leaky homes is about $180,000, but some cost more than $500,000, and most owners struggle to meet bank lending criteria. It's a catch 22 for honest homeowners, for without remedial work, their homes would be nigh-on impossible to sell.

Meantime, changes to the Unit Titles Act would bring thousands of apartments into the resolution process, and assessments would be broadened to cover likely, as well as known, weathertightness defects.

There is huge frustration at the length of time being taken to settle cases, but the Government said the current average of 14 months should be halved by the service's new approach.

Unfortunately, lack of confidence in the resolution service means that some owners are opting for court action instead: they get diverted for confidential mediation and the outcome remains secret.

Those who enter mediation often come out with less than half the money needed to repair their property. Some are then selling their properties without repairs and without disclosure. Buyer beware.

The Apartment Market

It's taken us a while to catch on to apartment living, but it's a permanent fixture now. By 2050, a quarter of Auckland's projected two million residents may be living in apartments, townhouses and high-rise buildings.

There are an estimated 13,400 apartments in Auckland's CBD and more than a quarter of those were built in the past year.

While psychologists warn that too-small living quarters isolate us and may mess with our minds, research shows that residents of multi-unit developments are generally content.

Nonetheless, Auckland City council has clamped down on "shoebox" apartments by setting minimum floor areas for studios (35m^2), one-bedroom (45m^2), two-bedroom (70m^2) and three-bedroom (90m^2) apartments to the central district plan. Other new minimum standards include ceiling heights of 2.4m, width of shared hallways (1.5m) and 20% of the floor area to have glazed external wall. In residential buildings of more than 20 units, no more than 70% of the units can be studios or one-bedrooms.

Martin Dunn, from apartment specialists City Sales, says 70% of apartment buyers are investors, enjoying typical net returns of 7%.

He says two new types of owner-occupier have emerged: city workers who can gain 90 minutes-plus a day by relocating from the 'burbs; and first-home buyers who can't afford even a "cheap" Auckland house but can get a CBD studio for under $100,000.

When choosing an apartment, Dunn recommends you consider:

- Whether the "culture" of the building is right for you - is it mostly student tenants, or settled owner-occupiers?
- Whether you are dealing with a reputable agent who knows the area and will be up to date with possible issues such as leaks?
- Where you will keep your car. An apartment with a carpark costs about $30,000 more.

Most apartments are owned under a unit title, which means you own the actual apartment but the common areas (eg car parks and gardens) belong to all owners.

A small number of Auckland apartments, including many in prime Viaduct locations, are leasehold – you need to find out how long the term is and what the annual lease costs.

Most apartment developments are managed by a body corporate – or an owners' committee – which makes decisions about maintenance, alterations and issues such as parking and pets. The body corporate can be the key to low-stress and relatively low-cost home ownership, or it can be the bane of your existence.

Apartment Checklist:

- Will your furniture fit through the doorways, up the stairs and into the rooms?
- Is there enough natural light?
- Will you enjoy the view and might it be built out? (Check with the council.)
- Will you be able to cool your living areas in the summer?
- How private is it?
- Is there enough storage?
- Does the bathroom have opening windows or a good extractor fan?
- Where is the neighbours' plumbing? (If it's in a shared wall it may be noisy.)
- Is there a balcony and is it sunny and big enough to use, or is it a token gesture?
- Is any communal outdoor space sunny and usable?
- What are the arrangements for rubbish and recycling?
- Is there an outdoor clothes-line so you can save power and money?
- Check the exterior for signs of leaks; small gaps around doors, windows and balconies where water can leak into the wall cavity;
- cracks and fine lines in plastered walls;
- large expanses of blank wall, which tend to show every flaw and make the building look scruffy.
- Ask existing owners how they find dealing with the body corporate. Ask for recent meeting minutes so you know what the burning issues are.
- What are the current body corp fees?
- Is there a sinking fund or savings plan to pay for big jobs like painting or re-roofing?
- Is there a long-term maintenance plan?
- You or your lawyer should get a Section 36 report under the Unit Titles Act to identify any outstanding levies or pending legal issues.

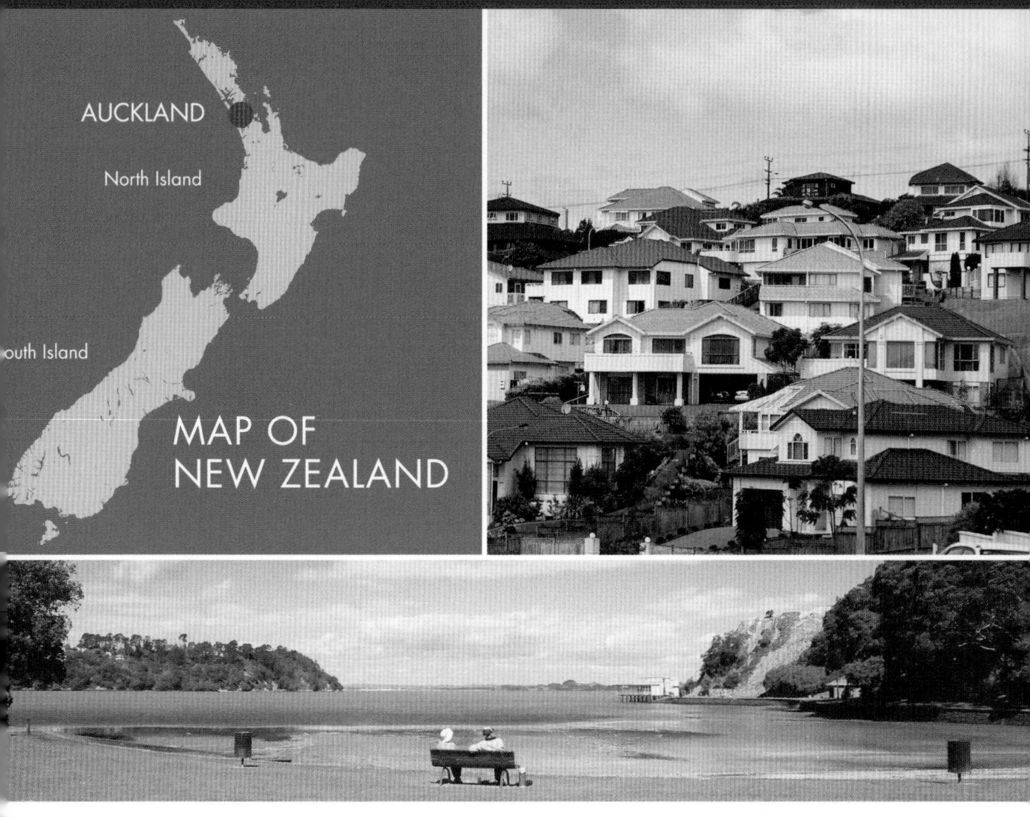

Where to Live in Auckland is split into five geographical areas - Central, North, West, East and South. Each area is, in turn, divided into neighbourhoods - a collection of suburbs and areas close to each other and similar in nature. To find the neighbourhood you are interested in, either refer to the Contents page or use the index at the back of the book.

Within each neighbourhood, we look at the character of the area, the people who live there, types of houses typical to the area, real estate trends and prices, as well as the amenities you can find there - the schools, shops, leisure facilities, open spaces, eateries and transport.

At the back of the book, you'll find more interesting facts – a full and comprehensive list of all Auckland schools, zoning maps for secondary schools, information about private schools and statistics giving a profile of Auckland's population.

Our star ratings: We've given the amenities a rating from one to five and we've also rated each neighbourhood from one to five, based on its desirability, house price level and general access to amenities.

Maps: Each neighbourhood has a map, coloured according to the types of people who live in the area. It's an intriguing insight into the habits, likes and dislikes of your potential neighbours - do they like drinking wine or beer, like sport, use the internet?

Each colour relates to a particular population sector based on demographics, lifestyle and preferences. For an explanation of those see page 226.

Prices: Property values and prices quoted within our Trends and House Prices sections are based on interviews with real estate agents and are anecdotal only.

Centra

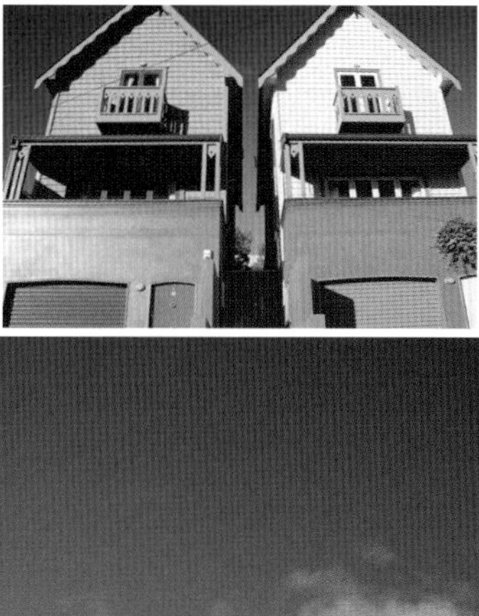

the sparkling Waitemata coffee and cáfées high energy nights high-ticket houses

The central suburbs of Auckland are where it all began. It's from here that Auckland has sprawled, around its two harbours and edging ever further north and south, to become the largest city in New Zealand. The central suburbs are where most of Auckland's history lies and where most of its prestige real estate can be found. The burgeoning number of apartments in recent years means that Auckland's central business district now has an energy it once lacked.

Auckland central encompasses a large area, from the southern edge of the Waitemata Harbour, west to Avondale, east to Panmure, south to Onehunga, and also captures the inhabited islands of the Hauraki Gulf.

With 320,000 new homes planned for Greater Auckland by 2050, 19 of the 51 areas tagged to take much of the growth are in Auckland City. The central suburbs are where

any new real estate trends are first felt, and in boom times, this is where price increases are at their highest. As areas like Ponsonby, Parnell, Remuera and Mt Eden become more expensive, attention turns to the next suburban ring as homebuyers' desire to remain close to the city remains strong.

The rest of Auckland's homeowners wonder why inner-city residents continue to pay huge sums for houses with no garaging that sit so close together you can hear your neighbour sneeze. Conversely, people who have prised themselves away from the inner areas marvel at the space they can buy for half the price out west or on the shore. And you can still get a decent cup of coffee.

Central Auckland is where you find the most of the truly luxurious real estate. Blue chip suburbs like Remuera, Herne Bay, Parnell and Epsom boast some gracious properties with large houses and plenty of room for the swimming pools and even tennis courts.

Central Auckland's traffic is a hot topic, with peak-hour congestion reaching crisis point and the city's public transport system not yet comprehensive enough to wean people off their cars. A daily fee for driving into the central suburbs and the CBD was mooted at the same time as motorists were reeling from record-high petrol prices, and neither were welcomed.

That helps to make the central city an attractive place for CBD workers to live. The abundance of new apartments and terraced houses mean that living near the city can be surprisingly affordable, to rent or buy.

The amenities for central dwellers are plenty and long-established. Great shopping, plenty of big parks, the sparkling harbour, top restaurants and cafés, plenty of sporting facilities and clubs.

The housing architecture is hugely varied. Much of it is older – villas, bungalows, state cottages – while many new and snazzy homes now share the land with their older neighbours. Whatever type or age of house you are seeking, you can find it somewhere in central Auckland.

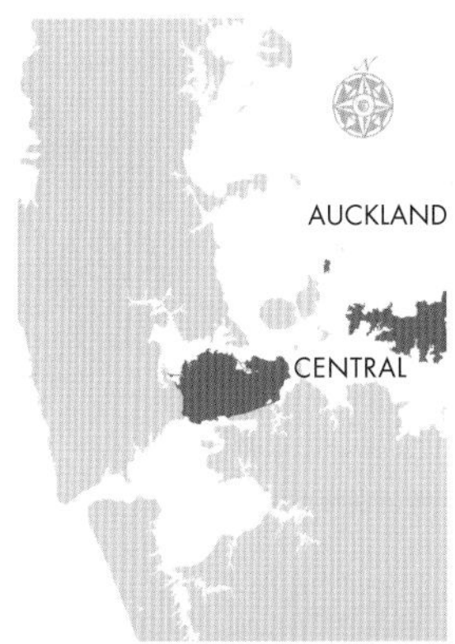

including the Central Business District, Newton and Grafton

A decade ago, you would have been thought mad to live in a city apartment. Why would you want to leave the green, green grass of the suburbs, that iconic quarter acre of Kiwi paradise that everyone else in the world so envies us for? Yeah, right, yadda yadda. Slightly mad then is hugely hip now... and rich, if that apartment happens to be at Viaduct Harbour. The non-lawn-mowing dwellers of our city CBD have bought themselves more time to play, in the many bars, restaurants and clubs that fight for imbibing patrons every evening of the week. It took us a while to cotton on but now, like other major world cities, we see our CBD as a place to live not just work and play. The popularity of city living is soaring, there's a wider array of apartment types to choose from and inner city addresses are in demand.

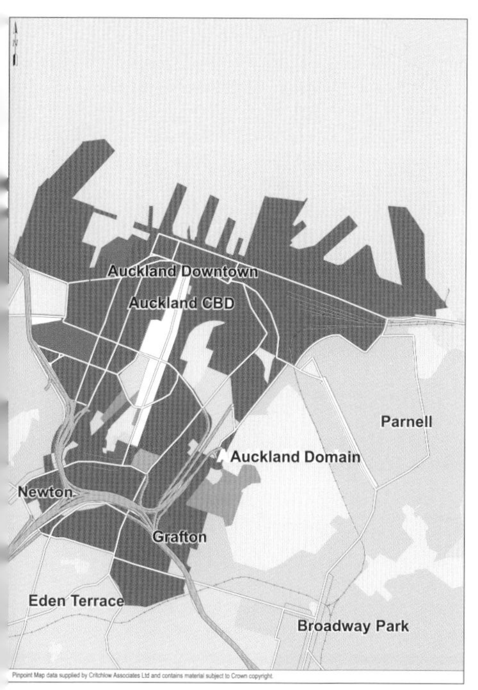

For colour key, see page 226

Population Profile

Population	11,193
% Aged Under 15 Years	4.02
% Aged Over 65 Years	4.10
% European	51.38
% Maori	5.49
% Pacific Peoples	3.46
% Asian	31.20

Who Lives There?

As well as the ageing baby boomers, central Auckland is home to many young people. Most rent, while others buy, disillusioned at ever being able to enter the conventional housing market (which starts at just under $300,000 for anything decent in the 'burbs) but who can buy a city studio for maybe $100,000.

The obvious attraction of walking to work and not having to take out a second mortgage to fill the car with petrol brings many young professionals who can toil, play, eat and sleep within a kilometre-wide circle. Despite recent immigration downturns, the city is still a magnet for new arrivals and ex-pats. The

numbers of Asian students may be less these days as language schools have diversified or closed down, but there are still plenty of students generally.

There are now "serial city residents", those who have tried it, liked it and have upgraded or just figured out exactly what they like about apartment living and bought to suit.

Typical Homes

As you'd expect, the city scene is apartments and more apartments, ranging in size and modernity. New apartment buildings keep emerging, albeit at a slightly slower pace than the past few years.

Many city apartments are of variable quality and not all are freehold. Leasehold apartments are found particularly around the Viaduct, Princes Wharf and the railway station developments and some owners have been stung by rising ground rents.

"Corporate crash pads" aimed at the short-stay business market have become a recent feature of the city, like the 18-level Columbard on Wyndham St, with 16sq m furnished units and hotel-style cleaning service. A second Columbard building is being built alongside Myers Park.

The council no longer allows proper apartments of less than 30sq m to be built, and banks generally won't lend on the smallest apartments (although other lenders may).

There are older-style houses in nearby Grafton and Newton, but many of the cute villas have been removed to make way for terrace housing developments.

Amenities

Schools ★★

Demand for schooling in the central city is not great, however the western part is in the Auckland Grammar School zone. The culturally diverse Freemans Bay School is close by and has a highly valued Maori immersion class, Whanau Ata.

Kadimah College in Greys Ave caters for children aged four to 13. A decile 10, private Jewish school (although children from all backgrounds are welcome) it continues to excel academically with small classes and ability, rather than age, groupings for key subjects.

ACG Senior College and Auckland Girls Grammar are in the CBD. Senior College has a strong academic focus and according to a recent ERO report "...is achieving outstanding results in national and international exams." At Auckland Girls academic standards are also high, and the school has a strong sporting reputation with more than 25 codes on offer.

For a full list, see page 270.

Shops ★★★★★

Queen St used to echo with the cries of tourists wondering were everyone else had gone, but after spending some time in the doldrums when people flocked to their local malls instead, Queen St shopping is once again on the rise. Trendy new chain stores sit alongside established outlets such as Smith & Caughey.

Newmarket and St Lukes are relatively close and two large supermarkets, the new Foodtown near Britomart and New World in Freemans Bay, give inner city locals plenty of choice for food shopping.

Leisure ★★★★★

Although still more of place to be at night time, the city has pleasant enough daytime activities, mostly centred around the waterfront. There's plenty of boat watching, strolling through Viaduct Harbour, or dining and drinking at one of the many cafés there while watching the world and its tourists go by.

There are quite a few green spaces, including Albert Park, Myers Park and Victoria Park – and if the lobbyists have their way, another substantial one along land currently occupied by the tank farm.

Real Estate

Trends

What wise investor needs a whole apartment? One CBD car park famously sold for $78,000 recently. Parking is in such high demand that some people buy an apartment just to get their hands on the accompanying car park: they immediately on-sell the apartment.

The city market is still about 70% investor, who currently expect about a 7% return on their money. Many invest in the smaller, cheaper apartments to rent to students or young city workers.

The leaky buildings scare means that most buyers now get building inspections done and most banks want to see a building report before they'll lend – this makes buying unconditionally at auction difficult.

The initial flurry of apartment-building in the CBD has slowed down but running out of full building sites doesn't stop development. There's always airspace – apartments are being built atop the Stamford Plaza hotel in Albert St, for example.

Best Buildings

Many of the apartment buildings in the Viaduct are considered good, including The Point, Lighter Quay and The Parc. Also in demand are new buildings in scenic spots, such as The Precinct on Lorne St, with views of Albert Park.

Converted loft-style apartments in heritage buildings are considered prime real estate for those who find new buildings too homogenised and soulless.

Local Hero: The Waterfront

Half of our city waterfront land may still be occupied by a container terminal, but we're getting there. The Viaduct Harbour has proved its staying power, sans an America's Cup challenge, and is a vibrant and fun place to be, now hosting various events (Auckland anniversary day fair, wine and food festival). The new 12,000-seat Vector Arena stadium at Quay Park is complete. Swish new apartment buildings have risen like phoenixes from the ashes of the yacht syndicate bases, and we wait with baited breath to see what happens to the old tank farm. The council planned to have it covered with yet more apartment buildings but opponents say that it should be a more public space with parks et al. Watch this space, literally.

Look Out (!)

Wise buyers will do their research before buying any property, but that's particularly true for apartments. Could your expensive view be built out? Are the walls so thin you can hear the neighbours' conversations? And, especially in the CBD, will you (or your tenants) be able to handle the noise of late-night revellers, loud bars, and construction/roading projects which don't stop at night for residents the way they would in the suburbs?

At a Glance...

Apartment Prices

Studio apartment

Apartment	
Price	$100,000 - $300,000

Entry-level apartment

Bedroom	🛏
Price	$130,000 - $400,000 +

Apartment with views and car park

Bedrooms	🛏 🛏
Price	$380,000 - $500,000 +

Heritage-style apartment

Bedrooms	🛏 🛏 🛏
Price	$600,000 - $750,000 +

Viaduct apartment

Bedroom	🛏
Price	$230,000 - $450,000 +

Larger Viaduct apartment

Bedrooms	🛏 🛏
Price	$600,000 - $1,000,000

Average Rents

Apartments

Bedroom	🛏
Price	$295/wk
Bedrooms	🛏 🛏
Price	$360/wk
Bedrooms	🛏 🛏 🛏
Price	$500/wk

Travel Times

With transport, everything starts and ends in downtown Auckland. The Intercity bus terminal is under Sky City Casino. Ferry travel has become a lot more attractive thanks to a $10.6m upgrade of the four piers. And Britomart has brought trains into the central city, as well as providing a central connection point for bus, ferry and rail.

The huge project to untangle spaghetti junction is now complete. The century-old Grafton Bridge will be closed for much of 2007 for strengthening and when it reopens, only buses, bikes and emergency vehicles will be able to use it during weekdays.

ncluding Rosebank and Waterview

How did such an innocent suburb get to be associated with horror? The middle-aged among us know Avondale for its Hollywood Cinema, and its amazing 10-year run of *The Rocky Horror Picture Show*. For others, the most enduring image is of the large hairy spiders that take their name from the suburb. But really, Avondale is far from scary. The well established suburb is close to the city and very popular with it's range of residents. It's one of Auckland's oldest suburbs, with the first European settlement as early as 1843. Waterview is a small and slightly more expensive area with a misleading name – very few of its ex-state houses actually see the water. Being that much closer to affluent Pt Chevalier and the city adds value, however.

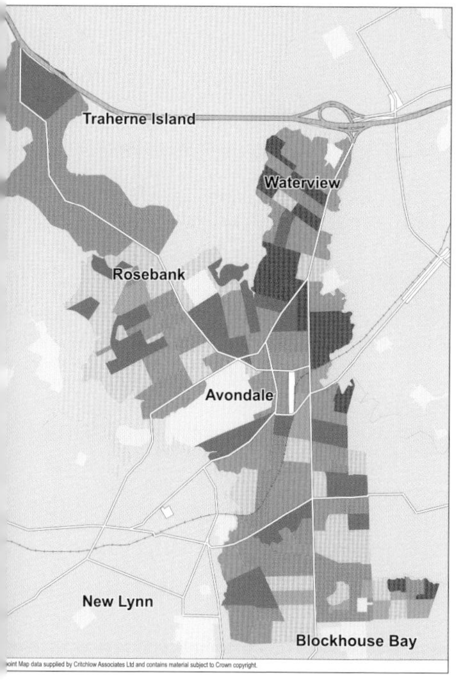

For colour key, see page 226

Population Profile

Population	25,206
% Aged Under 15 Years	22.80
% Aged Over 65 Years	10.08
% European	45.11
% Maori	10.93
% Pacific Peoples	24.57
% Asian	20.02

Who Lives There?

With trouble-free access to the city and an array of amenities on Auckland's west urban edge, the Avondale area is popular with a range of people, from city workers, families with teenage kids and immigrants (mostly Chinese), who like it for its good schools, job opportunities and lively community spirit. There's a large Polynesian influence – and Avondale College remains a draw card. Many residents are impressed by the magnificent potential of the area. Some initially rented in the suburb, but enjoyed the location so much, they eventually bought here.

Avondale's always been multi-cultural and in some parts it is staunchly blue collar. The influx of yuppies and dinkies who have been scared off by the prices of other inner city suburbs is changing the area's profile.

Typical Homes

There is probably no such thing as a typical dwelling in Avondale. There are numerous renovated villas and bungalows plus an abundant supply of 1930s, '40s, '50s and '60s brick and tile or weatherboard family homes. The past two decades have seen a number of modern infill plaster or brick and tile townhouses. Although created in 1861, Waterview was slow to develop. The area is now sought after however for its handy location and solid ex-state brick and tile houses.

Amenities

Schools ★★★

This mid to low decile neighbourhood is home to at least five primary schools. The multicultural Rosebank School is one of the largest primaries in the neighbourhood with a roll close to 700. Special features include four bilingual Samoan and two bilingual Maori classes.

Interestingly, the low-decile Avondale Intermediate was originally an American Army hospital during World War 2.

Avondale College is the only state secondary school in the area. The zoned college is very highly regarded and people will move into the suburb for this reason alone.

For a full list of schools, see page 270.

Shops ★★★

LynnMall and St Lukes are close by and that has had a negative impact on suburban strip shopping in Avondale itself. Avondale centre has been revamped with a newly paved town square, a stage, modern toilets and a 3m high spider sculpture, and that's attracted new shops and cafés. There's a library, a police station and community centre.

Every Sunday, the local market at the racecourse sells local produce, arts, crafts, foods and second-hand goods.

Leisure ★★★

Avondale is famed for its race course and jockey club in Ash St, but there are also other sporting clubs. There are plenty of parks and reserves ... for now. These will reduce in number once the SH20 extension cuts through Oakley Creek Esplanade and others.

Waterview has nearby mangrove wetlands accessible via Waterview Park and Howlett St Reserve. Backing Waterview is the Motu Manawa/Pollen Island Marine Reserve. P Chevalier beach is just down the road.

Local facilities include the Avondale Racecourse, an ice-skating rink, numerous gyms and sports clubs and a number of sports facilities at the college. Casual eateries abound. Avondale College runs an extensive community education programme.

REAL ESTATE

Trends

Prices have steadied, if not dropped bac slightly during the past year. One busy agenc recorded an average sale price of $340,00 at Christmas 2005 and a $320,000 average i June 2006.

Investors are still keen on Avondale, finding tha the suburb's accessibility to the motorway an city, as well as the presence of Unitec, bring a steady flow of tenants. They also feel this i a good market for capital growth. Immigrants mainly from China, are still a significant part c the buying market.

While many of the subdividable propertie have been split up, developers are still havin a busy time with the ones that are left.

Price-wise, Avondale Heights and Watervie are on a par, and slightly more expensive tha the flat areas of Avondale. The cheapest are is the group of residential streets near th industrial blocks of Rosebank.

Best Streets

The streets of Avondale Heights, on th west-facing slopes between Blockhouse Ba Rd and Great North Rd. Also Cradock S and Powell St.

Local Hero: Avondale Spider

Good on Avondale for embracing this hairy scary creature as the local emblem! The wee beasties in question are actually Aussie immigrants, but they've been here since the 1920s and it's pretty rare now to find one with a strong Australian accent.

Across the Tasman they're known as Huntsman spiders and, although they're harmless to humans, their appearance is impressive enough to have earned 374 of them starring roles in the 1990 horror movie *Arachnophobia*. Of course, they're not quite as large as they appeared on the big screen, but a span of up to 200mm, from the tip of one hairy leg to the tip of another hairy leg, is plenty big enough. Thanks, Australia.

Smart Buy ✓

Avondale and Waterview are colourful and relatively affordable city fringe options. Edged with water and close to good shopping, they are well worth a look, especially now that the route for the Waterview stretch of the Western Ring Route has been decided. It goes between Great North Rd and Unitec, through the Oakley Creek Esplanade, so doesn't affect existing housing that much but it will make the south-east, and especially the airport, much more accessible.

At a Glance...

House Prices

Unit or townhouse

Bedrooms: 🛏 🛏
Price: $210,000 - $240,000

House on the flat on half site

Bedrooms: 🛏 🛏 🛏
Price: $290,000 - $360,000

On the heights

Price: $400,000 - $470,000

Renovated bungalows

Price: $500,000 - $600,000

Average Rents

Flat

Bedroom: 🛏
Price: $210/wk
Bedrooms: 🛏 🛏
Price: $265/wk

House

Bedrooms: 🛏 🛏 🛏
Price: $345/wk
Bedrooms: 🛏 🛏 🛏 🛏
Price: $390/wk

Travel Times

From Avondale shops:

CBD	peak 30 min off peak 10 min
North-western motorway	peak 10 min off peak 2 min
Airport	30 min
LynnMall	5 min
St Lukes mall	10 min

Avondale is on one of a number of bus routes to the city, and has a railway station on the western line near the shops.

Blockhouse Bay ★★★★★

including Wesley, New Windsor and Lynfield

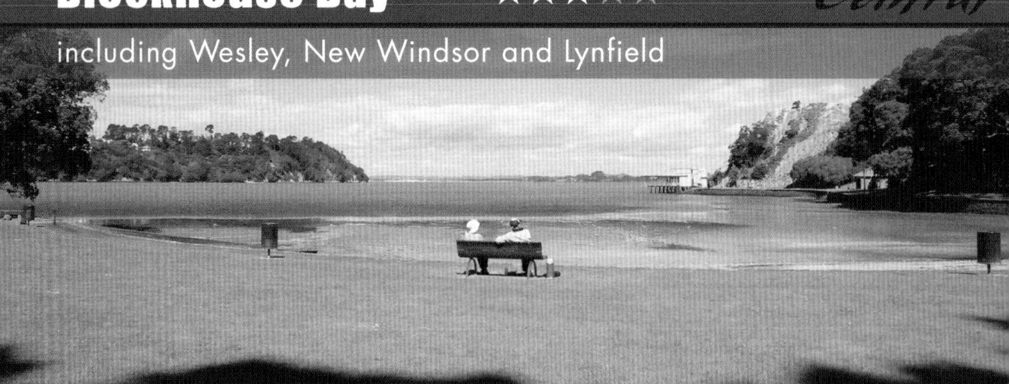

On the up and up is how you could best describe this once low-profile part of the city. Its previously hidden talents have now been brought more centre-stage as people discover the safe family lifestyle, sea views and even a spruced-up village-style shopping centre. Sitting along the southern edge of the Manukau Harbour, by day you can watch the ships and seabirds coming and going; by night the lights of Glenbrook Steel Mil sparkle on the southern horizon as a city alternative to a starry night. On the city side o Blockhouse Bay, some streets get a view of the Sky Tower. Lynfield is on a quiet point o land further up the harbour, which means there is no through traffic. The name Blockhous Bay refers to fortifications built to protect European settlers from Maori attacks.

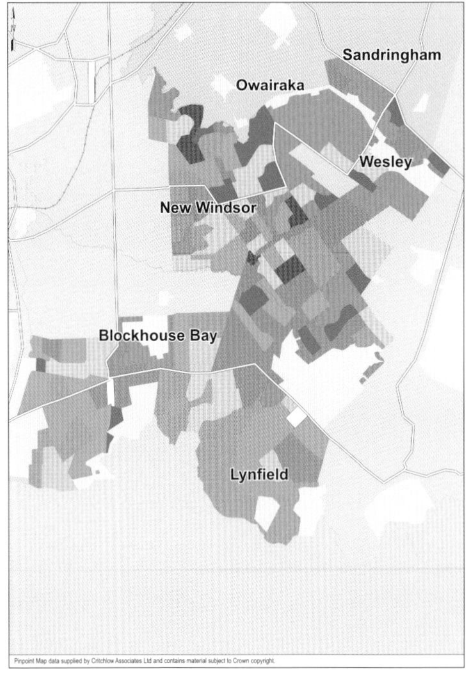

For colour key, see page 226

Population Profile

Population	26,283
% Aged Under 15 Years	22.44
% Aged Over 65 Years	12.24
% European	50.43
% Maori	5.95
% Pacific Peoples	14.67
% Asian	29.06

Who Lives There?

Good solid middle-class family-oriented Ne Zealanders are the traditional residents, with mix of ages and stages including retirees wh like the nice flat walk to the shops. It's mor cosmopolitan now, home to a mix of nationalitie including Fijian Indians and Asian immigrant Once popular with first-home buyers an investors, the recent property value increase have skewed that towards young families (ther are many good schools) and those with slight higher mortgage-paying capabilities. Mar owner-occupiers are in the 30-plus age grou and consider Blockhouse Bay a good steppin stone to trade up to suburbs closer to the cit

Lynfield College's strong reputation attracts education-conscious migrants who also see the district as a good starting point in the Auckland housing market.

Typical Homes

The most common houses in this area are weatherboard bungalows built between 25 and 35 years ago. There is some terrace housing at the bottom of Blockhouse Bay and rumours of low-rise apartments being built near the shops. Infill housing is common, typically with an older bungalow on the front section, and a 10 or 20-year-old house at the rear. There is a state housing area at the bottom of Blockhouse Bay.

Amenities

Schools ★★★

The area is well served with schools (there are nine within a 2.5km radius), including the well-regarded Halsey Drive School and Lynfield College.

Halsey Drive School is a decile nine school and was recently described by ERO as "very high performing."

Lynfield College boasts state-of-the-art technology and computer systems in all learning areas and has one of the largest English as a Secondary Language departments in Auckland. The college also provides strong community education and is a leading educator for foreign fee-paying students.

Hill Top School is also worth a mention. The successful private school caters for years one to 10 and was originally founded in 1915 in a Newmarket family home. The school relocated to its Blockhouse Bay character hill top location in 1959 and promotes a quality learning environment for boys and girls in small classes.

For a full list, see page 270.

Shops ★★★

The Blockhouse Bay shopping centre has a village atmosphere, with about 20 shops including cafés, a butcher, florist, medical centres and a supermarket. A lot of work has gone into beautifying the shopping area recently, with footpaths being improved and decorative sails erected to emphasise the connection with the sea.

Lynfield has a modern shopping complex including several new fast food outlets and a supermarket.

Leisure ★★★

Local sporting amenities include excellent recreational parks, a skateboard park, an ice skating rink, The Portage Trust Tennis Centre (indoor and outdoor), the refurbished Blockhouse Bay Boat Club, bowling clubs and rugby clubs. There is a good library and many artistic and creative events take place throughout the year.

There are several places with street access to the harbour. It's possible to swim at Blockhouse Bay and Wattle Bay - the beaches are tidal, but there are beautiful parks with play areas for children nearby. The region has many parks, including Craigavon, Avondale South Domain, Manukau Domain and Wattle Bay Reserve. It is also handy to the Waitakere Ranges.

The local restaurant and café scene is gradually improving. For a more trendy dining experience go to nearby Titirangi.

Real Estate

Trends

After a few years of spectacular increases (Blockhouse Bay and its surrounds seems to have been one of the bigger winners during the property boom), capital gains have slowed. A recent sale of a harbour-side Lynfield house was a record for the area at $1.3 million.

The new motorway extension is dragging down values of properties close by, but in the long-term the greater accessibility it brings will be a boon to the area.

Property values are now such that new developments are aimed at the affluent owner-occupier rather than investors, so it looks certain that the area will retain its respectability, and values will only increase.

There are still a few opportunities for in-fill housing, but they come available far less often. There's no high-density housing in the area yet, although there are rumours that some may be planned near the shopping area.

Best Streets

Gilfillan St, Mitchell St, Endeavour St and the seaward end of Blockhouse Bay Rd.

At a Glance...

House Prices

Unit

Bedrooms	2
Price	$240,000 – $340,000

House

Bedrooms	3
Price	$350,000 – $420,000

Older renovated house

Price	$450,000 – $650,000

Executive house with harbour views

Bedrooms	5
Price	$1 million+

Average Rents

Flat

Bedroom	1
Price	$200/wk
Bedrooms	2
Price	$265/wk

House

Bedrooms	2
Price	$275/wk
Bedrooms	3
Price	$340/wk
Bedrooms	4
Price	$390/wk

Travel Times

From Blockhouse Bay shops to:

CBD	peak 30 min off-peak 20 min
North-western motorway	10 min
Airport	20 min
St Lukes mall	10 min
Lynn Mall	5 min

Stagecoach Auckland provides a regular bus service from Blockhouse Bay and Lynfield. The SH20 motorway extension from Hillsborough through to the north-western motorway will be a benefit (drivers will get places faster) without the disadvantages (it's not close enough to be noisy).

Eastern Bays

including Mission Bay, Kohimarama, St Heliers, Orakei and Glendowie

The Eastern Bays reflect all that is aspirational about Auckland – history, a sense of grandeur, an interesting demographic range and a social structure which embraces both old and new money. Living in the Eastern Bays carries unequivocal, unshakeable status for Aucklanders, and it's all about lifestyle. The harbour views, the white sand beaches, the leafy bays offering delightful strolling...heck, even the drive to work in the city alongside the picturesque harbour is a pleasure. St Heliers, Glendowie, Mission Bay, Kohimarama and Orakei roll into one fabulous whole as the Eastern Bays, while retaining their own separate character and charm. The area is becoming even easier on the eye thanks to power and phone lines vanishing underground, the sand at St Heliers beach being topped up, and headlands being built to deflect coastal erosion.

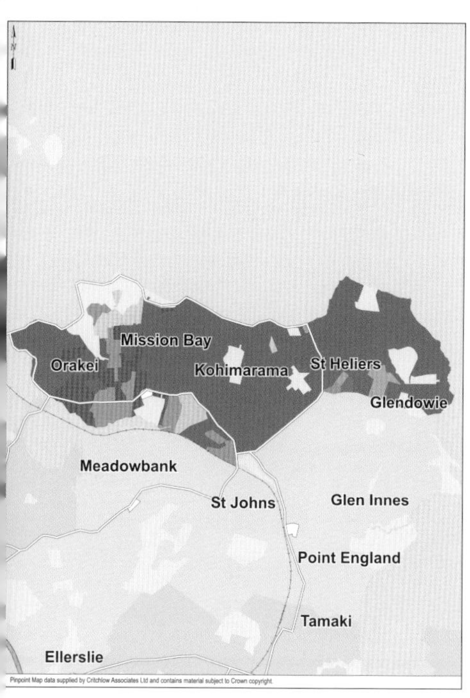

For colour key, see page 226

Population Profile

Population	24,801
% Aged Under 15 Years	17.54
% Aged Over 65 Years	14.47
% European	83.41
% Maori	4.68
% Pacific Peoples	2.03
% Asian	9.19

Who Lives There?

Many residents are second or third generation owners – and the wiser ones fully appreciate they're sitting on a goldmine. Newly wealthy Aucklanders and migrants aspire to live here as well. While it's close to the CBD, the lifestyle is utterly distinct from inner-city living.

Residents often move from bay to bay, or relocate from neighbouring suburbs. Older owners of large homes on big sections trade them in for an apartment with sea views or to move to retirement complexes such as the Grace Joel Village in St Heliers.

Kohimarama attracts both families and retired people with its facilities – locals enjoy being able to walk to the waterfront for casual strolls or more energetic runs, with superlative views of Rangitoto Island.

Mission Bay and Orakei are the locations to be seen in, and many choose to purchase in these suburbs for that reason alone. Bastion Pt is owned by the Ngati Whatua tribe, which hosts many cultural events including highly popular Kapa Haka concerts.

Typical Homes

The bays have every type of dwelling – from the opulent mansions of Orakei's Paritai Dr to humble state housing in some pockets of the various bay suburbs. A number of ex-state homes have been privatised and now command premium prices for their location – the modest state houses along Kitemoana St in Orakei have some of the best sea views in the entire city.

Apartments are increasingly becoming a feature of the Eastern Bays as developers pounce upon the last few remaining seafront sections on or near Tamaki Dr.

The Eastern Bays are not really the place to look for character villas or bungalows; stucco-and-tile is far more common.

Amenities

Schools ★★★★

Local schooling is high quality, with many sought-after primary and intermediate schools. The predominantly high decile area has at least nine primary schools, and while most include intermediate years some families prefer to send their children to Remuera or Meadowbank intermediate schools. Kohimarama School is popular and has a roll close to 500. According to a recent ERO report, the school provides "good quality education".

There are some low-decile schools in the neighbourhood including Glen Taylor School in Glendowie and Orakei School.

Co-educational Selwyn College, Glendowie College and Catholic boys' school Sacred Heart are the local secondary schools. Many students also attend private schools in Epsom and elsewhere. For a full list, see page 270.

Shops ★★★

Shopping facilities are spread throughout the bays, with a village atmosphere at St Heliers and a preponderance of eateries at Mission Bay.

There's limited grocery shopping locally – although the Eastridge shopping centre at the back of Kohimarama, and Meadowbank Foodtown are reasonably close. Many locals make weekend shopping trips to Newmarket and Botany Town Centre.

Leisure ★★★★★

There's plenty to do for both landlubbers and water sports enthusiasts alike. All the bays are tidal but suitable for swimming. Kohimarama Beach was upgraded with tonnes of new sand

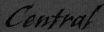

a year or so ago, and St Heliers beach is now in for a spruce up.

The reserve bordering Mission Bay is well frequented by picnickers, walkers and sunbathers. The Glendowie sandspit and Tahuna Torea bird sanctuary have fabulous walks. And then there's the harbourside Tamaki Dr for walking, running, cycling, roller-blading or stroller-pushing – in fact, it gets so busy you have to constantly beware of someone running you down.

There are numerous green areas including Orakei Domain, the quaint Dingle Dell, Glover Park, Madill's Farm, Kepa Bush Park, family friendly Churchill Park and many smaller reserves.

Local icons such as Tamaki Yacht Club, Kohi Yacht Club and Kelly Tarlton's Underwater World are well patronised.

Mission Bay is virtually all restaurants and cafés including the successful Mecca in the historic stone house, whereas St Heliers has a wider range of shops. With the café strip buzzing at night and all weekend, it's often said that locals leave the area for a bit of peace!

Real Estate

Trends

While there is no shortage of buyers, they are increasingly willing to wait for a vendor with realistic expectations – some are under the illusion that the buy-at-any-price property boom is still upon us. While the sky-rocketing prices of a couple of years ago are no longer in evidence, there are still examples of quality homes on good sections selling for top dollar. One $4 million-plus property recently sold very quickly, and a tired two-bedroom 1950s weatherboard home on Long Dr on a single dwelling site sold in April 2006 for $750,000.

Apartments are now spread across Orakei, Mission Bay, Kohimarama and St Heliers. Most of the dwellings along Tamaki Dr are apartment blocks with older two-bedroom apartments starting at $500,000 and new luxury apartments selling for between $1.75 million and $3 million, depending on size.

There are few small older units in the area, and they tend to be leasehold.

Turnover is low. Once people move to the Eastern Bays, they tend to stay put: of the12,000 properties in the area, 100 at the most change hands each month.

Best Streets

Paritai Dr in Orakei, Cliff Rd and Springcombe Rd in St Heliers and The Rise and Riddell Rd in Glendowie.

Local Hero: Movenpick Ice-Cream Gallery

Every seaside village needs a good ice-cream shop – strolling along the boardwalk at Mission Bay just wouldn't be the same without a cone clenched in hand.

And, of course, in this upmarket part of town, the shop isn't just any old parlour, but a swept-up and contemporary vision of loveliness, prominently sited on a corner in the middle of the shops. Inside, you can choose ice-cream of such delectable flavours as Tiramisu, Stracciatella, Lemon-Lime or Espresso Croquant, popped into a handmade Swiss waffle cone, no less. Take it to the beach, sit at one of the tables or admire the cool retro ice-cream cart parked in the front of the shop.

In winter, the store has hot chocolate brownies, hot fruit crepes and hot fruit sundaes. And, of course any food outlet wouldn't survive in Mission Bay, if it didn't serve good coffee.

At a Glance...

House Prices

Unit

Bedrooms	🛏 🛏
Price	$350,000 plus

Small freestanding townhouse

Bedrooms	🛏 🛏 🛏
Price	$580,000 - $665,000

Ex-state house on a half site

Bedrooms	🛏 🛏
Price	$550,000 - $650,000

Modest house

Bedrooms	🛏 🛏 🛏
Price	$600,000 - $680,000

House on full site or new townhouse

Bedrooms	🛏 🛏 🛏 🛏
Price	$800,000 - $900,000

Cliff-top home

Price	Multi-millions

Average Rents

Flat

Bedrooms	🛏 🛏
Price	$355/wk

House

Bedrooms	🛏 🛏 🛏
Price	$530/wk
Bedrooms	🛏 🛏 🛏 🛏
Price	$700/wk

Travel Times

From Mission Bay (add 5 mins for St Heliers)

CBD	peak 30 min off-peak 15-20 min by train 8 min
Greenlane interchange	15 min
Airport	30 min
Newmarket	15 min

There are regular buses through St Heliers and a train that runs along the bottom of Orakei Rd.

If Remuera is Auckland's best-known, richest suburb, Epsom is its august elder neighbour. Its elegant old houses recline in dignified silence behind stone walls and beneath mature trees. It almost seems charmed. This is where lawns seem to manicure themselves and dead leaves fly elsewhere to drop. Even the presence of some major arterial routes running through it towards the city can't dent the overriding feeling of peace and gentility. Epsom has some famous residences and, of course, the country's most highly regarded public boys school, Auckland Grammar. Its zoning restrictions lead many ordinarily upstanding parents to sneaky and creative address-fixing, and drives local real estate prices on a steady curve upwards. The southern reaches of the suburb may still be known as Epsom but have more of an affinity with the more lower middle class Royal Oak.

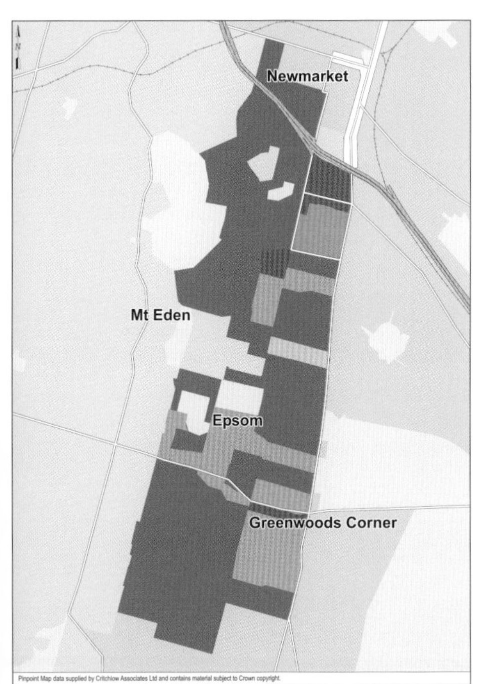

For colour key, see page 226

Population Profile

Population	9,849
% Aged Under 15 Years	20.32
% Aged Over 65 Years	9.53
% European	61.29
% Maori	2.56
% Pacific Peoples	1.83
% Asian	32.32

Who Lives There?

Well-heeled school age families are the backbone of Epsom, buying houses at premium prices to make sure their children are in-zone for Auckland Grammar and the equally well-thought-of Epsom Girls Grammar. Many of these are "education aware" Asian immigrants, whose off-spring tend to be true to studious form and make up the majority of the top streamed classes. So close are the schools that some children will even walk to school – a phenomenon virtually unheard of in recent years as we cotton-wool our kids.

There is a trend for families from inner-city suburbs such as Herne Bay – where schooling is a bit more hit-and-miss – to move here when their children reach secondary school age. They used to think Epsom was too staid and conservative, but now it stands for great, and free, education.

The suburb is definitely upper middle class in its outlook – and the impact of school zoning places even greater pressures on those wishing to buy.

Some of Epsom's decades old family names, finding the upkeep of their grounds costly and time consuming, have moved on. Rightly or wrongly, many of their homesteads have been flattened and replaced with modern townhouses.

Typical Homes

Epsom was settled mainly around the turn of the century, so there are many villas of 1900-1920s vintage as well as 1920s and 1930s bungalows. Most are large and beautifully renovated on substantial tree-studded sections.

Infill housing constructed during the past decade means there are now also many large townhouses in the area. They are mostly of brick-and-tile or plaster construction, and long-time residents say they signify new money and dubious design. Small units, sometimes in blocks, complete the spectrum of properties.

Amenities

Schools ★★★★★

Schooling in Epsom is excellent. This high decile area is home to at least two private and three public primaries and an intermediate. Epsom Normal Primary is a popular choice that includes separate gifted and talented classes. An English/Mandarin bilingual class has also been introduced to cope with a recent influx of students requiring language support.

The secondary schools in Epsom are some of the most sought after in Auckland, which is reflected in the inflated house prices for properties in-zone.

Auckland Grammar School (boys) and Epsom Girls Grammar consistently produce both

scholars and world class athletes. Auckland Grammar has produced 25 Rhodes scholars and 52 All Blacks since it first opened its gates in 1868.

Catholic St Peter's College and Marcellin College are also in the neighbourhood.

For a full list of schools, see page 270.

Shops ★★★★

Apart from the collection of antique and other small shops at Greenwoods Corner, Epsom itself is not big on shops. But with Newmarket down the road, and the city and the improved St Lukes mall close by, Epsom residents want for nothing when it comes to retail therapy. Also nearby are the charming villages of Mt Eden and Remuera.

Leisure ★★★★

Epsom has plenty of sports clubs covering hockey, football, bowling, croquet, tennis and netball as well as the Auckland Trotting Club. There is also the refurbished Lido Cinema, the Epsom library and Epsom Community Centre.

There's a wide choice of international cuisine available locally, including Indian, Italian, Chinese and Japanese. The gourmet fish and chip shop, Fish Café, at Greenwoods Corner is regularly voted as a top takeaway and the long-standing Eve's Pantry sees a steady clientele for its delectable cakes and savouries.

Real Estate

Trends

With its stately homes, large established gardens and wide tree-lined streets, Epsom would be a premium location even if it wasn't home to two of the country's most desirable public schools. This quirk of fate means a lot of ambitious parents who can't afford private school fees, or would rather use them to invest in a property that will hopefully increase in value, want to get into this area, and keeps real estate values high.

One- and two-bedroom units are the cheapest way to own a piece of Epsom. Investors like the one-bedders for the higher returns and less wear-and-tear from their professional couple or single tenants.

Two-bedrooms units are in most demand because they're more suitable for families – those chasing the school zones but can't afford a standalone house.

Being in-zone for Auckland Grammar puts an estimated premium of up to 25% on a property – and with Epsom prices, that's a considerable amount of money!

Epsom is a very family-oriented area so turnover of properties is not high. Despite the drop off in in-bound migration, demand for properties in all parts of Epsom is likely to remain strong for some time to come and houses sell steadily.

Best Streets

Mountain Rd, Shipherds Ave, Brightside Rd, Almorah Rd and Omana Ave.

Look Out (!)

With all the inner-city schools about to burst at the seams, it seems inevitable that another public high school will eventually be opened. The house values in this suburb are so heavily influenced by school zones that the effect of a new school on property values will always be an unknown.

At a Glance...

House Prices

Units

Bedroom	
Price	$250,000
Bedrooms	
Price	$380,000 - $420,000

House outside grammar zone, (half-site)

Bedrooms	
Price	early $500,000's

Large house in zone, (full-site)

Bedrooms	
Price	$1,500,000+

Average Rents

Unit

Bedroom	
Price	$240/wk

House

Bedrooms	
Price	$580/wk
Bedrooms	
Price	$660/wk

Schooling also drives a frantic demand for rentals.

Travel Times

CBD	peak 25 min off-peak 10 min
North-western motorway	10 min
Southern motorway	1 - 5 min
Airport	20 min
Royal Oak shops	5 min
Newmarket	5 min

Stagecoach Auckland has a regular bus service to Epsom, many traveling along the major roads of Gillies Ave and Manukau Rd. The major arterial of Gillies Ave is both a blessing and curse for local commuters; getting on at peak time is a tedious exercise but once on, you're well connected.

including Wai O Taiki Bay

Glen Innes and Pt England have a reputation for being rough with many state-owned rental houses, but these often overlooked suburbs have a richness of another kind. Like cultural diversity, a strong community spirit and, on a less touchy-feely note, a swathe of waterside land bordering the Tamaki River. Popular with first-home buyers and investors, the area was mainly paddocks until World War II but now has many 1950s two-storey duplexes, some lovingly renovated ex-State gems and pockets of infill housing. Pt England is the more upmarket suburb. Glen Innes has large sections and with most of the area zoned Res 5, few properties can be subdivided – more space to park the dead cars, perhaps. There are a lot of churches, which is always a good sign.

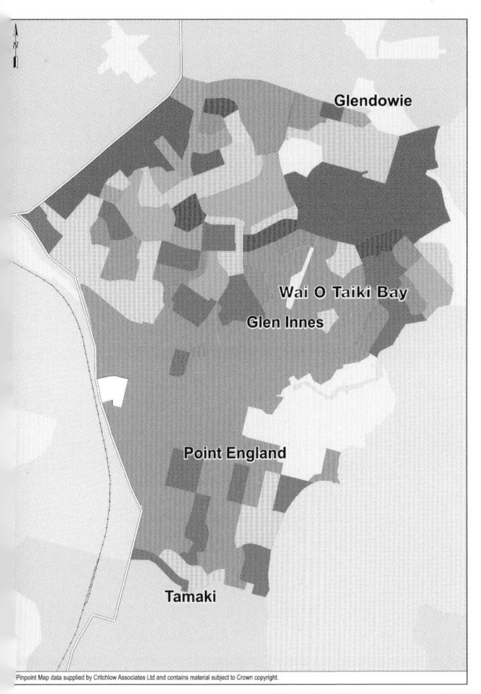

For colour key, see page 226

Population Profile

Population	16,125
% Aged Under 15 Years	26.98
% Aged Over 65 Years	11.81
% European	46.79
% Maori	15.50
% Pacific Peoples	31.83
% Asian	8.89

Who Lives There?

The area has great ethnic diversity – lots of Maori, Pacific Islanders and Asians. There are many immigrants including Arabs and Albanians. Many Asian immigrants have moved to Glen Innes and Pt England, attracted by the lower rents and house prices. Being home to the Tamaki campus of the University of Auckland, it is popular with students, especially on the hill at the St Johns Rd end of the suburb. Which, in turn, makes it popular with investors.

With the prevalence of state housing, it's an area of blue collar workers. Residents have lots of pride in the area and a strong community spirit. They love their beer and their sports.

Young couples and professionals have come into the area, buying up ex-state houses and restoring these solid little homes. Many of these first-time home buyers will move closer to the sea or the more affluent neighbouring suburbs of St Johns and Glendowie in subsequent moves.

Typical Homes

Archetypal houses are current and former state houses and bungalows of 1940s vintage onwards, including typical 1950s two-storey duplexes. Some ex-state houses have been nicely renovated. Wai O Taiki Bay is a pleasant mix of new houses and state homes.

Recent state housing developments have progressed in Maybury St and Rowena Cres. Since the late 1980s, some parts of Glen Innes, such as Ropata Ave, have seen a fair amount of infill housing. There are still many two-bedroom houses on large plots.

The Talbot Park area is under redevelopment by Housing New Zealand. The plan is to provide better housing by refurbishing units and homes and to make the general area safer with features such as good street lighting.

Amenities

Schools ★★

Glen Innes, which has predominantly decile one schools, is popular with families and there are at least three primary schools, one intermediate and a secondary school in the area, all within walking distance of most parts of the suburb. Glen Innes Primary is one of the most established schools in the neighbourhood and celebrates its 50th jubilee in 2006.

The secondary school, Tamaki College, has a reasonably small roll and is a popular choice for people in Glen Innes. The college's recreation centre is considered to be one of the best facilities of its type in any school in New Zealand.

For a full list, see page 270.

Shops ★★★

Known mostly for its food shopping, Glen Innes is packed with butchers, fruit and vegetable shops and a popular supermarket. It is a popular destination with residents from surrounding areas as well as the locals as a great place to do your weekly shop.

For residents who worry about the safety of local parks and streets (there have been some high-profile assaults), there's a sparkling new police station in Line Rd.

Leisure ★★★

The area has a great sporting complex with a pool, and it is bordered by the Merton Rd sports grounds which cater for rugby, cricket, soccer and tennis. Auckland University's Tamaki Campus, between St Johns and Pt England, continues to develop and impress, particularly with its new netball courts and other athletic facilities.

The estuary has a walking track from Mt Wellington along the coastline to Glendowie which passes a native bird sanctuary.

Real Estate

Trends

There is still a high proportion of state-owned housing in Glen Innes, which means the remaining housing stock is always in demand. Oddly, that hasn't resulted in a sharp increase in prices with the down-at-heel flavour prevailing for now. A two-bedroom home recently sold in Glen Innes for what was considered a whopping $270,000 – in other parts of Auckland that might be cheap for the most modest of homes, but here, it usually buys a house with three bedrooms, not two.

River-oriented Wai O Taiki Bay is still a hot area, with its views across the estuary. A five-bedroom former state house in "questionable condition" sold here for $630,000. Properties on the border of the more desirable Glendowie (eg Mount Taylor Dr, once the infamous "Mad Ave" before it was renamed) also carry high price tags.

The sought-after ex-state homes don't stay on the market for long.

The government housing project at Talbot Park (refurbishment of 108 units and creation of 98 new homes and two reserves) is due for completion in December 2006. Contrary to local resident fears, the anticipated negative effect on house prices nearby is negligible.

Best Streets

In Glen Innes, the top end off West Tamaki Rd, Weybridge Cres and Paddington St. In Pt England, Dunkirk Rd, and Riki Rd. In Wai O Taiki Bay, Silverton Ave and Inglewood St.

Smart Buy

Still relatively cheap in Auckland terms, the area is picking up. It is close to the waterfront, the city and Botany Downs. With Housing New Zealand likely to be a strong property owner for the near future, it may take a while to really come into its own, but it is still worth a look, especially around the edges.

At a Glance...

House Prices

For Wai O Taiki Bay, add $50,000

Unit

Bedrooms	2
Price	$200,000

Ex-state house

Bedrooms	3
Price	$280,000+

Modern townhouse

Bedrooms	3
Price	$400,000+

Basic house

Bedrooms	4
Price	$300,000 - $450,000

Average Rents

Flat

Bedroom	1
Price	$185/wk
Bedrooms	2
Price	$250/wk

House

Bedrooms	2
Price	$270/wk
Bedrooms	3
Price	$335/wk

Travel Times

Glen Innes shops to:

CBD	peak 40 min off-peak 20 min
Southern motorway	15-17 min
Airport	30 min

This area is well served by both buses and trains.

Grey Lynn ★★★★

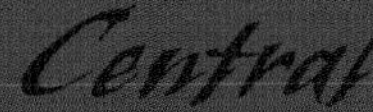

including Westmere, Pt Chevalier and Arch Hill

Once populated by bohemians who would happily turn their backs on riches, Grey Lynn is now home to a reborn breed - bohemians who have grown up, become cosmopolitan and now realise they need the cash they once spurned in order to afford the houses here. Where once they drank herbal tea, it's now lattes, albeit made with soy milk. They may stoop so low as to buy non-organic veges at Foodtown now, but they'll carry them home in a reusable calico bag. Grey Lynn is a desirable inner-city suburb, seen as a slightly cheaper alternative to neighbouring Ponsonby, and traditional home to free-thinkers and anti-establishment types. Westmere and Pt Chevalier exhibit some of the same tendencies but beneath the liberal veneer, there are more conservative concerns, while cheaper Arch Hill attracts younger homebuyers to its smaller villas.

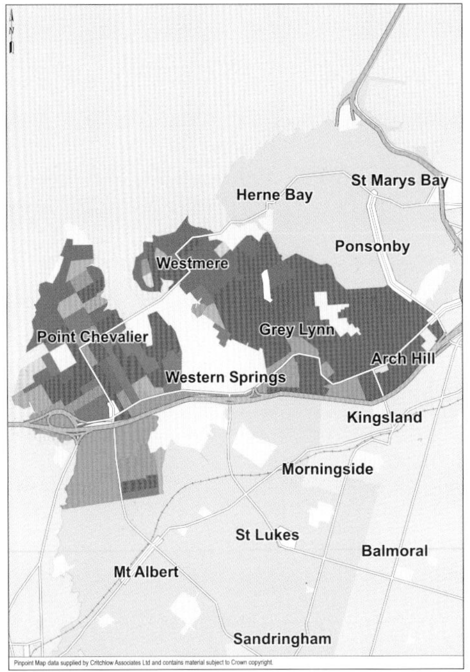

For colour key, see page 226

Population Profile

Population	23,781
% Aged Under 15 Years	18.09
% Aged Vver 65 Years	9.84
% European	73.05
% Maori	8.58
% Pacific Peoples	14.82
% Asian	8.14

Who Lives There?

Aside from the neo-hippies, Grey Lynn is where many of the artistically inclined and media types like to live (go celeb-spotting at the local supermarket). It's also the traditional home of gay women - gay men live in the more expensive neighbouring Ponsonby because men generally earn more money and don't have kids to support.

As with many of the inner-city suburbs, the trendy bohemianism has been replaced with more mundane concerns such as interest rates and school zones.

These suburbs attract young hipster renters who want to be close to the city centre, the clubs and cafés along Ponsonby and Karangahape Rds. Older people who have lived in the area for most of their lives choose to remain and there is a sizeable number of Maori and Polynesian families in long-held family homes.

Westmere and Pt Chevalier are not as outwardly arty as Grey Lynn, however the suburbs are full of trendy liberals, often with school-age child accessories.

Being a waterfront suburb, Westmere's attraction has increased markedly in the past decade.

Pt Chevalier has always been popular with older people. Before Meola Rd linked it to Westmere in the late 1970s, the peninsula suburb was a backwater. Now, it is in demand from young professionals and families as a commuter suburb and a great place to raise a family (parks, schools, tidal beaches).

Typical Homes

Grey Lynn and Arch Hill's villas and bungalows have undergone a steady spit and polish regime during the past decade. Most are now smartly renovated with modern interiors, leaving only a few remaining broken-down houses or those artistically embellished with weird colour schemes. There's a group of well-established terraced houses near the West Lynn shops and some apartment buildings on the main arterial Great North Rd. Arch Hill has narrower streets, smaller worker's cottages and more do-ups.

Westmere and Pt Chevalier were originally developed as bungalow suburbs in the 1920s and grew directly along the tram routes. Westmere has a variety of wooden bungalows, ex-state homes and the occasional stucco clad Art Deco house. Subdivision of larger sections has meant that there is a good smattering of designer townhouses.

Amenities

Schools ★★★

Grey Lynn adequately caters for all levels of schooling. There are at least six primary schools in the area, Pasadena Intermediate School and Western Springs College.

Pt Chevalier Primary School is highly-regarded. Despite being more than 100 years old the well-appointed school features high-quality new buildings and renovations, attractive gardens and well-developed play areas. Westmere Primary School is also very popular and just as old!

Western Springs College is one of the smaller secondary schools in Auckland with a roll of about 800. The decile 7 college has a reputation for innovative school drama productions, musicals and multi-cultural events. A new $4 million performing arts centre provides the perfect venue to support the students' creative talents.

For a full list, see page 270.

Shops ★★★

Grey Lynn Foodtown is a mecca for celebrity-spotters, it seems to be the supermarket of choice for numerous recording artists and famous TV folks.

Despite the high real estate values in the area, the main shopping centre at Surrey Cres is still rather shabby – the retro furniture shop Zeitgeist is unusually chic which might be a sign of things to come.

The West Lynn shops are more gentrified, with half a dozen trendy bars and cafés, organic store Harvest Wholefoods, a boutique wine shop and an organic baby clothes shop.

Westmere's little shopping centre had three antique shops not so long ago; it's now down to one. The others have become eateries and wine shops.

Pt Chevalier's main shops are as shabby as Surrey Cres, but a few more interesting shops are opening up towards the beach.

Leisure ★★★

The annual Grey Lynn Festival (held in Grey Lynn Park) in mid-summer attracts more than 40,000 people to its stalls and entertainment. Auckland Zoo, MOTAT (Museum of Transport and Technology) and Western Springs Stadium are just down the road. Grey Lynn Park has a free toddler pool and sports grounds and Cox's Bay Reserve has sports fields and a sea view.

Coyle Park at the end of Pt Chevalier peninsula is a lovely open space with plenty of parking. The beach is accessed here or further back off Harbour View Rd and is pretty but tidal. The bottom of Raymond St is popular for launching windsurfers.

Meola Reef, the point where some of the lava from Mt Albert's eruption met the sea, is a favourite spot for dogs and their people. There's a large off-lead area for socialising with other urban pooches.

Real Estate

Trends

Pt Chevalier has been a star performer during the past decade - according to the Auckland Central Property Hotspots Report produced by Hybrid Consulting it has had the highest capital gain (143%) of any suburb in Auckland during the 10 years to September 2005 (the average across all of Auckland was 106% during the same time). Reasons given are that it's mostly coastal, has a strong community spirit, is handy to the CBD and has been perceived as more affordable that Westmere and Grey Lynn.

Pt Chevalier houses north of Meola Rd used to be more expensive but that gap is closing with southern properties desired for their bigger sections and handy location.

Across the area, demand is strong from young families. In Grey Lynn, a new type of buyer has emerged for the apartment buildings that are popping up where car yards and old commercial buildings used to be on Great North Rd. They are a mix of young people, older people who want to retire close to the city without being in the thick of it, and empty-nesters who want to stay in the area.

As with all central city suburbs, demand will stay high and outstrip supply for the foreseeable future.

Best Streets

In Westmere, Rawene St and lower Garnet Rd. In Pt Chevalier, Harbour View Rd and Lynch St. In Grey Lynn, the upper reaches of Ariki St, Beaconsfield St and Elgin. Popular in Arch Hill is Cooper St, which is preserved under heritage status.

Why We Live There

Singer Jackie Clarke and film-maker Grant Lahood

When Grant and Jackie moved from Wellington some years ago, Grey Lynn was their choice of suburb. With their creative backgrounds, they typify the profile of the local residents.

Says Jackie: "The location is great. It's close enough to the city to still feel in touch with our wild youth [pre two children] when we used to go out a lot. It's a funky neighbourhood with a healthy mix of people. There are good schools, parks, and there are coffee places that are still a bit hokey. There are enough boutique shops to keep you interested but also Polynesian grocers and takeaways that sell everything from fish and chips to pizza. In 10 years time it might become too gentrified but it's good right now.

"Although we flirted for about 12 months with moving west for a bigger section, we can't seem to wean ourselves off the 'hood. We occasionally dip our toes into other parts of Auckland but really everything we need is here, including our work."

At a Glance...

House Prices

Spacious new apartment

Bedrooms	🛏 🛏
Price	\$300,000 - \$400,00

Cottage

Bedrooms	🛏 🛏
Price	\$450,000 - \$600,000

Tidy villa or bungalow

Bedrooms	🛏 🛏 🛏
Price	\$550,000 - \$750,000

Renovated house

Bedrooms	🛏 🛏 🛏 🛏
Price	\$800,000 - \$1.2 million

Executive house close to the water

Price	\$1million plus

Average Rents

Flat or apartment

Bedroom	🛏
Price	\$260 - \$300/wk
Bedrooms	🛏 🛏
Price	\$340 - \$420/wk

House

Bedrooms	🛏 🛏
Price	\$400/wk
Bedrooms	🛏 🛏 🛏
Price	\$490/wk

Travel Times

From Grey Lynn shops:	
CBD	peak 15 min off-peak 10 min
From Westmere shops	
CBD	peak 20 min off-peak 10 min
North-western motorway	5 min
Airport	30 min
St Lukes mall	10 min

Pt Chevalier's shape creates a bit of a traffic bottle-neck. Beach-end properties are more expensive partly because of the alternative route to and from the city via Meola Rd. There are excellent bus services to the entire area, especially along the major arterial roads.

Hauraki Gulf Islands  

including Waiheke Island, Great Barrier Island and Rakino Island

How many times can one island reincarnate itself? First Waiheke Island was a hippy hangout for dope-smoking escapees of urban life, then it became a holiday mecca dotted with quaint baches and now it's a commuter suburb with a colourful blend of all of the above. There are few major world cities boasting an island suburb like Waiheke, and fewer that have undergone the phenomenal property value rises of recent years as Aucklanders have flocked to buy coastal property. Beautiful beaches, grape and olive groves, a laid-back lifestyle, cafés and a quick ferry service to downtown Auckland are just some of the attractions of this romantic idyll. Great Barrier Island lies 90km northeast of Auckland and is 75 percent rugged conservation land. Rakino Island is near Waiheke, but has a much smaller population and more primitive facilities, ie no cafés or even shops.

Great Barrier Island
Otata Island
Rakino Island
Enclosure Bay
Blackpool
Onetangi
Man O'war Bay
Motuihe Island
Waiheke Island
Omiha
Cowes
Orapiu
Ponui Island
Beachlands
Cockle Bay
Pakihi Island
Wade Island
Karamuramu Island
Whitford
Ruakawakawa

For colour key, see page 226

Population Profile

Population	7,242
% Aged Under 15 Years	20.05
% Aged Over 65 Years	13.84
% European	86.12
% Maori	11.10
% Pacific Peoples	3.15
% Asian	2.03

Who Lives There?

Once the domain of retired folk, the unemployed and alternative lifestylers who had to float two hours in a boat to get to the city, Waiheke Island has become a commuter suburb and holidaying mecca. While plenty of locals could still be described as left-leaning and green, they're now more settled and middle class. The stauncher hippies have moved to Great Barrier Island or the Coromandel.

Waiheke has long been popular with artists and craftspeople. Now it's also a trendy haven for media and advertising personalities. The need to commute by ferry is no longer seen as a problem and many residents own apartments and cars in the central city.

Waiheke baches are being snapped up by wealthy professionals looking for something that doesn't involve a frustrating car trip out of town. During summer, the island's population rises from 10,000 to around 40,000.

Great Barrier Island's population is mainly farming based. Its 1100 or so residents live clustered in scattered coastal settlements, Port FitzRoy and Okiwi in the north, Okupu and Tryphena in the southwest and Claris and Oruawharo (Medlands) in the east. The numbers swell in the summer. Many business people who used to go to their Great Barrier homes only on weekends are now staying longer – even though the internet service on the island is painfully slow, it enables them to keep their business going while lingering at their holiday homes.

Rakino Island's permanent population is tiny, life here is for the hardy and adventurous only.

Typical Homes

The classic Waiheke bach is becoming rare, with many being bowled to make way for swanky modern creations. Most properties are on large sections and while there are do-ups available, anything with a sea view sells fast and at a price. The new house styles vary, with mud brick, board and batten, barn style and Mediterranean stucco available as well as swept-up creations in zincalume corrugated steel and concrete. There are also a number older houses relocated from the mainland.

It's not a place where you'd expect to find townhouses or apartment blocks; however in a few places zoning has allowed for medium density housing. Palm Beach has a group of four Kerry Avery-designed homes and The Sands is a lock-up-and-leave apartment complex with an on-site manager at Onetangi.

Houses on Great Barrier Island are more rustic with the odd discretely designed architectural number. Rakino's few houses are just rustic.

Amenities

Schools ★★★

Schooling on Waiheke Island is available for all ages, although many commute to schools in the city and on the North Shore. There is a pre-school, primary school and high school, with more primary schools proposed as the population expands.

After resolving some publicised governance and management issues, as documented in recent ERO reports, Waiheke High School is now performing well academically and its island location creates a unique learning environment.

There are three primary schools on Great Barrier Island, but once their children reach high-school age, families often move to the mainland.

For a full list, see page 270.

Shops ★★★

Waiheke Island's shops are now almost mainstream. The main shopping area is

in Oneroa with banks, restaurants, cafés, bookshops and the rest. There is a supermarket at Ostend, as well as numerous local shopping outlets and many arts and crafts stores.

Great Barrier has cafés, a pub and several stores. Rakino has nothing.

Leisure ★★★★★

In addition to the gorgeous white sand and pebble beaches, Waiheke Island is a great place for sea kayaking, horse riding, golf, fishing and diving, walks in the Forest and Bird reserve at Onetangi, or Whakenewha Park near Rocky Bay. Historic relics from Second World War years, including tunnels and gun emplacements at Stony Batter, can be explored. Waiheke has become famous for its vineyards and award-winning wines during recent years.

Much of Great Barrier is covered with second generation native trees with pockets of regenerating native forest and remnants of kauri forest in the north. There are the remains of New Zealand's last whaling station, plus the Kaiarara Kauri Dam.

Real Estate

Trends

During the latest round of council property valuations, these three islands showed the biggest increases of all the suburbs in Auckland: Rakino at 115%, Waiheke 94% and Great Barrier 86%.

While that has some owners rubbing their hands in glee, others (long-time residents on limited budgets) are dismayed at the resulting council rates increases.

North-side properties on Waiheke and north/east properties on Great Barrier are often double the price of their south-side equivalents: the north is warmer, sheltered from the prevailing southerlies, and boasts the best beaches. There are also some beautiful private baches that are only accessible by boat.

Most buyers are locals or Aucklanders; however, there are also many international buyers.

There's always a scramble for bare land. There are a few subdividible sites available, but they have to be big. An 800m² section is considered a small site and there is no infill housing allowed. Building consents are given for a specific number of bedrooms rather than size.

The new lifestyle blocks of up to 4ha are in demand for hobby farms or vineyards, and with these estates come architecturally designed dwellings.

Great Barrier is still not accessible enough for holiday-makers to open their wallets too wide.

Rakino Island has four residential areas, all surrounded by rural blocks of about 4ha. One local agent predicts that Rakino will one day become a very exclusive retreat, with all the charm of Waiheke, but without the mass of population or the infrastructure. It's hard to visualise.

Best Streets

On Waiheke Island, any beachfront road like The Strand, Beach Parade, Palm Rd or Waikare Rd. There are no best streets on Great Barrier.

Travel Times

From Waiheke Island:

Onetangi to ferry terminal	15 min
Ferry to CBD	35 min

Ferries between Waiheke Island and Auckland CBD run nearly hourly all day with extra sailings in peak times. Car ferries go from Half Moon Bay in Auckland and Kennedy Pt on Waiheke. There are regular bus services around the island.

There is a weekend ferry service between Pine Harbour (near Beachlands) and Rakino, via Waiheke, which takes about 35 minutes. Water taxis are also available from downtown Auckland ($46 return). Most Rakino-ites own a boat.

The trip to Great Barrier takes about two hours by ferry (a seasonal service) or 30 minutes by small plane.

Why We Live There

Winemaker John Dunleavy and Deborah Dunleavy

When winemaker John Dunleavy and his wife Deborah returned from overseas nearly 20 years ago, they wanted the perfect place to bring up a young family in a small caring community with open spaces and beaches, not too far from Auckland city. "We love Waiheke. We first came here for a weekend back in 1983, fell in love with the island's beauty and went away with a deposit on a one-acre section at Palm Beach. It had 180-degree sea views and was only $15,000."

Now they are fully immersed in Waiheke Island's best known industry, establishing the Te Motu vineyard and more recently The Shed restaurant, in Onetangi valley.

Deb commutes to Auckland daily. "We have the best of both worlds here – the city 35 minutes away for working, shopping, entertainment... and best of all the return to our island tranquillity.

Smart Buy ✓

Although Waiheke Island is now as expensive as the mainland, the heat has cooled considerably. Buyers can now shop around more and take their time making decisions. Coastal and island property will always hold strong appeal and a wisely bought property here will increase in value. The profiles of Great Barrier and Rakino are growing steadily, too.

At a Glance...

House Prices

Waiheke Island

Do-up bach	
Price	$280,000

Cottage with limited views

Bedrooms	2
Price	$400,000

Average house

Bedrooms	3
Price	$400,000 – $600,000
With good sea views	$800,000 + (north side)
	$600,000 + (south side)

Beachfront house (north side)

Bedrooms	4
Price	$2,000,000 - $3,000,000

Cliff-top house in new estate

Price	$2,500,000

Rakino Island

Basic bach	$300,000
Coastal property	$500,000

Great Barrier Island

Entry level	$300,000
Bedrooms	3
Price	$300,000 – $900,000
Close to the water	$1,000,000

Average Rents

Flat

Bedrooms	2
Price	$290/wk

House

Bedrooms	2
Price	$270/wk
Bedrooms	3
Price	$335/wk

Of course, these rents are for your average weekly grind. Casual holiday rentals can be up to $500 a night.

Kingsland ★★★½

including Eden Terrace, Western Springs and Morningside

Kingsland used to be a grungy inner-city haunt of students and their ilk. These days it's the stamping ground of the modern incarnation of the yuppie. They're carrying the mantle of all that is fab about inner-city living; shopping at the local boutiques and being seen at the cafés. Kingsland is also seen as the cheaper alternative to Ponsonby and Grey Lynn. Kingsland's tastefully groovy shops, galleries and cafés, narrow streets, villas and its closeness to the CBD are very alluring. Western Springs is less frantically trendy but is being just as steadily gentrified. Eden Terrace is an eclectic mix of residential and commercial properties; an idiosyncratic, bohemian character and a number of student flats. The north-western motorway runs at the foot of these suburbs which, depending how far you are down the hill, is a plus or a minus.

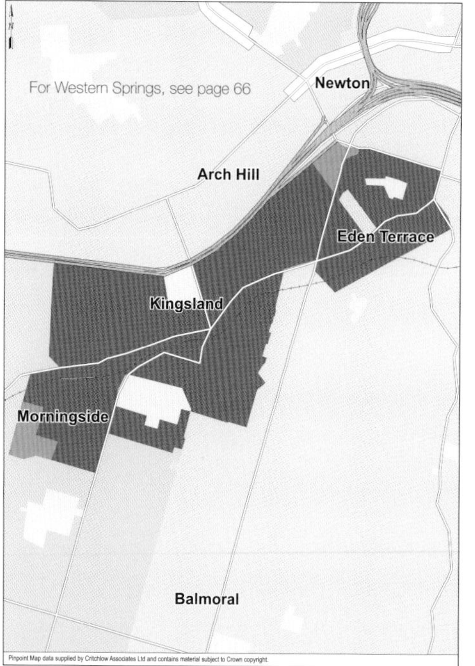

For colour key, see page 226

Population Profile

Population	5,421
% Aged Under 15 Years	13.61
% Aged Over 65 Years	3.98
% European	65.52
% Maori	8.36
% Pacific Peoples	15.05
% Asian	9.96

Who Lives There?

This once less-than-desirable area is now humming to the sound of coffee machines and the cry of wee ones following in their trendy parents' footsteps. Professionals have moved in, as traditional blue collar residents move out. It's telling that Kingsland now boasts an "urban pet accessories" store (Fur), with such canine must-haves as von Dutch hoodies and bowWOW Butter Balm for sore paws.

Western Springs has moved from a rental suburb to a thriving family area. The do-ups that renovators have bought in the past are now ripe for re-sale and are being snapped up by willing buyers.

Gentrification of the whole region has been fuelled by those making the jump across the north-western motorway from the more expensive Grey Lynn. Some of the older Polynesian families remain, many living in homes owned for several generations.

Typical Homes

These suburbs were established over time and there is a range of house styles, from turn-of-the-century villas, cottages and onwards. Most Kingsland houses are villas and the suburb is a protected area under the council's district scheme.

There's also a number of contemporary homes. Although many of the houses in Western Springs are on larger sections (by inner-city standards) subdivision opportunities are scarce.

There are some apartment complexes, such as those near the railway line in Morningside, the new block in Kingsland or further up New North Rd in Eden Terrace.

There are some tatty blocks of flats, particularly down Don Croot St between Kingsland and Western Springs, but even this area is being slowly spruced up.

Amenities

Schools ★★

If living close to schools is a high priority you may want to look elsewhere. There are no primary or secondary schools in Kingsland – the closest are Mt Albert Primary in Morningside, and Newton Central School in Grey Lynn.

The decile six Kowhai Intermediate is just around the corner from the Kingsland shops. Established in 1922, Kowhai was the first intermediate school in the country. Maori bilingual and immersion classes are a special feature.

The nearest secondary schools are Auckland Girls Grammar and Western Springs College.

For a full list, see page 270.

Shops ★★★

This area has the perfect mix of trendy village-style shops in Kingsland and mega-mall style shopping down the road at St Lukes. With Kingsland's boutique shops, restaurants and cafés appreciated by trendy types from all over the city, it's often hard to find a car park on this stretch of New North Rd during dining hours.

There's an excellent array of eateries and drinkeries, including cosy wine bar Ruby and alternative café Roasted Addiqtion. You can get arguably the city's best burgers at Handmade, a burger joint in a converted petrol station.

Practical service shops, such as Carters and Briscoes, are close by off Morningside Dr and there are supermarkets in Grey Lynn, St Lukes and Mt Eden.

Leisure ★★★★

Eden Park stadium is, of course, a major draw card and Western Springs has outdoor concerts and annual festivals, and until recently, the

speedway – although its eviction may not be a done deal.

Western Springs Park with its huge central lake is a fabulous place for a family outing. The zoo and MOTAT are right next to the park. Chamberlain Park Public Golf Course is on St Lukes Rd.

The area's parks also have skateboarding ramps, basketball hoops and rugby grounds.

Real Estate

Trends

Kingsland now has an apartment block, aptly, but perhaps unimaginatively, called The Kingsland, where units sell for up to $570,000 for three bedrooms, two bathrooms and tandem covered garaging. Not long ago this area had abundant rentals, but these days owner-occupied is more the norm. Local DIY and garden stores do a roaring trade.

Don Croot St, which runs between Kingsland and Western Springs, is a good place to get a toehold in the area. The street was home to some rough characters years ago, and that reputation has lingered. A good two-bedroom unit in very good condition will only cost you little more than $200,000. Just don't expect to flick it on quickly: as one agent says, "everything eventually sells, it's just a heck of a lot harder in this street".

Best Streets

First and Second Ave in Kingsland and Springfield Rd in Western Springs. Properties along Western Springs Rd, on the ridge overlooking Grey Lynn and Fowlds Park, now command $1 million plus.

Smart Buy ✓

Kingsland is just a stone's throw from the now expensive Grey Lynn, yet the north-western motorway seems to act as a psychological break point – meaning that savvy buyers can take advantage of the inevitable flow-on effect. Although not as undiscovered as it once was, Western Springs still has a bargain or two.

At a Glance...

House Prices

Unit

Bedrooms	🛏 🛏
Price	$270,000

Cottage

Bedrooms	🛏 🛏
Price	$400,000 - $520,000

Bungalow or villa do-up

Bedrooms	🛏 🛏 🛏
Price	$520,000 - $600,000

House

Bedrooms	🛏 🛏 🛏 🛏
Price	$650,000 +

Average Rents

Flat

Bedroom	🛏
Price	$230/wk
Bedrooms	🛏 🛏
Price	$280/wk

House

Bedrooms	🛏 🛏 🛏
Price	$420/wk

Travel Times

From Kingsland shops:

CBD	peak 20 min off-peak 10min by train 15 min
North-western motorway	5 min
Airport	30 min
Westfield St Lukes mall	5 min

Stagecoach provides a good bus service, particularly along Great North Rd. Commuter trains en route from the west stop at Kingsland station, right by the shops, and at Morningside. The Kingsland train station was gussied up in time for the 2005 Lions matches at Eden Park. Although the lift tower happened (wonder who uses it), the planned overbridge hasn't happened yet. There's talk of upgrading the neighbouring stops at Mt Eden and Morningside before the 2011 Rugby World Cup. Thanks, rugby!

Including St Johns and Ellerslie

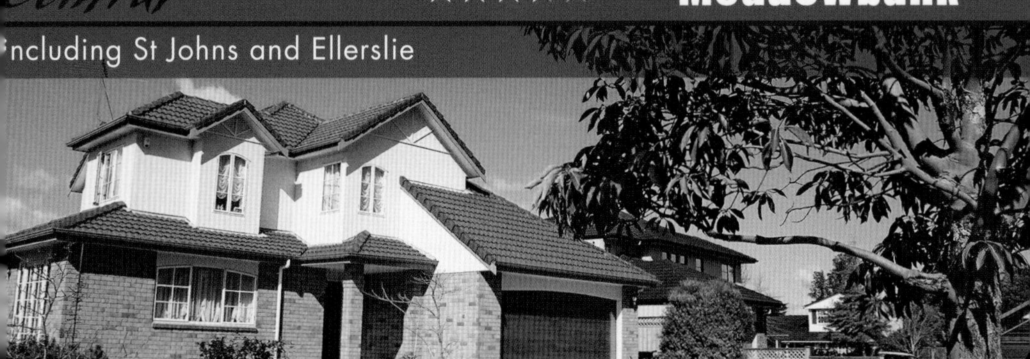

Hanging tenaciously onto the skirts of its ritzier neighbour Remuera, this area can't help but be appealing. You may not be as handy to the CBD, but heading east for your major shopping is an easy option, the Eastern Bays beaches are a tumble down the hill and the motorway's fairly accessible. Meadowbank has plenty of green spaces with the sizable Waiatarua Reserve and Remuera Golf Club rubbing shoulders. Ellerslie is a much older suburb with affordable villas and bungalows, but that's changing and it's become increasingly popular with professional couples. St Johns – including the fashionable St Johns Park - is a more recent addition to the city's landscape. A notable St Johns landmark is the theological college with its pleasant, parklike grounds. As well as giving the suburb its name, it provides tertiary level education for both the Anglican and Methodist churches.

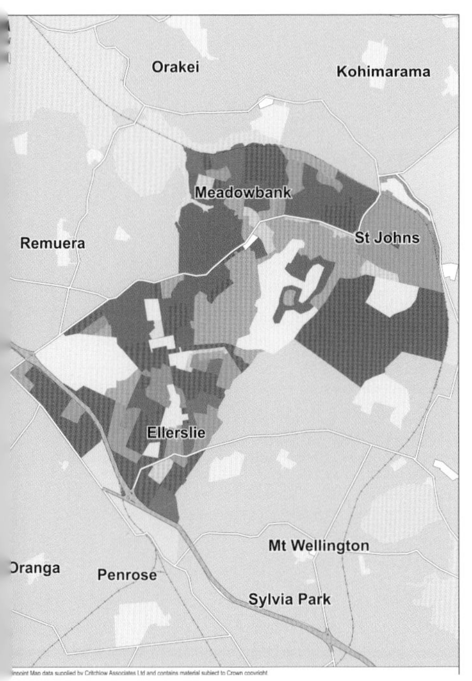

For colour key, see page 226

Population Profile

Population	24,351
% Aged Under 15 Years	17.51
% Aged Over 65 Years	10.95
% European	71.15
% Maori	4.92
% Pacific Peoples	4.36
% Asian	18.60

Who Lives There?

Many families with school-age children buy in Meadowbank. The local primary schools are excellent and when the children get older, their parents will either turn their backs on the grammar zone fights that take place in Remuera next door and enrol their children in private schools ... or they'll upgrade to Remuera and join in the scrum.

If you want a stable area, friendly neighbours and a relaxed lifestyle, then Meadowbank's hard to beat. You have to have a reasonable amount of money for these suburbs; this is not usually the domain of first-home buyers.

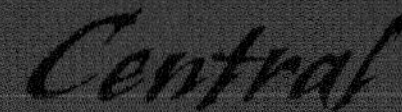

There's a wide multicultural mix as well, with many migrants making these suburbs home, especially St Johns Park.

Typical Homes

Meadowbank underwent a building boom 30 years ago when the houses were roomy and sprawling and well-designed for family living. This was the era of the rumpus room, barbecue patio and conversation den. The 1970s.

These homes, and the mix of older established homes – including 1940s bungalows and many ex-state houses – together with recent townhouses and developments, blend well into the landscape, and give the region a lived-in, friendly feel. The sense of spaciousness is one of the suburb's most attractive features. Generally, sections are fenced and tidy and not cramped up against their neighbours.

St Johns has many rental properties, while St Johns Park has large, modern, multi-bedroom family dwellings on good-sized plots of land. Ellerslie has some old villas as well as terrace housing complexes near the village. The Ladies Mile/Pukerangi Cres area still has some grand old merchant's houses.

Amenities

Schools ★★★

Meadowbank is not inundated with schools, however the local primary schools have solid reputations, including the high-decile Mt Carmel School and Ellerslie Schools. Being on major bus routes makes traveling to nearby secondary schools easy; Glendowie College is popular. Many students also attend private schools in Epsom and elsewhere.

Ellerslie is home to one of only two Rudolf Steiner schools in Auckland, the Michael Park School, which goes from preschool through to high school. For a full list see page 270.

Shops ★★★

Meadowbank has one of the best supermarkets in Auckland – the Foodtown nestled in the small Meadowbank mall.

Marua Rd in Ellerslie has the wonderful Mexican Specialties shop, which is only open Fridays and Saturdays, and sells authentic Mexican groceries, café food and handcrafts.

There's also easy access to Newmarket, Pakuranga/Howick and Botany Town Centre. Just around the corner on the Mt Wellington Highway there's a busy mega centre including The Warehouse, Noel Leemings, Rebel Sports, Briscoes, Plastic Box and an Ezibuy retail store. And, of course, there is now the huge Sylvia Park retail centre in neighbouring Mt Wellington.

Leisure ★★★

One of Meadowbank's great benefits is its easy access to the waterfront, with beaches and myriad water sports. Auckland Domain and One Tree Hill are just down the road. Waiatarua Reserve is popular with joggers and weekend strollers, and has a small bird sanctuary. Remuera Golf Club is well patronised (there's a long, long waiting list). The impressive university sports fields and McDonald's tennis centre on Merton Rd are local assets. Ellerslie

Ellerslie Racecourse

Racecourse is also here, and is the site of the busy Sunday morning car fair. There's also a small par three golf course and driving range in the infield.

Real Estate

Trends

Although Ellerslie and Meadowbank have traditionally been seen as cheaper locations than neighbouring Remuera, the price gap narrowed during the recent property boom. Even with a moderate softening in demand, prices remain stable here. Meadowbank's, and especially Ellerslie's, handiness to the city, with good rail and vehicle access, has meant many people favour this area when relocating.

Prices can vary widely in this area with some of the variation being due to swathes of St Johns Trust leasehold land. Depending on the terms of the lease and ground rents, leasehold properties can be sometimes much cheaper and therefore more attractive: in St Johns you might get a two-bedroom leasehold unit for $120,000 while freehold would be nearer $350,000.

Prices increase appreciably in St Johns Park and in Ellerslie Heights where there are some fine old homes.

Best Streets

Temple St is seen as Meadowbank's best. Ellerslie has no real standout streets. In St Johns and St Johns Park, anything near the golf course demands top dollar as well as Panapa Dr, Coldham Cres and Charles Fox Pl.

Look Out (!)

The planned 2200 new homes to be built in the substantial Mt Wellington Quarry area, across the road from Meadowbank and St Johns, has some people despairing that the already busy main roads will become traffic congested nightmares. The first sections are due to be built on in early 2007 and the quarry is expected to fill up during the next six years, eventually becoming home to 6000 to 8000 people.

At a Glance...

House Prices

Unit

Bedrooms	🛏 🛏
Price	$260,000 +

Ex-state house

Bedrooms	🛏 🛏 🛏
Price	$500,000

Newer house

Bedrooms	🛏 🛏 🛏 🛏
Price	$650,000 – $850,000

Property with golf course views

Price	$1 million+

Average Rents

Flat

Bedrooms	🛏 🛏
Price	$280/wk

House

Bedrooms	🛏 🛏 🛏
Price	$405/wk
Bedrooms	🛏 🛏 🛏 🛏
Price	$530/wk

Travel Times

CBD	peak 25-30 min off-peak 45 min by train from Ellerslie 18 min
Southern motorway	7 min
Airport	20-30 min

Buses run regularly along main roads and there are train stations at Ellerslie and Meadowbank.

Mt Albert 

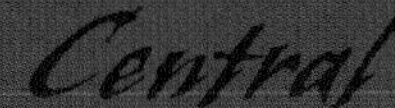

This suburb is a real melting pot – from well-off families in grand houses and tree-lined streets on the slopes of Mt Albert, to students flatting near Unitec and relatively poor migrants renting in Owairaka. It's diverse, vibrant and cosmopolitan, with the sprawling Unitec campus on one boundary and the teeming St Lukes shopping mall on the other. Mt Albert was Auckland's second suburb settled by well-to-do families in the late 1800s. Although parts of it nip at the heels of more expensive neighbouring Mt Eden, this is Toyota Corolla country, and not generally the preserve of European 4WDs. St Lukes is less a suburb and more a home to the mall. Locals debate just where it belongs - is it part of Morningside, Kingsland, Mt Eden or Mt Albert? Owairaka, towards Mt Roskill, is seen as the poor cousin of the area.

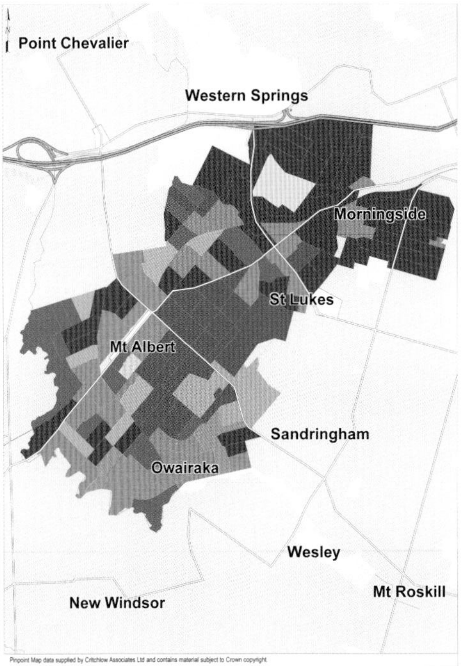

For colour key, see page 226

Population Profile

Population	18,591
% Aged Under 15 Years	19.40
% Aged Over 65 Years	9.29
% European	62.27
% Maori	6.99
% Pacific Peoples	11.46
% Asian	18.28

Who Lives There?

Mt Albert has always been a good, solid suburb, great for raising the children. There was a recent blip as Asian student numbers swelled at nearby Unitec and the AIS St Helens campus but with that phenomenon in recession the leafy streets and character wooden bungalows now echo once more to the cries of toddlers and teens.

The suburb has become popular with ex Ponsonby and Grey Lynn dwellers who want bigger sections for the kids but still want to be fairly close to the CBD.

The faces of those families aren't all white and shiny – this is a culturally diverse suburb with

Polynesians, Indians, Sri Lankans and Chinese. There's also a Somali community in Owairaka.

Typical Homes

Most houses were built during the 1920s to 1940s and many of these gracious bungalows remain, spruced up and beautifully renovated. There has been a fair amount of infill housing so there are also units and modern townhouses, and a development opposite Westfield St Lukes shopping mall which has injected 282 apartments into the market.

St Lukes housing reflects the lifestyles of the inhabitants. Many locals live in townhouses and smaller apartment-style accommodation. Renovated villas and bungalows are available as well; however, they tend to be smaller, with only two to three bedrooms.

Owairaka has more modest housing, with current state and ex-state homes.

Amenities

Schools ★★★★

Mt Albert is well served with schools. Gladstone Primary School is very popular and, with a roll close to 900, is one of the largest primary schools in New Zealand.

Many children from Mt Albert go to Kowhai Intermediate in Kingsland for years 7 and 8, and then progress to the impressive Mt Albert Grammar which recently became a co-ed school (though not in the classrooms). It is one of the 12 biggest schools in Auckland and has a strong tradition of academic and sporting excellence. A unique feature is the School Farm and Horticulture unit offering student's agriculture based learning programmes.

Hebron Christian College and the Catholic girls school Marist College are also in the neighbourhood. For a full list, see page 270.

Shops ★★★★

Mt Albert's main street is now dominated by Chinese signage and internet cafés. Valiantly continuing with its daily muffin bake is the Triniti of Silver café in the old Post Office.

If your tastes are more homogenised, there's Westfield St Lukes mall where you'll find plenty of shops, a big food hall, a cinema complex and more car parks, although we'd like to know at which time of the day you can ever get one. Around the corner, Briscoes and Carters are well patronised and across the road there's a collection of bulk retail style shops for appliances, bedding etc.

Leisure ★★★

There are plenty of family-friendly amenities. The Philips Aquatic Centre in Alberton Ave is hugely popular, with its wave pool, waterslide and baby pools.

Rocket Park in Wairere Ave is well used by young (the playground) and old (the community centre). For walking, you can't beat the volcanic slopes of Owairaka (otherwise known as Mt Albert). For walking while hitting a small white ball with a stick, you can't beat the public Chamberlain Golf Course (gets a bit crowded sometimes and you can't book a tee time).

Hebron Christian College

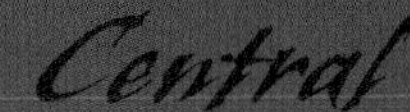

Also in the area are many sports clubs and recreational facilities. Other green areas include Owairaka Park around the Mt Albert summit, Alan Wood Reserve, Unitec's landscaped grounds and many others. Eden Park is within walking distance of St Lukes.

Real Estate

Trends

The recently extended St Lukes mall and the commercial centre surrounding it has spawned a crop of low-rise apartments for those who want to do their mall-crawling by foot not car. Across the road, the St Lukes Garden apartment project is nigh-on finished. With 282 units, sales have been for $350,000 and up, to a mix of buyers – of all ages and ethnicity – with about half being owner occupied. The classy brick-clad St Lukes development Tremont – whose promoters claim the area will be "the next Newmarket" – will be complete in September 2007, with 106 apartments (ranging from $255,500 for one bedroom to $676,500 for three bedrooms).

Further out, houses in-zone for Gladstone Primary carry a small price premium and renovated villas and bungalows in the Golden Triangle, on the leafy north-facing slopes of Mt Albert itself, are very sought-after: in late 2005 a property in Summit Dr sold for $1.38 million; in 2004 another in the same street sold for more than $1.5 million.

Best Streets

Mt Albert's Golden Triangle, with its leafy streets and elevated views, has the most valuable properties, including Stilwell Rd, Summit Dr and surrounding streets.

Smart Buy ✓

House prices in areas with good schools and a reputation for being solid community suburbs, with good amenities, may ease off at times, but they'll never plummet. There are also good investment opportunities with the increase in apartments – what tenant wouldn't want to live across the road from a mall, on various bus routes and a couple of gear changes to a motorway?

At a Glance...

House Prices

Unit	
Bedrooms	🛏 🛏
Price	$250,000
Terrace house	
Bedrooms	🛏 🛏
Price	$280,000
Ex-state house	
Bedrooms	🛏 🛏
Price	$350,000 - $450,000
Villa or bungalow	
Bedrooms	🛏 🛏 🛏
Price	$400,000 - $600,000
Renovated villa or bungalow	
Price	$500,000 - $700,000
In the Golden Triangle	
Price	$750,000 - $1,500,000

Average Rents

Apartments	
Bedrooms	🛏 🛏
Price	$280/wk
House	
Bedrooms	🛏 🛏 🛏
Price	$420/wk
Bedrooms	🛏 🛏 🛏 🛏
Price	$490/wk

Travel Times

CBD	by car peak 20 min off peak 10 min by bus peak 25 min
North-western motorway	5 min
Airport	30 min

Mt Albert has excellent public transport, with regular buses, and the train running through Mt Albert on the Waitakere route.

Mt Eden

★★★★½

including Three Kings, Balmoral and Sandringham

Mt Eden is family-ville for the financially comfortable. The sort of place where you risk being run over by expensive three-wheeled strollers if you step beyond the gate, or jostled off the road by a bevy of SUVs as you drive past the local school at 3pm. Nestled at the base of its namesake mountain, the suburb's other defining feature is its iconic village. It may not be the biggest suburban block of shops in Auckland, but it has heaps of atmosphere, bustles with shoppers and has a hearty smattering of cafés (many with child-friendly sandpits and courtyards). Balmoral and Sandringham now merge seamlessly into Mt Eden but will always be seen as the more affordable neighbourhoods. A few minutes further along Mt Eden Rd, and more elevated, Three Kings is still more affordable, due mainly to pockets of state housing.

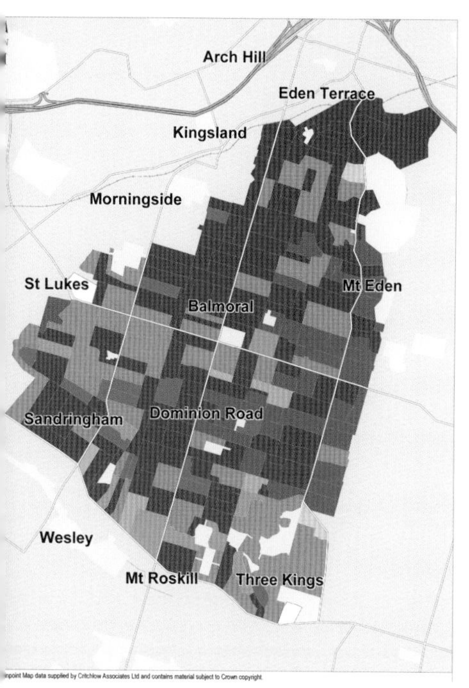

For colour key, see page 226

Population Profile

Population	36,075
% Aged Under 15 Years	19.53
% Aged Over 65 Years	7.97
% European	66.15
% Maori	6.61
% Pacific Peoples	8.79
% Asian	18.99

Who Lives There?

The arty bohemian era that Mt Eden has been famed for is definitely passing – raising families in desirable school zones comes with materialism and middle class values these days. Although more ethnically and socio-economically diverse than its neighbour Epsom, Mt Eden is still full of middle- to upper-middle-class families pursuing the quiet life.

Mt Eden is predominantly European, but with significant numbers of Asians, Polynesians and Indians (there's a Hindu temple in Balmoral Rd). All the local primary schools appear to be bursting at the seams due to the district's numerous young families.

In Three Kings the mix of residents is changing with new terraced housing blocks and infill housing being built. Cynics sometimes refer to Sandringham as a "poor man's Mt Eden". It's a highly cosmopolitan area with a wide mix of ethnic groups and nationalities and many young families.

Typical Homes

Mt Eden is famous for its supply of fabulous turn-of-the-century villas, interspersed with Californian bungalows and other period homes. Moving away from the city and across Balmoral Rd or into Sandringham, the sections tend to be slightly larger and there are more 1930s bungalows.

Mt Eden has its share of low-level blocks of flats and one- to two-bedroom brick and tile units, as well as terrace apartment blocks. There are some unattractive examples of 1960s and 1970s single and double-storey blocks of flats jarringly sited in streets of classic villas and bungalows.

The old state housing area of Three Kings and the southern part of Sandringham is now a mix of owner-occupied housing and tenanted homes, with many ex-state homes receiving trendy renovations. These solid houses are snapped up as soon as they hit the market and are attracting young working couples and professional singles to the area.

Amenities

Schools ★★★★

Most of the schools in this high decile area are very good. There are at least three primary schools for years one to six, four full primaries with intermediate Auckland Normal. Kowhai Intermediate sits on the Mt Eden border.

Balmoral School is popular and caters for years one to eight, although check with the school as the intermediate zone could be tightened for 2007.

While there are no secondary schools, some parts are in-zone for Auckland Grammar School and Epsom Girls Grammar School – check the zones carefully before buying. Other parts of the area are zoned for Auckland Girls Grammar, Mt Roskill Grammar and Mt Albert Grammar, which also have good reputations. For a full list, see page 270.

Shops ★★★★

There's plenty of shopping locally, with a range of shops at Eden Quarter including a well-stocked supermarket. Mt Eden village has interesting specialty shops and boutiques.

Along Dominion Rd there are several Asian specialty groceries; Sandringham has Indian and Pakistani groceries and two halal butchers. The Three Kings shopping centre includes a supermarket and a library.

St Lukes mall is right next door to the east and the busy Newmarket shopping precinct a few minutes down the road west.

Leisure ★★★

As well as the Mt Eden Domain, the area has many smaller parks and reserves, including Edenvale Reserve, Potters Park and Centennial Park. In Three Kings, the quarry site has interesting walks up to the Three Kings Reserve, with great views from the top. The suburb is well catered for sports lovers too with successful soccer and athletics clubs.

There is also Mt Eden Swimming Pool and Eden Park, the famed stadium battleground for local and international rugby and cricket games.

Mt Eden village is well known for its cafés and restaurants which draw diners from all parts of the city, particular Molten restaurant. Dominion Rd and Sandringham Rd have a wide range of ethnic eateries, including the tiny but superb Satya for southern Indian food, and ZapThai and Tusk for Thai food. At the city end of Mt Eden there's a cluster of quirky cafés and pubs.

Real Estate

Trends

The major demarcation in this neighbourhood relates to Auckland Grammar and Epsom Girls Grammar zones with houses in-zone always commanding a hefty premium. There is still a noticeable migration of families across town from the likes of Herne Bay, drawn by the schooling. This isn't always for the grammar schools, it's often to be closer to the many private schools in Epsom and Remuera. Spacious sections are important to Mt Eden buyers, given that many have young families.

Desire to be close to the village, and north of Balmoral Rd, is stronger than ever for buyers upgrading from outlying streets. There has been a substantial increase in sales in north Sandringham, close to Eden Park, a cluster of streets with some fabulous renovated villas and a stone's throw from Kingsland's bars and cafés.

There are still do-ups to be had but they are attracting good prices – a villa, untouched for 50 years, in Woodford St recently sold for just over $1 million. Once beautifully renovated, however, it might sell for $1.7 million, as have similar houses in Woodside Ave and Pencarrow St recently, the latter for $1.82 million.

Three Kings and the southern end of Sandringham are the cheapest areas in this neighbourhood, but properties are always in demand because of that. You can buy an ex-state house for around $500,000; a renovated version would cost around $600,000.

Best Streets

Anything in the grammar zones and the streets close to Mt Eden village. Fairview Rd and Woodside Rd have some big gracious houses, as do Horoeka Ave and Bellevue Rd at the northern end of Mt Eden. In Sandringham, roads north of Balmoral Rd, like Burnley Tce and Royal Tce, and in Balmoral, those near desirable Maungawhau Primary.

Smart Buy ✓

The northern part of Sandringham may be out of grammar zone but it provides easy access to the CBD and it's close to St Lukes mall and Kingsland's restaurants. The area is rightly increasing in popularity and renovated villas on the eastern side of Sandringham Rd are now selling for big bucks. It's only a matter of time before the streets west of Sandringham Rd attract strong buyer interest.

Local Hero: Our Volcanoes

Mt Eden, Mt Albert, Mt Wellington, Three Kings, One Tree Hill... we proudly call them mountains, but on the worldwide scale, they're really only hills. The fact that there are so many of them, however, makes our volcanoes quite different. Auckland's volcanic field contains about 50 volcanic features, 23 of them in Auckland City.

Auckland's volcanoes may be small in statue, but they're a big part of Auckland's tourist marketing. Regional authorities have created "viewing protection planes" so that no large buildings obscure the views from key vantage points and the Auckland City Council is proposing changes to the district plan which would include:

- Controls on the height of new buildings. Homes next to open space on volcanic cones must be either no more than 8m tall or the same height as adjacent buildings, whichever is lower.
- Landscaping assessments to show the impact of new development on the surrounding landform, trees and vegetation, and a requirement for new developments to have landscaping or planting that helps them blend in.
- Restrictions on retaining walls and on the amount earthworks (maximum $5m^3$).
- New homes not to be built any higher up the slope of a volcanic cone than existing developments.

Before the mountains were protected, they were quarried for scoria to the extent that Three Kings, originally five peaks, is now just one. Mt Eden dates back 23,000 years and Mt Wellington was formed about 10,000 years ago. Rangitoto Island is Auckland's most recent volcano, formed some 600-700 years ago.

At a Glance...

House Prices

Unit

Bedroom	🛏
Price	$200,000
Bedrooms	🛏 🛏
Price	$350,000 – $400,000

Bungalow or villa

Bedrooms	🛏 🛏 🛏
In grammar zones	$950,000 plus
Out of zone	$600,000 - 800,000

Large renovated home by Mt Eden village

Bedrooms	🛏 🛏 🛏 🛏
Price	$1.4 million plus

Average Rents

Flat

Bedroom	🛏
Price	$235/wk
Bedrooms	🛏 🛏
Price	$305/wk

House

Bedrooms	🛏 🛏 🛏
Price	$455/wk
Bedrooms	🛏 🛏 🛏 🛏
Price	$565/wk

Travel Times

From Mt Eden village:

CBD	peak 30 min off-peak 10 min
North-western motorway	10 min
Southern motorway	5 min
Airport	30 min
St Lukes mall	5 min

Dominion Rd, Mt Eden Rd, Sandringham Rd and Balmoral Rd are all major bus corridors. Priority peak-hour bus lanes make bus commuting into the city much quicker.

Mt Roskill

including Hillsborough and Waikowhai

The cross proudly displayed on top of Mt Roskill at Christmas and Easter says it all – this is Bible country. God is worshipped diversely these days with the influx of migrants from various ethnic groups. Unfortunately His presence didn't stop Mt Roskill being named recently as the most grafittied suburb in Auckland city. Look more deeply into the solidly suburban streets of Hillsborough as you whip through on your way to the airport and you'll find some real estate gems hugging the Manukau Harbour coastline in leafy sections. The great gashes in the land caused by the SH20 extension roadworks will soon heal, making properties a couple of gear changes away more desirable for their easy access. Nearby Waikowhai has pretty much lost its separate identity and quietly merged with Hillsborough.

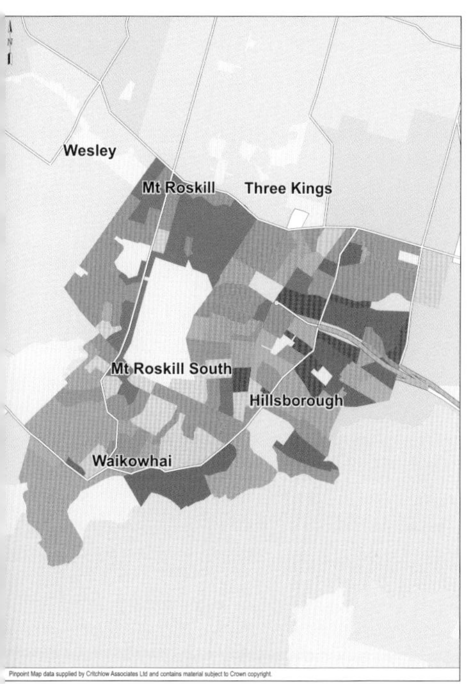

For colour key, see page 226

Population Profile

Population	21,936
% Aged Under 15 Years	20.90
% Aged Over 65 Years	13.09
% European	50.56
% Maori	5.44
% Pacific Peoples	13.65
% Asian	30.06

Who Lives There?

Mt Roskill and Hillsborough have sizeable immigrant populations, with many from India, Korea and China. The neighbourhood and it's Samoan residents have even been immortalized in the successful local film, Sione's Wedding. Families love the big rambling houses on decent sized sections and are attracted by Mt Roskill Grammar School's good reputation.

Others appreciate the handiness of the area – only 20 minutes, off peak to the CBD. It's close to the airport, Manukau and Onehunga and, soon, thanks to the SH20 extension, even West Auckland. Just as well located but half the price of, say, bluechip Remuera.

Typical Homes

Salt-of-the-earth suburban homes, kids running hither and thither, open friendly front yards (no high keep-away walls here) - that's Mt Roskill. Developed mostly in the 1950s and 1960s, modest bungalows and solid ex-state houses are also common, interspersed with newer townhouses on half sites as the once ubiquitous quarter-acre sections are sliced up. There's also a new apartment block called Key Stone Ridge. Mt Roskill South is a subdivision developed from the 1980s onwards, with executive-style homes.

Amenities

Schools ★★★★

Mt Roskill is well served with schools and demand for properties in-zone is high, especially for Mt Roskill Primary, which includes The Endeavor Centre. The expertly staffed centre provides specialist programmes catering for the learning needs of children with varying degrees of disabilities.

At the intermediate level there is Mt Roskill, Wesley and Waikowai intermediates.

Mt Roskill Grammar is a very popular with a student roll close to 2500. Lynfield College isn't as high-profile but is still well-regarded. The private and co-ed Marcellin College is a popular choice with Hillsborough residents.

For a full list, see page 270.

Shops ★★

Lynfield Mall is now a drawcard for the entire area. There's a new complex of medical offices and shops at White Swan Rd and Richardson Rd, developed, in fact, by one of the local doctors.

Apart from the Mt Roskill shops on Dominion Rd, there's Royal Oak, Mt Eden and Blockhouse Bay shopping centres, the DressSmart outlet centre at Onehunga and Westfield St Lukes mall all close by. Plenty of places to spend your hard-earned dosh.

Leisure ★★★

Parks and reserves are plentiful, although on one side the lower slopes of Mt Roskill have been trimmed for motorway extensions.

Green belts and sports grounds include Keith Hay Park, the War Memorial Park and Winstone Park. The area is a walker's paradise, and a golfer's dream – there are three local golf courses. There are two beaches, which are muddy and tidal so not great for swimming, but are popular with boaties and windsurfers.

For fitness enthusiasts there's the Lynfield Recreation Centre (YMCA) and Cameron Pool (Roskill Aquasport). Local sports clubs include those for hockey, cricket, bowling, rugby, soccer and tennis.

With the area's multinational composition, there is more culinary variety in Mt Roskill than ever before.

Real Estate

Trends

Trends in the past have tended to follow school zones, with houses in Mt Roskill Grammar

selling at a premium. Lynfield College has a rising reputation however, so the price gap may start to narrow.

There is strong demand for all types of property in the area, especially at the cheaper $400,000 end. The area is very much favoured by families and the residences reflect this – there are many larger homes on decent-sized sections. Subdivision is slowing in Mt Roskill, simply because almost all of the subdividable parcels are taken.

Most Hillsborough and Waikawai properties get views of some kind, be they Manukau Harbour or west to the Waitakere Ranges. Many a view-loving buyer has rubbed their hands in glee at the relative bargains to be had.

Best Streets

In Hillsborough, any streets near the sea. In Mt Roskill, Stamford Park Rd and Oakdale Rd.

Local Hero: The SH20 Extension

Car-fixated Aucklanders just love seeing a nice new road being built. Although it's pretty hard to imagine what the new four-lane 4km State Highway 20 extension from Hillsborough Rd to Maioro St will look like, it's sure to make getting around faster and easier, especially if you're heading west.

Designed to ease through-traffic congestion on local roads in Mt Roskill and Avondale, it will be finished in 2009 and will cost Transit New Zealand around $169 million. Real estate agents report that properties that back onto the construction site are, naturally, hard to sell but the roadworks haven't otherwise affected housing prices one way or the other.

At a Glance...

House Prices

Unit

Bedrooms	2
Price	$250,000 - $300,000

Bungalow

Bedrooms	3
Price	$330,000 - $450,000

Top end Mt Roskill townhouse

Bedrooms	3
Price	$500,000 +

Hillsborough house

Bedrooms	3
Price	$450,000 +

Executive-style house

Bedrooms	4
Price	$500,000 - $600,000
With sea views	$1,000,000 +

Average Rents

Flat

Bedrooms	2
Price	$285/wk

House

Bedrooms	3
Price	$375/wk
Bedrooms	4
Price	$475/wk

Travel Times

From Mt Roskill shops to:

CBD	peak 20 - 45 min off-peak 10 - 15 min
Airport	15 - 20 min
St Lukes Westfield mall	5 - 10 min
Royal Oak shops	10 min

Hillsborough is handy to get to the airport, but otherwise it's a bit landlocked. The area is well-serviced by buses and the peak-time bus lanes along the major roads into the city have improved travel times – for those on the buses anyway.

Onehunga ★★★½

including Oranga, Te Papapa and Penrose

Funny, really, that a suburb with such a long and interesting past is best known for its big and brash outlet store complex, Dressmart. But whether it's cheaper frocks or cheaper villas you're after, this is the place. The suburb has a history that goes back deep into the 19th century when retired English soldiers were posted here to help protect the locals. Today, its older houses are seen as affordable alternatives to those closer to the CBD. It's a suburb in the middle of everywhere, handy to two motorways, most points of Auckland, the huge Cornwall Park, Auckland International Airport and a 15-minute drive to the CBD on a good day. Oranga is a slightly more rugged version of Onehunga while Penrose and Te Papapa are traditionally industrial and commercial suburbs.

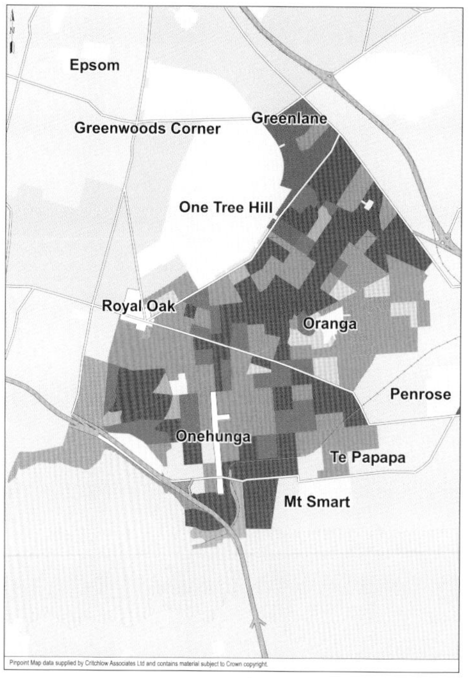

For colour key, see page 226

Population Profile

Population	25,890
% Aged Under 15 Years	20.03
% Aged Over 65 Years	10.76
% European	61.45
% Maori	8.90
% Pacific Peoples	17.46
% Asian	14.77

Who Lives There?

Onehunga's population is very diverse. Singles love the affordability and the shops, families love the big sections and immigrants love the easy access to some of Auckland's largest industrial, and therefore employment, areas. That mix gives it a relaxed and unpretentious air.

Traditionally Onehunga is solidly working class and has been home to many Maori and Polynesian families over the years, many of whom still live there. A wide range of ethnic groups are represented here – over 50 different nationalities are currently enrolled at Penrose High School.

Typical buyers into the suburb include young local couples seeking their first home do-up and migrants from Asia – as well as from Europe and South Africa. It's also popular with those who work at the airport but who don't want to live in deepest South Auckland.

Typical Homes

Many of Onehunga's earliest homes were built by, and for, Fencible soldiers looking to settle with their families on their own patch of land. This suburb is still full of the classic villas, bungalows and worker's cottages which are much cheaper than those you would find in inner-city suburbs like Ponsonby, and on larger parcels of land. For a long time Onehunga was tipped as the "new Ponsonby" but, frankly, that's a bit of an insult for a suburb with such a clearly defined identity. There are also a number of historic properties, including the one-time residence of Governor Grey, in Symonds St.

While many of the older homes have already been renovated, there are still occasional vintage homes requiring restoration. There is also a range of more modern housing. There are 1950s brick and tile bungalows and contemporary family homes. Weatherboard state houses and ex-state houses are plentiful, as well as stucco duplexes. Infill housing is common and larger properties are now harder to find.

There are a number of terraced houses which have been built predominantly on industrial land during the past five to 10 years and now an apartment complex, called Atrium on Main.

Amenities

Schools ★★★

This low decile area has adequate schooling for all ages. Onehunga Primary is well-regarded and steeped in history. Established in 1873, it has become part of the fabric of Onehunga, changing and growing along with the revitalising community it serves. Te Papapa School is also in the neighbourhood and is a multi-cultural primary school with a history of positive ERO reports.

Royal Oak Intermediate is close by, and the two co-ed secondary schools are the zoned Onehunga High School (which includes a unique Business School) and Penrose High School.

For a full list, see page 270.

Shops ★★★★

The retail scene is dominated by the Dressmart outlet centre which just got even bigger with the addition of yet more shops.

Onehunga Mall has been rejuvenated since the early 1990s when greater access for cars was restored. The local shopping embraces an assortment of retail and service stores, banks and increasingly trendy restaurants and cafés.

Leisure ★★★

Open spaces include One Tree Hill Domain and Cornwall Park as well as Jellicoe Park and Waikaraka Park and the motorway-edged Onehunga Wharf. Waikaraka Park cemetery

is historically interesting, and there are a number of heritage walks in the area.

Sporting facilities include the Onehunga War Memorial Pool and the Manukau Cruising Club, as well as clubs catering for bowling, soccer, rugby, squash and rowing.

There are some excellent ethnic restaurants in Onehunga as well as artistic and cultural facilities and a modern library.

Real Estate

Trends

Prices and number of sales are holding their own in Onehunga, and the biggest trend continues to be younger couples, priced out of the likes of Ponsonby and Kingsland, buying old houses for renovation. These houses are generally well maintained but in need of a modern look.

Local real estate agents say Onehunga is less likely to be affected by a downturn in the market because of its diversity of houses, old and new, big and small. There's been a lot of recent sales activity near the $1 million mark and even above.

New apartments are selling for around $250,000 for a one-bedroom unit and around $330,000 for a two bedroom.

There has been a revival of interest in older brick-and-tile units (selling in the low to mid $200,000) because of their solid construction in the wake of the leaky building syndrome scandal. Especially popular, are homes with internal access garages and small gardens.

Generally, the top area of Onehunga, nearest One Tree Hill, commands higher prices than the lower part, with its busy roads and proximity to the industrial area.

Best Streets

Onehunga Heights and properties west of The Mall (streets like Forbes, Norman Hill, Quandrant and Arthur) often get Manukau Harbour views so are more desirable, as are the streets closer to One Tree Hill. The closer you get to Rockfield Rd and the industrial area of Penrose, the less desirable the streets.

At a Glance...

House Prices

Unit
(add $40,000 for those closer to One Tree Hill)

Bedroom	🛏
Price	$190,000 – $220,000
Bedrooms	🛏 🛏
Price	$230,000 +

Old workers cottage

Price	$350,000 – $420,000

House on a half site

Bedrooms	🛏 🛏 🛏
Price	$400,000 +

Renovated villa or bungalow on full site

Price	$650,000 +

New townhouse close to One Tree Hill

Price	$700,000 – $750,000

Average Rents

Apartment

Bedrooms	🛏 🛏
Prices	$310/wk

Flat

Bedrooms	🛏 🛏
Prices	$275/wk

House

Bedrooms	🛏 🛏
Prices	$305/wk
Bedrooms	🛏 🛏 🛏
Prices	$360/wk

Travel Times

From Onehunga Mall:

CBD	peak 60 min off-peak 20 min
Airport	10 min
Royal Oak shops	2 min
Southern motorway	5 min

Stagecoach Auckland provides regular services to Onehunga, with many buses intersecting at this point from different parts of the city. The SH20 motorway extension in neighbouring Hillsborough will be a boon to those travelling west.

One Tree Hill

ncluding Royal Oak and Greenlane

If you take a map of greater Auckland and stick a pin in the middle, One Tree Hill and its surrounding suburbs are pretty much at the centre. One of Auckland's iconic landmarks, One Tree Hill – or rather None Tree Hill since it's lone pine was attacked by a Maori activist in 1994 and then removed – gives some of the best views of Auckland and is encircled by beautiful parkland. The surrounding suburbs are well established, tree-filled and pretty. The confusing and busy Royal Oak roundabout is like the centre of a compass and a place of loathing for the hesitant driver. Greenlane is sandwiched between the motorway and Cornwall Park, and has suffered an image problem due to an abundance of car dealerships, it's close to but traditionally much cheaper than both Epsom and Remuera.

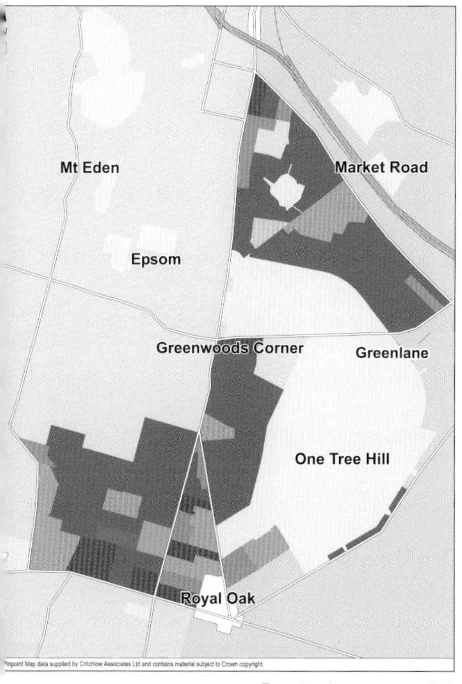

For colour key, see page 226

Population Profile

Population	11,271
% Aged Under 15 Years	19.11
% Aged Over 65 Years	12.86
% European	70.91
% Maori	4.07
% Pacific Peoples	3.09
% Asian	23.02

Who Lives There?

The flat terrain (with the exception of the hill itself) makes these suburbs ideal for the elderly who bravely negotiate the Royal Oak roundabout (Zimmer frames must make great bumper bars) en route to the homely Royal Oak mall.

The reputable local primary and intermediate schools make the area a drawcard for young families. With most of these suburbs just missing out on Auckland and Epsom Girls Grammar zoning, families tend to use them as stepping-stones to Epsom when their children reach secondary school age.

Many young professionals make their home in One Tree Hill because of its relatively central location. It is less than half an hour's drive to the city, a 15-minute drive to the airport and south Auckland and a five-minute drive to the industrial area of Penrose.

Typical Homes

Established in the 1930s, when neighbouring Onehunga with its thriving port became crowded, One Tree Hill and Royal Oak have many period bungalows, now often on half-size sections. Although both villas and period bungalows can be found in One Tree Hill itself, villas are less common in Royal Oak and Greenlane. Virtually every era of family home is represented in the leafy streets.

There are some big bungalows still on large sections nearer Onehunga and on the Greenlane streets bordering Cornwall Park (many of these are on leasehold land so may look grand but aren't exorbitantly expensive).

There are still many state houses as well as brick and tile units, concentrated in streets like Te Rama Rd. There has been a general increase in townhouses throughout the area, due to infill housing.

Amenities

Schools ★★★

There are at least three public primary schools in the area. Cornwall Park School and Royal Oak Primary are well regarded with high deciles and are performing well academically. Royal Oak Intermediate is an adequate local intermediate school.

If you're not in-zone for Auckland Grammar School or Epsom Girls' Grammar, other local secondary schools are the co-ed Catholic Marcellin College, Onehunga High School or Penrose High.

For a full list, see page 270.

Shops ★★★

Royal Oak is a thriving shopping hub for locals, although it looks a little scruffy in parts. Several new cafés and restaurants, including many ethnic ones, have opened locally in the past five or six years.

Nearby Greenwoods Corner has an interesting stretch of shops and cafés, and Newmarket is less than 10 minutes' drive north along Manukau Rd.

The eastern side of Cornwall Park has very little aside from car yards, a huge Foodtown supermarket and a McDonalds. Oh, and a clever little venture by ex-rugby league player Matthew Ridge, called Car-fe. Watch your car being valleted while you have a coffee.

Leisure ★★★

The area's biggest recreation asset is Cornwall Park and One Tree Hill Domain. This expanse of country amid suburbia has lambs gamboling on the green hillside, chickens clucking in the sun and huge groves of historic trees. The Monterey pine which gave One Tree Hill its name has been gone since October 2000; a planned replacement grove of nine native trees is on hold until a Treaty of Waitangi claim on the site is settled.

Cornwall Park has recreational areas, barbecues, a restaurant, an information centre and a working farm that families can walk through. On the One Tree Hill Domain side of the mountain there's a planetarium and a popular playground.

At peak times the park can be busier than Queen Street, with bumper-to-bumper power walkers pushing designer buggies or being dragged along by over-zealous canines. But if you get off the beaten track there's plenty of peace to be found in this beautiful place.

Other attractions include Alexandra Park and also Ericsson Stadium, where hope springs eternal for the New Zealand Warriors.

Real Estate

Trends

Demand for houses is always steady in these suburbs, especially near the Epsom border. Royal Oak recently had a record sale: $880,000 for an upmarket, contemporary, stand-alone townhouse on 400m^2, bought off the plans and not in grammar zone. In mid 2005, $625,000 was top dollar for similar properties.

Bungalows, villas and ex-state homes are snapped up quickly by those buying their first or second homes. Plaster townhouses and terraced homes which are looking dated are very slow to sell, largely because of "leaky building" fears, but also because they often don't offer the same high level of specs as newer homes.

The classic brick-and-tile unit from the 1960s and 1970s is popular at both ends of the home-buying life-cycle: as well as their traditional pensioner buyers, young couples or singles may buy one as a first home.

Being just in-zone for Auckland Grammar or Epsom Girls Grammar will put a premium of at least $100,000 (or 10 – 15%) on a property.

Best Streets

The area's best streets include Maungakiekie Ave and Wapiti Ave in Greenlane, Haydn Ave, Raurenga Ave and Lewin Rd in Royal Oak and Kowhatu Rd and Irirangi Rd in One Tree Hill.

At a Glance...

House Prices

Unit

Bedrooms	2
Price	$300,000 – $350,000

Bungalow on half site

Bedrooms	3
Price	$500,000 – $600,000

Bungalow on full site

Bedrooms	4
Price	$550,000 – $680,000

Townhouse

Bedrooms	4
Price	$500,000 – $800,000

Large freehold house bordering park

Price	$800,000 - $1,800,000

Average Rents

Flat

Bedroom	1
Price	$225/wk
Bedrooms	2
Price	$280/wk

House

Bedrooms	3
Price	$400/wk
Bedrooms	4
Price	$530/wk

Travel Times

CBD	peak 30 min off-peak 15 min
Southern motorway	5 min
Newmarket	10 min
Airport	10 min

There's a regular Stagecoach bus service to these suburbs and the roundabout points drivers in all directions.

Panmure

including Mt Wellington, Sylvia Park and Tamaki

Panmure is one of the few Auckland suburbs that can be compared with London and Paris. Unfortunately it's not for the shopping. The infamous Panmure roundabout is at least as difficult for drivers to navigate as Hyde Park Corner or the Arc de Triomphe and best approached with trepidation and a steady hand on the wheel. But Panmure deserves to be talked about for its other attributes; like its varied housing, proximity to the city and good motorway access, as well as the large and exciting projects afoot. Mt Wellington will soon become home to New Zealand's biggest shopping centre – the sprawling 24ha Sylvia Park (stage one is open). Next, is the proposed development of the old Mt Wellington quarry, which will pump 2200 new houses and 8000 new souls into its re-sculpted crater. This is an area undergoing a transformation.

For colour key, see page 226

Population Profile

Population	26,049
% Aged Under 15 Years	23.62
% Aged Over 65 Years	8.81
% European	45.02
% Maori	16.01
% Pacific Peoples	24.42
% Asian	18.93

Who Lives There?

A relatively affordable suburb fairly close to town, Panmure appeals to first-home buyers. Mt Wellington is seen as an aspiring man's Ellerslie, while Tamaki is fairly scruffy with lots of renters. On the flip side, there are some very expensive homes, owned by captains of industry, peppered throughout the area, especially near the river estuary.

Many migrants – from a huge range of countries – also live here, attracted by the lower prices and major employment areas in Mt Wellington and further south.

The townhouses and terrace blocks around the Panmure Lagoon and near the shopping centre attract young professional couples seeking reasonably priced modern accommodation. Despite this, it's still a working to lower-middle-class area that acts as a gateway to the eastern suburbs. In Panmure and Tamaki, the University of Auckland's Tamaki campus attracts students and lecturing staff to live nearby.

Typical Homes

The types of houses in Panmure are as diverse as the suburb itself. There are turn-of-the-century villas and renovated bungalows, but the houses are predominantly 1960s and 1970s family homes and state houses. Many of the latter have been sold by the Government in recent times, although this trend has slowed with current policy. With many sizeable sections (between 600m^2 and 950m^2), it's an ideal spot for families.

Spacious executive-style houses can be found along the Tamaki River, and on the hill heading towards Pakuranga, where they have views towards St Kentigern's College, Farm Cove and Mt Wellington.

Amenities

Schools ★★★

There are at least eight primary schools in this low-decile area as well as Portland House Montessori and the special needs Somerville School. Tamaki intermediate is popular and shares grounds with Tamaki Primary.

While Panmure is well stocked with primary and intermediate schools, parents will need to look elsewhere for a suitable secondary school. Tamaki College is close by but is actually located in neighbouring Glen Innes.

Carey College is also in the neighbourhood, for the more devout. The Christian school's website describes the institution as "...uncompromising in its commitment to biblical schooling." For a full list, see page 270.

Shops ★★★

If you're a southern motorway motorist, you just can't miss it – the emergence of the huge 24ha, $538 million Sylvia Park shopping centre development near the south-eastern highway off-ramp. Blocks of shops will progressively open (stage one opened in June 2006) during the next few years, combining strips of shops and giant anchor tenants in big-format areas. One of these giants will be the first "The Warehouse Extra" with a fresh food department.

Panmure's main street is full of shops and a bustling place at any time of the day. Major retail outlets are also dotted along the Mt Wellington Highway

Leisure ★★★

Stage one of the new Auckland Netball Centre at Ngahue Reserve in Mt Wellington (total cost $13 million) is now complete, with 26 outdoor and three indoor courts. Stage two will add another 20 outdoor and five indoor courts.

The popular Lagoon Gymnasium is well patronised and the lagoon itself is host to many maritime activities as well as being pleasant to stroll around.

The landmark of Mt Wellington provides panoramic views of Auckland and its harbours. This spot is popular with both visitors and locals, keen to walk the dog at the weekend. Views from the summit include the impressive array of local amenities, starting with the superbly landscaped university playing fields for rugby, cricket, tennis, netball and soccer on Merton Rd.

A miniature train runs in Peterson Reserve next to Waipuna Lodge on Sunday afternoons. Panmure's main drag has plenty of eateries with a variety of foods.

Real Estate

Trends

Traditionally lingering below average on the desirability level, the area is showing signs of increasing in value – it's still affordable but has good access to the water, is close to desirable eastern suburbs and reasonably close to the CBD. It's still a viable option for the investor, with a good number of established tenants. Terrace houses show considerable range in pricing and while most of the properties in these suburbs are at the mid to lower end of the market, there are some on the Tamaki River banks – especially at the boat yard end – worth more than $1 million.

Panmure's downfall is its schooling with a steady exodus of families leaving the area when their children reach secondary school age.

Landco already has approval for about 300 sections on the edge of the old Mt Wellington quarry, and has now applied for a plan change to cover the remainder of the quarry, including 2200 homes, a commercial centre, school and 9ha of open space. The first sections are due to be built on during the 2006/07 summer and the quarry is expected to fill up during the next six years. When completed, it will be home to 6000 to 8000 people.

Best Streets

Bridge St in Panmure; Marine Lane in Mt Wellington and Dunkirk Rd in Tamaki.

At a Glance...

House Prices

Unit

Bedroom	
Price	$175,000 - $190,000
Bedrooms	
Price	$200,000 +

House

Bedrooms	
Price	$280,000 - $500,000

New executive townhouse

Price	$550,000 +

Waterfront property

Price	$1,000,000

Average Rents

Flat

Bedroom	
Price	$200/wk
Bedrooms	
Price	$250/wk

Apartment

Bedrooms	
Price	$310/wk

House

Bedrooms	
Price	$285/wk
Bedrooms	
Price	$330/wk

Travel Times

Panmure roundabout to:

CBD	peak 40 - 60 min off-peak 13 min
Southern motorway	5 - 7 min
Airport	25 min

The new Panmure train station and park-and-ride facility is now completed.

For a small place, Parnell has a huge impact on the city's culture and property values. It has always been the centre of all things fashionable, but in a more confident and cultured way than that young upstart, Ponsonby. Boutiques demurely offer the latest couture, galleries glow with contemporary art and furniture stores display an artful scattering of imported European sofas. This is also where those exasperating Auckland property booms usually start, rippling ever outward in concentric bands. Now Newmarket's a different story – big glitzy shops stretching as far as the eye can see and a sea of people on a retail mission, whether it's to the roadside shops or the Two Double Seven mall. Although there have been some prosperous residential real estate developments in recent years, all those shops don't leave much room for housing.

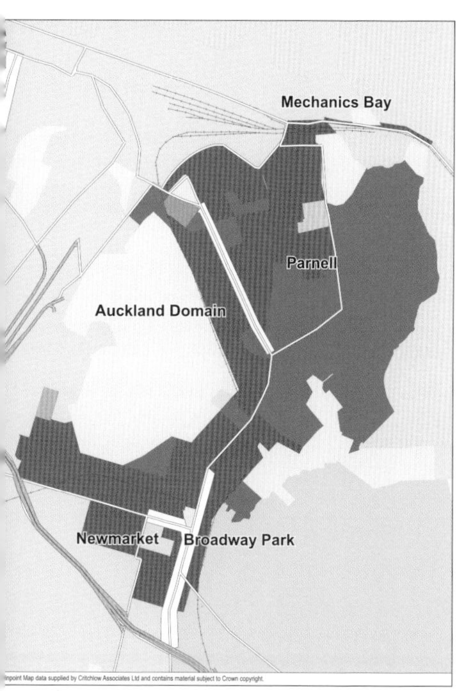

For colour key, see page 226

Population Profile

Population	7,593
% Aged Under 15 Years	10.27
% Aged Over 65 Years	8.06
% European	81.59
% Maori	4.27
% Pacific Peoples	1.82
% Asian	8.85

Who Lives There?

Parnell is Auckland's Beverly Hills. Residents tend to be wealthy socialites, surgeons, financiers and (oh, dear) property developers. Martini-toting Parnell Girls and their Prada bags are in evidence at the bars of Parnell Rise most nights of the week.

The suburb has also long been an established centre for the artistic intelligentsia (literati meets the glitterati); and – as with Ponsonby and other inner city suburbs – many residents are categorised as bobo, or bourgeois bohemians. Artists and writers may live in Parnell, but they're not the starving in a garret types.

There are many old Auckland families in Parnell, who have lived here for generations, and many families with secondary school-age children – it's in-zone for Auckland Grammar and Epsom Girls' Grammar and close to many private schools.

The many new luxury townhouses and apartments are popular with affluent empty-nesters - older couples whose children have left home and who have discovered a new and active life in which to indulge. They travel unencumbered and entertain at leisure. Going by the quality of these properties, the nests may be empty but they are well-feathered.

Buyers in Parnell are mainly white Europeans. By comparison, Newmarket attracts more Chinese buyers; it is a cosmopolitan professional area favoured by business people wanting to live close to their offices and the shopping.

Typical Homes

Parnell boasts some of Auckland's grandest old homes, and is brimming with turn-of-the-century villas and bungalows. Modern architecture has also made its mark here, with sleek townhouses tucked behind older houses and many apartments, from designer studios to luxury abodes. Although many of the sections are small and neighbouring houses are only a stone's throw away, Parnell oozes atmosphere. Many Parnell houses enjoy spectacular sea views of Rangitoto Island and the Auckland Harbour Bridge.

While Newmarket has fewer houses than Parnell, there are numerous 1840s worker's cottages in the area. These tend to be too small for family living, but attractive for singles and childless professional couples. Broadway Park, with its arrangement of terrace homes, duplexes and mid to high-rise apartments also serves this sector.

Amenities

Schools ★★★★

Parnell and Newmarket are both well served with quality, high decile schools.

Parnell District School is a full primary with a new library building which contains thousands of books, state-of-the-art audio/visual equipment comfy cushions and underfloor heating! Story time never sounded so good.

Newmarket Primary School is equally well regarded; the colourfully designed school recently celebrated its 125th jubilee.

The only secondary school is the private ACG Parnell College (formally Junior College). But fear not, most of the neighbourhood sits comfortably within the Auckland Grammar and Epsom Girls schools zones.

For a full list, see page 270.

Shops ★★★★★

Gracing the shopping strip in Parnell are most of the leading fashion houses, art galleries and some of Auckland's best restaurants and trendiest cafés. With its cobbled paving and heritage buildings, the area mixes chic retail with a village atmosphere. It is a great

place to while away an afternoon or a whole day. Be prepared to watch the credit card bend however, as the offerings are far from bargain basement.

Newmarket's shopping strip is busier and more commercial, with a mix of boutique retail and chain stores, and a high number of overseas visitors. The big Two Double Seven mall is set to double in size over the next two years.

The elegant former Mercury Energy building on Nuffield St is being restored with a mix of restaurants and shops at street level.

Leisure ★★★★★

In an area where leisure generally equals boutique browsing or mall trawling, there is a surprising array of other activities on offer. There are three tennis clubs, the fun Parnell Baths and the Olympic Pool & Fitness Centre.

There are plenty of open spaces – the Auckland Domain, Parnell Rose Gardens and Dove-Myer Robinson Park, and a number of smaller reserves. Newmarket Park has undergone major upgrading and Lumsden Green, the park at the bottom of Khyber Pass, is being upgraded and slightly enlarged. The Wintergardens complex at the Domain has been restored to its former grandeur during the past couple of years.

Both the Auckland Museum and Auckland's Trinity Cathedral are major centres of cultural activity. The museum extensions and its Grand Atrium are due to finish in December 2006. Parnell library is located in the former Foundation for the Blind building. Newmarket has two large cinema complexes.

Real Estate

Trends

Supply is not keeping pace with demand in this area: with publicity about the end of the boom, residents assume they won't get a high price for their property, so they're not putting them on the market. It's the land that's valuable here: the most ramshackle do-up on a small site will fetch between $650,000 and $700,000.

Having originally been developed for lowly workers, Parnell sections tend to be small, so there never was a lot of subdivision potential. New apartments and townhouses at the end of St Stephens Ave and on Crescent Rd never seem to be short of willing buyers despite being priced in the multi-millions.

Despite some local protest, the $150 million two-tower intensive apartment and shopping project on the corner of Broadway and Remuera Rd is going ahead, due for completion at the end of 2008. A three-bedroom, two-bathroom third-floor apartment with two carparks sells for $500,000.

These aren't suburbs for first-home buyers (unless it's a well-paid young advertising type buying a small apartment).

Best Streets

The lower end of St Stephens Ave and the streets that run off it, such as Bridgewater Rd, Crescent Rd and Judge St.

Auckland War Memorial Museum

Local Hero: Shoe Sheriff

Despite his shop name, Shoe Sheriff owner Peter Croad didn't resort to shoot-outs in his fight to keep his Newmarket shoe repair shop open.

Instead, he used lawyers and the court system, to win his battle with the developers who considered his shop to be a blot on the glossy Broadway landscape.

Croad has been running the shop for 25 years, and his father ran it before him. Now virtually engulfed by its ultra-modern new neighbours, the 1930s building, at no 332, looks as though it's been transplanted into the wrong movie set. Nonetheless, the Shoe Sheriff plans to be doing what he does best at least until his next rent review, in 2020.

Travel Times

From Parnell Rise:

CBD	peak 15 min off-peak 5 min walk 15 min by train (Newmarket) 10 min
Southern motorway	3 min
Airport	25 min
Remuera	5 – 6 min

Buses run regularly through this part of town (including the Link service), as well as a train line. The Newmarket train station is due for major improvements so that the train doesn't have to back out (we kid you not).

At a Glance...

House Prices

Apartment

Bedroom	🛏
Price	$280,000
Bedrooms	🛏 🛏
Price	$350,000

New apartment

Price	$600,000

Broadway Park terrace house

Price	$550,000

Renovated character home on half site

Price	$800,000

Renovated character home on full site

Price	$1,000,000 +

Blue-chip Parnell house

Bedrooms	🛏 🛏 🛏 🛏
Price	$2,000,000 - $3,000,000

Average Rents

Flat

Bedroom	🛏
Price	$270/wk
Bedrooms	🛏 🛏
Price	$375/wk

Apartment

Bedroom	🛏
Price	$315/wk
Bedrooms	🛏 🛏
Price	$455/wk

House

Bedrooms	🛏 🛏 🛏
Price	$630/wk
Bedrooms	🛏 🛏 🛏 🛏
Price	$810/wk

There are many people who want to live in this trendy area, but don't have enough money to buy here. This continues to fuel the rental market.

including Herne Bay, St Marys Bay and Freemans Bay

Ponsonby is home to the pink dollar and good coffee. Yummy mummies sip skinny lattes with their designer-clad toddlers or their gay neighbours. To live in its narrow, double-parked streets you've probably sold your successful organic food company for millions, drive a late-model European and know what a Ghost chair is (a designer, see-through plastic number). Almost all of the tumble-down houses have been renovated to within an inch of their lives and spawned a new language: brown is mocha and a back verandah is a loggia. Herne Bay is more blue-chip and less arty, with harbour views, grand old homes and leafy streets. St Marys Bay has even better views than Herne Bay, but smaller sections and a noisy motorway beneath it. Freemans Bay has great city views, but a reputation for losing the sun early in the day.

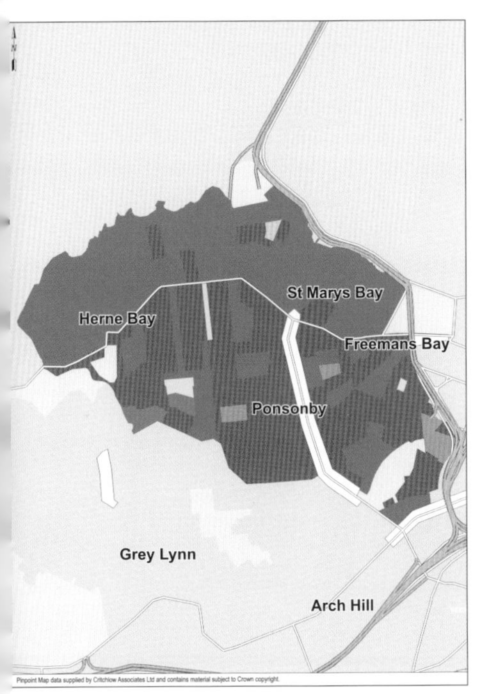

For colour key, see page 226

Population Profile

Population	14,415
% Aged Under 15 Years	14.19
% Aged Over 65 Years	7.62
% European	82.39
% Maori	6.66
% Pacific Peoples	8.14
% Asian	4.79

Who Lives There?

Ponsonby is not the eclectic mix of races and economic strata it used to be. Professional sportspeople, media celebrities, advertising types, trendy business owners and icons of Auckland's gay subculture rub shoulders in Ponsonby Rd's trendy cafés, but that's about as varied as it gets. There's no shortage of people clamouring to live here but they have to have money and the mindset to do so. Very few Asian migrants buy into Ponsonby – mainly due to the higher upkeep older homes.

While it's true the area has a warm social conscience and an appetite for all that is trendy, there's also an obvious hankering for the finer

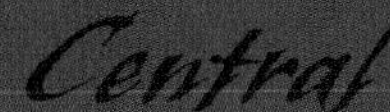

things in life. Ponsonby residents are what the rest of New Zealand is visualising when they seethe on about "Dorklanders." And Ponsonby residents love it.

Typical Homes

Ponsonby people love their houses, lavishing them with architect-inspired renovations then filling them with designer fittings and furnishings. This is where towels are folded onto the rail, not slung. Where pillows are for decoration not comfort.

Most houses are old villas and workingman's cottages, nestling cheek-by-jowl on tiny sections in the narrow streets. You certainly get to know your neighbours well around here, even if you don't want to.

Off-street parking is rare so be prepared to get a scratched Saab or two.

Herne Bay has larger villas, more stately homes and bigger sections. In recent years, some older homes here and in St Mary's Bay have been removed to make way for swept-up new designs but Auckland City laws now protect anything built before 1940.

Freeman's Bay has a broader mix of house styles. Old villas, a smattering of 1930s bungalows, many 1960s ex-council flats (now being fought over tooth and nail by buyers for their retro appeal) and some new townhouses.

Amenities

Schools ★★★

This high-decile area is well served by primary and intermediate schools but the secondary schooling is scant for boys. The attractive and well-resourced Ponsonby Primary is very popular and according to a recent ERO report, continues to provide,"...high quality education."

At secondary level, the area is in-zone for Auckland Girls Grammar and conveniently close to Western Springs College. Many of the moneyed residents prefer to send their kids to private schools across town.

While most Ponsonby residents would rather choke on their brioche before moving across to what they see as the staid part of town – Remuera and Epsom – some are forced to once the children reach secondary school age to get them into Auckland or Epsom Girls Grammar.

No such problems for Catholics – St Mary's College (girls) and St Paul's College (boys) are in the neighbourhood.

For a full list, see page 270.

Shops ★★★★★

This area is famous for its shopping. Ponsonby and Jervois Rds are lined with trendy specialty stores selling designer clothing and

Local Hero: The Ponsonby Belgian Beer Café

When the Ponsonby Post Office was built in 1912, many proud local residents contributed funds towards the cost of its clock tower.

You have to wonder what would they think of the fact that it now presides over the consumption of bizarre foreign alcoholic beverages rather than the purchase of postage stamps.

Current locals, however, seem perfectly satisfied with the ornate landmark's conversion into a Belgian beer bar. New Ponsonby enterprises usually tend towards funkiness and minimalism, so the bar's lush

1930s European ambience is a delicious surprise. The traditional Belgian fruit beers – one made with fresh cherries, another with raspberries – are equally delicious.

homewares heavily interpersed with cafés and restaurants catering to all tastes and styles. Ponsonby Rd has its own website www.ponsonby.co.nz

There are supermarkets in Richmond Rd and College Hill and plenty of bakeries, flower and fruit shops. Downtown Auckland, St Lukes mall and, in fact, Takapuna shops, are all close by.

Leisure ★★★★

Many local parks, including Victoria Park, Western Park, Grey Lynn Park and Cox's Bay, are great places to relax and get some fresh air. The famous local rugby club sharing the suburb's name now plays just down the road in Western Springs. Residents enjoy being close to the zoo, MOTAT and Western Springs Park as well.

The Pt Erin Baths are well patronised, as are a collection of little beaches along the waterfront. Local sports clubs include bowling, yachting, rugby, soccer, snooker, tennis, petanque and squash. However, if we're being honest, the only game in town is people-watching while sipping a trim latte.

The 1970s Gables pub in Herne Bay looks likely to follow in the esteemed footsteps of Ponsonby's former iconic boozer The Gluepot, and be demolished to make way for 15 upmarket apartments, offices, two shops and a small restaurant and bar. Building is expected to start in late 2007.

Real Estate

Trends

Serious vendors are recognising that the astronomical price rises of the past few years have cooled to a simmer; the opportunists, with a "we'll only sell if we get a ridiculously high price" mentality just aren't selling their properties.

There are very few do-ups left in this area and, when they do come available, they sell very quickly and for very good prices, often before they're even officially on the market. A three-bedroom Ponsonby villa do-up will easily fetch a price in the early $600,000s.

Large, top-quality townhouses with very high-end specifications are a new phenomenon in Ponsonby and they're fetching between $1.1 million and $1.3 million.

If you're aiming at the upper echelons of the Herne Bay housing market, $2 million won't buy you much of anything: best to have around $3 million in your back pocket.

Demand is always high for three- and four-bedroom houses thanks to more families wanting to live here.

Ponsonby's narrow streets and closely-spaced dwellings mean that off-street parking is sought-after: an apartment with a parking space will cost about $20,000 more than one without.

Perspective, the swanky apartment building on College Hill which was finished (eventually) at the end of 2005, has 81 apartments in seven low-rise buildings which surround a plaza, giving these well-heeled apartment dwellers some outdoor space (and a lap pool). Prices range from $360,000 to about $750,000.

It was the end of an era when New Zealand's only dedicated yeast factory left its huge site at the end of Ponsonby Rd, which it had occupied since 1921. The developer wants to replace it with Soho Square, a $200 million mix of retail, offices and apartments. Many local artists, businesspeople and residents are roundly opposed to the scheme, which they say will undermine the historic nature of the area (and create traffic nightmares).

Best Streets

Marine Pde, Sarsfield St and Argyle St in Herne Bay; Vermont St, O'Neill St and Summer St in Ponsonby. Dunedin St, Hackett St and London St in St Marys Bay, and Arthur St, Paget St and Hepburn St in Freemans Bay.

At a Glance...

House Prices

Apartment

Bedroom	
Price	$220,000 +
Bedrooms	
Price	$350,000 - $750,000

House in Freeman's Bay

Bedrooms	
Price	$600,000 - $700,000

Villa or cottage in Ponsonby

Price	$750,000 +

House in Herne Bay or St Marys Bay

Bedrooms	
Price	$1,200,000

Top-end house

Price	$2,000,000 - $3,000,000

Average Rents

Flat

Bedroom	
Price	$280/wk
Bedrooms	
Price	$340/wk

Apartment

Bedroom	
Price	$320/wk

House

Bedrooms	
Price	$560/wk
Bedrooms	
Price	$660/wk

Travel Times

From Three Lamps shops:

CBD	peak 15 min off-peak 5 min
	on foot 15 min
North-western motorway	5 min
Airport	35 min
St Lukes mall	15 min

The area has excellent bus services, especially with the Link buses that run on a continuous circuit from Ponsonby Rd to Newmarket via the city.

Ask anyone in New Zealand what "Remuera" means to them and, chances are, their answer will have something to do with snobbery or enviable wealth. This is where late-model European cars slip quietly down tree-lined streets and into boutique-side carparks in the village. Where anything above a rounded-vowel whisper is frowned upon and where captains of commerce come home to couture-clad wives and their silver-spooned children. The suburb's traditional make-up is changing however, with a steady stream of new money wanting a slice of the suburb's status – the well-heeled at last meet the high-heeled. While Remuera now faces strong competition in the top property-price bracket from trendier suburbs such as Herne Bay and coastal North Shore, it would take a brave commentator to predict that it will be toppled from its top spot in the foreseeable future.

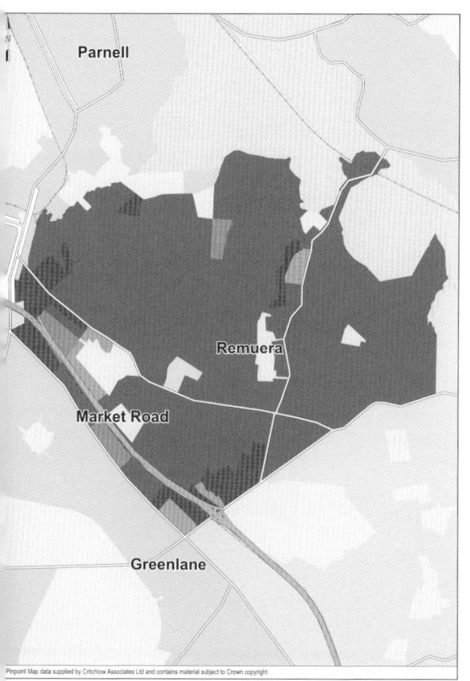

For colour key, see page 226

Population Profile

Population	18,660
% Aged Under 15 Years	19.98
% Aged Over 65 Years	12.28
% European	81.74
% Maori	2.17
% Pacific Peoples	1.53
% Asian	12.68

Who Lives There?

It's no secret that Remuera is home to the medium-to-high socio-economic bracket. Nowadays it's increasingly a mix of the nouveau riche and old money families – much to the chagrin of the latter. It has long been established as the residential area of choice for successful businesspeople and their families. Much of the country's old money is housed within these impressive villas and bungalows, although inter-generational loyalty to the suburb does seem to be dying off.

Because Remuera is within the Auckland Grammar School zone and close to a number of private schools, it is popular with affluent,

education-conscious families seeking a comfortable suburban home. School zoning is a also a definite attraction for large numbers of wealthy migrant families. There are also numerous retired people living in Remuera's apartments.

The suburb retains some sort of youthful balance, with a large number of professional people aged under 40 trying to establish a foothold. For couples on a high joint income, the area's excellent resale prospects make a necessarily large mortgage still look like a good bet.

Typical Homes

Remuera has some of the largest old homes in Auckland, some on extensive grounds. Heritage zones protect the character of certain streets – parts of Bassett Rd, Arney Rd, Portland Rd and Seaview Rd.

During the past decade, contemporary, minimalist designer homes and luxury low-rise apartments have taken pride of place on the suburb's famous north-facing slopes. This, combined with the many renovated character villas and bungalows has added to the selection of housing styles available.

The undulating geography of the suburb means that views of the city, the Hauraki Gulf and One Tree Hill are commonplace. Nearly every pocket of land has been filled, with many older-style homes being relocated to make way for new developments – typically we're talking about well-designed, quality developments, not bargain basement ticky-tacky, so this has not detracted from the area. It has enhanced it, by offering people a wider variety of residences.

Amenities

Schools ★★★★★

The schools in Remuera are top notch. There are at least seven high decile primary schools, including the impressive St Kentigern's and Kings Prep private schools.

Victoria Avenue School is well regarded. According to a recent ERO Report, "students receive a high quality education." Remuera Primary School also has a strong reputation, and includes specialist learning programmes for talented and gifted children. Both schools operate tight zoning restrictions.

The neighbourhood is in zone for both the hugely popular Epsom Girls' and Auckland Boys' Grammar Schools. Remuera's young ladies often attend Diocesan School for Girls or St Cuthbert's in nearby Epsom (both private). The Catholic girls school, Baradene College, and the charitable trust school of Dilworth are also in Remuera.

For a full list, see page 270.

Shops ★★★★

Remuera's popular shopping strip is dominated by banks, antique shops, real estate agents, boutique clothes stores and cafés. A great place for the locals to catch up, it is regularly humming despite being so close to the thriving shopping mecca of Newmarket. Banque gastrobar, in the town centre, is a very welcome recent addition to Remuera's previously sparse restaurant scene.

Further east on Remuera Rd is Remuera Village, where there are wall-to-wall wine bars and casual eateries. This part of Remuera, and Benson Rd down the hill, is a popular destination for caffeine addicts at the weekends.

Leisure ★★★

Remuera is home to numerous parks and reserves. Proudly poised overlooking its residents is Mt Hobson, where walking tracks offer a challenging workout.

There are numerous sports clubs in or near Remuera, including cycling, lawn and court tennis, bowling, squash, badminton, netball and football. Remuera Golf Club is actually located in neighbouring Meadowbank. Ellerslie Racecourse is nearby.

Remuera has an excellent library, at least three medical centres and two hospitals nearby. The beginning of Remuera Rd is New Zealand's medical mile, the New Zealand equivalent of Harley St. Three popular retirement homes are St Vincent's, Remuera Gardens and the Remuera Life Care Retirement Village.

Real Estate

Trends

Remuera Rd has traditionally been a dividing line, with homes on the "northern slopes" being worth much more than those on the other side. On the southern side, Armadale Rd, from the motorway back, has more bungalows. Relatively speaking, it has been the cheaper end of Remuera. Tired bungalows are of little value in Remuera, but the land on which they sit is at a premium.

The cheapest residences in this affluent suburb start in the early $400,000s – and that's for a two-bedroom unit.

A three-bedroom house with negative aspects such as being on a main road, having no off-street parking, or within coo-ee of the motorway will be around $650,000; take away any such negatives and the price quickly soars to well over a million.

Many new homes with luxury fittings and designed for modern family living, now compete with the area's gracious old homes. The latter generally hold their value better as they never become outdated. The trend in low-rise luxury apartment blocks also continues with more being built. They fulfil the need for older retired or semi-retired couples wanting all the mod-cons but without the maintenance hassle.

Whichever way you look at it, this suburb is likely to continue to be a residential destination of choice (and aspiration) for many years to come.

Best Streets

All the streets north of Remuera Rd are desirable. Of special note are Victoria Ave, Arney Cres, Arney Rd, Eastbourne Rd, Waiata Ave, Tirohanga Ave, the upper part of Portland Rd, Seaview Rd and Westbourne Rd.

Why We Live There

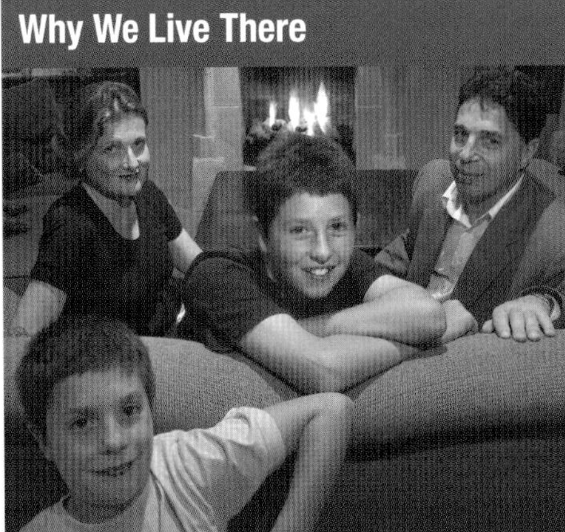

Cardiologist Warwick Jaffe and Megan Jaffe

Cardiologist Warwick Jaffe, his wife Megan and their two children Samuel and Elliot moved to Remuera more than five years ago. Having lived in Epsom and Mt Eden, where they found the in-fill housing and traffic congestion of those suburbs frustrating; Remuera was a logical option being close to work and school. "The move has been most successful and we are extremely happy living here," says Warwick.

Finding the village atmosphere welcoming and friendly, the couple felt they had a wide choice of excellent schools, both public and private. "The boys currently attend King's School and we are very much part of the King's 'family'. As our two boys move to secondary school, we are zoned for some of the best schools in Auckland."

Minutes to work, the CBD, Parnell, Newmarket, and only eight minutes to St Heliers, the family also enjoy the local shopping at Remuera and Newmarket, the restaurants in Parnell (especially Cibo) the viaduct and Ponsonby.

At a Glance...

House Prices

New apartment

Bedrooms	🛏 🛏 🛏
Price	$1,000,000 +

New townhouse

Price	$900,000 +

Do-up on a half site

Bedrooms	🛏 🛏 🛏
Price	$650,000
Bedrooms	🛏 🛏 🛏 🛏
Price	$800,000 +

Bungalow on northern slopes

Bedrooms	🛏 🛏 🛏 🛏
Price	$1,500,000 - $2,500,000

New mansion

Bedrooms	🛏 🛏 🛏 🛏
Price	$3,000,000 +

Average Rents

Apartment

Bedrooms	🛏 🛏
Price	$450/wk

House

Bedrooms	🛏 🛏 🛏
Price	$540/wk
Bedrooms	🛏 🛏 🛏 🛏
Price	$715/wk

The eastern suburbs rental market can only be described as chaotic, with many people chasing an address in the Grammar zone.

Travel Times

CBD by car	peak 25 - 45 min off-peak 10 - 15 min
Britomart CBD by train	10 min
Southern motorway	1 - 5 min
North-western motorway	10 min
Airport	30 min
Newmarket	5 min

There are regular bus services, plus the area is on the Papakura train line.

Many of Auckland's inner-city suburbs are testaments to the housing styles of their times with streets of turn-of-the-century villas and rows of 1930s bungalows. While many have been sympathetically renovated, just as many have met the wrecker's ball or been subjected to nasty "modernizing".

Not wanting to leave the protection of those that remain to chance, the Auckland City Council has proposed sweeping changes to the District Plan. The changes, if they go ahead, will restrict what owners of some 16,300 character homes in Residential 1 and 2 zones can do to their properties.

The Residential 1 zone is intended to protect the "built historic character" of Auckland's early established residential neighbourhoods, including large portions of Ponsonby, Grey Lynn, Herne Bay, St Mary's Bay, Freemans Bay, and Mt Eden, with smaller pockets in Ellerslie, Onehunga, Parnell, Avondale and Otahuhu. These areas are dominated by large numbers of villas and bungalows.

The Residential 2 zone is intended to protect "the spacious and tree-filled qualities of sites characterised by generously sized lots, wide roads and lower densities often with period housing". These zones are mostly in Mt Albert, Herne Bay, Epsom, One Tree Hill, Parnell, Remuera, Kohimarama, and St Heliers.

The proposed plan changes for these zones include:

- Requiring resource consent as a restricted discretionary activity for the demolition or removal of any building built before 1940.
- Requiring resource consent as a restricted discretionary activity for external additions and alterations to existing buildings and all new buildings. "Inappropriate" designs can be declined.
- Introducing architectural design guidelines for new developments, sympathetic to the character of the neighbourhood.
- New "height to boundary" controls will result in less dominant buildings on corner sites.
- Lower front fences and walls in the Residential 2 zone: for solid walls/fences, a maximum height of 1.4m (compared to the present 2m), or 1.8m if 40% of the entire structure is transparent.

Zone 8

In 2003 Auckland City Council created a new zone, Residential 8, encouraging more intense development in specified areas – with a view to accommodating the estimated 140,000 extra people expected to be living in Auckland by 2021. It was a toss-up between this and letting Auckland keep going until it hit Hamilton.

The zone will not be applied in character or heritage areas, and public transport options must already be in place for permission to be granted. The new rules will typically apply around town centres (where apartment blocks may be up to four storeys), or within 2km of the CBD (up to five storeys), on areas over 1ha.

West
LYNNMALL

Dominated by the moody, bush-clad Waitakere Ranges and a dramatic wild coastline, west Auckland has a character quite unlike the region's other areas. Its residents are independent thinkers and creative – this is home to a film and TV industry, top comedians and one of our best-known fashion designers. This was the first city in New Zealand to declare itself nuclear free and its greenie reputation is well-established. Waitakere City is an "eco city", which means it strives to do everything from producing less rubbish and planting more trees to containing urban sprawl and reducing traffic accidents.

West Auckland never seems to stop still. Its population is young and forward-thinking. Current initiatives include updated transport centres, new libraries, new civic centres and a technical institute campus. It's a major centre of tourism, arts and culture,

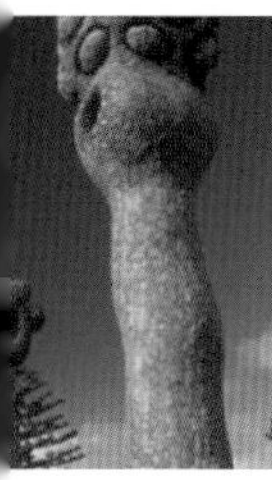

and the landscape includes everything from gentrified lifestyle blocks to fabulous native bush gardens.

People here are both down-to-earth and idealistic; they can laugh at themselves and the "Westie" label (supposedly all about fast cars, a hippy-ish outlook and black jeans) given to them by the rest of Auckland; and they're becoming more ethnically diverse.

West Auckland was shaped by rapid post-war expansion, and is now a series of town centres. Henderson is its undisputed CBD, and a vibrant retail and civic centre. Areas of industrial land add to the mix and further out you'll find orchards, market gardens, viticulture, rich farmland and majestic black-sand beaches surging with pounding surf. The

raindrippednativebush
pounding surf beaches
blackjeansandbigdogs
green, green, green

area has always had a strong industrial base, beginning with timber and flax milling, and kauri gum digging, followed by brick works and pottery industries. During the 1970s, New Zealanders ate their dinners off the heavy crockery produced by the now defunct Crown Lynn factories in New Lynn.

Back in 1902 Assid Corban helped to kick-start west Auckland's wine industry. Viticulture is becoming an ever-more significant industry here with much of the activity now based at Kumeu.

The houses are diverse, from original farmhouses, 1970s cedar-clad homes in the bush and suburban bungalows to palatial mansions. This is where you can live in the 'burbs, hang out at the beach, cloister yourself in the bush, or fulfil your lifestyle dream on a few hectares of semi-rural paradise.

At the weekend, many Aucklanders head to west Auckland's beaches or bush for walks, picnics, gannet-watching, fishing, surfing or to experience the notorious west coast rips. The 10,000ha Centennial Memorial Park includes a large chunk of the Waitakere Ranges and some of the beaches.

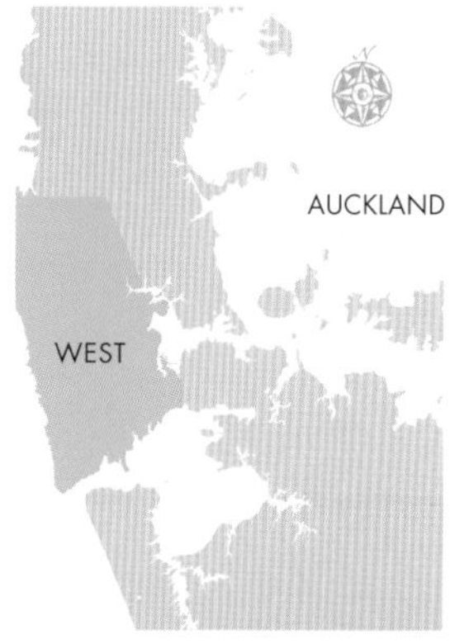

West Auckland – it's spirited, a bit brash and has some of Auckland's best natural assets.

Helensville

including Parakai, Kaukapakapa and South Head

Where else can you walk from town to your lifestyle block but in Helensville? Set in the rolling rural heartland in the Kaipara River valley, Helensville is catching the eye of ifestylers who've been priced out of the likes of Kumeu and Huapai. Once conservative and solated, Helensville used to suffer from bypass status. Nobody took much notice of the place; people just passed through. Now thriving again, Helensville is a mix of country town and heritage charm. One born-and-fled, but now-returned Helensville woman couldn't believe the change when she came back six years ago: "I drove out from Auckland, saw this huge signpost – 'Helensville' – and I thought, 'Oh my goodness, we are on the map!'" Nearby Parakai is gradually benefiting from the spin-off in residential interest and the community of Shelly Beach is a gem on the South Head Peninsula. Kaukapakapa township s the hub of the surrounding rural area.

Tauhoa
Hoteo
Mangakura
South Kaipara Head
South Head
Glorit
Lake Ototoa
Araparera
Kakanui
Waioneke
Makarau
Shelly Beach
Kanohi
Motukuru Island
Kaukapakapa
Parkhurst
Loch Norrie
Parakai
Helensville
Ohirangi
Wharepapa
Rewiti
Huapai

For colour key, see page 226

Population Profile

Population	6,819
% Aged Under 15 Years	25.34
% Aged Over 65 Years	8.84
% European	83.99
% Maori	15.35
% Pacific Peoples	3.52
% Asian	1.54

Who Lives There?

Lifestylers, artists, self-confessed eccentrics, families and elderly people come together happily in a community that expresses the best of what small-town New Zealand is all about. The children of born-and-bred locals generally stay and raise their own families. Newcomers from West Auckland and the North Shore will happily get into their cars for the commute to Auckland, when not long ago they'd baulk at struggling through urban motorways and traffic lights. As one puts it: "It takes my friends the same time to get from Titirangi to Dominion Rd as it takes me to get from Helensville, 35 minutes – and my drive is much better than theirs."

Typical Homes

Helensville is best known for its villas. Those in the township are originals; out in the back blocks there are some relocated from Auckland's inner-city suburbs. Auckland buyers widen their eyes in delight at the price tags, considering what a similar home might cost in Mt Eden or Devonport.

Other homes include weatherboard houses of all shapes, sizes, styles and conditions. There are smart brick-and-tile house in Amberly Heights close to Kaipara College.

Parakai's older housing stock includes basic family homes on the typical quarter acre sections. The new brick-and-tile homes in the River Valley estate behind Palm Springs pools are bringing a modern look to the township.

South Head is largely lifestyle blocks. Kaukapakapa is a mix of lifestyle block and large farms.

Amenities

Schools ★★

There are at least seven primary schools in the neighbourhood, and like many other semi-rural parts of Auckland the majority include intermediate years. Helensville Primary School is one of the largest with a roll close to 400.

Kaipara College is the local secondary school. Relatively small by Auckland standards, according to a recent ERO report, that size contributes to providing a supportive learning environment. The report also indicates high quality teaching practices and above average NCEA qualifications. For a full list, see page 270.

Shops ★★

The arrival of a Woolworths supermarket several years ago is credited with revitalising the shopping centre and the town itself. As well as the usual furnishing, gifts, craft, appliance and chemist shops, there are a number of antique and collectables shops including the Global Village and River Cottage. Parakai's shops include a grocery store.

Leisure ★★★

Parakai is famous for its two thermal pool complexes. Woodhill Forest has trails for motorbikes, mountain bikes and horses. It's popular for orienteering and tramping.

The Helensville Showgrounds host an annual A&P show. Boating is popular along the Kaipara River.

Helensville's eateries include the Café Regent in the art deco Regent Cinema building and the Ginger Crunch Café at the railway station. Kaukapakapa has its hotel restaurant and café. Parakai has Black Pete's Bar and Grill. At Shelly Beach South Head the Shelly Beach Store has takeaways and café-style food. The Macnut Macadamia Farm Café is at South Head.

For golfers, there's the charming Helensville Golf Club and South Head Golf Club which has impressive views of the Kaipara Harbour.

Real Estate

Trends

The bad news is that Helensville villas no longe cost $100,000. The good news is that they sti cost a heck of a lot less than those in othe parts of Auckland. For under $500,000 yo should be able to get something comfortabl and character-filled, perhaps even with a vie of the river or the harbour. There is alway strong demand for these character houses which means they are the least affected b prices easing off across the market generall One of the town's grandest villas, Ahukaroro was on the market at the time of writing fo around $700,000. Beautifully restored with four five bedrooms, it sits on 2560m² (in two titles on a hill in the middle of town overlooking th Kaipara Harbour.

There are no more sections left in Helensville which leads to new subdivision homes holdin their value very well.

Many families have relocated here from th North Shore and, especially, west Aucklan during the past few years, drawn by the rur ambience and the affordable house prices Agents note, though, that since petrol price have escalated, demand from would-b commuters has dropped off.

Near Helensville, lifestyle blocks with villas are rare and always in very high demand. Lifestyle blocks in Kaukapakapa with average condition houses fetch around $600,000. Top dollar in Parakai is about $350,000.

Best Streets

Rimmer Rd in Helensville for its lifestyle blocks; Garfield St in town for its quaint villas. Fordyce Rd in Parakai.

Why I Live There

Entertainer Jools Topp

Jools Topp is one half of the hilarious Topp Twins. While twin sister Lynda is something of a townie, Jools is anything but. "I never have been and I never will." Jools' patch is 6.8ha of rolling pasture on the outskirts of Helensville which is also home to her horses, cows, chooks, dogs and cats. It's close enough to Auckland for her gigs and the airport is just over an hour away. "It can take that long to get from Ponsonby to Newmarket!"

She loves Helensville for its sense of openness and the riverside location. She doesn't worry about the possibility of some day waking up to acres of brick-and-tile sprawl. "You can't stop progress, but I think Helensville will still be a small town with all its old charm for a long time yet. Most people living here have realised that there's sense in slowing down a bit. They're getting away from the idea that life is only about rushing around making money."

At a Glance...

House Prices

Helensville

Cottage

Bedrooms	2
Price	$250,000 - $300,000

Villa Do-up

Bedrooms	3
Price	$300,000 - $350,000

Renovated

Price	$450,000 - $550,000

On lifestyle block

Price	$650,000 - $750,000

New house

Bedrooms	4
Price	$425,000 - $475,000

Parakai

Basic house

Bedrooms	2
Price	$220,000 - $250,000
Bedrooms	3
Price	$280,000 - $320,000

Average Rents

Flat

Bedrooms	2
Price	$220/wk

House

Bedrooms	3
Price	$320/wk
Bedrooms	4
Price	$420/wk

Travel Times

From Helensville:

CBD	peak 45 min off-peak 30 min
Parakai	5 min
Kumeu/Huapai	12 min
Muriwai	20min

Ritchies Coachlines runs a six day a week bus service between Helensville and Auckland's CBD. There is mounting public pressure for the Auckland to Waitakere passenger rail service to be extended to Helensville. In the meantime some locals drive to Waitakere, then commute by rail from there.

Henderson 

including Lincoln, Sunnyvale, Western Heights and Henderson Valley

Henderson is a big suburb going big places. This is heartland West Auckland, and the thriving cosmopolitan CBD of Waitakere City. Progress on many fronts make it the envy of other big centres. There's a new civic centre and a "Baby Britomart" transport centre underway. The overhauled Waitakere Hospital, on Lincoln Rd, has been named one of this country's most advanced "green" buildings. There's a Henderson Vineyards Business Campus planned for central Lincoln, and Mayor Bob Harvey plans to make Henderson the Hollywood of the South Pacific. The old apple coolstore which was converted to a film facility in 2002 is pretty well booked solid for film and TV productions and was used for major films including *In My Father's Den* and *The Chronicles of Narnia*.

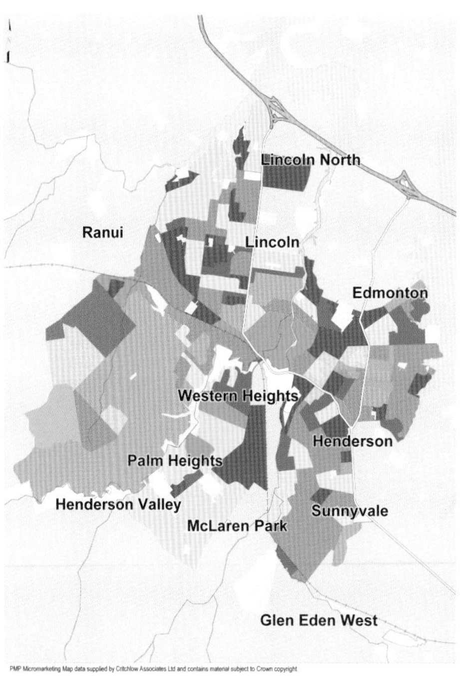

For colour key, see page 226

Population Profile

Population	33,156
% Aged Under 15 Years	23.96
% Aged Over 65 Years	10.54
% European	63.32
% Maori	13.83
% Pacific Peoples	15.08
% Asian	12.54

Who Lives There?

About 160 years young, Henderson was where Yugoslav migrants brought their skills as orchardists and viticulturalists in the days when the countryside was a vista of orderly vineyards and orchards.

There are still strong multi-generational links throughout Henderson. Children are born and schooled here and if they do move away, they'll often be drawn back to its lifestyle, schools and amenities to raise their own children.

This is largely solid working-class territory, with some more moneyed folk in the comparatively prestigious estates of Henderson Heights.

Typical Homes

Henderson's houses are synonymous with the famous "Dally palaces", built by Croatian migrants from Dalmatia during the 1970s. They were big with white wrought-iron balustrades and orderly rose gardens on generous 700m² sections.

Brick continues to be the cladding material of choice, as the developers who've moved into the old vineyards and orchards have created enclaves of prestigious brick homes. In Burgundy Park, Western Heights and Palm Heights, brick homes adorn streets with mouthwatering names, such as Chardonnay, Semillon, Cognac and Shiraz – a nod to Henderson's famous wine-making heritage.

Amenities

Schools ★★★

Henderson is well served with schools with at least 18 primaries, four intermediates and four secondaries.

The high decile and well appointed Summerland Primary is one of the newest to the area, opening in 2002 with a predetermined enrolment zone due to its popularity.

Waitakere College is the largest secondary school here and very popular - so much so that an enrolment zone was introduced in 2004 to manage growth. Henderson High School and the Catholic schools Liston College (boys) and St Dominics (girls) are also in the neighbourhood. For a full list, see page 270.

Shops ★★★★

The WestCity mall in the heart of Henderson's busy shopping precinct has grown in size and sophistication in recent years. Lincoln Rd has several retail centres, boasting just about every big-name store. Urban sprawl brings with it the need for local shops, and these are dotted throughout the suburbs.

Waitakere Central Civic Centre is the council's shiny new eco-friendly home, on Henderson Valley Rd. With features such as a green (planted) roof to help reduce stormwater and improve insulation, solar water heating, rainwater for flushing toilets and high levels of natural light, this building is a flagship for Waitakere's eco-ideals.

Leisure ★★★

A brick archway in Central Park is a memento of an eccentric early Henderson resident, Henry Swan: it was originally the entranceway to a cave where he stored fruit.

The new Henderson library is very user-friendly and open long hours. It's a joint project between Unitec and the Waitakere City Council.

At the city end of Henderson Valley Rd, Opanuku Reserve offers a restful playground area for weary parents. The 7.2ha Kiwi Valley complex in Henderson Valley Rd includes farm tours, an equestrian centre and Old MacDonald's travelling farmyard.

The West Wave Aquatic Centre is in the heart of Henderson. The new Waitakere Trusts Stadium is located on Central Park Dr. For eateries try Moka on Great North Rd, along with the wide range of Indian, Asian and Middle Eastern restaurants along the main street. The lively Corban Estate Arts Centre operates in historic winery buildings, and has 15 working studios.

Real Estate

Trends

Although Henderson is still very affordable compared to much of the Auckland region, things are hotting up here. Developments such as the Unitec campus mean that more people are wanting to live in Henderson, and that will naturally drive prices up. Anything in the mid- to high-$200,000s is already hotly contested by investors, families and first-home owners. Many first-home buyers have grown up here, traveled, then returned. "Once a Westie, always a Westie," says one such buyer.

There aren't a lot of sections available in Henderson: existing properties generally aren't big enough for subdividing, but homeowners will often settle for adding a sleep-out instead.

Henderson Valley is great for those who want a country lifestyle near town. Council restrictions on subdivision protect its rural ambience.

Best Streets

Burgundy Park Ave in Henderson Heights, Frank Evans Pl in Henderson.

Local Hero: The Westie Image

It's so frustrating when the people you're trying to poke fun at embrace your sneering and turn it into something to be proud of. "Westie", for example, used to be such a handy term of derision, conjuring up images of long hair shaped into ridiculous mullets, scrawny bodies encased in black jeans or long tie-dyed velvet skirts, roll-your-own ciggies and tough-as dogs wearing studded collars.

Blame the media and the mayor for shameless Westie pride: Waitakere mayor Bob Harvey reminds us at every opportunity that's he's a proud Westie, and Waitakere's version of white trash now even have their own award-winning TV series, featuring the lovable and chronically criminal West family. We're gonna have to find another group to look down on...

Smart Buy ✓

With developments like Unitec and the new transport hub, Henderson is becoming a real focal point for West Auckland and it's bursting with civic pride. If you like the sound of a three-bedroom house for $250,000 it might be time to consider getting some black jeans and signing up to the Westie register.

At a Glance...

House Prices

Unit

Bedrooms	2
Price	$200,000 - $250,000

House

Bedrooms	3
Price	$260,000 - $325,000

Better quality house

Bedrooms	4
Price	$375,000 - $400,000

Executive house

Bedrooms	4
Price	$400,000 - $450,000
With views	
Price	$600,000 +

Average Rents

Flat

Bedrooms	2
Price	$240/wk

House

Bedrooms	3
Price	$315/wk
Bedrooms	4
Price	$390/wk

Travel Times

CBD	peak 30-40 min off peak 15 min
West Coast beaches	30 min
Airport	35 min

By the end of 2006 the new rail and bus interchange (including an improved train station) should be operating, with airbridges linking it to the civic centre.

A train ride to the CBD takes about the same time as a motorway trip.

Kumeu/Huapai

including Coatesville, Riverhead, Waimauku, Dairy Flat and Taupaki

This bustling part of rural West Auckland is where townies can go country without having to give up their city-life refinements. Ex-suburban dwellers flocking to buy their bucolic piece of paradise have wineries and cafés at their door to lessen the shock, and can now buy smaller lifestyle blocks for country ambience, without having to feed any livestock. The area supports everyone from horticulturalists and viticulturalists to hobby farmers and we-really-take-it-seriously lifestylers. Ten years ago, no one thought the sight of the local chap chugging along the main road on his tractor would ever change. Now, that main road has traffic lights for the first time and is a bustling arterial route for the SUV monsters driven by well-polished parents and their pony-riding offspring.

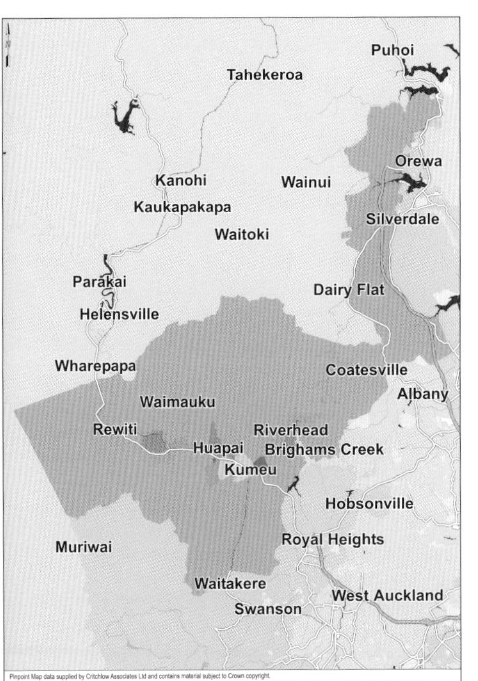

For colour key, see page 226

Population Profile

Population	14,748
% Aged Under 15 Years	24.13
% Aged Over 65 Years	8.18
% European	90.01
% Maori	6.81
% Pacific Peoples	1.75
% Asian	2.58

Who Lives There?

Kumeu/Huapai has a community with a spirited mix of all ages and interests. Well-established professionals continue to be significant buyers here. They arrive with their young children and take to the land with a passion for its lifestyle rather than its productive appeal. They're easily spotted in their SUVs and accept in good humour the ribbing they get for driving their "shinies".

The area is a popular base for the self-employed working from home and those who can vary their commuting times to avoid peak periods on the non-internet superhighway that is the main drag into Auckland city.

Typical Homes

With new subdivisions under construction and palatial homes dotting the rolling landscape of lifestyle blocks, the flavour of the wider area is continuing to change. Among the older housing stock, there are original farmhouses and small cottages, plus villas that were relocated from city suburbs. Tucked among the horticultural countryside, the best homes include tennis courts, pools and stables, providing their owners with all the trappings of the modern country luxury lifestyle. Now that buyers are paying higher prices for land, the houses they build have to be an appropriate quality.

Amenities

Schools ★★

Here you'll rediscover everything that's great about rural schools, including "ag days" when children show off their pets and produce. There are four primary schools which means children have to travel outside the area at secondary school age. The high decile and well appointed Waimauku School is one of the largest primary schools in the area.

At secondary level, the neighbourhood is in-zone for Massey High School. Private co-ed schooling is offered at Kristin School in Albany. For a full list, see page 270.

Shops ★★★

There's energetic commercial and retail expansion going on in Kumeu. Huapai and Kumeu each have their own shopping areas with plenty of parking in a forecourt off the main road. The sprawling array of shops sells everything from envelopes to antiques; there's even a place to get your lawnmower fixed. There are market garden outlets and vineyards with cellar door sales along the highway.

For more substantial shopping, the Westgate shopping mall is about 10 minutes' drive away at the beginning of the north-western motorway link to the city.

Leisure ★★★★★

Kumeu's enviable choice of leisure activities reflects a location that's close to both rural and suburban facilities. Woodhill and Riverhead forests offer ideal terrain for motorcycling, orienteering and horse riding. Rimmers Rd, near Muriwai Beach has motorcycle tracks. In Kumeu/Huapai proper, sporting facilities include golf, squash and tennis courts and a driving range. For moviegoers, there are theatres at Westgate shopping centre.

Kumeu/Huapai has several quality restaurants tucked among the vineyards, including River Mill, Allely House, Gracehill Vineyard Restaurant, Settlers Lodge, The Hunting Lodge and the Soljans Estate restaurant. For top café fodder, tuck in at the Carriages restaurant, Blossoms Café or Misada, or visit the stylish BeesOnline honey centre and café complex.

Real Estate

Trends

As with many of Auckland's outlying areas, Kumeu property values had some outstanding growth in recent years. For three years running, Quotable Value figures showed annual rises over the 20% mark. That has now slowed along with the rest of the market.

There are plenty of 1ha blocks on the market but a dearth of 4ha, and very few in the $800,000 to $1.2 million range. Top end sales have hit $3 million for a palatial house on a lifestyle block with swimming pool, stables etc.

Disaffected suburbanites who come to Kumeu to buy are from throughout West Auckland and there are still ex-pats coming to town.

A few minutes down the road, Waimauku has seen a surge in popularity – maybe from those people who thought the coming of Kumeu's first set of traffic lights was the beginning of the end. Buyers are keen on its smaller size and there is a wider choice of properties to buy. Bigger residential sections have come on to the market here, selling for around $330,000 for 1500m².

Best Streets

Matua Rd and Sunny Cres in Huapai; Pomona Rd in Kumeu; Solan Estate, Freshfields and Cloverfields in Waimauku.

Local Hero: BeesOnline Centre and Café

Whoever thought honey could be sexy? BeesOnline is a sleek concrete and glass building on SH16 which houses a manufacturing centre, development kitchen and casual licensed café. Honeygar (honey and naturally fermented wine vinegar) and flavoured honeys are used extensively in the café menu, as are uniquely New Zealand bush foods such as piko piko, horopito and kawakawa. So that you can see how the honey arrived in your meal, there's also a demonstration area complete with bees, hives and a keeper.

At a Glance...

House Prices

House near town

Bedrooms	3
Price	$400,000 - $550,000

1 ha bare land

Price	$450,000 - $550,000

1ha land with house

Price	$600,000 - $1,000,000

4 ha bare land

Price	$600,000 - $800,000

4 ha land with house

Price	$700,000 - $1,400,000

Average Rents

House

Bedrooms	2
Price	$285/wk
Bedrooms	3
Price	$350/wk
Bedrooms	4
Price	$460/wk

Travel Times

From Kumeu:

CBD	40 mins
Muriwai beach	15 min
Airport	peak 90 min off peak 45 min
Westgate shopping centre	15 min

New Lynn ★★½

including Glendene, Kelston and Glen Eden

New Lynn is solid suburbia from its heart to its heights. The suburb's focus is its signature mall and it's fitting that this is were the iconic Crown Lynn potteries for years produced tough, serviceable crockery for New Zealand's dinner tables. Nothing fancy, no pretense. In recent years, the suburb's status as the civic hub of the west has been usurped by its gung-ho neighbour Henderson but the locals don't care. They have all that they need. Glen Eden is shaking off its backwater status thanks to the enviable energies of forward-thinking locals. They have revitalised its playhouse theatre, smartened up its RSA, acquired an excellent library and put in a railway station café. Don't get Glen Eden confused with Glendene though. That's a newer area that sprouted during the 1960s and 1970s.

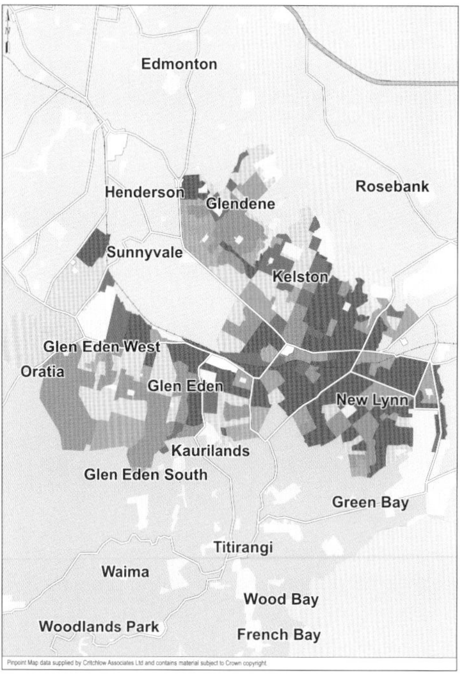

For colour key, see page 226

Population Profile

Population	42,216
% Aged Under 15 Years	23.94
% Aged Over 65 Years	9.77
% European	58.91
% Maori	12.49
% Pacific Peoples	18.80
% Asian	14.83

Who Lives There?

New Lynn and its environs is real New Zealand, heartland stuff with families of all ages and stages working to make an honest living.

First home buyers, long-term elderly residents and migrant families from throughout Asia are all part of the population mix. The suburb's flat topography suits older folk and pram-pushing parents.

Glen Eden continues to be a traditional first home buying area, and is used as a stepping stone to the more desirable neighbouring Green Bay and Titirangi. Older houses attract investor interest. Kelston is a family suburb famous for its secondary schooling.

Typical Homes

Older homes on large sections are common, built in the days when weatherboard and corrugated iron were the building materials of choice for affordable homes. These properties have been snapped up for their subdivision potential and the result is of modern brick and tile in-fill houses. Glen Eden and Kelston both have the odd original farmhouse, some Art Deco homes, post-war bungalows and the more recent weatherboard styles. Glen Eden also has new terrace housing and older group housing. In New Lynn, the old brickworks and potteries land by the railway continues to be developed with high-density housing.

Amenities

Schools ★★★★

Kelston is especially well served with schools, boasting seven schools within a 1km radius.

The decile five Arahoe School in New Lynn is one of the largest primary schools in the area with a roll close to 600. The well appointed school has a history of positive ERO reports.

Kelston Boys' High School and Kelston Girls' High School are the local secondary schools. Kelston Boys' High is well known for its rugby prowess. For a full list, see page 270.

Shops ★★★★

Each community has its own shopping centre, including the expanded Kelston Shopping Centre, Glenmall in Glen Eden and the Glendene village shops at the roundabout. The Lynnmall shopping centre is the hub of the wider retail area with more than 120 shops. It's complimented by some street-side shopping, plenty of car yards and more bulk-style retail outlets on Margan Rd.

Leisure ★★★

There are plenty of neighbourhood parks. New Lynn's pride is the 2ha Manawa wetland reserve created from a defunct clay quarry.

Glen Eden has its famous Glenora Rugby League Club, the swimming centre at Parrs Park, the Ceramco Park Functions Centre and a smart new library building.

Both New Lynn and Glen Eden have a large selection of ethnic eateries but for fine dining, locals head to Titirangi and Henderson.

Real Estate

Trends

New Lynn is now a "destination" suburb and not one homebuyers simply make do with because they can't afford elsewhere. In a generally flat market, this area has been steadily rising according to figures from the Real Estate Institute of NZ. During 2005 the median price hovered around $280,000 but during 2006, it hasn't fallen below $300,000. That amount of money will buy you a good solid family home, and attracts plenty of first-home buyers.

Within New Lynn there is continued strong interest from developers in all properties with subdivision potential. Even when a section is carved up, it's likely to still measure a healthy 500m², which is larger than the average full section in Auckland's inner-city suburbs.

New Lynn's apartment and terrace houses are popular with the wide mix of Asian nationalities

as well as younger workers who like being close to the rail line to the CBD.

Glendene is a quiet place without the through-traffic of other western suburbs and elevated houses get views of the Whau River estuary. Kelston has historically been cheaper, so has been popular with investors looking for rental properties and families attracted to the schools. Glen Eden's highest prices are for the older, more established homes. Prices rise as you get closer to Titirangi and Green Bay, where homes are also of higher quality – think granite kitchen benches rather than laminate.

Best Streets

In New Lynn, any road near the Titirangi border or Titirangi golf course. Pleasant Rd in Glen Eden. All of Manhattan Heights in Glendene. Anything on the water's edge in Kelston.

Local Hero: DFM Clean Lynn-Avon Utd

Photo: Jeremy Ruane

The DFM Clean Lynn-Avon United Premier Women's team, based at Ken Maunder Park, is unequivocally the best women's football team in New Zealand at the moment. Since the club was formed in 1996 Lynn-Avon has won the Northern Women's Premier League eight times, finished runners up twice, and won the national SWANZ Cup six times. Over the past decade Lynn-Avon has boasted two women's national coaches, and consistently provides five to seven national players every year. The club is also home to a successful men's team playing in the Northern Federations First Division and 26 other teams ranging from midgets through to over 35's. New members are always welcome, visit www.lynnavon.org.nz for more information.

At a Glance...

House Prices

Unit

Bedrooms: 2
Price: $250,000

Older basic house on half site

Bedrooms: 3
Price: $290,000 - $330,000

Newer house

Bedrooms: 3
Price: $350,000 - $450,000

Executive-style house closer to Titirangi

Bedrooms: 4
Price: $600,000 - $750,000

Average Rents

Flat

Bedrooms: 2
Price: $245/wk

House

Bedrooms: 3
Price: $315/wk

Travel Times

CBD	peak 40 min off peak 15 min
Airport	peak 40 min off peak 20 min
Henderson	peak 15 min off peak 10 min

The New Lynn transport centre is next door to the New Lynn Railway station and from there buses run to the CBD and other parts of West Auckland, Otahuhu, Panmure and Manukau City. Trains run to the CBD.

including Ranui, Waitakere and Massey

Swanson's enviable location in the foothills of the Waitakere Ranges defines its identity. The hills are home to Swanson's creative folk – probably the ones who used to live in Titirangi before it became too upmarket and crowded. The restfulness of the bush and the good-sized blocks of land are a lure for families wanting a more laidback semi-rural lifestyle. They're happy, progressive people who put energy and time back into the community. Waitakere township has all the charm of a country town. Massey North folk like to call themselves Westgate, an area which is considered to be more modern, upmarket and urban.

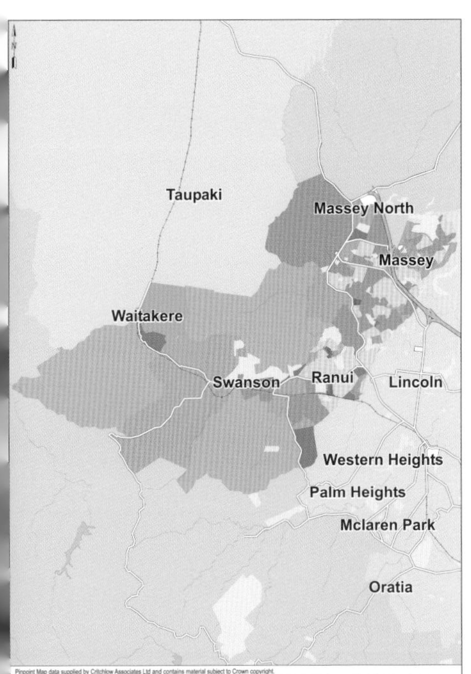

For colour key, see page 226

Population Profile

Population	31,485
% Aged Under 15 Years	27.59
% Aged Over 65 Years	6.03
% European	64.70
% Maori	15.46
% Pacific Peoples	18.11
% Asian	7.37

Who Lives There?

Swanson's community reflects the alternative lifestylers who live there – both the hippie types and those seeking a less crowded alternative to the city. Ranui has a solid mix of Maori and Pacific Islanders and an equally solid mix of first home buyers and renters. Waitakere is popular with larger families and their gaggle of farm animals and household pets, wanting a down-to-earth lifestyle for the children.

They are typically very community spirited. An example is The Swanson Station Café, established by an energetic bunch of locals who bought the land and moved the old Avondale rail station building to the site.

Typical Homes

Swanson has a mix of older weatherboard homes and newer brick and tile homes. Ranui has some newer brick and tile houses to complement the area's original weatherboard homes and the flush of group homes built during the 1960s.

In Waitakere, section sizes range from residential on 1012m², semi-rural on 1350m² and rural on large acreages, often sporting a relocated villa or cottage. Massey North, around the Westgate area, has the Rush Creek development built by Fletcher Homes and Universal Homes' Stonegate enclave. Royal Heights has some architecturally designed homes with views across the upper Waitemata Harbour.

Amenities

Schools ★★★

The mid to low decile area is well served by schools at all levels, especially primary schools (there are at least 10), most of which include intermediate years.

There is one secondary school – Massey High School – although teens who live in Swanson, Ranui or Waitakere township tend to travel by train or bus to Waitakere College in Henderson. Both secondary schools have enrolment zones. For a full list, see page 270.

Shops ★★★

There's retailing for every kind of lifestyle here. Swanson has its car boot, plant and produce sales and craft market. Waitakere township has its dairy. Royal Heights mall in Royal Rd includes the well-known Swiss butchery. The Westgate shopping centre is the retail focal point for Massey and surrounding communities.

Leisure ★★★

The Massey Leisure Centre is a fine example of the Waitakere City Council's artistic input into community facilities. Everything from the carpets to the palm mosaic, the clock to the children's play sculpture benefited from the creative input of local artists commissioned by the council.

The Auckland Outdoor Health Club in Ranui is a private naturalists' (as in nudists) club set in parklike grounds. Golf courses include the Waitakere Golf Club, the Massey Golf Club and the Redwood Park Golf Club in Swanson. There are pony clubs in Massey and Waitakere townships. Massey also has archery and athletics clubs.

At the foot of the Waitakere Ranges is Crystal Mountain gallery which houses the country's largest selection of crystals and minerals from around the world, and has a café. The Swanson Station Café is the top stop in Swanson for all commuters - by rail or by car.

Top eateries in the Waitakere Ranges include the Waitakere Park Lodge and Devines. The highly-regarded Elevation Café and Restaurant has a deck with views over the rainforest and back to the city. There are several casual eateries in the Westgate shopping centre.

Real Estate

Trends

Poor old Ranui remains a bargain-hunter's dream, with its run-down properties and population of lower socio-economic tenants. For a do-up on a half-site you'll pay just $220,000, although these are becoming rare. As one agent says, "$300,000 to $350,000 will buy something quite nice in Swanson, and something spectacular in Ranui!"

The better parts of Massey fetch similar prices to Swanson, and top dollar is around $700,000 which will buy a four-bedroom, two-bathroom character villa on 1600m² with heated landscaped swimming pool, garaging and sleep-out.

For the ambience of rural Swanson, and Waitakere township, you'll pay an extra $50,000. Lifestyle blocks in this area have soared in price: from $350,000 a few years ago to around $600,000 now. A warning, though: although the surrounds are very picturesque, the land is often too steep for grazing (and a lot of the bush is protected), so it's not the place for people who want a horse in the back garden.

Best Streets

Christian Rd, Swanson; White Heron Dr and Petrel Pl in Royal Heights.

Smart Buy ✓

If you have a hankering for the rural life but don't want to pay through the nose, the land around Waitakere township is for you. It's about as rural as you can get, as close to town as you'll ever want to be and you'll be among truly community-spirited people. And as Auckland spreads, land values can't help but grow.

At a Glance...

House Prices

House (deduct $50,000 for Ranui)

Bedrooms	🛏🛏
Price	$260,000
Bedrooms	🛏🛏🛏
Price	$310,000 - $340,000
Bedrooms	🛏🛏🛏🛏
Price	$340,000 - $380,000

2ha - 4ha lifestyle block

Price	$600,000 - $650,000

Average Rents

Flat

Bedrooms	🛏🛏
Price	$260/wk

House

Bedrooms	🛏🛏🛏
Price	$320/wk
Bedrooms	🛏🛏🛏🛏
Price	$400/wk

Travel Times

From Westgate:

CBD	peak 40 min off peak 25 min
Airport	45 min
North Shore via Upper Harbour Dr	20 min

Waitakere township is the last stop on the train line from the CBD. Buses run from Massey, Ranui and Swanson to the CBD.

Te Atatu ★★★½

including Te Atatu Peninsula and Te Atatu South

You can't put a suburb on a peninsula surrounded by water and not have it be a real estate success. For years, Te Atatu North as it used to be called, was regarded as one of the roughest suburbs in the west. Now it's called Te Atatu Peninsula and like all waterfront property in Auckland has had its own mini-boom. Smart houses have sprung up on land that looks up the harbour to the city, and the people now living here have money to spend. The peninsula may be fringed with mangrove wetlands rather than beaches but there are plenty of places to launch a boat, and walkways meander through the reserve that edges the coastline. The peninsula's sister suburb, Te Atatu South, is more aligned in style and price to main-stream, blue-collar Henderson and offers good, solid family homes close to good shops, schools and motorway access.

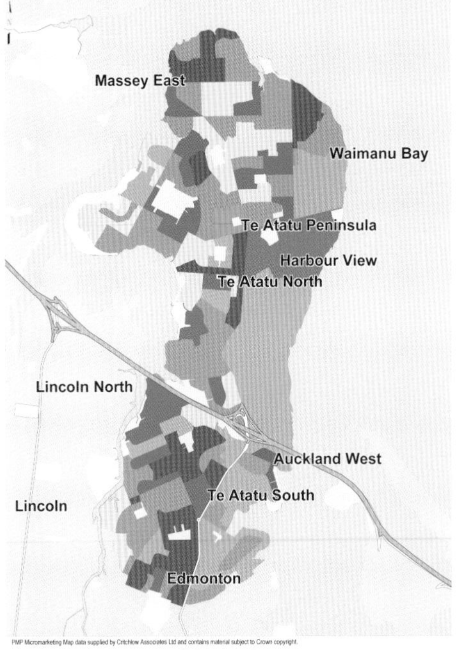

For colour key, see page 226

Population Profile

Population	16,857
% Aged Under 15 Years	23.24
% Aged Over 65 Years	11.78
% European	66.95
% Maori	17.73
% Pacific Peoples	13.22
% Asian	9.79

Who Lives There?

As a suburb in transition, Te Atatu Peninsula is home to a variety of people. There's the traditional crowd made up of salt-of-the-earth families and retirees living on a tight budget then there are the more affluent newcomers who have bought the swanky new houses and who have disposable cash in their pockets. They are a mix of families and professional young couples, keen on mod cons but also aware of the relative value of waterside living in this area.

They also like the fact that it's not a "through" suburb, so has comparatively less traffic.

Te Atatu South has many families with its good-sized homes and plentiful schools as well as being close to both Henderson civic centre and the motorway.

Typical Homes

On the peninsula, there are generally two types of housing – the older family homes from the 1950s and 1960s, and the new brick and plaster-finish and terrace houses, with not much in between. The general lift in interest in the area, has seen a revival of popularity in those earlier homes for their solidity and accompanying family-sized sections.

In Te Atatu South, the houses are standard suburban weatherboard numbers, very similar to those in Henderson.

Amenities

Schools ★★★

As with other west Auckland suburbs, there are plenty of schools catering for the many young families in the area, with at least five primary schools, two intermediates and a large co-ed secondary school. It's predominantly a decile five area.

Rangeview Intermediate is the largest intermediate on the peninsula with a roll close to 900. A recent ERO report described the school as, "attractively presented... providing good quality educational and learning opportunities". For a full list, see page 270.

Rutherford College is the local secondary school, located at the base of the peninsula.

Shops ★★

The peninsula has a relaxed village-style centre but as one local puts it "now we just need the shops to catch up". They're referring to the lack of restaurants and boutique-style shops in the strip that don't yet reflect the newness of the surrounding houses. For coffee, try Compass Point Café or Peninsula Palms. For a more unusual spot, Servo Café is in a converted old petrol station just off the main road.

Te Atatu South only has a small collection of shops and a large supermarket but it is close to Henderson with its huge selection of stores and the mall.

Leisure ★★★

A creative, marine-themed kids playground and skate park sit next to the community centre in the village. There are plenty of sports grounds, and you can virtually walk around the whole peninsula, along the sea-front, watching the many birds flit amongst the trees and mangroves. There's a yacht club, numerous boat ramps and a pony club. Boating buffs get the best views from the Te Atatu's Taikata Sailing Club at the tip of the peninsula.

Waitakere City Council is consulting on what to do with the run-down historic McCormick's Cottage, built on the sea-front in what is now Harbour View Reserve in the 1880s – it could become a café, restaurant or

information centre. There are plans to develop the 80ha of water's edge land looking across to Auckland city into a "People's Park" which will link up with the peninsula walkway. In Te Atatu South there are various local parks and sports grounds, including those on the banks of the Whau River, where many boaties have sheltered mooring for their craft.

Real Estate

Trends

Te Atatu Peninsula has been called "the next Pt Chev", and it's definitely living up to that title. Properties commonly sell for between $600,000 to just over $1million (especially in Harbour View Estate and Waimanu Bay). The little 1950s bungalow you might have bought for $200,000 in 2001 is now valued at closer to $400,000.

There's a real premium on one-level units on the peninsula, because of demand from retired couples (and singles) who want to buy something low-maintenance without leaving the area where they've raised their families. They'll pay around $300,000 for a unit near the shops.

There are a few sections available: 400m² with a peep of the water and just 100m from the beach is expected to fetch almost $330,000; a couple of sea-view sections have sold recently on Spinnaker Dr for between $500,000 and $600,000.

Over in Te Atatu South, prices are steady but definitely a step below those on the peninsula. Most buyers – be they investors, first-home buyers or families – are looking in the $330,000 to $350,000 range. Many ex-rental properties have been bought and spruced up by young couples.

Best Streets

The closer to the water, the more expensive the real estate, so the vote goes to Waikura Dr, Spinnaker Dr and Karemoana Dr on the peninsula.

At a Glance...

House Prices

Unit

Bedrooms	🛏 🛏
Price	$300,000 +

Older house

Bedrooms	🛏 🛏 🛏
Price	$340,000 - $400,000

Modern peninsula house

Bedrooms	🛏 🛏 🛏 🛏
Price	$600,000 - $1,000,000

(add $100,000-plus for sea views)

Average Rents

Flat

Bedrooms	🛏 🛏
Price	$250/wk

House

Bedrooms	🛏 🛏
Price	$275/wk
Bedrooms	🛏 🛏 🛏
Price	$325/wk

Travel Times

CBD	peak 40 min off peak 15 min
Airport	40 min
St Lukes Mall	10 min

Te Atatu South and the peninsula are divided by the north-western motorway and while that's handy, it can be hellish in peak hours. Buses run into town but hopefully some entrepeneurial spirit will establish a ferry service between the peninsula and the CBD soon.

including Oratia, Green Bay, Wood Bay, French Bay, Konini, Waiatarua, Parau, Kaurilands, Huia, Cornwallis and Laingholm

The wooded suburb of Titirangi is inextricably linked with certain enduring images: tree-huggers, potters in home-spun jumpers, old Rovers in British-racing green with Greenpeace stickers disappearing up bush-lined driveways. Trees are to Titirangi as coffee is to Ponsonby. Mention the place and most people think "bush", and the 1970s vintage timber houses tucked out of sight, and often out of sun, amongst the trees. Many of Titirangi's homes sit high above the Manukau Harbour with glorious sea views and distant city vistas. The suburb's little village emphasises the feeling that you're far from the madding crowd. Just five minutes up the road Oratia, with its big flat sections and views back towards the city, is one of the best-kept secrets of these parts.

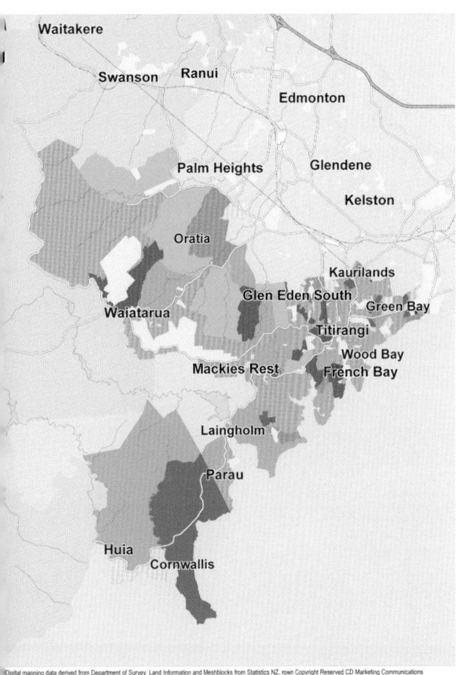

Digital mapping data derived from Department of Survey Land Information and Meshblocks from Statistics NZ, rown Copyright Reserved CD Marketing Communications

For colour key, see page 226

Population Profile

Population	24,120
% Aged Under 15 Years	24.07
% Aged Over 65 Years	8.67
% European	87.82
% Maori	7.25
% Pacific Peoples	3.96
% Asian	4.17

Who Lives There?

Traditionally, Titirangi has appealed to the artistically inclined and to bush-lovers. Alternative lifestylers and commuting professionals and every philosophy in between is represented here today. There's continuing interest from British migrants and even holidaymakers who become so smitten with the bush, the village and its laidback lifestyle that they move here. It represents green city living without the cheek-by-jowl housing of other suburbs. Green Bay is one of Auckland's most affordable family suburbs and has a core of elderly residents who can move to Pinesong Retirement Village when their needs change.

Typical Homes

The typical Titirangi house is all about timber. Homes perched on poles, clad in weatherboard and finished inside with cathedral-style beamed ceilings and tongue-and-groove paneling. The 1960s and 1970s style that defined Titirangi's development found new favour when buyers turned their backs on modern but leaky stucco dwellings. Titirangi people who buy to renovate, generally do so with skill, style and sympathy. Building extensions have to conform to strict Waitakere City Council regulations to protect trees on residential properties.

In Oratia, cottages and weatherboard bungalows grace the large sections. Several small enclaves of new housing give a broader choice for home buyers.

Baches, cottages and weatherboard family homes are among Laingholm's housing stock, which makes it popular for those stepping onto the home-ownership ladder for the first time.

Green Bay has a mix of units, group housing stock and larger, well-appointed houses to suit all tastes, needs and financial bottom lines.

Amenities

Schools ★★★

There at least eight primary schools in this high-decile area, including a Rudolf Steiner School.

The popular Kaurilands School is one of the largest primaries in the neighbourhood with a roll close to 800. Parents will move to specifically be within its enrolment zone. The equally well-regarded Konini School does not have an enrolment zone, and according to a recent ERO Report, provides students with "high quality education".

Glen Eden Intermediate caters for years seven to eight, although children at Green Bay Primary School need not change schools; it includes intermediate years and has a history of very positive ERO reports.

Green Bay High School is the local co-ed secondary although children also travel to Kelston's two single sex high schools. For a full list, see page 270.

Shops ★★★

Titirangi's quaint shopping village has cafés spilling outdoors, stone walls and cobbles. Dyed-in-the-wool Titirangi-ites would never venture forth to the likes of Ponsonby – there's simply no need. There are plenty of restaurants and cafés including the Hardware Café and a German/Italian bakery.

For a real sense of community, rub shoulders with the early birds to peruse the 100 stalls that make up the Titirangi Village market on the last Sunday of every month. There is art, craft and collectables, but precious little parking because of its popularity.

Leisure ★★★★★

Aside from the stunning Waitakere Ranges Regional Park, there are numerous small

neighbourhood green areas. There's also the coastline within the Manukau Harbour, although this tends to be tidal. The entire area has easy access to the sandier but wild west coast beaches of Piha and Karekare, or remote Whatipu at the harbour entrance.

Titirangi's links with art were strengthened recently with the opening of the renovated Colin McCahon cottage in French Bay. A feasibility study is underway on extending Lopdell House. The gallery sits at the far end of the village and runs a variety of exhibitions.

Real Estate

Trends

With Titirangi prices out of reach for many who want to live in the area, Laingholm (less than 10 minutes further out) has become more attractive – so attractive that its prices are often now very similar to those in Titirangi proper. Well-appointed waterfront homes in Huia and Cornwallis, a little further out than Laingholm, are regularly selling for close to $1 million. Also in the million dollar plus bracket are some of the designer homes in Titirangi's more prestigious sites, with double views of city and sea.

With no more subdividable properties in Titirangi, those wanting to build have gravitated towards sections in Oratia. Now that area is almost out of sections, prices are starting to rise there too. While it remains desirable for its larger sites, some buyers are concerned about the health effects of living on ex-orchard land that was heavily sprayed for decades.

Green Bay is as popular as ever with families, for its excellent schools, reputation for safety, proximity to several little beaches and to Titirangi village itself. It's prices don't reach the heights of Titirangi, however.

Best Streets

South Titirangi Rd and Kohu Rd in Titirangi. Cliff View Dr in Green Bay; Carter Rd in Oratia.

Local Hero: The Bush

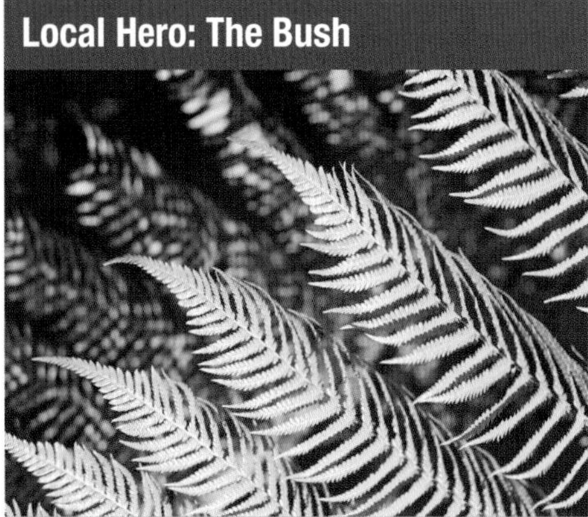

The thing that defines Titirangi most in the minds of all Aucklanders is its bush. Protected by local by-law, you can only clear as much as you need for a house site. The one-ness with nature, the birdlife and the cool green-dappled shade is offset by a lack of views and sun for some properties ... but Titirangi residents don't seem to mind at all. They love this Jurrasic Park kind of lifestyle.

Legislation to further protect the Waitakere Ranges and its foothills has been through its first reading in Parliament (February 2006). The Waitakere Ranges Heritage Area Bill would restrict further development in the Waitakere Ranges Regional Park, residential areas around Titirangi, the foothills area, coastal villages such as Piha, Karekare and parts of south-west Rodney District. During consultation, nearly three-quarters of written responses supported the bill.

If you want to get out and experience the bush, there's a hugely popular walk within easy reach of the village, starting at the Woodlands Park water treatment station. It used to be a bush maintenance track, which gets referred to as the pipeline road. On your street maps it's marked as the Exhibition Dr walkway, taking you through the bush of the Woodlands Park residential area to an exit near Laingholm. One hour 15 minutes is a reasonable estimate for the return work. Don't bother rushing - that's not what bush-walking is about. Take time to appreciate what makes Titirangi unique to Auckland.

At a Glance...

House Prices

Unit in Green Bay

Bedrooms: 2
Price: $240,000 - $270,000

Cottage in Laingholm or Oratia

Bedrooms: 2
Price: $300,000 - $350,000

House

Bedrooms: 3
Price: $360,000 - $380,000
With good views: $400,000 - $500,000

Executive house

Bedrooms: 4
Price: $500,000 - $800,000

Average Rents

House

Bedrooms: 2
Price: $280/wk
Bedrooms: 3
Price: $350/wk
Bedrooms: 4
Price: $430/wk
(drop about $20 for Laingholm and Huia)

Travel Times

From Titirangi village:

CBD	peak 60 min plus off peak 30 min
North-western motorway	15 min
Airport	40 min
Lynmall shopping centre	10 min

The nearest train link is Glen Eden. Buses serve most of the main streets of Titirangi.

West Coast Beaches

including Muriwai, Bethells Beach, Anawhata, Piha and Karekare

Wild and rugged, the beaches to the west of Auckland have a particular reputation linked to raw beauty, rolling surf and black sands. It's a place for rejuvenation and inspiration drawing holiday makers and an increasing number of city escapees to savour its disconnection with all that's stressful about suburbia. Its soleful beauty inspires the arty and has helped put this part of New Zealand smack on the world map. Karekare's beach was the backdrop for the 1993 movie *The Piano*, Xena has had more than a few sword and sandal moments here and now the boys in Speedos even have their own surf lifesaving TV show. Piha is the most exclusive neighbourhood and the only one with houses right on the beach. Muriwai appeals for its accessibility to Auckland. The mystical remoteness of Bethells Beach, Anawhata and Karekare just increases their appeal.

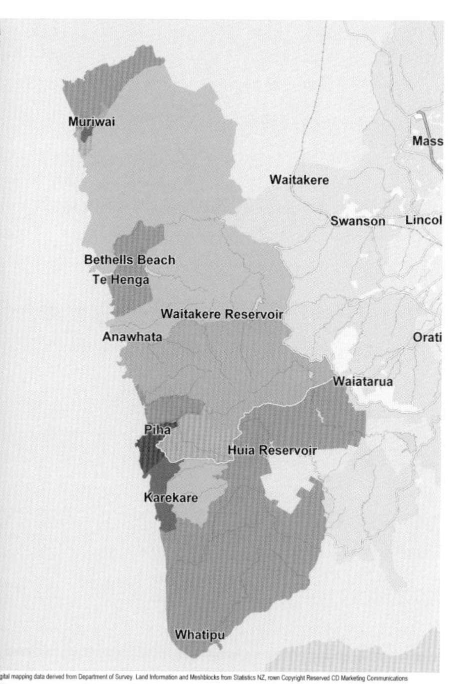

igital mapping data derived from Department of Survey. Land Information and Meshblocks from Statistics NZ, rown Copyright Reserved CD Marketing Communications

For colour key, see page 226

Population Profile

Population	6,894
% Aged Under 15 Years	24.76
% Aged Over 65 Years	5.87
% European	88.99
% Maori	8.96
% Pacific Peoples	2.61
% Asian	1.65

Who Lives There?

The West Coast beaches are not for the faint hearted - the drive to Piha alone needs to be undertaken with respect for the terrain, and a good gearbox. It's also not the place for faux lifestylers who think they can transplant their city designs on the landscape. As one real estate agent put so eloquently: "Start talking like that at a party out here and the music would stop all on its own."

An increasing number of citysiders are choosing to relocate here and commute, replacing the bling with bare feet. The middle-aged affluent want to revisit the surfie haunts of their teenage years with their own kids.

Migrants, including many English, add to the rich character of the area.

Muriwai has its share of return surfies, too. The 30-40 minute commute to Auckland city makes it popular with business people. All of the beaches have populations that swell in summer, and while the ratio of permanent residents continues to climb, there are still those with the spare cash to afford a holiday home ... and the props to enjoy their entertainment and their water sports. Surf the waves, surf the internet - they do it all.

Typical Homes

It's a heartening sight to see rustic baches tucked into the bush alongside stylish modern homes. The original houses – board-and batten, 1930s Art Deco and the post-war bach – are mostly getting the makeover treatment. New houses are usually sympathetically designed for the surroundings. This is given bureaucratic weight by the ever tightening regulations regarding subdividing land (you virtually can't do it) and the removal of trees (only enough to make space for the dwelling). City considerations just don't cut it here. As one resident put it: "It'd be an insult to build a big fence out here."

These settlements are small. Piha has some 700 titles; Anawhata has only about 30 houses, some relying on solar and wind power. Karekare has comparatively few properties with sea views. Up the coast, Muriwai has a colourful diversity of houses from baches to mansions and with every price tag imaginable.

Amenities

Schools ★

Primary, intermediate and secondary schools are a bus ride away from the west coast beach communities, although there is a thriving local pre-school at Piha. It was recently extended to cope with an increase in young families living in the neighbourhood and the latest ERO report described the school as a "warm" and "welcoming" environment.

For primary and intermediate schooling, Piha kids go to Oratia, and then to Henderson for secondary school. From Muriwai, children bus to Waimauku. The Lone Kauri Community School at Karekare is officially part of Oratia Primary School. For a full list, see page 270.

Shops ★

The general store is what these communities are all about, selling all sorts of household wares and foodstuffs, freshly baked cakes (at Piha's store) and displaying notices about local services. Supermarkets are at the nearest major suburb - for those at Muriwai Beach its Kumeu for Piha it's Henderson.

Leisure ★★★★★

Rolling surf, stunning beaches, rocks to fish from, freshwater lakes, waterfalls, hills to hang glide from and miles of bush walks – if the outdoors is your thing, this is heaven.

Both Piha and Murawai have surf clubs and there are golf courses nearby - Waitakere Golf Club and the excellent Murawai Golf Club. Murawai has an off-road motorcycle track and Woodhill Forest is close for off-road or mountain-biking. Murawai is popular for horse-riding and its famous gannet colony.

Piha has a saltwater lagoon and Bethells has freshwater lakes set in the sand dunes.

In March each year, weather permitting, the Karekare Volunteer Fire Brigade runs its beach races.

Piha and Muriwai both have community libraries.

Posh nosh means a trip towards town. Both the Piha RSA and the Piha Surf Club put on good meals throughout the year and there are deli foods and German-style pastries available at the Piha Store and good take-aways and take-home meals at the Muriwai Lodge Store. The Sand Dunz Beach Café at Muriwai is practically on the beach and its hearty and affordable café-style meals are popular.

During summer, a Ponsonby-class pie cart parks up at Bethells Beach.

Real Estate

Trends

Don't tell anyone who lives in Muriwai, but Piha is probably the most popular of the West Coast beaches, because of the consistently good surf and easy access to the beach (it's the only one with a road running alongside). It's also a bigger settlement, so there are more properties on the market at any one time.

Rustic baches have become an endangered species here: one recently sold for $1.5 million but it was the spectacular site the buyers were really after, so that little bach probably won't be around for much longer.

Views fetch big bucks out here; a great one will add a premium of up to $200,000 on a property's price.

As examples, are two recent North Piha sales, both just across the road from the beach: a one-bedroom basic bach went for $789,000; the other a large executive home fetched $1.06 million.

Top dollar at Muriwai is about $800,000. A few sections are available, starting at $220,000 for a bush-clad site sans sea views. Expansive sea and coastal views will set you back twice as much.

The highest sale price so far at Karekare has been $940,000, but many very attractive homes have been built in the past couple of years and when they eventually sell, could easily fetch well over a million.

Best Streets

Oaia Rd and Ngatira Rd at Muriwai Beach; Marine Pde and Garden Rd at Piha; Tasman View Rd at Bethells Beach.

Smart Buy ✓

A bach is the one to aspire to out here, whether it's high profile on the beach or something uniquely Kiwi that no-one can see in the bush. Prices are pushing them out of the reach of many buyers, but if you're lucky enough to be able to buy one you'll be onto a lifestyle and an investment winner.

Local Heros: The Piha Surf Lifeguards

Every summer, thousands of people flock to Piha – New Zealand's most dangerous beach – to play the seaside version of Russian roulette. Most stick between the flags where they are overseen by the bronzed and heroic troops of the Piha Surf Life Saving Club. An astonishing number like to stack the odds – against themselves – by swimming outside the flags.

You can understand tourists and new immigrants being completely unprepared for the vicious rips that Piha can serve up without a moment's notice. But it's astonishing that Aucklanders are so blasé about it all.

These heroes have now been recognised for their work, with a documentary series screening on national television. Whether this will make people more aware of the dangers and be more cautious has yet to be seen.

At a Glance...

House Prices

Piha bach

Bedrooms	
Price	$500,000 - $600,000

By the beach

Price	$800,000 plus

Muriwai/Bethells/Karekare bach

Bedrooms	
Price	$400,000 - $500,000

With views

Price	$500,000 - $600,000

Designer house

Bedrooms	
Price	750,000 - $1 million plus

Average Rents

Piha / Murawai bach

Bedrooms	or
Price	$240/wk

House

Bedrooms house	
Price	$380/wk
Bedrooms	
Price	$450/wk

Travel Times

From Piha:

CBD	peak 70 min off-peak 45 min
Henderson Centre	30 min

From Muriwai

CBD	off peak 45 min

Public transport is non-existent in Piha and Muriwai; it's either yours or the neighbour's car or the bike. Then again this is the sort of place where locals will happily stop and offer you a lift.

ncluding Hobsonville, Whenuapai and Herald Island

This used to be a disparate group of suburbs - the shiny new West Harbour, the hippy settlement of Herald Island and the airforce base of Whenuapai. Now this area at he top of the Waitemata Harbour is happily morphing into a unified spot offering lots f lifestyle choice for its residents. It's the sort of edge-of-suburbia living meets sea with arket garden stalls, big plant nurseries and a fabulous marina. West Harbour's elegant nclaves of big brick-and-tile homes have aged nicely. Whenuapai is one of Auckland's est-kept secrets, with some of our finest waterfront properties hidden beyond its tall rees. In Hobsonville, rural properties along Scott Rd offer prestigious buying on what was ttle more than rural land 25 years ago. And the baches of Herald Island are virtually all eplaced with new designer houses.

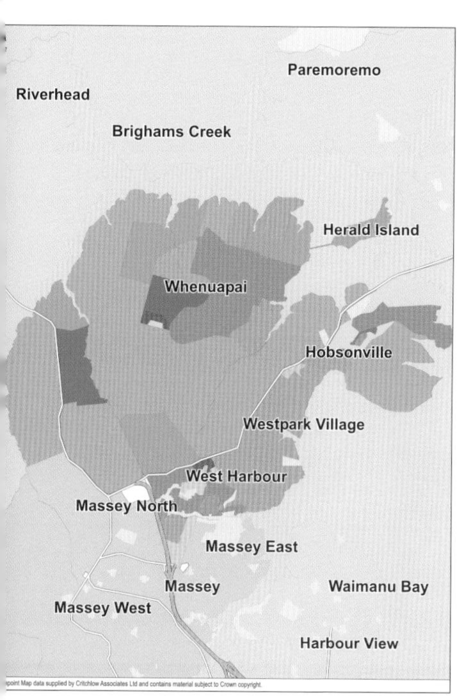

For colour key, see page 226

Population Profile

Population	16,062
% Aged Under 15 Years	25.35
% Aged Over 65 Years	5.96
% European	73.91
% Maori	9.76
% Pacific Peoples	7.99
% Asian	12.61

Who Lives There?

This is lifestyle territory and the suburbia of the upwardly mobile. Buyers upgrade from other parts of Auckland, particularly from other less affluent western suburbs. They'll come with their water toys, mountain bikes and horse-riding gear to enjoy the wealth of recreational treats on offer.

Boaties love it naturally, with the good water access and West Harbour marina. It's popular with young families although the lack of a local secondary school dulls the attraction for those with teenage kids.

The suburbs are a healthy mix of ages and ethnicities. Asian buyers like the modern low-maintenance homes and retired rural landowners like the culture shock buffer it gives compared to inner city living.

Typical Homes

There's a great contrast between the duplex dwellings and wire fences that define housing owned by the airforce, and the elegant, brick-and-tile executive houses of West Harbour's finest enclaves.

Just a stone's throw from airforce land, Scott Rd has some stunning water's edge properties. Whenuapai has hidden million-dollar homes with views across the upper reaches of the Waitemata Harbour.

Herald Island has rapidly lost its traditional baches to make way for new houses. For an area only developed during the past 15 years, West Harbour has already become noted for its stylish homes and gardens.

Amenities

Schools ★★

Schooling is one of the biggest issues here – there's no local secondary school. Ex-airforce land has been purchased for a state secondary, but a decision on its future is yet to be made. Plans for a private secondary school, to be known as Sutherland College in Brighams Creek Rd are awaiting resource consent.

In the meantime, older children bus to the secondary schools in Takapuna, Te Atatu and Henderson and to the private Kristin School in Albany. Younger children are well catered for with at least five well-respected primary schools.

For a full list, see page 270.

Shops ★★

Westgate is the big retail centre of choice. Local shops in Hobsonville and West Harbour cater for most needs, whether veterinary, beauty therapy, flowers or takeaways. Whenuapai has its local shops, including a butchery, a dairy and a grocery store.

At the 600-berth Westpark marina, a full range of marine-related services include engineering, boat building and painting, chandlery and sail making.

Leisure ★★★★

Stroll through Westpark Marina for boating eye-candy or take the coastal walkway from the marina and enjoy the beautiful water views. Throughout West Harbour there are playgrounds and green restful spaces, including the Luckens Reserve that meanders down to the water opposite the Mariner View School.

At the Hobsonville end of Upper Harbour Dr there's a vintage car display at the Monterey Park Motor Museum. Sports facilities include the Hobsonville Bowling Club and the Belvedere Tennis Club. There is a good choice of restaurants and cafés in the area.

Real Estate

Trends

The big modern homes of West Harbour entice a steady flow of buyers, especially from other parts of West Auckland. A recent luxury house with great sea views sold for $2.23 million but that was unusual; normally you can spend $750,000 for a near-new house and get a sea view. Try going house shopping with that sort of money in St Heliers and see how far you get. There are now very few sections left in West Harbour.

The area near the top of the north-western motorway is somewhat cheaper, but if you head the other way towards Hobsonville prices can easily nudge $3 million for water's edge land along Scott Rd. Whenuapai's lifestyle waterside sections command big prices too.

The ex-hippy hangout of Herald Island has now gone well and truly upmarket. All the old cottages have disappeared and prices start at $400,000.

Whenuapai sales have been up and down because of talk of the air force base becoming a commercial airport – jet planes overhead anyone? It's not going ahead for now but the project still has some influential support. Also, there are fears that a large portion of the old Government-owned Hobsonville air base, which has potential for 3000 house sites, may be used for state housing and lead to a potential drop in property values and a rise in crime.

Best Streets

Mansion Court and Courtneys in West Harbour; Scott Rd in Hobsonville; Pohutukawa Rd and Totara Rd in Whenuapai.

Smart Buy ✓

Good value for money, plentiful recreational pursuits (even it that only means wine-tasting or bulk retail shopping), harbour views and attractive new houses. With expressways and secondary schools in the offing, this has to be a go-ahead area.

At a Glance...

House Prices

Basic entry level house

Bedrooms
Price $300,000 - $370,000

Away from motorway

Price $370,000 - $450,000

Newer house

Bedrooms
Price $450,000 - $570,000

Executive-style house with sea views

Bedrooms
Price $700,000 - $1,300,000

Lifestyle block with older house

Price $1,000,000 +

Lifestyle block on the water with new house

Price $1,800,000 - $3,000,000

Average Rents

House

Bedrooms
Price $310/wk
Bedrooms
Price $400/wk
Bedrooms
Price $520/wk

Travel Times

From West Harbour:

CBD	peak 60+ min off peak 25 min
Takapuna	30 min
Westgate/north-western motorway	5 min
Glenfield Mall	20 min

Commuters have a choice of three routes to Auckland city – via the North Shore, down the north-western motorway, or on the new commuter ferry service. Buses run to the city, New Lynn and Takapuna. The second Greenhithe bridge is now finished and locals look with anticipation towards the proposed Upper Harbour Expressway, linking Albany to Westgate.

North

The North Shore is synonymous with golden beaches, water sports and big shopping malls. It evokes a sense of lifestyle potential, epitomised by the stunning million-dollar beachfront and clifftop mansions of Takapuna and Milford's Golden Mile. Even those living in deepest suburbia are within easy reach of the beaches.

The Shore has a reputation for being a very white, middle-class city, a safe and secure place to raise children, with great amenities and schooling. Around 70% of schools on the Shore are decile eight or above and it was a coup for the area when Massey University established its gracious campus at Albany.

Whatever the attraction, new residents are pouring in, particularly to Albany, which is the fastest growing area on the North Shore. It's commercial and retail centre now threatens

Takapuna's status as the central business district of the shore – and that's without the huge new mall Westfield has started to build. Albany's growth is also credited with raising the profile of the upper East Coast Bays, which have traditionally been the poor relations to suburbs nearer Takapuna.

The North Shore's amenities have developed along with the population. Sporting facilities, leisure centres and shopping complexes have grown rapidly across the city. A lesser known attraction is the shore's green areas – there are 454 reserves covering 1579ha.

Real estate values reflect this diversity. Multi-million dollar waterfront properties aside, there are plenty of suburbs packed with modest first homes.

sun-kissed sands
rangitoto island's silhouette
family-friendly
schools aplenty

Devonport was the first area of the Shore to be populated by Europeans. Settlements grew as paddle steamer ferry services began plying their way across the Waitemata Harbour into areas such as Bayswater, Takapuna, Northcote and Birkenhead.

When the Harbour Bridge opened in 1959, the North Shore woke up with a start. Within 10 years housing developments were sprouting up everywhere – and that's still the case, with new subdivisions emerging in Albany and one planned for Long Bay.

The northern motorway extension is doing for Orewa and the Whangaparaoa Pensinsula what the Harbour Bridge did for the more southern suburbs.

The main thorn in the side of North Shore-ites is the gruelling peak hour traffic which crawls along the main arterial routes, the motorway and over the bridge. The new busways project is already helping, and is hugely popular.

Who knows, by the time we're publishing the 2030 edition of this book, the powers-that-be may be announcing plans for a busway to Cape Reinga to reach the apartment blocks and cafés huddled around the light house. Now there's a frightening thought.

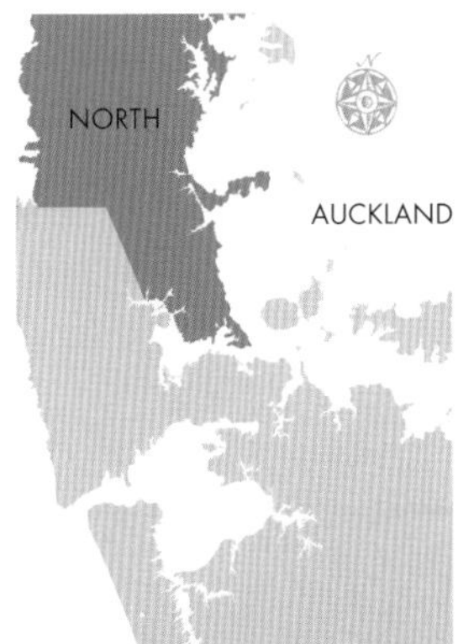

Including Greenhithe, Paremoremo, Brookfield, Rosedale and North Harbour

Like a runaway train, Albany seems unstoppable. Its development as the undisputed commercial, retail and light industrial CBD of the North Shore continues unabated. There's barely any land that hasn't already been earmarked for housing. Albany and Greenhithe are a picture of contrasts. Albany village is still quaint, saved by the new motorway north heading off in another direction, but most of the area is shiny and new. Greenhithe has kept its rural charm. There may be new houses and new roads being cut nearby, but this bush-clad waterside spot is idyllic. Brookfield and Bushlands are more established, while North Harbour is predominantly commercial. Paremoremo has its share of big lifestyle properties ... and a maximum security prison.

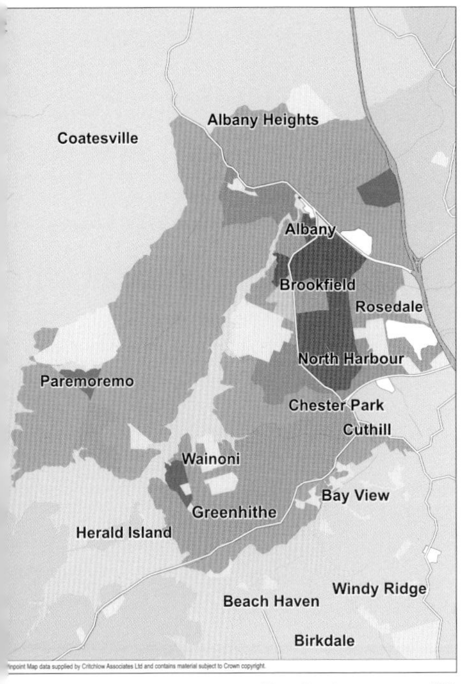

For colour key, see page 226

Population Profile

Population	11,634
% Aged Under 15 Years	24.29
% Aged Over 65 Years	5.65
% European	84.01
% Maori	7.14
% Pacific Peoples	1.88
% Asian	8.38

Who Lives There?

There's a broad population base here, ranging from urban professionals to lifestylers, but mostly it's families, keen on the new, well-planned houses and ever-increasing amenities and the fact that you can live your life well without having to venture too far afield.

Some students of Massey University's Albany campus live locally in the terrace houses and apartments, which also appeal to the semi-retired and singles.

The inflow of Asian migrants has slowed and Greenhithe has virtually no Asian presence.

Affluent lifestylers are not bothered about living near Her Majesty's tenants at Paremoremo Prison.

Typical Homes

There's a broad range of houses, but the overall impression is one of newness.

Bushlands has a much wider range of styles, reflecting its development some 10 years ago. The largest homes are those in the prestigious The Oaks and Oak Manor developments next to the golf course.

Greenhithe has a mix of rural and upmarket residential properties, all sitting on a minimum of $1200m^2$ sections. Oteha Valley Rd has new houses of all types terrace, duplex and stand-alone. There is a new apartment block in Albany Village.

Paremoremo has million-dollar homes on lifestyle blocks and the fairly new Goodlands Country Estate is a farm park concept with properties selling for up to $2 million.

Amenities

Schools ★★★

Huge population growth has been matched by growth in good schooling. Two private schools, Kristin and Pinehurst, cater for all levels.

Upper Harbour Primary opened within the past year on Kyle Rd, near Greenhithe, and Oteha Valley Road primary school opened in 2004.

In 2005, Albany Junior High School opened on the corner of Appleby Rd and Albany Highway as a new concept for New Zealand, for pupils from Year 7 to 10. See page 244 for more information.

Older pupils travel out of the area for state secondary schooling, either to Long Bay College or Glenfield College. For a full list see page 270.

Shops ★★★

In a very short time, Albany has become a shopper's dream. Not only is there the Mega Centre selling everything imaginable, but Westfield is soon to build a mall here. Plans include 90 shops and a multiplex cinema, to open in late 2007. Greenhithe's shops include a bakery, a takeaway and a garage and Albany village has a handful of shops, and a new library.

Leisure ★★★★

Despite the burgeoning subdivisions, there are plenty of reserves, including Lucas Creek Reserve, Wainono Park and the Albany Scenic Reserve. Lucas Creek is great for those who love kayaking and want to paddle their way down to the harbour. A special spot is the Wharf Reserve, where you can listen to the birds .

Horses are part of the rural scene, with pony clubs and equine centres aplenty. For golfers, the North Shore Golf Club borders Albany Highway. For those who like to watch rather than participate, there's the North Harbour Stadium.

Eateries with character, like The Wine Box tend to be in the village while the cafés and fast food outlets in the mega centre are of the "quick refuel between shops" variety.

Real Estate

Trends

Albany has shown steady growth during the past year, with the median price barely dipping

North Harbour Stadium

below $500,000. Some industry commentators predict it is due for retrenchment, however.

With a ready student market and long-term capital gain in mind, investors are always keen buyers.

Families continue to buy here (some trading up from neighbouring Glenfield), and with improved schooling that trend will continue (the junior high is a particular attraction). The area is too pricey for the first-home owners market but the area around Bass Rd attracts families who have less to spend.

Greenhithe always holds a steady attraction. Immigrants from England and South Africa see the big houses on large sections as good value for money. Entry level here is now $550,000 for a bach-type of house. There is some movement away from Greenhithe among buyers who don't like the new motorway development by Wainoni Park. Water views command top dollar because so much of the land bordering the upper harbour is reserve land. Lifestyle buyers are moving beyond Paremoremo towards Coatesville and the more affordable land as far out as Kaukapakapa.

Best Streets

Oak Manor Dr (aka Millionaires Row) in Albany; Vanderbilt Pde in Brookfield; Sycracuse Pl in Northwood; Rame Rd and Kingfisher Gr in Greenhithe and the new homes in Kitiwake Dr.

Travel Times

From Albany:

CBD	peak 60 + min off peak 20 min
Airport	60 min
North Shore Hospital	15 - 20 min

The new park-and-ride bus station off Oteha Valley Rd is one of the first on the new Northern Busways project, making for a speedy trip to town. Buses also go from here to Takapuna. The new Upper Harbour Bridge is now complete and will eventually join up with the Albany Expressway via a 5km Greenhithe deviation due for completion in a year.

At a Glance...

House Prices

Albany

Terraced house (entry level)

Bedrooms	2
Price	$275,000 - $295,000

Older house

Bedrooms	3
Price	$450,000 +

New executive house

Bedrooms	4
Price	$650,000 - $1,000,000 +

Rural 1ha to 2ha blocks on Albany fringe

Price	$500,000 - $800,000

Greenhithe

1200m2 bare land

Price	$430,000 - $470,000

Older house on large site

Bedrooms	3
Price	$700,000 - $800,000
With water views	$950,000 +

New house

Price	$580,000 - $650,000

Average Rents

Apartment

Bedroom	1
Price	$270/wk
Bedrooms	2
Price	$340/wk

House

Bedrooms	3
Price	$430/wk
Bedrooms	4
Price	$500/wk

The highlight of an Albany landlord's year is the seasonal influx of tertiary students at the end of the summer holidays.

Beach Haven/Birkdale ★★★★★

including Island Bay and Mariner's Cove

The thing that people first loved about this place is the very thing that's fuelling its resurgence in popularity. Once upon a time, Beach Haven and Birkdale were holiday destinations with a relaxed seaside feel, then they fell heavily from favour - real estate agents wouldn't even include their names in advertisements. North Shore snobs likened the area to the Bronx in New York and, although there is still some stigma attached to these neighbourhoods, people are waking up to the fact that coastal properties here can still be bought for under $1 million – for the time being. There's more coastline here than in any other Auckland suburb, lots of Titirangi-style bush and harbour views across the upper Waitemata Harbour to Hobsonville and beyond.

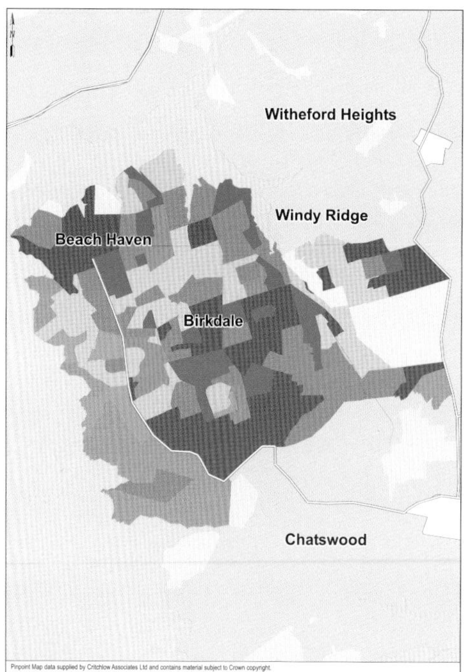

For colour key, see page 226

Population Profile

Population	18,603
% Aged Under 15 Years	24.35
% Aged Over 65 Years	7.76
% European	74.07
% Maori	14.06
% Pacific Peoples	9.19
% Asian	8.40

Who Lives There?

Singles, couples and first-home buyers are among the broad mix of people here, buying older houses and beginning the renovation treadmill that is Auckland's rite-of-passage into home ownership. The investment necessary is relatively modest for an area that's near to the city and – thanks to the Kaipatiki Bridge – to Glenfield and Albany.

There's a steady influx of buyers and families from other parts of the North Shore, especially the East Coast Bays. On the back of persuasive real estate marketing and good prices, they're trading morning sunrises over Rangitoto Island for homes with land and native bush around them. Interest from British buyers is steady because of the appeal of the bush-clad coastline. Grey north Yorkshire will soon become a distant memory in such an exotic location.

Typical Homes

Baches in original condition, and those that have been souped up into impressive family homes, dot the streets. There's a significant amount of infill housing now. On the harbour side of Rangatira Rd, new townhouses with sea views sit at the back of just about every original home.

Beach Haven is much newer than Birkenhead and Northcote, with their 19th-century villas, and owes its development to the opening of the harbour bridge in 1959. This is 1960s and 1970s, Hardiplank cladding and aluminium joinery country.

Amenities

Schools ★★★★

The mid decile area has plenty of adequate primary and intermediate schools, while older kids head to neighbouring Birkenhead for secondary schooling. Birkdale Primary is one of the most established and includes four Maori Immersion classes. Birkdale North School is small, but boasts a large attractive swimming pool and playing fields.

Birkenhead College is a Goodman Fielder School of the Year winner and has added to its academic successes a strong reputation in sport (orienteering and hockey) as well as music, drama and arts.

For a full list, see page 270.

Shops ★★★

Birkdale and Beach Haven each have local shops. The opening of the Kaipatiki Bridge link from Beach Haven to Glenfield has created a welcome direct route to the Glenfield Mall.

In the other direction there are the shops and mall in Birkenhead. At Verrans Corner there's an antique shop and Verrans Espresso and Food Café, which is a popular local meeting place.

Leisure ★★★

For leisure activities, Shepherd's Park has sports grounds, tennis and squash facilities. For fresh-air fiends, there's a coastal walkway and parks and reserves to wander through. Beach Haven's best-known eatery is the Au Bon Coin, which offers courtyard dining beneath a big pohutukawa tree. For those needing to eat and rush, there is an Asian bakery, a fish and chips takeaway and a pizza shop.

Boat trips on the harbour are an easy leisure option. The Beach Haven wharf is scheduled for upgrading within the next five years.

Real Estate

Trends

Beach Haven and Birkdale are clearly coming of age, with buyers realising that sea views will only ever increase in value. These suburbs were among the last on the North Shore to take off but it's happening now. Investors looking for bargains under $300,000 are turning their attention from Beach Haven to the poorer parts of West and South Auckland. Likewise, some first home buyers are being priced out of the market.

Homes on full sites are especially popular. In some cases, auction prices are exceeding real estate agents' expectations. Quality homes with water views continue to gain value and water's edge homes worth $650,000 five years ago are now selling for up to $1.5 million. On the main arterial route of Rangitira Rd, prices go up as much as $200,000 for a house on the coastal side of the street.

Overseas interest includes migrants from South Africa and England; they're not bothered about the traffic crawl to the CBD compared with life in the world's busier cities. A big part of the attraction is the geography, which makes Beach Haven free of noisy through-traffic.

Best Streets

Water's edge Brigantine Pl and Aeroview Dr in Beach Haven; Valkyria Pl in Island Bay; Rosecamp Rd in Mariner's Cove; Gatman Pl in Birkdale; Tramway Rd and Japonica Dr in Beach Haven.

Why I Live There

"King of the Castle" Ron Reid

Ron Reid wasn't joking when he decided to build "something that no-one else in the street has" on his Verbena Rd, Birkdale, property. Inspired by a picture of an English castle, he drew up plans for the five-bedroom, three-storey Lymington Castle. It stands on "two or three acres" of land that was part of a 100-acre dairy farm bought by Ron's father-in-law in 1919.

One of the founders of Reidbuilt Homes, Ron hand-cut the Hinuera stone for the castle; new stone was delivered in eight-tonne truckloads twice a year. Ron can't remember how long his DIY project took but he thinks it stretched from the 1950s to the 1970s. All he remembers of the completion date was pulling on his beret to keep the stone dust out of his hair, tucking his ruler into his pocket and heading out to cut more stone – until his wife Dee reminded him that he'd finished the project the previous day!

At a Glance...

House Prices

Unit without views

Bedrooms	🛏 🛏
Price	$275,000 - $300,000

House on a half site without views

Bedrooms	🛏 🛏 🛏
Price	$380,000 - $450,000

House on full site with views

Bedrooms	🛏 🛏 🛏
Price	$480,000 - $520,000

Renovated coastal home on full site

Price	$600,000 - $900,000

Premium clifftop home

Price	$1,000,000 - $1,500,000

Average Rents

Flat

Bedrooms	🛏 🛏
Price	$260/wk

House

Bedrooms	🛏 🛏 🛏
Price	$325/wk
Bedrooms	🛏 🛏 🛏 🛏
Price	$370/wk

Travel Times

From Birkdale:

CBD	peak 45 - 60 mins off peak 20 min
Birkenhead shops	5 - 10 min
Glenfield mall	5 - 10 min
Airport	45 min

Peak-hour priority lanes for buses and car-poolers cut the driving time to the city by a third. Buses loop the area before heading into the city through Birkenhead. It takes less than five minutes to get from Beach Haven to the Glenfield mall over the Kaipatiki Bridge.

Belmont/Bayswater

including Narrow Neck

Belmont and Bayswater are very much more than a gaggle of streets off the main drag between higher profile Takapuna and Devonport. When you're squashed between two illustrious neighbours, something's gotta happen, and happen it has. The average little houses on the flat, wide streets are being spruced up big time as residents recognise the potential for capital gain. Shops and beaches are handy, there's boating down at the Bayswater marina, coastal walks, and schools nearby. Five minutes' drive in either direction gets the theatre/restaurant goers to whatever their cultural urges desire. Bayswater Pt has wonderful views across to the city; Belmont's eastern shoreline has the same golden sands and Rangitoto Island views as Cheltenham and Takapuna. Narrow Neck has both clifftop and beachside properties and a status that's more aligned with sought after Devonport.

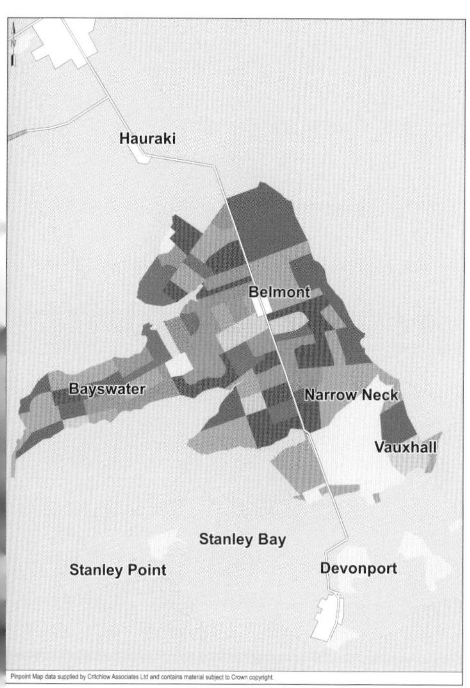

For colour key, see page 226

Population Profile

Population	9,015
% Aged Under 15 Years	21.76
% Aged Over 65 Years	13.91
% European	87.05
% Maori	9.35
% Pacific Peoples	2.56
% Asian	4.99

Who Lives There?

These suburbs are a good healthy mix of all sorts of people, from retirees who have lived here for yonks, young aspiring families who perhaps can't afford Devonport yet, and sophisticated young professionals getting into the home ownership market. There's the sort of cultural diversity you only get when an area has its grounding in solid blue-collar workers. With such a mix, community life and pride is alive and well.

With the area on the up and up and prices rising, that lively mix is likely to start skewing towards those who are more financially well-off.

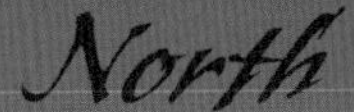

Typical Homes

Belmont/Bayswater was established long after Devonport so the houses date from 1920s bungalows and are representative of most decades since: 1930s art deco stucco homes, 1950s ex-state houses, 1960s brick-and-tile units and 1970s weatherboard houses. Of course, 21st century renovations are giving all of the above a new, improved twist. Something for everyone.

The scruffy state houses on Lake Rd, driving into Belmont, aren't an indication of the flavour of the area. The best homes are tucked off the side streets and along the water's edge streets on both coastlines. With homes built originally on large 900m^2-plus sections, this area has attracted its share of infill housing which at least gives choice to prospective purchasers.

Amenities

Schools ★★★★

The high decile area is adequately served by schools, catering for all ages. The neighbourhood includes at least two primary schools, Belmont Primary School and Bayswater Primary School. Belmont Intermediate is very well-regarded. As well as offering "high quality teaching" a recent ERO report also described the school as "...attractive and well resourced..."

The area is in zone for the well-appointed Takapuna Grammar School.

For a full list, see page 270.

Shops ★★

Belmont's busy shopping precinct includes several hairdressers, a bakery, shoe repair shop, and the art supplies/gallery shop Palette. There's a chemist and a medical centre with the closest supermarkets being New World stores at Hauraki Corner and in Devonport. And what more proof do you need that this is a family neighbourhood than the popularity of the local McDonalds and Pizza Hutt?

Leisure ★★★

Boating and other water activities are right on your doorstep. The Takapuna Boating Club is based at Bayswater Marina where you can spend time ogling the big yachts. Bayswater boat ramp is a mecca for windsurfers who zip up and down this part of the harbour on a brisk and breezy day.

Outdoor jaunts include beach walks along the beautiful sands of Narrow Neck Beach where there's a playground and a shop. Some 5ha of former naval land at Takapuna Head is being developed into public open space by the North Shore City Council. On the opposite side of the peninsula there are reserve walks amongst the mangroves and mudflats. If the wetlands appeal, then try the boardwalk jaunt off the Kawerau Reserve for a change.

Eateries include Thai, Italian and Indian plus excellent food at the popular Vanilla café.

Real Estate

Trends

There's a distinct pride in the air around Belmont these days, with people no longer feeling they have to make excuses for not living in neighbouring Takapuna.

Many newcomers are ex-pat Kiwis who are drawn back to the area, hankering after a fair dinkum kiwi upbringing for their kids that includes climbing trees, fossicking on the beaches, messing about on boats and learning to swim by falling off the local wharf!

The commuter ferry service from Bayswater and the express bus service into the city are big drawcards, along with quality schooling and sea views. Lake Rd divides Belmont (seaside) and Bayswater (harbourside) and has become a physical price demarcation – houses on the seaward side fetch a premium, although Bayswater's harbourside homes have now climbed to well over the million dollar mark. Each suburb offers wonderful choice for buyers with all depths of pockets.

Smart buying has been most evident off the Eversleigh Rd area where renovations abound. Prices have jumped significantly with a three-bedroom house rising from high $300,000s two years ago to low $500,000s this year.

Best Streets

Norwood Rd, Beresford St and Marine Tce in Bayswater have great harbour views, and in Belmont, Williamson Ave, Seacliff St, Hamana St and Merani St overlook Narrow Neck Beach.

At a Glance...

House Prices

Brick and tile unit

Bedrooms	🛏 🛏
Price	$300,000

Renovated ex-state house

Bedrooms	🛏 🛏
Price	$400,000 - $500,000

Renovated character house on half site

Bedrooms	🛏 🛏 🛏
Price	$530,000 +

Modern house near the water

Bedrooms	🛏 🛏 🛏 🛏
Price	$800,000 - $1,000,000 +

Premium clifftop home

Price	$2,000,000 - $3,000,000

Average Rents

Flat

Bedrooms	🛏 🛏
Price	$280/wk

House

Bedrooms	🛏 🛏 🛏
Price	$380/wk
Bedrooms	🛏 🛏 🛏 🛏
Price	$475/wk

Travel Times

From Birkdale:

CBD	peak 40 - 50 min off peak 10 -15 min
North Shore Hospital	15 min
Hauraki Corner	5 min
Devonport	10 min
Airport	45 - 60 min

There's a regular bus service (including an express) into Takapuna and the CBD. Best of all, there's a ferry service that leaves from the wharf by the Bayswater Marina.

Devonport ★★★★★

including Stanley Bay, Stanley Pt, Cheltenham and Vauxhall

Devonport is a unique combination of classy historic town and seaside village, with a bit of arty bohemian thrown in for good measure. This suburb is the iconic, historic face of the North Shore – and its future is well assured, thanks to the passion of residents who strive to keep Devonport true to its Victorian heritage. Devonport is steeped in maritime history, with the Royal New Zealand Navy base at Stanley Bay and gun emplacements on North Head and Mt Victoria. You're never far from either the sea or the village here, but you're a long way from the madding crowd, the motorway hum and the high rises that now typify the city side of the harbour. Devonport's physical isolation may make it a commuting headache by car but residents wouldn't have Devonport any other way. Anyway, you can forget traffic hassles with a gentle harbour ferry ride to the CBD. Very civilized.

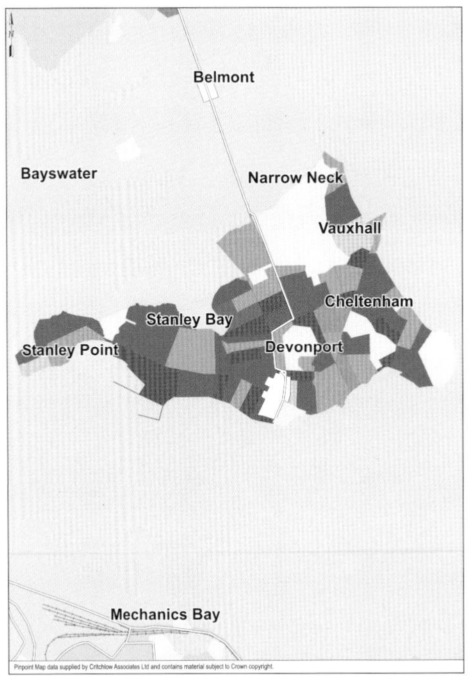

For colour key, see page 226

Population Profile

Population	7,374
% Aged Under 15 Years	21.20
% Aged Over 65 Years	10.78
% European	92.76
% Maori	5.53
% Pacific Peoples	1.91
% Asian	2.03

Who Lives There?

Arty, creative types have always favoured Devonport for its peaceful atmosphere beautiful coastline and historical charm These days the area attracts many young professionals, often with school-age children looking for large homes, big sections and a laid-back community-minded lifestyle close to beaches, parks and good schools. It's popular with those often relocating from overseas or other parts of New Zealand. Residents are a pro-active lot who will fight to protect the uniqueness of their suburb.

There's a saying that Devonport brings people home and this trend is truer than ever before

Young professionals who grew up here are returning with their own families. Along the way, many expansive properties long-held in family ownership have been subdivided for sons and daughters in a low-key twist on the "old money" theme.

Typical Homes

Devonport boasts many elegant, picturesque Victorian and Edwardian villas and cottages, large and small, along the water's edge and down the little streets beyond the village. It has the North Shore's largest collection of villas. Inconspicuously dotted among the older houses are a smaller number of 1960s units and homes.

Devonport's heritage character is strongly supported by the North Shore City Council and zoning regulations require renovations to enhance the historical flavour of individual buildings, the immediate neighbourhood and the wider suburb. Street facades pre-1930 can't generally be altered and rear additions and alterations must be done using sympathetic materials. But inside, you can do what you wish. There are few apartment blocks - and that's considered a big attraction.

Amenities

Schools ★★★★

Quality schooling is one of the attractions of this high decile area. There are at least four state primary schools feeding into the well-regarded Belmont Intermediate - Devonport School, St Leo's School, Stanley Bay School and Vauxhall School. According to a recent ERO report, children at Devonport School are achieving above expectations for their age in the core curriculum areas. The well resourced, attractive and equally high performing Stanley Bay School has excellent sporting and cultural facilities including a recently built sports hall, outdoor pool, sandpits , playgrounds and large playing fields.

At secondary level, students move onto Takapuna Grammar School in Lake Rd, which is the only co-ed secondary school in the area and one of the oldest high schools on the North Shore.

For a full list, see page 270.

Shops ★★★★

Shopping here is more than just filling your basket with life's necessities, it's about relaxing and enjoying the village charm that sets Devonport apart from other suburbs. Most shops still have their original facades, including the grand old Esplanade Hotel at the bottom of the main street. Once you've dealt with the shopping list at the supermarket (discreetly tucked down a side street), there are all the little galleries, boutique-style shops and bookshops to distract you on the way home.

Leisure ★★★★★

There's plenty of scope to enjoy the outdoors here, whether it's lazing on one of the beautiful beaches or a jaunt up North Head or Mt

Victoria to take in the harbour and city views. Water sports are popular, with five boat ramps around the Devonport shoreline, and tennis, cricket and bowls are also well catered for.

If looking at all the beautiful old homes makes you want to know more about local history, the hour-long Old Devonport Walk is well worth the time and effort. There's also a museum at the naval base.

Devonport is well supplied with restaurants and other eateries, including Manuka, the Stone Oven Bakery and Café and the award winning Ice It Café in Church St. The historic cinema has been bought by the council and will be run by a trust.

The rusting and disused Devonport Wharf building is an embarrassment from which ferry users avert their eyes as they pass – like a drunk on a street corner. It has just been bought by the council, which will now ponder the building's future and do some much-needed maintenance.

Real Estate

Trends

Devonport has notched up some significant sales during the past year with properties close to the water - and not necessarily on big sites - reaching comfortably past $2 million. Down Stanley Pt, property values are in the $3 million plus bracket, and houses with city views carry values up to and over $4 million.

At the Cheltenham end of Devonport, sales of $2 million and $2.5 million plus are being achieved for well-renovated houses that would have sold for less than $1 million a few years ago, unrenovated.

Figures of $2 million plus have even been paid for properties on which new, heritage-appropriate homes are planned, where the value is in the land rather than the dwelling.

At the humble entry-level end of the market, there's a recent and rare example of a modest home that was untouched for 50 years and in the same family for a century selling for $505,000. More often, the price for a small Devonport villa is around $800,000.

Best Streets

Jubilee Ave, Cheltenham, the peninsula end of Stanley Pt Rd and First and Second Ave in Stanley Pt.

Look Out ⓘ

If slick, minimalist architecture is your style, then Devonport definitely isn't for you. A rash of so-called "renovations" that have seen brand new homes arise from the rubble of near-demolitions have attracted the wrath of locals concerned at the threat to Devonport's heritage. Now the rules that govern building design are under review by the North Shore City. Changes to subdivision, minor units and garages have already been made. Meanwhile, much misinformation surrounds what owners of older homes can and can't do during renovations. Town planning criteria refers to pre-1930 homes as adding historical character to a neighbourhood that needs to be retained, but homes built subsequently and deemed by council to add character to the area can still be bound by resource consent requirements especially in regard to the street frontage.

At a Glance...

House Prices

Brick and tile unit

Bedrooms: 2
Price: $300,000

Basic villa

Bedrooms: 3
Price: $800,000 - $900,000

House without views

Bedrooms: 4
Price: $800,000 - $1,000,000

House with sea and city views

Bedrooms: 4
Price: $2,000,000 - $4,000,000

Average Rents

Apartment

Bedrooms: 2
Price: $320/wk

House

Bedrooms: 3
Price: $465/wk
Bedrooms: 4
Price: $590/wk

Travel Times

CBD	peak 50 - 60 min off peak 20 - 25 min
By ferry	12 - 15 min
Northern Motorway	peak 45 - 50 min off peak 15 - 20 min
Airport	peak - anyone's guess off peak 45 min
Takapuna shops	10 min

The ferry is the saving grace for Devonport's commuters, with some 30 sailings every weekday to the city. It's also great for party-goers - from Monday to Thursday the last ferry leaves the city at 11pm. On weekends it leaves at 1am. There's also bus services into the city. People who love this place don't see the one-road in, one-road out of Devonport as a commuter's nightmare. To them, it makes Devonport a destination of choice rather than a noisy, anonymous transit suburb.

Glenfield ★★½

including Wairau Park, The Palms, Unsworth Heights, Bay View, Marlborough and Witheford Heights

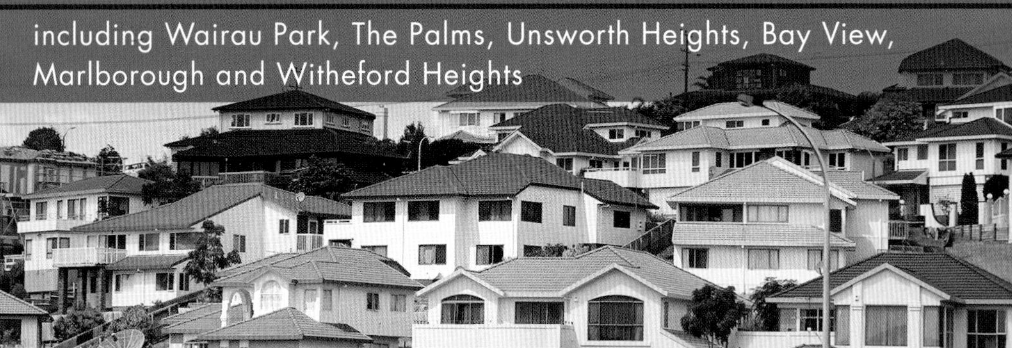

Glenfield's claim to fame is twofold. Firstly, its population is said to personify average New Zealand. Secondly, "our" Rachel Hunter, model and ex-wife of ageing rocker Rod Stewart, came from Glenfield. She may live in Hollywood now but she's Glenfield girl through and through. Glenfield is the heart of North Shore suburbia, where the buzz of the lawnmower is alive and well. Its affordable houses make it attractive to people who are not suburb snobs, many of whom work on the shore or from their vans as self-employed tradespeople. Glenfield may not have a beach on its doorstep but it's not far to either coast, has an amenity-crammed sports and community centre, is handy to all of the North Shore, has some of the best shops in Auckland and a firm community spirit. If this is life in the 'burbs, bring it on.

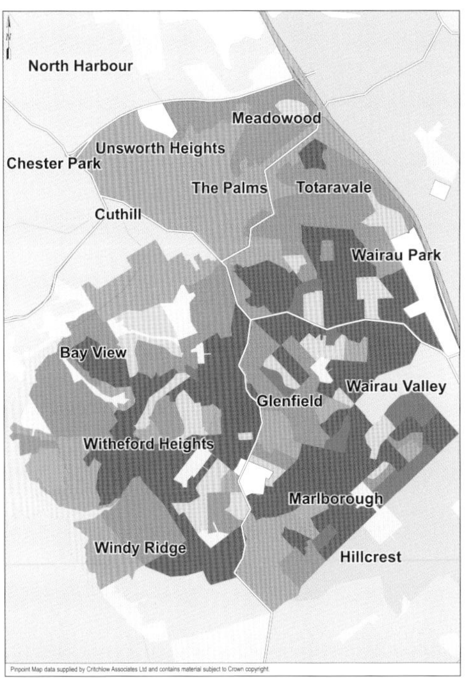

For colour key, see page 226

Population Profile

Population	33,099
% Aged Under 15 Years	22.34
% Aged Over 65 Years	6.73
% European	69.65
% Maori	8.04
% Pacific Peoples	4.59
% Asian	18.01

Who Lives There?

Glenfield has now lost many of its traditional first home buyers. People moving here now are more likely to be second home buyers. The number of local trade vehicles confirms the perception that this is a hearty self-employment area, with residents who give a lot back to their community.

Newer housing developments are attracting professionals from within and from outside Glenfield. Some prefer to think of themselves as living in more upmarket Albany rather than Glenfield.

Typical Homes

There's huge choice in Glenfield, from the well-known traditional group houses with their simple design to the newer developments. The group houses built, street by cul-de-sac street in the 1960s and 70s, have come back into favour. They may not be the height of architectural style, but they're popular with homeowners at the middle to lower income spectrum.

There are larger executive homes in Unsworth Heights and The Palms. Glendhu Rd has an almost rural feel, a striking contrast to the busy Glenfield Rd thoroughfare.

Amenities

Schools ★★★

Glenfield is a mid to high decile area well served with schools, especially at primary level. There are at least eight primaries, including Westminster Christian School and Wairau Valley School (a special school).

Glenfield Primary school, with a roll of around 500, is a popular choice; according to a recent ERO report, the school provides "good quality learning programmes".

Glenfield College is the main state co-educational high school in the area. It was one of the first secondary schools to attract fee-paying international students and it has a strong pastoral emphasis to its curriculum. For single-sex education, the secondary boys' and girls' high schools at Westlake are the closest, but it's important to check zones. For a full list, see page 270.

Shops ★★★★

Glenfield shoppers are spoilt for choice, whether it's the many little surburban blocks of shops, the mall or the Link Dr retail area at Wairau Park. On Glenfield Rd, the Westfield mall is the largest on the North Shore (although soon to be outdone by the one in Albany). Its "family destination" style includes 114 shops, department stores, a food hall, cafés and two supermarkets.

Leisure ★★★

Glenfield has many small parks and a coastal walkway as well as the nearby East Coast Bays beaches. Rosedale Park is close to the wastewater treatment park, but you'd never know now that the odours have mercifully been eliminated by new technology. The walkway around the Manuka Reserve has had a recent upgrade. There's a boat ramp for use when the tide is right and a children's playground.

The Glenfield Leisure Centre is hugely popular for its indoor heated pools, hydroslides and diving boards, saunas and spas. Facilities include conference rooms and a gym.

The North Shore Events Centre, that has seen many a Silver Ferns netball tussle, is also in Glenfield.

Wairau Park has a cinema complex and bowling alley. There are several cafés for a chance to check the shopping list. Eateries include Asian restaurants and Valentines on Wairau Rd. The Glenfield Tavern is a quaint watering hole opposite the Glenfield mall.

Real Estate

Trends

As first home buyers drift west, local real estate agents are selling to buyers trading up from other areas, and long-established residents and self-employed people investing in rental property. Consequently, buyer competition is strongest at the entry level bracket of $300,000 to $330,000 where quick sales are being made.

Many people trade up within the wider suburb (to larger houses in places like Marlborough or Glendhu and Daldys Lane) as they work their way towards the more upmarket east coast bays

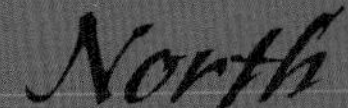

suburbs on the seaward side of the motorway. Houses in areas like Bay View, which has long laboured under a downbeat image with lots of rental properties, are now being bought by young couples and those with young children.

The influx of Asian buyers into Unsworth Heights and The Palms has eased off, as it has elsewhere throughout Auckland.

Best Streets

High Rd and Glendhu Rd in Glenfield; Calypso Way in The Palms; Westminster Gardens in Unsworth Heights and Pemberton Ave in Witheford Heights.

Local Hero: Westfield Glenfield

How can you drive past it? It's big, it's on top of the ridge along Glenfield Rd and it's the hub of the retail area that services the western area of the entire North Shore. Westfield Glenfield is the biggest mall on the North Shore, with 114 shops including major department stores such as Farmers, The Warehouse and two supermarkets. There's every specialty shop you'll ever need, a foodcourt and cafés to suit all appetites and an area for young children to be supervised while parents shop. The mall as we know it officially opened in Oct 2000 following massive redevelopment. It's close to bus routes, local businesses and the Glenfield Leisure Centre. It's also smack in the middle of residential Glenfield, which is great for the locals.

At a Glance...

House Prices

Unit

Bedrooms
Price $275,000 - $295,000

House on half site

Bedrooms
Price $320,000 - $350,000

House on full site

Bedrooms
Price $350,000 - $380,000
Bedrooms
Price $420,000 - $460,000

House in Pemberton with estuary views

Bedrooms
Price $500,000 - $600,000

Average Rents

Flat

Bedrooms
Price $280/wk

House

Bedrooms
Price $365/wk
Bedrooms
Price $480/wk

Travel Times

CBD	peak 60 min off peak 20 min
Glenfield mall	5 min
Airport	25 - 30 min

The widening of Glenfield Rd is on track for completion by 2010, at which point a bridge will be installed to link the two parts of Glendhu Rd. This will give Bayview (west Glenfield) residents a route north through Albany instead of the current route south through Manuka Rd and onto Glenfield Rd.

Hibiscus Coast

including Whangaparaoa, Orewa, Silverdale, Red Beach and Gulf Harbour

Once upon a holiday time, this region was Auckland's summer playland. People would head north to their baches at Orewa and the Hibiscus Coast for summer; these days they don't bother to go home afterwards. They're settling here lock, stock and barrel. The beaches are where it's all happening, and Orewa's 2.5km stretch of white sand is one of the best. Along both sides of the Whangaparaoa Peninsula a dozen or so beaches run from Red Beach to Shakespear Bay. Gulf Harbour has the marina as its focus, with a canal development for apartment dwellers and a planned harbour village. The rural landscape is fast disappearing into suburbia.

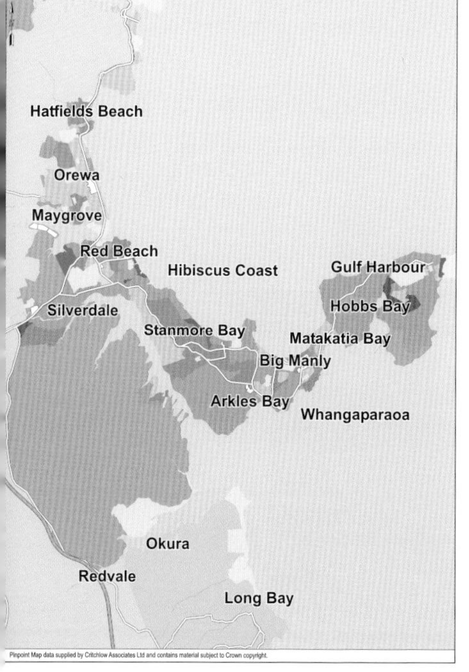

For colour key, see page 226

Population Profile

Population	31,488
% Aged Under 15 Years	21.34
% Aged Over 65 Years	19.83
% European	90.39
% Maori	6.67
% Pacific Peoples	1.45
% Asian	2.49

Who Lives There?

Orewa has always been popular with retired people who appreciate the flat walk to the beach and the shops, but the largest blip on the population graph of late is professional families settling in for a year-round seaside lifestyle. The extended motorway now makes commuting easier, there are good schools, a strong community spirit, superb beaches, and more green space around the houses.

On the peninsula there's a mix of families and couples including retired people who've often lived here a long time. Many young elderly (in their 60s rather than 80s) live in semi-retirement at Gulf Harbour. Migrants like the

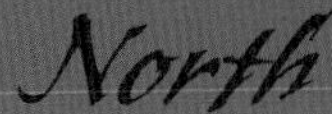

coastline – the Brits for its Kiwi-style homes; South Africans for the Gulf Harbour lifestyle and big houses.

Typical Homes

Near the motorway, Orewa's elevated new housing developments have wide sea views. Within the township, there's a mix of modern contemporary homes and old holiday baches. Orewa got its first Gold Coast-style semi high rise a few years ago – some people love it, some hate it.

Throughout the peninsula the mix includes baches, weatherboard 1960s-70s homes and new contemporary homes. Many homes have great sea views. As well as the marina and apartment complex, Gulf Harbour has subdivisions with large homes and terraced apartments, and more apartments are planned for the Eastern Boat Harbour.

At Waiwera a hotel/apartment complex is planned for land between the beachfront and the thermal pools complex. Local retirement villages include Maygrove Village at Orewa and Pine Haven Retirement just north at Hatfields Beach.

Amenities

Schools ★★★

There's plenty of choice for children of all ages. The Hibiscus Coast is well served with high decile schools, and most are growing to accommodate the increasing number of families living in area - Gulf Harbour School has added 14 new classrooms since opening in 1998. There are at least seven other primary schools in the area, including Whangaparaoa School, which, with a growing roll close to 700 is one the largest.

Kingsway School offers schooling for all ages, providing high-quality education in a non-denominational Christian learning environment.

Hibiscus Coast Intermediate is well-regarded; according to a recent ERO report, the principal and teachers at the school, "... set high educational standards and strive for excellence."

Secondary schools include Wentworth College, Orewa College (just 100m from Orewa Beach) and Whangaparaoa College. For a full list, see page 270.

Shops ★★★

Orewa's town centre has a friendly small-town feel. It is, however, a little disjointed and local business owners would love to see a mall come to town. It's also the headquarters of the Rodney District Council.

Whangaparaoa township has the Pacific Plaza complex which includes some big stores such as Farmers. There are shops at Red Beach, Manly Village and Gulf Harbour. Heading inland, the popular Silverdale shopping centre offers plenty of options for bargain hunters with its mix of designer label factory outlets,

boutique shops and an industrial park. The weekly Saturday markets are also popular.

Leisure ★★★★

Relaxing in this part of Auckland is easy. By Orewa Beach is a reserve with a skating rink, playgrounds and a surf club. There are numerous sandy beaches along the peninsula and Red Beach has a surf club, making it a hugely popular teen surfie beach. The Whangaparaoa Coastal Walkway goes from Amorino Reserve in Red Beach to Matakatia Beach.

If the beach isn't your style, the Hibiscus Coast Leisure Centre at Stanmore Bay has an indoor heated swimming pool, squash courts and fitness facilities, or there's the Snowplanet in Silverdale for year-round indoor skiing. There are two golf courses, including the Robert Trent Jones Jnr designed Gulf Harbour Country Club, and there's a miniature steam railway at Whangaparaoa and activities such as rock climbing, 10-pin bowling, mini golf and horse riding.

At the tip of the peninsula, Army Bay has a heritage trail of World War II Army defences and Shakespear Regional Park has sheltered bays, pastureland, regenerating native forest and a lookout with views to die for. Wenderholm Regional Park and the Waiwera Thermal Resort are a short drive north.

Eating out is improving. Local restaurants include The Rock Salt Restaurant and Café Kaizen Coffeehouse, both on the Hibiscus

Coast highway in Orewa. Manly Village has some well patronised little restaurants.

Real Estate

Trends

"Old" Orewa, near the beach, was temporarily overshadowed by the new houses being built on the slopes behind town but in the past two years it has returned to popularity. Many older properties here are being demolished or undergoing major renovations. Anything within a whiff of the sea sells for big bucks. A double site with an old bach, stretching from the beachfront to the Hibiscus Coast Highway sold recently for $3.525 million. A north-facing clifftop house on the peninsula with wide sea views would go for a similar amount.

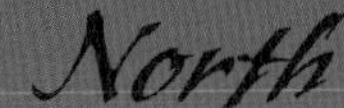

Prices tend to be lower along the peninsula than in Orewa simply because of the limited access. The recent upgrade of the sole route in and out, that is Whangaparaoa Rd, has raised real estate spirits somewhat and with Government funding decisions pending on the proposed Penlink toll road, speculators are buying in the belief that this area will lift in value.

Construction of the new European-inspired Eastern Boat Harbour is underway with completion due by early 2008. It will have a mix of apartments, a hotel, restaurants, cafés, boutiques and bars right on the water's edge. The Puriri Park Motor Camp at the northern end of Orewa was sold recently and is to be subdivided for housing.

Best Streets

In Orewa any of the beachside cul-de-sac streets off the Hibiscus Coast Highway; also Grand Dr and West Hoe Heights. Along the peninsula, anything on the beachfront or clifftop in any of the bays. Chalverton Tce in Red Beach; Duncansby Bay Rd in Stanmore Bay; Tiri Rd in Big Manly.

Smart Buy ✓

With access along the Whangaparaoa Peninsula improving by the minute, older properties in the more established settlements can be bought relatively cheaply and will no doubt improve in value. With a spruce-up, they will meet the ever-heightening tastes of the peninsula's "new", more affluent residents.

Average Rents

Flat

Bedrooms	2 (bed icons)
Price	$260/wk

House

Bedrooms	3 (bed icons)
Price	$345/wk
Bedrooms	4 (bed icons)
Price	$420/wk

At a Glance...

House Prices

Basic house

Bedrooms	3 (bed icons)
Price	$350,000 - $500,000
Bedrooms	4 (bed icons)
Price	$550,000 - $700,000

Near beach with sea views

Price	$700,000 - $1,000,000 +

Executive house

Bedrooms	4 (bed icons)
Price	$700,000 - $1,000,000

Gulf Harbour

New duplex	$380,000
Waterfront apartment	$900,000 - $1,000,000
Large apartment with marina berth	$2,000,000+

Travel Times

From Orewa:

CBD	peak 60 min off peak 40 min
North Shore Hospital	30 min
Airport	60 min
Motorway	2 min
From along the peninsula	30 - 45 min

Regular bus services run from Orewa and the peninsula to Takapuna (taking about an hour) and central Auckland. The Kawau Kats commuter ferry service between the CBD and Gulf Harbour has been extended to three sailings daily each way.

The northern motorway extension from Orewa to just south of Puhoi is on schedule for completion by mid-2009. Meanwhile the Weiti toll road project (or Penlink as it is known) could start soon pending confirmation of supplementary Government funding. The 7km route is an alternative out of the peninsula running from Stanmore Bay, across the Weiti River and past Stillwater before joining SH1. All for the cost to the user of a gold coin.

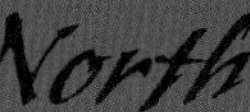

Lower East Coast Bays

Including Castor Bay, Campbells Bay, Mairangi Bay, Murrays Bay and Rothesay Bay

If there was a poster-boy suburb to be used by agencies attracting immigrants to Auckland, this string of beach-side communities would be it. Its X-factor attributes include access to the sea, views of the gulf, a heady choice of great schools and the CBD a quick nip over the harbour bridge. The area's laid-back residents claim it's more demure than the showy suburbs of Milford and Takapuna down the road. It's certainly more affordable, but if you're after lifestyle you can't really go wrong here. Many of the houses have sea views and there's a pretty little bay just down the road. Who wouldn't love living so close to the water, whether it's taking a workday lunch break at the beach or packing an evening picnic for the family?

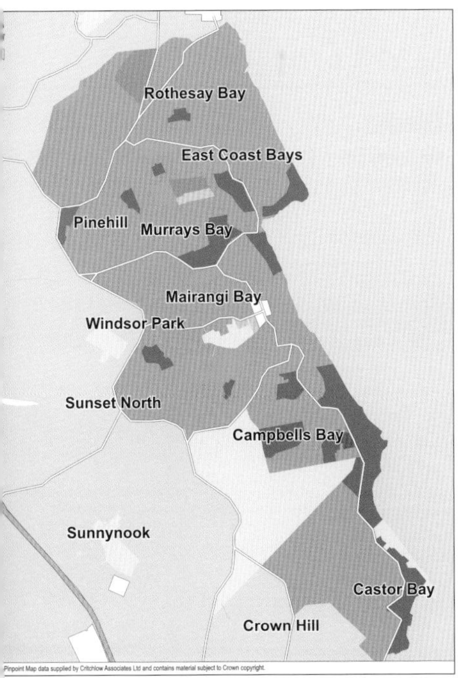

For colour key, see page 226

Population Profile

Population	18,456
% Aged Under 15 Years	19.64
% Aged Over 65 Years	11.64
% European	87.29
% Maori	2.57
% Pacific Peoples	0.75
% Asian	9.56

Who Lives There?

Those who move here fall in love with the place and are reluctant to leave. The community spirit is part of the area's appeal, helped by geography that naturally creates little communities within the wider area that hugs the coastline north of the more sprawling suburbs of Milford and Takapuna. They're also very outdoors orientated here with the focus on the beach, the surf club, walking and picnics.

A large number of South Africans and Asians have settled here in recent years as much for the school zoning as for the quiet, restful appeal of the area.

Typical Homes

As many as two-thirds of East Coast Bays homes enjoy impressive outlooks. Throughout the bays, homes have been built to make the most of the picture-postcard eastern aspect and elevated topography with ridges and gullies leading down to the waterline. The houses are a more eclectic mix than the older areas of the North Shore, with architecturally designed homes, redevelopments, updates and well-maintained older homes. In Mairangi Bay, apartments add to the buzz of the village.

Amenities

Schools ★★★★

Schooling in this predominantly decile 10 neighbourhood is very good, with ample primaries and New Zealand's largest secondary school. One of the primary schools, Campbells Bay, has stunning sea views!

At secondary level, the highly desired co-ed school, Rangitoto College, has a tight zone so always check with the school to confirm you are buying within the catchment area if that's your motivation. As the country's largest school, it has a roll close to 3000. For a full list, see page 270.

Shops ★★★

Village shopping in Mairangi Bay has a Parnell-on-the-Shore appeal with several fashion boutiques, jewellery and homewares boutiques among the cafes – and it's a only a block away from the beach. There' a supermarket in Hastings Rd, a grocer store and stationery shop in the block arounc the corner.

Leisure ★★★★

The sacred Rahopara Reserve has a uniqu handcrafted Maori-style viewing platform tha takes in the wider Hauraki Gulf. It's a shor walk from the southern end of Kennedy Par in Castor Bay. Recreational walking is a treat through Centennial Park and along littl foreshore spots that dot the coastline.

For golfers, there's the Pupuke Golf Club o East Coast Rd. World-class facilities are on offe at the Millennium Institute of Sport and Health For the more culturally minded, the Mairang Arts Centre offers a range of classes.

Throughout the Lower East Coast Bays ther is a wide choice of cafés and restaurants, whil Mairangi Bay has the pick of the eateries. Ther are quality takeaways and plenty of beachfron pohutukawa trees to scoff them under.

Real Estate

Trends

The two big market drivers here are schoo and sea. Highly reputable Rangitoto Colleg continues to pull families, as evidenced with th sale of sections in the Rangitoto Ridge Estat on surplus college land. Buyers, predominantl

sian, paid $305,000 to $425,000 for the land hat will ultimately support million dollar omes. The 10 sections of stage three are to o on sale shortly.

here are huge price variations in the three-edroom house category, and it's all to do vith the sea. An inland house might cost 300,000 to $400,000 while an identical one n elevated site closer to the beach will be loser to $600,000. East Coast Bays Rd is he demarcation line where you can tack 100,000 on to the price of a property on the eaward side. A view of the sea assures a plus 1 million price tag, with the most sought-after xecutive homes falling into the $900,000 to 1.4 million range.

est Streets

nything on the seaward side of Beach Rd. he Esplanade in Campbells Bay, Brighton Rd, idmouth St and Whitby Rd in Mairangi Bay, hurchill Rd and Portal Pl in Murrays Bay.

Local Hero: East Coast Bays Coastal Walkway

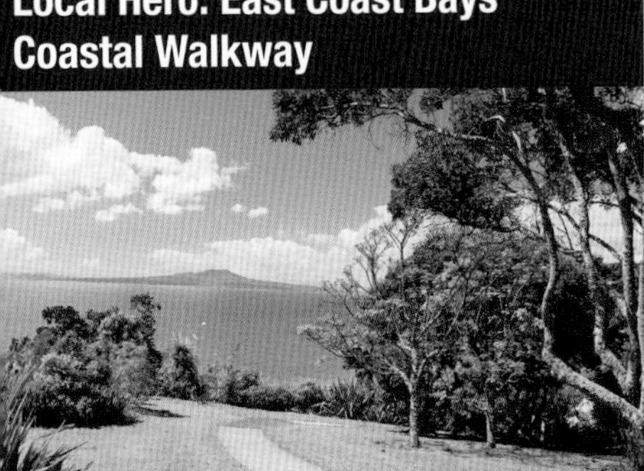

When they've seen enough of their "local" – the beach, not the pub – energetic East Coast Bays people love to tackle the length of the coastline in what must be one of Auckland's most glorious coastal walks. The walkway begins at Long Bay and has views of Rangitoto Island and the Hauraki Gulf. It's a great activity for a weekend, especially knowing there's good coffee to be supped at the far end in Takapuna.

At a Glance...

House Prices

Unit

Bedrooms
Price $315,000 - $390,000

House

Bedrooms
Price $430,000 (inland) - $600,000 (seaward)

House with a peep of the sea

Bedrooms
Price $950,000 - $1,000,000 +

Large cliff top house

Price $2,500,000 - $4,000,000

Average Rents

Apartment

Bedrooms
Price $335/wk

House

Bedrooms
Price $390/wk
Bedrooms
Price $495/wk

Travel Times

From Mairangi Bay:

CBD	peak 45 - 60 min off peak 20 - 25 min
Northern Motorway	5 - 10 min
Airport	45 - 60 min
Albany Mage Centre	10 min

Buses regularly run along East Coast Rd on the ridge and Beach Rd down below.

Northcote ★★★½

including Birkenhead, Chatswood and Hillcrest

This area includes a couple of Auckland's niche market real estate gems. With their harbour views across to the city and elegant villas, Birkenhead Pt and Northcote Pt tend to be described in the same breathless tones as Devonport and, of course, have the price tags and status to match. The rest of the area is well-established and has good quality homes. The big difference is accessibility. Disregarding the often congested Onewa Rd, this is the closest the shore comes to Auckland's CBD – you can be there in a matter of minutes. There's lots of bush (in fact, second only to Titirangi), open space and family-friendly spots. There's a rich Asian influence in these suburbs, as you can see at the Birkenhead shops.

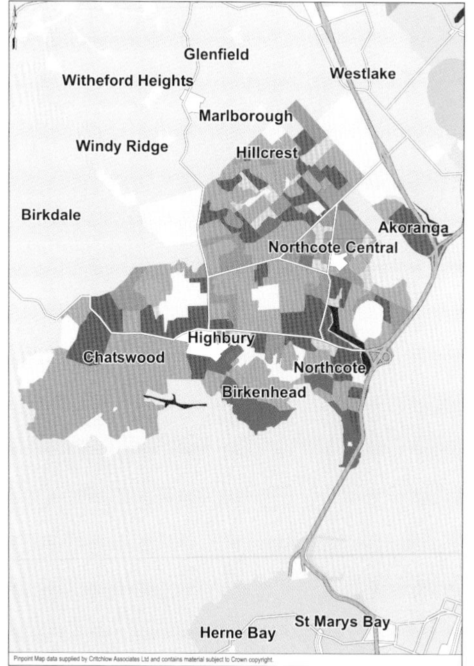

For colour key, see page 226

Population Profile

Population	32,346
% Aged Under 15 Years	19.23
% Aged Over 65 Years	11.78
% European	73.51
% Maori	7.94
% Pacific Peoples	3.74
% Asian	16.11

Who Lives There?

Northcote Pt and Birkenhead Pt attract buyer who love old homes. There's been a migratior from the southern shores, people looking fo similar character to Ponsonby but who wan to pay less. Northcote Pt is considered more conservative than Birkenhead Pt. There is a lo of trading up - it's not unusual for families tc move three, four or five times as their lifestyle budget, tastes and aspirations change.

Families like Northcote central for its gooc schooling, while Birkenhead central's apartments are popular with commutinc executives. Chatswood's large homes or good-sized sections attract families, includinc Asian buyers.

ypical Homes

listoric cottages that were built for Chelsea ugar Refinery workers are still dotted round ne suburb. The original brick cottages built or the shift managers on the road down to the efinery can be leased.

haracter homes define Northcote Pt and irkenhead Pt, which were established in the ate 1880s. Near the centre of Birkenhead there re a number of apartment buildings.

hatswood estate was developed as an xecutive subdivision in the early 1970s, with nodern homes on big sections. Northcote entral and Hillcrest have styles ranging from enovated ex-state houses, townhouses and lder weatherboard homes. The best of the nore modern homes are in the Onepoto Basin rea of Northcote and along Sylvan Ave.

menities

chools ★★★

here are at least eight primary school in this igh decile neighbourhood, two intermediates nd three secondary schools. Willow Park chool is one of the largest primaries here with roll close to 600 and has a history of positive RO reports.

ocal co-ed secondary schools Birkenhead ollege and Northcote College both have igh profiles, with sporting, cultural and cademic achievements. Northcote's acclaimed azz band regularly wins regional awards. he decile two Maori-Katorika school Hato etera College is also in the area. Auckland Jniversity of Technology's Akoranga campus is n Northcote. For a full list, see page 270.

Shops ★★★

Birkenhead Pt has a scattering of boutique shops and cafés while Birkenhead central is a mix of street-front and mall with plenty of undercover parking.

Northcote has a busy shopping centre and now boasts the largest range of Asian food stores on the North Shore. Down the road, the Fox Outlet Centre's 50 shops are off Akoranga Dr for bargain hunters.

Leisure ★★★★

The historic Northcote Point Walk encompasses old villas, coastline and spectacular views. The Harbourside Art Trail through Birkenhead and Northcote visits artists' studios and workshops.

The Chelsea Sugar Refinery grounds are a beautiful spot for a picnic. Birkenhead has numerous bush reserves, including Kauri Glen Reserve near Little Shoal Bay. For youngsters there's rock climbing at the Birkenhead Leisure Centre and a skate park next door. In Akoranga Rd, there's the Takapuna Athletics Club and the YMCA.

There's the famous Bridgeway cinema on Northcote Pt and the cool new, award-winning eatery The Engine Room across the road.

Real Estate

Trends

City-siders priced out of the likes of Herne Bay, Ponsonby and Westmere are crossing the bridge in steady numbers to buy in Northcote and Birkenhead. During the past three years prices in both Northcote and Birkenhead

Pts have doubled in value. Northcote Pt is slightly more expensive for being closer to the city but Birkenhead Pt has had a couple of record-breaking sales recently – an historic home in Hinemoa St sold for just over $2 million and further along the same street a sizeable clifftop section changed hands for $1.3 million in early 2006.

Ferry services to the CBD from the Northcote Pt and Birkenhead Pt wharves are a drawcard.

Chatswood continues to attract Asian buyers for the grand style of its 1970s and 80s houses.

Hillcrest, on the ridge, is often a step-up for those who have been living on the flat in Northcote. A townhouse here will be priced in the early $400,000s. Elevated homes with views are fetching $500,000 to $600,000.

Best Streets

Clarence Street, Queen St and Princes St on Northcote Pt; Tizard Rd, Wanganella St and Palmerston Rd on Birkenhead Pt, Puawai St in Northcote; seaward Onetaunga St in Chatswood; Mountbatten Ave and Lynngate Pl in Hillcrest.

Local Hero: The Bridgeway Cinema

Actually it's two cinemas, thanks to entrepreneurs Heather and John Hart, who have revitalised the landmark Queen St, Northcote Pt, building into an award-winning boutique cinema complex.

The 1920s Art Deco originally only had one auditorium. What is now the second 100-seat cinema was once the local bus station. The main auditorium has been reduced from 400 seats to 200, to allow wider aisles, more comfortable armchairs and generous leg room. The Bridgeway's crossover movie selections (chosen by Heather) attract a sophisticated, arty audience from all over Auckland.

At a Glance...

House Prices

Apartments or terrace houses

Price	$240,000 - $450,000

House

Bedrooms	
Price	$400,000 - $500,000
Bedrooms	
Price	$450,000 - $550,000
With sea views	$700,000 +

(add $100,000 for a Chatswood house with sea views)

Executive Onepoto basin house

Price	$700,000 - $800,000

Clifftop historic house on the Points

Price	$1,500,000 - $2,000,000 +

Average Rents

Flat

Bedrooms	
Price	$285/wk

House

Bedrooms	
Price	$365/wk
Bedrooms	
Price	$440/wk

Travel Times

CBD	peak 20 min off peak 7 - 10 min
Northern Motorway	5 min
Airport	40 - 45 min
North Shore Hospital	10 - 15 min
Glenfield Shopping Centre	10 min

For buses and car poolers, peak-hour priority lanes cut the driving time into the city considerably. Northcote Pt's big plus is the sole traffic light allowing traffic to flow into Onewa Rd for the straight run over the harbour bridge. There are bus services throughout Birkenhead and Beach Haven. City-bound ferries go from Birkenhead and Northcote wharves.

ncluding Milford and Hauraki

This is Auckland's own little piece of the Gold Coast – without the brashness, the high rises or the Australians. An address in Takapuna or Milford signifies prestige and ffluence. Life here centres around the two gorgeous beaches – whether it's about the tunning views from the high-rise apartments that are comparatively new to the area, r being able to step right onto the sand from one of the elegant homes that line the eachfront. Location is everything in these suburbs and parochialism abounds. Tell Milford wellers that Takapuna has the edge and you'll get the pointy finger. The closer to the each or the more expansive the sea view, the greater the kudos. For those who want he lifestyle without the big beach house, apartments offer resort-style living, with cafés, estaurants and entertainment all within walking distance.

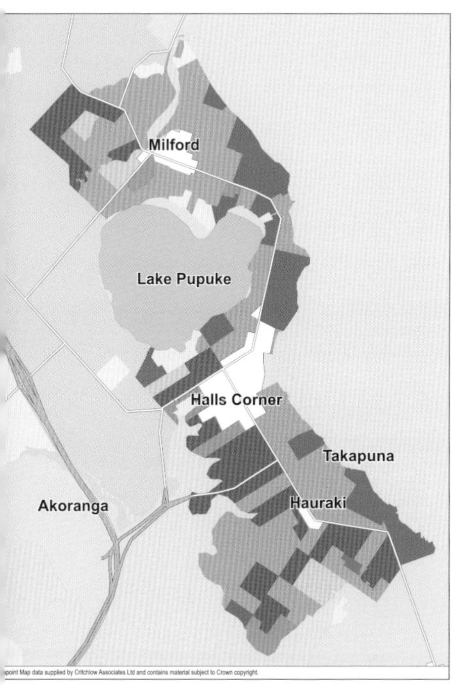

For colour key, see page 226

Population Profile

Population	12,819
% Aged Under 15 Years	14.84
% Aged Over 65 Years	19.10
% European	83.10
% Maori	4.05
% Pacific Peoples	1.31
% Asian	10.45

Who Lives There?

The smart, the stylish and the suitably suntanned all live here. Takapuna and Milford are the suburbs that everyone else on this side of the bridge aspires to move to. A stroll along Takapuna beach tells you lots about the locals, whether it's the gold that adorns the beachgoers or the fabulous homes that abut the beach.

In Milford there are affluent families with boating in their blood, and many older people who like the flat walk to the mall and the beach.

Anywhere along the seaward side of Lake Rd, this country's high rollers have put down a small portion of their net worth for water's edge properties. The city side of the landscape is where the upwardly mobile are settled – for the meantime – until they can edge their way street by street towards the water.

Typical Homes

For all its affluence, Takapuna has many basic weatherboard houses as well as larger family homes, palatial mansions and high-rise apartments. Many original cottages have been renovated beyond recognition or demolished. Along Clifton Rd, the trend is to build new rather than renovate. Takapuna's popular modern high-rise apartments include Promenade Terraces, the Takapuna Sands, the Rocks and the Mon Desir.

At the other end of the market, brick and tile units built during the 1960s and 1970s are still in demand for buyers seeking a foothold in Takapuna, and for investors. Inland Hauraki Corner is a popular first entry into the area, and its appeal is evident in the new homes and extensive renovations along the quiet leafy streets off the main road.

Amenities

Schools ★★★★★

Takapuna is a high decile area well served with quality schools, at all levels, with at least six primaries, an intermediate and three secondary schools.

The well-appointed Sunnynook School is on of the largest primaries, with a roll close to 500 According to a recent ERO report, Sunnynook teachers provide children with "high qualit learning programmes." The other primar schools also receive positive ERO reports.

As the only co-ed secondary school in th immediate area, Takapuna Grammar School i a popular choice. Westlake Boys and Westlak Girls zones include some parts of Takapuna Catholic schools Carmel College for girl and Rosmini College for boys are also in th neighbourhood. For a full list, see page 270.

Shops ★★★★★

The revitalised resort-style shopping strip alon Hurstmere Rd provides boutique retail therap and quality cafés and eateries for locals an tourists. On Sunday mornings there's a marke in the Lake Rd carpark offering a colourful mi of entertainment, fruit and veges, seafood artisan foods, bric-a-brac, etc.

Westfield Takapuna has more than 70 fashion and lifestyle stores with a boutique flavou There's also a substantial mall at Milford To the south, there's a shopping block a Hauraki Corner.

Leisure ★★★★

The long, sandy beaches of Takapuna an Milford offer swimming, boating and plenty o strolling. The Takapuna Boating Club on Th Strand hosts international regattas and th

/lilford Cruising Club and marina are much-oved fixtures.

'here's a popular coastal walk between 'akapuna and Milford with plenty to see, ncluding stunning harbour views and multi-nillion dollar seaside mansions.

Vhile the beaches are popular with the jet ki set, Lake Pupuke is a favourite for sailing, vindsurfing and rowing. For swimmers oreferring the indoors, there's the Takapuna \quatic Centre on the lake's edge. Other local ports facilities include the 18-hole public 'akapuna Golf Course and driving range and a 0-pin bowling centre.

ndoor amenities include the Pumphouse 'heatre and gallery by Lake Pupuke, the Bruce /lason Centre and the Berkeley Cinema.

'he flourishing dine-out scene includes estaurants, gourmet takeaways and cafés long Hurstmere Rd and down the side streets. /lilford has fewer eateries - but Takapuna is nly a stone's throw away. Nighclubbers have he Poenamo Hotel on Northcote Rd.

Real Estate

Trends

'he newest apartment block The Sentinel in the entre of town is bringing more affluent "empty esters" into Takapuna. The 117-apartments in he 30-level development include a two-level 8 million penthouse and two $4.5 million sub-penthouses; the rest are expected to sell for $1million to $2.5 million ahead of a late 2007 completion date.

There's significant growth in the $700,000 to $1 million price range and again in the $2 million to $3 million whether it's the handful of apartments being on-sold in the more established developments or homes on the clifftop, lake side or near the water. The off-shore percentage of high-end buyers is only around 20% of all sales, down from some 30% a few years ago.

The record $12.78 million sale on a beach-side Gibbons Rd property still stands, but significant water's edge sales include one for $6.35 million and another for $7.75 million.

Pricewise, Takapuna is slightly more expensive than Milford and anything on the Golden Mile, east of Kitchener and Lake Rds, can be literally millions dearer. Prices go up virtually by the house the closer they are to the sea and sales of $3 million to $4 million for homes only one or two back from the beach are no longer the exception.

Best Streets

Any street east of Lake Rd towards Takapuna Beach, for example Minnehaha Ave, Brett Ave and O'Neills Ave. In Milford, the streets between Kitchener Rd and the beach – Tiri Rd, Cecil Rd. At Hauraki, it's Clifton Rd, overlooking the beach.

Why I Live There

Entertainer Tina Cross

For a girl who grew up in South Auckland, the suburb of Milford was, Tina says, "somewhere else on the planet". She knew nothing about the North Shore as a place to live until she spotted the Milford house on the market that has now been her family's home for 14 years. Tina and her husband Wayne fell in love with the 1970s-style house and its picturesque cul-de-sac location running down to Milford beach. It's the only home their children Sean (16) and Leah (13) have ever known, and they've made wonderful friendships among the swag of kids who were always playing in the street. Says Tina: "It's the beach, the location, the kids and the fact that we're all like-minded people, which makes Milford really special to me."

Travel Times

CBD	peak 45 min off peak 15 min
Airport	off peak 40 - 45 min
Harbour bridge	off peak 5 - 10 min

Regular bus services into the city help peak-time traffic flows a little. By car it can be a slow trip. Urban Express runs a bus service from Bayswater through Hauraki and from Milford into the CBD.

At a Glance...

House Prices

Unit

Bedrooms	2
Price	$350,000 +

Unit on seaward side

Bedrooms	3
Price	$600,000 - $700,000

Seaward townhouse

Bedrooms	3
Price	$800,000 - $1,200,000

Basic inland house

Bedrooms	3
Price	$500,000 - $600,000

Modern house inland

Price	$700,000 - $1,500,000

Near the sea

Price	$1,500,000 - $3,000,000 +

Average Rents

Apartment

Bedrooms	2
Price	$420/wk

Flat

Bedrooms	2
Price	$320/wk

House

Bedrooms	3
Price	$465/wk
Bedrooms	4
Price	$590/wk

At the top end, exclusive X-factor homes will command $2000 to $3500 a week for corporate types relocating from overseas.

Upper East Coast Bays

including Browns Bay, Waiake, Torbay, Pinehill, Long Bay, Northcross and Okura.

This part of Auckland is a seductive mix of city living and casual beachy lifestyle. The beaches and bays are pretty, and easily accessible. Long Bay Regional Park is a favourite location for extended family picnics and touch football games and the shops at Browns Bay have a laid-back feel that makes you slow down to an amble. The schools are excellent and the houses more affordable than in the bays closer to town. This area still has the wide-open feel you get at the edge of suburbia – even though the city is growing beyond it, the sea to the east and Okura River to the north will always make it feel special. It's a great place to bring grandma for a weekend drive. Just don't expect her to understand any of the new locals - they'll be speaking in heavily accented English, or Afrikaans.

For colour key, see page 226

Population Profile

Population	28,626
% Aged Under 15 Years	21.21
% Aged Over 65 Years	10.68
% European	86.08
% Maori	4.37
% Pacific Peoples	1.36
% Asian	8.79

Who Lives There?

A couple of local events say it all: in March, there's the African street festival dubbed From Cairo to Cape Town and the Best of British Day is held in June. South Africans and Brits happily decamp here from their home countries for the schooling, the kinship and holiday-style living.

There's a wide cross-section of ages, but it's a strong young family area (as evidenced by the budding gymnasts who whirl about the boat-shaped playground by the beach). Buyers here are often trading up to a coastal lifestyle from cheaper inland North Shore suburbs. Those concerned about schooling will settle for any style of house in the desired zone. Browns

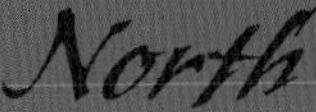

Bay is the North Shore's second significant town centre after Takapuna (with Albany in the wings) and appeals to those working in the Albany basin.

Typical Homes

Sea views are the big focus of all the homes built anywhere along the bays. The large numbers of 1970s architecturally-designed family homes give the area a sense of individuality that is lacking in some parts of Torbay/Glenvar, where streets were defined by the housing development company of the day. Pinehill has big new homes popular with Asian buyers.

Browns Bay's village now includes several apartment developments that have brought 300 more permanent residents into the thriving retail centre. At the other extreme are the lifestyle blocks of Okura at the northern edge of the area for those preferring wide, open spaces.

Amenities

Schools ★★★★★

The predominantly decile 10 neighbourhood is well served with at least six primary schools. Northcross Intermediate is the main intermediate for the northern bays.

The local high school, Long Bay College is nationally known for its creative arts and technology teaching. It's much smaller than the huge Rangitoto College further down the bays, but that appeals to many parents keen for their children to get what they see as more personalised schooling. Some homes at the southern end of the upper bays are in-zone for Rangitoto College, but it pays to check with the school for the latest boundary changes. Local private schools include Corelli School in Browns Bay which specialises in the arts, including music, dance and drama. For a full list, see page 270.

Shops ★★★

Browns Bay's shopping village is the retail hub of the East Coast Bays. With the beach just 100m away, it's a casual beachside shopping strip that has everything – and everyone – covered, whether you're a tweenager, a surfie beach bum, a lady who lunches or the pooch of such a lady who needs a diamante collar. There are two supermarkets, Whitcoulls, Farmers, banks, boutique shops and cafés. On Sundays, there's a market.

Torbay has a small shopping centre and several restaurants and takeaway bars. For Okura and Long Bay residents, the nearest shops are Torbay, Albany and Northcross. From Browns Bay, Albany is only a quick drive along Oteha Valley Rd.

Leisure ★★★

All the beaches are beauties, but Waiake Beach is the best. Its 1ha beachfront reserve has an impressive block of Phoenix palms and Norfolk Island pines, as well as being home to Torbay Sailing Club.

The hugely popular Long Bay Regional Park has a 1km long golden beach, with a restaurant and playground and is within the Long Bay-Okura Marine Reserve. The Browns Bay beach has a reserve, playground and well-patronised boat club. A service lane between the shops is to be redeveloped with a pedestrian boardwalk and the council hopes to prompt commercial

property owners to add a beachfront focus to their properties with cafes and the like.

The northern East Coast Bays area has plenty of typically Kiwi sports grounds and clubs as well as the East Coast Bays Leisure Centre in Browns Bay. The Pupuke Golf Course is a couple of bays along at Campbells Bay.

Art Ducko at Torbay is a popular local restaurant. Browns Bay has a great selection of eateries including Sp'getti and Speakers Corner Ale House. Long Bay beach restaurant has simple, honest food in a stunning beachside setting.

Real Estate

Trends

For many years the Upper Bays lacked the lustrous appeal of those bays closer to Takapuna, but the tide is turning as premium clifftop properties here start to pull in ever-higher prices. The area's buoyancy is driven, in part, by its burgeoning neighbour Albany, which provides good job opportunities.

In the heart of Browns Bay, proposed zoning changes will free up light industrial properties for "mixed use" which will translate into more apartments in the retail strip. Established apartments are beginning to on-sell now for significant capital gain.

On the northern fringe, there's significant public interest in the North Shore City Council's "Long Bay Structure Plan" designed to achieve an integrated, rather than piecemeal, development of some 360ha of land between Glenvar and Vaughans Rds. It is still subject to appeals, but the plan allows for a residential community with a village green and village centre, a mix of housing types and densities, and an integrated network of streets and reserves with pedestrian and cycle access. The Long Bay-Okura Great Park Society is pushing for a chunk of the land to be used to extend the Long Bay Regional Park.

Best Streets

All the coastal top-spots, including Sharon Rd in Browns Bay and Cliff Rd and Gilberd Pl in Torbay.

At a Glance...

House Prices

Beach/reserve front apartment

Bedrooms	🛏 🛏
Price	$440,000

House

Bedrooms	🛏 🛏 🛏
Price	$380,000 - $450,000
Bedrooms	🛏 🛏 🛏 🛏
Price	$500,000 - $700,000

House on Torbay clifftop

Price	$1,500,000

Clifftop mansion

Price	$2,500,000 - $3,500,000

Average Rents

Apartment

Bedrooms	🛏 🛏
Price	$335/wk

Flat

Bedrooms	🛏 🛏
Price	$290/wk

House

Bedrooms	🛏 🛏 🛏
Price	$390/wk
Bedrooms	🛏 🛏 🛏 🛏
Price	$495/wk

Travel Times

CBD	peak 45 - 50 min off peak 25 - 30 min
Airport	50 min
Northern Motorway	10 min
Milford mall	15 min
Albany Mega Centre	10 - 15 min
Massey University in Albany	15 min

Bus services run to Takapuna and to Auckland's CBD. There's a new park-and-rise bus station at nearby Oteha Valley Rd, as part of the Northern Busways project.

Warkworth ★★★½

including Matakana, Leigh, Snells Beach and Omaha

Service towns don't come much prettier than Warkworth. It's in an idyllic spot that hugs the languid curves of the Mahurangi River. Little more than 2.5 square kilometers in area, it fizzes with community spirit and is 15 minutes drive away from 15 beaches. Warkworth is the self-proclaimed heart of the Kowhai Coast. It's also the gateway to the busy road to Matakana, Omaha, Leigh and Kawau Island. Less than 10 years ago, Matakana was a two-shop, pub stop, Holden and Harley Davidson drive-thru town but while the laid-back character is intact, it now has a high-profile market and plans for an expanded village. Omaha is best know for its monolithic modern holiday homes that spring forth from the sand dunes. Snells Beach is the hub of the Mahurangi peninsula and has a coastal/suburban flavour to match.

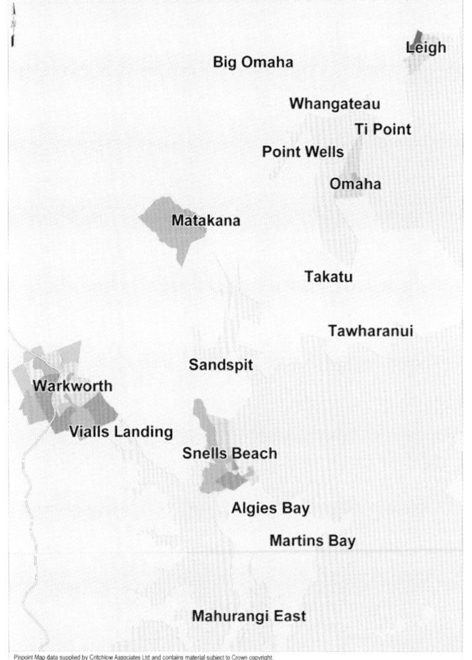

For colour key, see page 226

Population Profile

Population	7,836
% Aged Under 15 Years	20.52
% Aged Over 65 Years	20.75
% European	91.42
% Maori	7.27
% Pacific Peoples	1.34
% Asian	1.91

Who Lives There?

Warkworth, Snells Beach and Leigh have a mix of young families and long-term older residents. It's popular with elderly people retiring from Auckland and professionals commuting to work in Albany and the North Shore. There's a great community spirit. Local people stumped up $50 a plank to fund the riverside boardwalk; sausage sizzles and garage sales pay for the museum building's upkeep.

Omaha is a high profile spot for those with enough cash to fund a sophisticated holiday home (not a bach). It had some 110 permanent families at the last unofficial count, but the population swells to more than 1000 during summer. Matakana has some 250 residents and 60 houses, about half of which are long-time residents.

Typical Homes

There's a wide mix of housing in each community. Warkworth has villas, weatherboard houses and stylish renovations of these, as well as new houses in subdivisions.

Matakana's mix of traditional bungalows, farm cottages and relocated villas now includes a group of new brick and tile houses in a development behind the bakery. Famous for its rural lifestyle, Matakana also has acreage properties around the fringes.

Leigh has everything from caravans to large coastal lifestyle blocks. There's also the Wonder-view subdivision of large executive homes.

Old Omaha to the north was developed in three stages from the 1960s to the 1980s, so there's everything from board-and-batten, group-style housing to two-storey houses that were the fashion of the day. To the south, houses continue to sprout up in the 600-section The Dunes development. Their design has to meet strict criteria for this upmarket beach resort.

Amenities

Schools ★★★

While Warkworth, Leigh and Matakana have a primary school, Snells Beach children travel to Warkworth for their education. A primary school is scheduled to be built on Dawsons Rd, Snells Beach, opening in 2008. The well resourced Warkworth School is one the largest in the area with a roll close to 550.

The co-ed Mahurangi College in Warkworth is the local secondary school. According to a recent ERO report "although there is a range, some high quality teaching is evident across the school."

For a full list, see page 270.

Shops ★★

Warkworth's main shopping area runs through the centre of town, and offers everything from fishing gear to flooring, home appliances to chiropractic care. There are also numerous art galleries.

There's a dairy on the road to Omaha, but no shops in Omaha itself. Five shops and a restaurant have been designated in the latest Omaha development but they haven't been built yet.

Snells Beach has its Mahurangi Shopping Centre. Leigh has a general store and a fish and chip shop

Leisure ★★★★★

Being outdoors is everything here, whether it's canoeing down the Puhoi River or riding horses, admiring the tuatara at New Zealand's only reptile zoo at Leigh or peering at the fish at Goat Island Marine Reserve from the glass-bottom tourist boat.

Boat tours of the Mahurangi River are popular. The less adventurous can stroll along the river's edge.

The jewel in the crown is Tawharanui Regional Park, a pest-free haven for native plants and animals. Scandrett Regional Park, which opened in 2004, is a short drive beyond Snells Beach.

The ferry to Kawau Island leaves from Sandspit. Omaha has bowls, a harbourside golf club and an ocean beach.

Warkworth has many historical treasures, including the Warkworth Museum, the Parry Kauri Park, the site of New Zealand's first Portland cement operation and the Kowhai Park limestone kilns dating back to the 1880s. Foodies have the Matakana Village Farmers' Market for artisan foods and wine, and Ascension vineyard restaurant for lazy lunches. There's also the Matakana Country Park for art, crafts and entertainment.

Warkworth cafes include the River View Plaza Café and the Queen St Café. Cafés and winery restaurants are scattered throughout the outlying area. At Leigh, the Sawmill Café is particularly popular as an eatery and venue for live music.

Real Estate

Trends

Warkworth is home to an increasing number of Auckland refugees. Many are happy to make the 60- minute commute simply because it's much prettier than 60 minutes staring at someone else's bumper from one side of suburban Auckland to the other.

Older character homes are scarce, so are keenly sought after. Top prices in the township are now reaching $700,000+ for modern executive-style homes.

The Dunes development at the southern end of Omaha has been sold out, with many of the properties bought by Aucklanders for long-term development.

Leigh is still a sleepy village but the appearance of the first homes in Wonderview is changing the visual character slightly. They're being bought by Aucklanders to enjoy during semi-retirement.

The $213 million Whisper Cove development at the northern end of Snells Beach is underway with the first of the 28 villas and eight apartments scheduled for early 2007 completion. Villas sell from $950,000 right up to $2.5 million which hasn't dampened keen interest from North Shore buyers seeking a mix of holiday home lifestyle and permanent home base.

Best Streets

Westpark Glen and Coquette St in Warkworth (winners of Warkworth's annual Best Street competition).

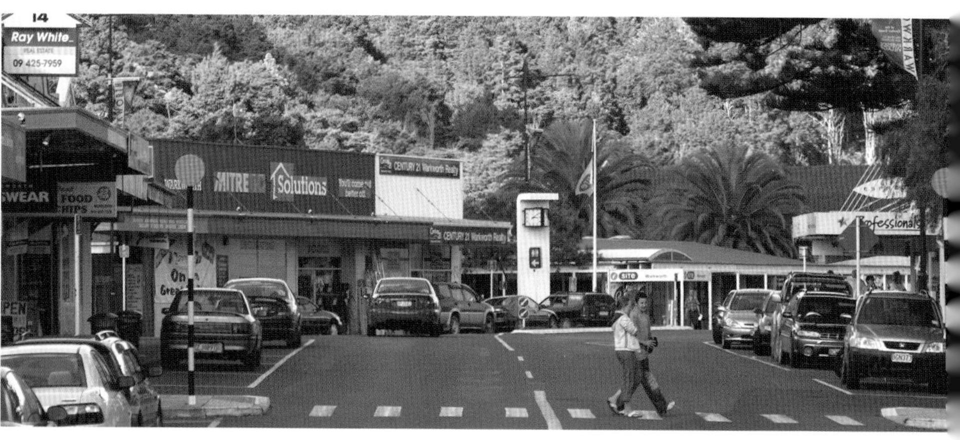

Local Hero: Matakana Village Farmers' Market.

Everybody who is anybody comes to the farmers' market for the artisan breads, sausages, fruits and vegetables and the wine, the coffee and the entertainment. It's the trendy outdoorsy way to shop. Located in purpose-built rustic stalls down by the river, the market needs no signage. Just follow the European cars from Auckland and Omaha. The market is part of Matakana's quest for international Slow Town status, which is about savouring food harvested from local soils and prepared with pride to local recipes. The system is strict, so don't expect to be handed your produce in a plastic bag – you'll need to buy a canvas one to carry you're goodies. And don't expect to trot your designer dog around in its diamante collar either - yours will just have to people-watch from the doggie creche beside the carpark.

Travel Times

From Warkworth:

CBD	peak 90 min off peak 50 - 60 min
Snells Beach	peak 20 min off peak 10 min
Leigh	25 min
Matakana	8 min
Omaha	10 - 15 min

Intercity Coachlines and Northliner Express Coachlines operate bus services seven days a week between Warkworth and Auckland's CBD. There is no public transport serving Leigh, Snells Beach and Matakana.

At a Glance...

House Prices

Warkworth

Basic house

Bedrooms	
Price	$280,000 - $300,000
Bedrooms	
Price	$370,000 - $450,000

Executive house

Bedrooms	
Price	$500,000 - $700,000

1.2ha sections

Price	$230,000 +

Matakana/Leigh

Caravan on 600m2

Price	$280,000 - $300,000

House on a larger section

Bedrooms	
Price	$420,000 - $450,000

Villa on 2ha

Price	$500,000 - $600,000

Large coastal properties

Price	$3,000,000

Omaha

Older house

Price	$500,000 - $700,000

Modern house with beach or reserve frontage

Price	$2,000,000

Average Rents

House

Bedrooms	
Price	$318/wk
Bedrooms	
Price	$339/wk

Westlake ★★★

including Sunnynook, Forrest Hill and Crown Hill

Westlake is the name synonymous with its two local secondary schools – both excellent institutions. It's quiet, solid and, well, just downright handy to everything that's important to the people of the North Shore. – shops, beaches, motorways and cafés. It's only a few minutes north of Takapuna, which makes it pretty special to start with but it's far more affordable which makes the picture even brighter. Sunnynook used to be one of the shore's "nappy valley" suburbs but it now attracts a wider cross-section of people. Forrest Hill and Crown Hill are more upmarket with many elevated properties having fabulous views of the city.

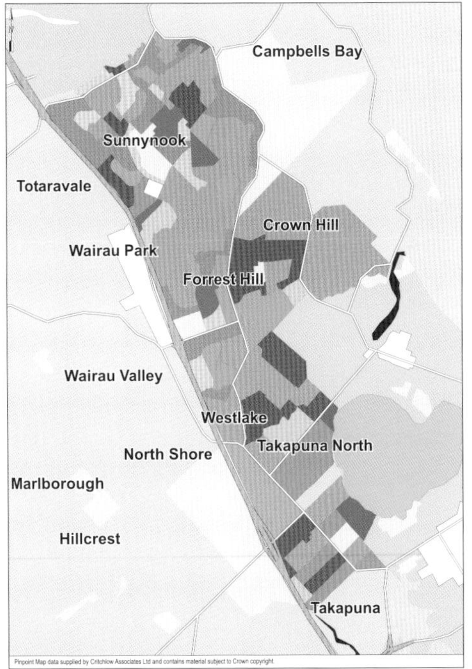

For colour key, see page 226

Population Profile

Population	20,631
% Aged Under 15 Years	18.44
% Aged Over 65 Years	14.70
% European	74.76
% Maori	4.57
% Pacific Peoples	2.02
% Asian	18.92

Who Lives There?

Families, families and more families – that's who lives here. The houses are more affordable than neighbouring Takapuna and Milford so appeal to families looking to get established. For those for whom it's "the shore or nothing", this is a choice location that's still close to Milford, CBD-style amenities in Takapuna and the beaches along the east coast bays. An influx of affluent professionals is adding to the demographic profile in the newer areas of the suburb.

Modest income-earners who can't afford bay prices opt for Forrest Hill and Crown Hill. Sunnynook was created as a subdivision of affordable housing and is a natural stepping stone for young families moving up from neighbouring Glenfield.

Typical Homes

Sunnynook's stock, standard houses have lasted the distance. Originally built by developers, they may all be much of a muchness but make good solid family homes. In Forrest Hill there's more choice in housing styles, reflecting the era in which sprawling farmland was carved up into residential plots 40 years ago.

There are plenty of 1970s houses which, when renovated, suit the clean-lined contemporary look of today. They generally deliver good-sized basement garaging and storage and several bedrooms with flexibility for families of all shapes and sizes.

Forrest Hill has new executive houses off Manutara Ave, which bring some welcome diversity to the area and lifts its profile somewhat.

Amenities

Schools ★★★★

The high-decile neighbourhood is well served with quality schools at all levels. High Schools are a major attraction. The area is zoned for the reputable single-sex Westlake Girls' High and West Lake Boys' High. Note, though, that the boundaries for West Lake Boys' High is slightly different to West Lake Girls' High. If teens are wanting to rub shoulders on a regular basis with the opposite sex, their options are more limited. The area is not zoned for neighbouring co-educational Rangitoto College, the largest high school in New Zealand. However "Rangi" does have an out-of-zone enrolment scheme.

For a full list, see page 270.

Shops ★★★

Sunnynook's shopping centre includes a Foodtown supermarket as well as a bakery, video, chemist shops and the like. Forrest Hill doesn't have its own shops. Large-scale retail therapy is easily satisfied with a short drive to the Westfield malls in Glenfield and Takapuna, and a mall at Milford. Good streetside shopping is provided in Takapuna.

Leisure ★★

Parks and facilities include Becroft Park for rugby and soccer and Greville Park which has soccer grounds. The beach is only a short drive from everywhere here. A couple of eateries in Sunnynook include a large Chinese restaurant. There isn't exactly a café scene as such; that requires a trip to Takapuna, Milford or Mairangi Bay which are all nearby. These are also the places to head to for restaurant dining.

Real Estate

Trends

This continues to be one of the North Shore's most sought-after family areas. It has great secondary schools, is affordable (compared

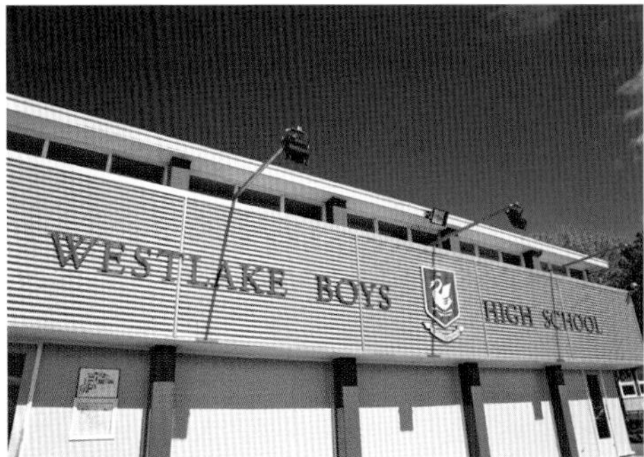

to its pricey neighbour suburbs) and has some elevated properties with sea and city views.

It is very popular with education-conscious migrant Asian families who value the quality schooling, with prices holding firm as a result. Some use it as a stepping stone to more esteemed suburbs.

Rambling streets such as Nile Rd, that run from Forrest Hill through to Milford, can show significant price variations simply because of the suburb name tacked onto the bottom of the street address - and the higher status that comes with being in Milford.

Sunnynook's group houses are holding their appeal among first home buyers. They'll then move up to the 1970s homes of Forrest Hill for more space, a bigger section, an ensuite bathroom and garaging.

That trend is in keeping with the north-to-south drift down the bays and the general pattern of buyers moving from the west towards the eastern sea shore.

Best Streets

Sycamore Dr in Sunnynook; Knightsbridge Ave, Grenada Ave and Ravenswood Ave in Forrest Hill; Gordon Ave in Crown Hill.

Look Out (!)

The schooling here is great but double-check the zones if that's the main reason you're buying in a particular street – see the school zones at the back of this book, check the school's website and contact the school direct.

At a Glance...

House Prices

Unit

Bedrooms	🛏 🛏
Price	$300,000 - $330,000

House on half site

Bedrooms	🛏 🛏 🛏
Price	$410,000 - $460,000

House on full site

Bedrooms	🛏 🛏 🛏
Price	$450,000 +

Large modern house

Bedrooms	🛏 🛏 🛏 🛏
Price	$500,000 - $700,000

Average Rents

Flat

Bedrooms	🛏 🛏
Price	$280/wk

House

Bedrooms	🛏 🛏 🛏
Price	$365/wk
Bedrooms	🛏 🛏 🛏 🛏
Price	$480/wk

Travel Times

CBD	peak 45 min off peak 15 - 20 min
Shopping malls	5 - 10 min
Airport	50 min

The long-awaited upgrade of the Taharoto/Wairau Rd corridor has started and is scheduled for completion in 2010/2011. This project will see Taharoto Rd widened from Northcote Rd to Forrest Hill to create an intersection at Smales Farm for the planned bus station and to remove the traffic bottle-neck at the Wairau Rd intersection near Westlake Girls High School.

Aucklanders are slowly but surely relinquishing their love affair with the motor vehicle, especially those disillusioned North Shore commuters who creep nose to tail across the Harbour Bridge each weekday morning. Good news, help is at hand.

Anyone who has ventured across said bridge lately cannot fail to have noticed the massive site works beside the motorway - at the Onewa Rd interchange into Birkenhead/ Northcote and a minute down the road at the Esmonde Rd interchange. There are colonies of orange cones, men in hard hats and huge earth moving machinery further where a separate two-lane busway is being built on the eastern side of the motorway.

Welcome to the Northern Busway Project. Part of it is up and running with the completion of two of the planned five bus stations at Albany and Constellation Drive, where commuters can park their cars and catch the Northern Express bus (one every 15 minutes) into the CBD.

It's already popular. The carparks are full and, in the month of March alone, the express service notched up some 50,000 trips.

Next on the completion schedule (May 2007) is the new Esmonde Rd interchange that feeds commuters up off Akoranga Dr to the western suburbs, north into Takapuna and east into Devonport. Once that's completed, work will start on widening Onewa Rd to create the bus lane that will link up with the new Onewa Rd interchange.

Meanwhile, the motorway busway from Constellation Drive to the Esmonde Rd interchange is due to open in February 2008 along with three more bus stations at Sunnynook (near the Link Drive commercial and industrial area), at Westlake (at Smales Farm to the east of the motorway) and at Akoranga close to the AUT campus.

Along the way, plans are unfolding at a local level for improved suburban bus routes and upgraded bus stops towards creating a wholly user-friendly public transport service for the entire North Shore.

Beyond that, there's talk of an extension of the busway through to Albany and even beyond to Orewa.

All this progress is being keenly watched by home owners and developers alike, knowing that improved public transport has perhaps the biggest influence on regional development and real estate values.

East

These are some of the scenes evocative of east Auckland: families swimming at safe beaches lined with pohutukawa and Norfolk pines; hectare after hectare of new cloned houses; millions of dollars'- worth of boats bobbing in marinas.

The suburbs of east Auckland have long been the embodiment of New Zealand suburbia. Pakuranga was known as Vim Valley in the 1970s, after the cleaning product endorsed on TV by housewives in Pakuranga – everything was shiny, new and clean.

Botany Downs has taken over the mantle of super-suburbanness now, and it's emblematic in another way. The eastern suburbs have long been part of Manukau City but, until Botany Downs and its neighbours were developed, the eastern and southern parts of that city were physically separated by farmland. Now the

farmland has become suburbs, and the division has become blurred.

A major drawcard for this part of Auckland is the proximity to the sea. The area is so built-up that you often can't see the ocean until you're right next to it, but it's still very accessible.

The beaches have white sand and are, in general, safe for swimming. The convoluted coastline and nearness of the islands of the Hauraki Gulf make it a haven for boaties too, as the number of boat clubs and boat ramps, (and two large marinas) testify.

The horsey set is well established in the east, too. Whitford, Clevedon and Brookby are particularly known for being havens for horse-lovers. Clevedon is home to the busiest polo club in the country; Brookby has a top-rate

safe and secure
settled suburbia
a boatie's dream
new, new, new

equestrian centre; and some days in Whitford you can't move for horse floats.

Many residents who commute to Auckland's CBD for work or study have the option of doing so by ferry, from Pine Harbour near Beachlands, or from Half Moon Bay. It makes a very pleasant alternative to a long journey by road. And the fact that the Pine Harbour operators have just invested in a second boat, for a more frequent service, shows that it's appreciated.

Suburbs such as Howick have attracted many Asian immigrants in the past decade – and while inter-racial relations were strained in many quarters initially, there doesn't seem to be an issue now. Indeed the NZ European population now probably wonders how they survived without the Asian food shops and restaurants which now abound.

Further evidence of the integration of Asians into this area is the fact that many schools and community facilities now offer information and courses in various Asian languages. Visit the website of Pakuranga College, for example, and you can download their newsletter in English, Korean or Chinese. There's also an impressive new Buddhist temple in town.

With its quintessential Kiwi lifestyle appeal, the area also attracts many South Africans and English – to them this is a perfect blend of seaside living with access to world-class shops and amenities.

In the days when we travelled at a leisurely pace – not by choice, just because we had to – Beachlands and Maraetai were the preserve of farmers and holidaymakers. These settlements managed to feel slightly removed from the madding crowd for an impressively long time, but times are a-changing.The area's desirable seaside location and relative ease of access to the city, means farms are being sold and subdivided. Ironically, the rural landscape provided by the remaining farms helps make the place look attractive to weary city-dwellers.For those who can afford it, these seaside hamlets are still a great way to hang on to traditional Kiwi family values, where you know the neighbours by name and kids can safely ride their bikes to school. Being at the end of a road, Beachlands is especially appealing and the one likely to see the most development.

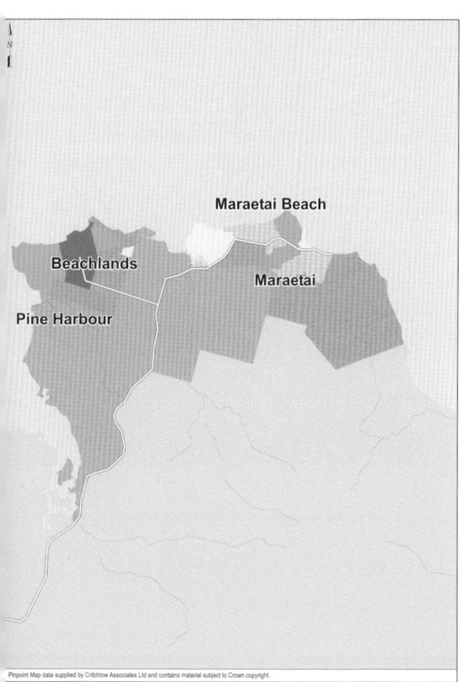

For colour key, see page 226

Population Profile

Population	4,419
% Aged Under 15 Years	25.19
% Aged Over 65 Years	10.39
% European	89.61
% Maori	7.60
% Pacific Peoples	1.97
% Asian	1.70

Who Lives There?

These two seaside hamlets are family-oriented communities, popular with lifestylers who want access to the city without having to tolerate crowded suburbs. Indeed, many people moving here are coming from other eastern suburbs. There isn't a lot of employment here, so most people commute. But this is still an area where you can expect to know your neighbours and be part of a strong community network.

Although occupants of each of the two hamlets tend to identify closely with their community, there's a strong spirit that unites the two parties, proud as they are of the area in general.

Typical Homes

The fibrolite baches which were the norm here 20 years ago are now a rare and quaint sight. Many have been demolished and replaced with very substantial modern homes. Until recently, the area had a fairly even selection of housing styles from every decade since the 1920s, but new subdivisions mean that large quality contemporary homes now dominate.

Amenities

Schools ★★

Beachlands and Maraetai each have a combined primary/intermediate school catering for years one to eight. Interestingly, these high decile schools are not strong on zoning, so you can choose between them.

Both schools are well appointed, with strong ties to the local community. Beachlands is the larger of the two with a roll close to 400, although Mareatai is the oldest, celebrating its centennial 25 years ago!

For secondary schooling, a free school bus takes half an hour to transport teenagers to Howick College. For a full list, see page 270.

Shops ★★

Most residents take advantage of the fact that they're out of the area almost daily by doing the bulk of their shopping where there's more choice and lower prices. But if you were marooned here indefinitely, it wouldn't be so bad. All the basics are covered, including grocery, hardware, baked goods, alcohol, pharmaceuticals and videos.

Leisure ★★★

Part of the great Kiwi dream this area provides, is the easy access to outdoor activities. Beachlands and Maraetai both have great swimming beaches (hence the endless line of day-trippers heading out to Maraetai every sunny summer weekend), fishing and boating. Omana Regional Park, between the two hamlets, has beach, bush and farm. Neighbouring Te Puru Park has sports fields. Nearby Whitford Forest has tracks for mountain biking, walking and horse riding.

After years of community fundraising, Te Puru Community Centre opened between Beachlands and Maraetai in mid-2005. It has a fitness centre, function rooms for hire, and a clubroom for sports teams.

The Formosa Golf Resort has a golf course, a small gym, tennis courts and a swimming pool and spa pool with sea views.

As for dining out, the focus is on takeaways rather than silver service here – reflecting the family-oriented culture rather than any down-at-heel demographic. And let's face it, if you don't feel like catching the ferry into the CBD to make your selection from hundreds of dining establishments, then a picnic on the beach is probably just the ticket.

Real Estate

Trends

Ten years ago, the gruff laid-back locals of Beachlands and Maraetai would have laughed themselves silly if you'd shown them sketches of the palaces that would soon be changing the look of their unpretentious seaside neighbourhoods. When they'd finished laughing, you could tell them today's prices – and they'd probably choke. Nowadays, anything under $400,000 is likely to be described as "entry-level".

These suburbs certainly earn their great reputations, with their excellent swimming beaches, friendly communities and jaw-dropping gulf views. A view will add up to $100,000 to a home's price tag.

Intensive subdivision (particularly at Beachlands, although there is also a new 64-section development at Maraetai) is making space for the increased demand.

Many of the new residents are immigrants, often from the UK, or Kiwis returning home from overseas to raise families, and wanting the space, sun and sand they've spent many a grey London winter reminiscing about.

Best Streets

There's really no unfortunate street in Maraetai. In Beachlands, the clifftop streets are still the favourites: Hawke Cres, Ealing Cres and First View Ave. A good address doesn't automatically guarantee top dollar – it's still very dependent on the quality, age and style of the residence.

Local Hero: Pine Harbour Marina

Arriving at Beachlands by ferry you have the bonus of a tour of the rather splendid Pine Harbour Marina, home to 600 beautiful boats. The marina has a full complement of on-site tradespeople, 24-hour security, a 24-hour fuel service, and a complete haul-out and hard-stand facility, with a boatlifter capable of handling 28m boats up to 44 tonnes.

All of this doesn't come cheap: to buy a maritime parking space for your humble nine-metre yacht will cost at least $25,000 a year plus operating fees. For a 20-metre yacht the website says POA: if you need to ask, you probably can't afford it.

Look Out (!)

If you're after a quiet bucolic retreat, this probably isn't it. Sure, it's prettier than most parts of Auckland, but the population is growing very rapidly and it's not the backwater (no seaside pun intended) it was until a few years ago.

At a Glance...

House Prices

Basic bach without a view

Bedrooms	🛏 🛏
Price	$380,000

Bach with a sea view

Bedrooms	🛏 🛏 🛏
Price	$550,000

New executive house

Bedrooms	🛏 🛏 🛏 🛏
Price	$600,000

Section in a new subdivision

Price	$220,000 +

Average Rents

Flat

Bedrooms	🛏 🛏
Price	$275/wk

House

Bedrooms	🛏 🛏 🛏
Price	$375/wk

Travel Times

From Beachlands:

CBD	peak 60 min off peak 40 min by ferry 35 min
Southern motorway	20 min
Airport	30 min
Manukau City shops	20 min
Botany Town Centre	20 min

There are 11 return ferry trips between Pine Harbour Marina and Auckland's CBD on weekdays. There are services to Rakino and Waiheke islands at weekends. From Beachlands, you can stroll to the ferry along the clifftop reserve or along the beach. For timetables and ticket prices, visit www.pineharbour.co.nz or phone 09 536 4725. Buses run to and from Maraetai and Beachlands and Auckland on weekdays.

Botany Downs ★★★½

including Northpark, Somerville, Pt View Park, Dannemora, Cumbria Downs and Burswood

It was inevitable that the easy-on-the-eye rural landscape between south and east Auckland would be gobbled up by developers. On the whole, they've done a great job. Facilities are good, especially considering how recent this all is, and the Botany Town Centre has become renowned throughout Auckland. To some, the newness and myriad copy-cat residences can be overwhelming but others love it. The fast growth and the variety of residents are well illustrated by a local primary school. Baverstock Oaks opened in Botany Downs in 2005 with just 90 pupils; a year later it had more than 300, and by the end of 2007 it's expected to have 700. Three-quarters of the school's parents, and more than half of the children, were born overseas, in South Africa, Asia, Russia, Switzerland, England and Scotland.

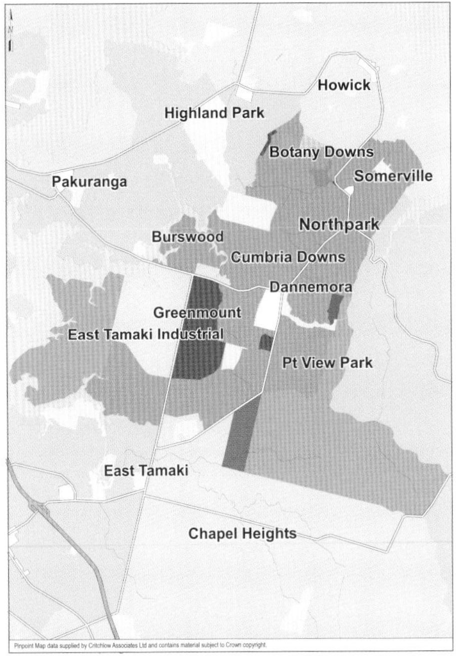

For colour key, see page 226

Population Profile

Population	26,064
% Aged Under 15 Years	22.43
% Aged Over 65 Years	7.38
% European	62.43
% Maori	3.36
% Pacific Peoples	1.55
% Asian	31.64

Who Lives There?

This is a racially mixed middle-class area with many immigrants – the variety of nationalities was obviously expected by those who dish out the street names: they include Billabong Pl, Kilimanjaro Dr and Napa Ct! Whatever the nationality, the family profile tends towards those with teenagers or older.

Immigrants and locals alike are drawn by the newness of the houses and the amenities. Many people have relocated here from more established parts of east Auckland, seeking low-maintenance homes with desirable features such as internal-access garaging, ensuites and walk-in wardrobes.

Typical Homes

Because this area was farmland just a few years ago, the houses are all virtually new. The modern brick-and-tile, four-bedroom, one-level house dominates, although apartments are creeping in. There's a definite sense of the homogenous American suburban dream: although the reality of land prices (and desire for big houses) means that the sections are small.

The style of some of the more dramatic homes, where classical-style columns support two-storey-high porticos, seems ostentatious to some while appealing to others, particularly immigrants from the east.

The Sacramento terrace houses by Botany Town Centre, was seen as innovative at the time but is fraught with leaky building problems.

Amenities

Schools ★★★

Options are limited in Botany Downs itself but there are plenty of quality schools in neighbouring Howick and Pakuranga for this highly mobile community.

Botany Downs School is popular and Point View School has a new performing arts centre and IT suite with dedicated music and technology teachers.

Somerville Intermediate is decile 10 and has a roll close to 1000. At secondary level, Botany Downs College opened in 2004, and won an award from the NZ Institute of Architects, who described it as "a spectacular learning environment". On a smaller and less dramatic scale, Catholic high school Sancta Maria College also opened in 2004. For a full list, see page 270.

Shops ★★★★★

They sure know how to do retail therapy around here! Botany Town Centre endeavours to deliver the best of both retail worlds – it's mall and mainstreet, all bundled into one mega shopping experience. It feels a little like you've stepped into a movie set but there's lots of architectural variety in the shop fronts, which should help it to age more gracefully. The centre includes an eight-screen cinema complex and is home to Manukau's flagship library. Biblio-purists might not approve, but it blends into its commercial habitat by being designed like a retail space, complete with café.

Leisure ★★★

Botany Downs will soon be rivalling Ponsonby Rd for the number of cafés per kilometre.

And as long as shopping is your idea of leisure, you won't put a foot wrong here. There is also 10-pin bowling and ice skating on offer just over the road from Botany Town Centre.

All manner of land sports and maritime activities are available in nearby Howick. Lloyd Elsmore Park in Pakuranga has excellent recreational facilities, including a swimming pool complex.

Real Estate

Trends

The busy real estate market of past years has levelled off now. A couple of years ago everybody wanted to live near the Botany Town

Centre; now Botany College (which opened at the beginning of 2004) is the big draw card.

What they call "established Dannemora" is in very strong demand, largely because it's in-zone for the highly desirable trio of schools: Point View Primary School, Somerville Intermediate, and Botany Downs College.

Prices for newer four-bedroom properties in nice areas and with larger than average sections regularly sell for $580,000 or more, and five-bedroom quasi-mansions on 1200m² sections (which seems huge in this densely populated area) sell for up to $1.2million.

Best Streets

Fairfield Lane is sought-after because it has a good number of masonry homes which look established and respectable. Also popular are John Brooke Cres, Brook Ridge Rise, and anything near Botany College.

Local Hero: Fo Guang Shan Buddhist Temple

After the eye-numbing blandness of Botany's residential streets, doing a double-take is a natural reaction when the Fo Guang Shan Buddhist temple looms into view. It's huge and, being built in the style of an ancient Chinese palace, very distinctive. The architecture, interiors and numerous statues and sculptures are fascinating. And when you step into the cool calm of the main courtyard, it's hard to believe you're in the midst of one of the fastest-growing areas in the country. If it rains when you visit, you'll notice that the traditional architecture has not been compromised by the addition of guttering: in typically hospitable style, umbrellas are provided.

At a Glance...

House Prices

Unit

Bedrooms	2
Price	$280,000 - $340,000

House

Bedrooms	3
Price	$350,000 - $450,000

Executive house

Bedrooms	4
Price	$500,000 - $650,000

Average Rents

Flat

Bedrooms	2
Price	$280/wk

House

Bedrooms	3
Price	$335/wk
Bedrooms	4
Price	$445/wk

Travel Times

From Botany Downs:

CBD	peak 50 - 60 min off peak 25 min
Southern motorway	10 min
Airport	25 min

The regular bus service takes about an hour from Botany Town Centre to the CBD. Another option is to bus to the Half Moon Bay ferry and get into town by sea.

Look Out (!)

Only time will tell how well this area will mature. The newness of everything is quite attractive, but obviously won't last – there is a certain sameness to the area which might become claustrophobic for many Kiwis.

including Eastern Beach

Bucklands Beach and Eastern Beach occupy a spectacular little peninsula – but the area is so built up that it's perfectly possible to be unaware of the fact that you're on such a narrow piece of land. That is, until you reach Musick Pt at the tip of the peninsula and the almost surreal vista of the Hauraki Gulf opens up before you. Browns Island looks so close you could almost leap down on to it. (No, please don't try it.) Apart from the hidden drama of the geography, it feels like any established eastern suburb. It's a very settled place, with people staying put for a long time because they love it so much. It also has some real estate gems – streamlined nods to modern architecture - on the clifftops looking out to sea.

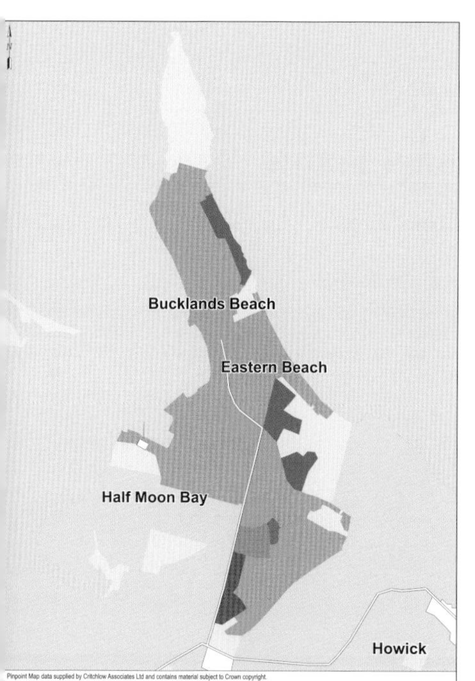

For colour key, see page 226

Population Profile

Population	10,875
% Aged Under 15 Years	21.63
% Aged Over 65 Years	9.57
% European	72.30
% Maori	2.57
% Pacific Peoples	1.32
% Asian	23.48

Who Lives There?

Families who appreciate being near the sea have long gravitated to this area. They also appreciate the good schooling available (this is Macleans College zone) and, to a certain extent, the relative isolation of the peninsula where there is no through-traffic and therefore less noise and fumes than nearer to Pakuranga Rd.

While many properties are the preserve of the wealthy, there is also a range of more affordable properties, which means a good mix of residents. They are predominantly NZ European, and Asian. Another significant part of the population is older couples

who are financially very comfortable and enjoy spending their semi-retirement in this pretty environment.

Typical Homes

Because the area has been developed over many decades, there is no such thing as a typical style of home. Many houses, though, are large and set on lovingly landscaped sections. Those with sea views make the most of them with huge expanses of window. Away from the sea views, there are more modest townhouses and units.

Amenities

Schools ★★★★

There are several good primary schools in the neighbourhood, including the high-decile Bucklands Beach Primary and Macleans Primary. Both schools are performing well and regularly receive positive ERO reports. The equally well regarded Bucklands Beach Intermediate caters for years seven and eight.

The local secondary school Macleans College is the big cheese among high schools in the eastern suburbs, and a major drawcard for families to the area. Being in the right zone means a lot to people (and to the prices they're prepared to pay for real estate). For a full list, see page 270.

Shops ★★

All the basics are catered for at small centres dotted around the peninsula, but for anything major you will need to venture further afield to Highland Park, Howick, Pakuranga or Botany Downs. A couple of marine-themed cafés and restaurants, The Beach House and Barracuda, make the most of their setting on The Parade by the water on the western side of the peninsula. Otherwise, Howick village is the closest and best bet for good food.

Leisure ★★★★

The Howick Golf Course at Musick Pt is a treat, even if you have no interest in golf. It looks like an old-fashioned park, complete with pot-holed road wending its way through the golf course. Right at the tip of the peninsula is a wonderful Art Deco building, built in 1939 as a base for marine radio communications and now leased by a group of amateur radio hams.

Yachties are well served, of course, with the Bucklands Beach Yacht Club and the Half Moon Bay Marina, as well as public boat ramps at both Bucklands and Eastern Beach. The latter has a water ski lane, picnic area and children's playground.

There are tennis clubs and, not far away, the various delights of Lloyd Elsmore Park in Pakuranga.

Real Estate

Trends

Bucklands Beach and Eastern Beach are comparable in price to neighbouring Mellons Bay and Cockle Bay, which puts the whole coastline one notch up from other eastern

suburbs like Half Moon Bay. Properties on the northeast-facing slopes, in particular, have vast sea views out into the gulf and good sun.

The area has seen a lot of redevelopment and renovations. Cliff-top homes, in particular, are always sought-after thanks to those unbeatable sea views, and a lot of money is being spent on making them into top-notch contemporary homes.

Popular Macleans College continues to attract families to the area, as well as South African and English immigrants. There appears to be a slight drop-off in Asian buyers, who prefer the newness of suburbs like Dannemora.

Best Streets

The Parade (west side of the peninsula) and Clovelly Rd (east side) are the places to be if you've got big money to spend on a huge view.

Musik Point

At a Glance...

House Prices

Unit

Bedrooms	
Price	$300,000 +

House

Bedrooms	
Price	$450,000 - $550,000

Executive house with sea views

Bedrooms	
Price	$650,000 - $2,000,000

Average Rents

Flat

Bedrooms	
Price	$280/wk

House

Bedrooms	
Price	$295/wk
Bedrooms	
Price	$335/wk
Bedrooms	
Price	$445/wk

Travel Times

CBD	peak 50 min off peak 30 min
Southern motorway	25 min
Airport	35 min
Botany Town Centre	15 min

There are regular buses to the CBD and to Manukau. There is also a regular ferry service from the adjacent suburb of Half Moon Bay.

Half Moon Bay 

including Farm Cove and Sunnyhills

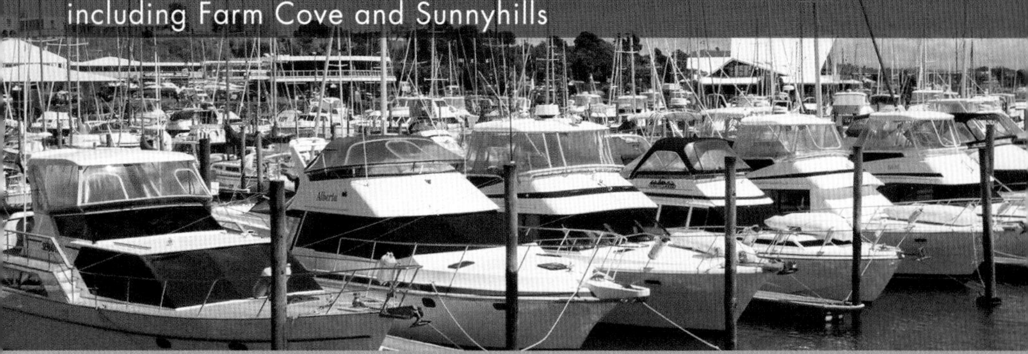

Beautiful but not bland, Half Moon Bay has much to boast about - beaches, boat ramps and a marina, a large park and several great shopping centres close by. With its waterside areas and views along the Tamaki River and into the Hauraki Gulf, it typifies the modern Kiwi suburban dream in many ways. Developed in the early 1970s, Half Moon Bay was soon joined by its neighbours Sunnyhills and Farm Cove, which share in the waterside location. Unlike other newer eastern suburbs, the streetscapes are leafy and the houses diverse and interesting - parts of the area feel like a set from the 1970s TV show The Brady Bunch, while elsewhere, whole streets have been modernised and bedecked with swimming pools and smooth plaster facades.

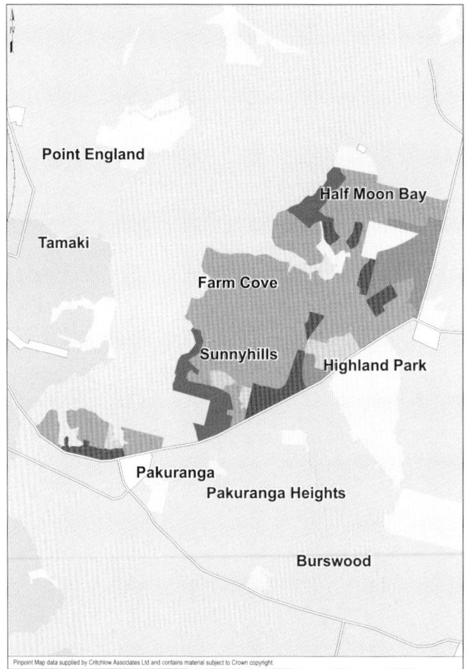

For colour key, see page 226

Population Profile

Population	9,150
% Aged Under 15 Years	20.79
% Aged Over 65 Years	10.62
% European	71.64
% Maori	4.33
% Pacific Peoples	9.05
% Asian	21.74

Who Lives There?

People who appreciate the sea and the beach feel right at home here. It's considered a great place to raise children; the schools are good and the house prices not astronomical. Hence, it's filled with many families mainly with school-age and teenage kids. Residents are very comfortable financially and own their own homes.

Once the kids have grown up, people tend to stay put, so there is a good mix of generations in the area.

ypical Homes

\lthough there is a huge range of styles from he past four decades of development, those hat really stand out are the palatial waterfront esidences, many of them with a nod to Aediterranean style.

here are certainly many 1970s and 1980s ouses on generous sections, many now pdated and refurbished. But if you're into etro style, you can also easily find a 1970s hree-bedroom home in fairly original condition.

he only apartments in the area are in a small ow-rise block on the corner of Sunderlands Dr bove the Half Moon Bay marina.

f you want new, there's the Compass Pt levelopment (see Trends section).

\menities

chools ★★★

)ptions are limited in Half Moon Bay self but there are plenty of quality chools in neighbouring Bucklands Beach nd Pakuranga.

Vakaaranga Primary School caters for years ne to six. The high decile school has a history f positive ERO reports and was recently lescribed as delivering "a good quality ducation" to it's students. Other nearby rimary schools include Pigeon Mountain rimary in Bucklands Beach and Sunnyhills rimary in Pakuranga.

There are two intermediates - Farm Cove and Pakuranga. At secondary level, the area is in zone for Pakuranga College and the co-ed private school St Kentigern College is close by. For a full list, see page 270.

Shops ★★★

There's no huge mall here, but you're never far from a shop in these suburbs. If you need more than a video, loaf of bread, bunch of flowers or bottle of sauvignon blanc, you only need to head to nearby shopping meccas such as Westfield at Pakuranga, The Hub or, of course, Botany Town Centre. The marina offers a surprising range of goods and services, including a pharmacy, doctor and hairdresser.

Leisure ★★★★

Residents are spoiled for choice, starting with the beautiful 500-berth marina. There are reserves and parks in every direction, and public boat ramps at Bramley Dr Reserve in Farm Cove and at the Ara Tai Reserve in Half Moon Bay.

Sunnyhills has its own well-regarded tennis club, and there's another nearby in Pakuranga.

Lloyd Elsmore Park is an absolute asset to all the eastern suburbs. Half Moon Bay residents wanting to dine out can catch the ferry to the many splendoured offerings of the CBD, or enjoy the international cuisine at neighbouring suburbs Pakuranga, Highland Park and Howick.

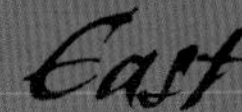

Real Estate

Trends

While the look of these suburbs seem to stay the same from one year to the next, according to industry statistics and local real estate agents, the prices keep creeping upwards in a generally flat Auckland market.

There are few subdividable sections left and homeowners continue to quietly modernise their 30-year-old houses. One noticeable and recent change on the landscape was Compass Pt where about half of the 64 sections have homes (luxury homes) on them. Most of the sections initially sold for between $400,000 and $500,000; one larger one with extremely good views fetched $1.5 million. Subsequent on-sales have been high; one palatial home sold for $2.8 million.

Some fairly luxurious properties are tucked out of sight by the water and on the clifftops. A Venus Pl, Farm Cove, property currently for sale on an acre of waterfront land with seven bedrooms, pool and tennis court may break records when it sells.

Best Streets

Takutai Ave residences have an impressive view over Half Moon Bay and the Hauraki Gulf. In Farm Cove and Sunnyhills, desirable streets include Sanctuary Pt, Bramley Dr and Fisher Pde.

Smart Buy ✓

A "nice" neighbourhood by the sea with a range of attractive houses on decent-sized sections set down wide leafy streets. This area was the suburban dream when it was developed 30 years ago and will continue to be the dream destination for many. Values will hold, and grow, along with the many families who love life here. The small waterfront area of Farm Cove is definitely worth checking out if you want to live in the area – it's substantial homes are surprisingly affordable.

At a Glance...

House Prices

Unit

Bedrooms: 2
Price: $290,000 - $320,000

House

Bedrooms: 3
Price: $390,000 - $460,000

Modernised house

Bedrooms: 4
Price: $500,000 - $1,000,000

Luxury house on Compass Pt

Price: $2,500,000

Average Rents

Flat

Bedrooms: 2
Price: $270/wk

House

Bedrooms: 3
Price: $350/wk
Bedrooms: 4
Price: $415/wk

Travel Times

CBD	peak 50 min off peak 20 min by Ferry 30 min
Southern motorway	10 min
Airport	25 - 40 min
Botany Town Centre	10 min
Manukau City shopping centre	15 min

There are regular buses to the CBD and to Manukau. There is also a regular ferry service to the CBD from Half Moon Bay marina (reduced at weekends and public holidays), as well as a vehicle ferry to Waiheke Island.

ncluding Mellons Bay, Cockle Bay and Shelly Park

Howick's a bit of a paradox. To many it's that newly developed area out east. Today, by the sheer volume of new suburbs that have sprung up around it, it's seen as the lder kid on the block. To those in the know, it's a place with a strong history. Old, new, ake your pick. It has it all. Now a leafy, affluent seaside area, it was settled in the 1850s by encibles: retired British soldiers brought here to defend Auckland in return for land. For ne next 100 years the town was dominated by holiday homes and farms. The rural land as developed into residential during the 1950s and 1960s – much like Botany Downs in ecent years, but in a more gradual manner. Today, it has a provincial feel more in common ith Hamilton than Auckland. Maybe it's because a drive to the CBD in rush hour seems o take just as long.

For colour key, see page 226

Population Profile

Population	18,888
% Aged Under 15 Years	20.90
% Aged Over 65 Years	12.74
% European	86.47
% Maori	3.72
% Pacific Peoples	1.41
% Asian	9.15

Who Lives There?

The area was particularly popular with Dutch and English immigrants in the 1950s and 1960s, and it has long been more "exotic" than other, more staunchly Kiwi areas.

It still attracts folk from distant shores. Asian immigrants came in droves but now prefer the newer eastern suburbs of Dannemora and Cumbria Downs. Many English and South Africans have dipped their toes into the Howick waters and pronounced them worthy of a long-term soak. There's a strong sense of community here. Not all of the youngsters move out of the area when they leave home – there's certainly a good percentage of young professionals and

students near the town centre. It's a great spot for sailors, and as you'd expect, around the waterfront properties, you'll find some folk with fairly deep pockets.

Typical Homes

Howick's gradual development over many decades has resulted in a vibrant mix of architectural styles. There are century-old cottages and villas, but the majority are mid-20th-century brick-and-tile or weatherboard homes. This has long been a comparatively wealthy area, so the homes tend to be well built and well maintained.

The influx of Asian buyers has meant that many of the homes built in the past decade have Botany Downs-style features of grandeur such as double-height porticos and classical-style pillars.

A heritage zone has been imposed on the seaward side of Bleakhouse Rd, which means the sections can't be smaller than 1400m². In other areas, large sections have succumbed to in-fill housing, particularly in the popular Macleans College zone.

Amenities

Schools ★★★★

Howick is a high-decile area well served with quality schools for all ages. There are at least eight primary schools, two intermediates and three secondaries.

Cockle Bay School is one of the largest primar schools here, with a roll close to 700 childrer The two new schools Point View School an Willowbank School are also very popular bu have tight zoning restrictions.

At secondary level, the highly regarde Macleans College in Bucklands Beach is a attraction, although only the northern pa of Howick is in zone. Howick College, whic also has a strong reputation, is in th neighbourhood along with the fairly ne Catholic Sancta Maria College. For a full lis see page 270.

Shops ★★★★

Howick Village has a wide range of shop offering everything from the basics to upmarke luxuries, as well as a new supermarket. Th footpaths are wide, making this pleasant villag style mainstreet shopping for pedestrian At the beginning of 2005, Howick's olde building, the 99-year-old Rishworth Buildin was demolished to make way for a new reta development on the corner of Picton St an Park Hill Rd.

The range of eateries reflects the ethni diversity and the cosmopolitan nature c locals – there are Asian restaurants of mar flavours, including Japanese, Vietnames Malay, Korean and Indian.

Leisure ★★★★

Beautiful beaches below pohutukawa-cla cliffs are a major drawcard for relaxing local

Howick Beach is a five-minute walk from the shops. Although they do get crowded in summer, there are numerous small coves accessed by steep pathways which only a few know about.

The reserves are plentiful and beautiful here, too. The Mangemangeroa Reserve walkway from Somerville Rd to the Shelly Park Yacht Club, part board-walk over mangroves, part beach-walk and part bush-walk, is well worth the effort.

The number of moored yachts and boat ramps testify to the popularity of sailing. Howick also has sports clubs for cricket, netball, rugby league, squash and tennis, and Cockle Bay has a petanque pitch.

There is an active cultural scene, too, with Howick Little Theatre and the Howick Operatic Society. Howick Historic Village (physically in Pakuranga, but spiritually in Howick) is a fascinating showcase of olde worlde everyday life. Here are gathered, and restored, some 30 buildings built between 1840 and 1880. Regular live days, when the voluntary staff dress the part and perform such mysterious acts as making butter and writing on slates, are deservedly popular.

Real Estate

Trends

Prices have been steady during the past year but sales numbers have been buoyant. Some industry commentators say that satellite

suburbs that have seen a lot of market activity, like Howick, are due for a slight recession.

House-proud and spurred on by high real estate values, many Howickians are renovating their 1960s and 1970s era houses often to the point where they are no longer recognisable. Some, especially those on the desired northern slopes of Cockle and Mellons Bay, are being removed to make way for new, contemporary homes.

Most sections which can be subdivided, have been. Howick now also has apartment complexes near the main street. Many people still find Howick an attractive option compared to the newer, characterless eastern neighbourhoods such as Botany Downs.

Best Streets

The north-facing slopes of Mellons and Cockle Bay have sea views and therefore the best streets. In Howick, Island View Tce, Marine Pde, Seaview Tce, Bleakhouse Rd, Burford Pl, Seymour Rd and Pah Rd.

Local Hero: Uxbridge Centre

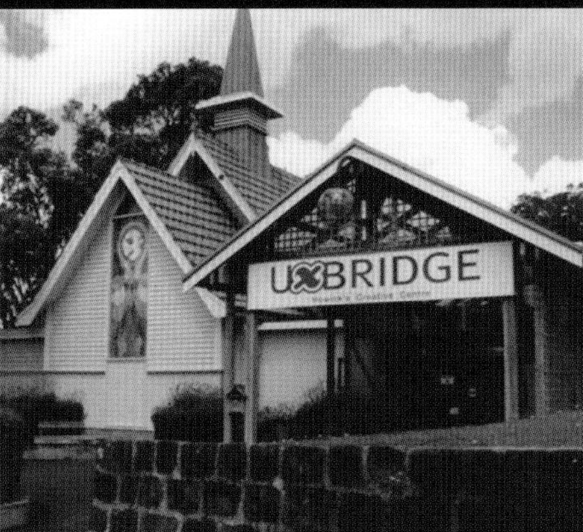

Bustling and diverse, Uxbridge Centre is the very model of a community arts and leisure centre. Every year some 40,000 people attend its programmes and events. A couple of the more unusual offerings are: a drawing and painting class mainly for Mandarin speakers (non-Mandarin speakers are also welcome); making moulds from body parts; belly dancing and painting on to corrugated iron.

The Uxbridge Centre was founded in 1981, when the former Howick Borough Council purchased the Uxbridge Presbyterian Church and associated buildings – extensive redevelopment is planned for the future once funding is organised.

At a Glance...

House Prices

Unit

Bedrooms	2
Price	$300,000

House

Bedrooms	3
Price	$400,000 - $550,000

House with sea views

Bedrooms	4
Price	$550,000 - $3,000,000

Average Rents

Flat

Bedrooms	2
Price	$280/wk

House

Bedrooms	2
Price	$295/wk
Bedrooms	3
Price	$335/wk
Bedrooms	4
Price	$445/wk

Travel Times

CBD	peak 45 min off peak 25 min
Southern motorway	20 min
Airport	40 min
Botany Town Centre	10 min

There's a regular bus service for the area and if you don't relish rush-hour commuting, you can catch the ferry from nearby Half Moon Bay marina.

ncluding Highland Park and Edgewater

Pakuranga is the Botany Downs of the 1960s. That's when the farmland in this area was subdivided and turned into the great Kiwi suburban dream. Families loved it then and, although it's been mocked relentlessly over the years for being embarrassingly suburban, it's still got a lot going for it. It's relatively affordable for east Auckland, and has easy access to good beaches, boating and schools, and is the closest eastern suburb to Auckland's CBD. Simply by merit of the era in which it was developed, sections are family-sized – a rare commodity in newer parts of the city. To the north-east, Highland Park is more elevated, with some houses having views across suburbia to the city. As a result, prices are also more, well, elevated. On the map, it looks as though the whole area is enfolded by coastline but it looks out over tidal mangrove-filled mudflats not white sand beaches.

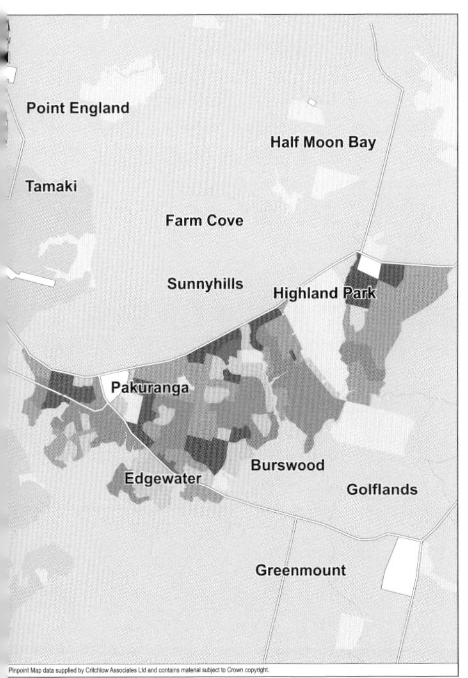

For colour key, see page 226

Population Profile

Population	23,451
% Aged Under 15 Years	20.21
% Aged Over 65 Years	13.06
% European	66.18
% Maori	6.95
% Pacific Peoples	4.35
% Asian	24.36

Who Lives There?

After being THE place to bring up kids for many generations, Pakuranga's population has aged in recent years: new generations have grown up and moved on to more desirable areas. But now the well-built and well-maintained homes on large sections with mature trees are starting to be seen by young families as a compelling alternative to a tiny townhouse on a small section. As well as the NZ European families who've been here since it was first developed, Pakuranga has proven attractive to immigrants from a variety of countries in the last decade, especially Asians. And it's a perfect spot for those who love to be near the sea.

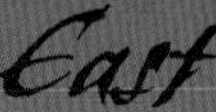

Typical Homes

If you're after a solidly built, three- or four-bedroom weatherboard or brick home with internal-access garaging, which has hardly been altered since it was built in the mid to late 1960s, you'll have plenty of choice. Many have been modernised but houses of that era were actually built with harmonious family living in mind (think rumpus rooms, second living areas, even ensuites) so the layouts themselves haven't had to change much.

Highland Park, which developed more recently, has homes of a similar style, but the prices are generally higher. More modest homes are available in Edgewater, southeast of Pakuranga.

Amenities

Schools ★★★

Appropriately for such a family-oriented area, Pakuranga abounds with schools at all levels. Be warned however, that decile ratings vary wildly from one school to the next and this, unfortunately, can impact on the quality of the education. As always, do your research.

The high-decile Elm Park School has a history of positive ERO reports and sound teaching practices. The Education Review Office also described the quality of teaching at Pakuaranga Heights School as, "generally…very good".

Pakuranga Intermediate and Farm Cove Intermediate are in the area. For secondary students there is Pakuranga College and Edgewater College. The highly regarded co-ed private school St Kentigern College is also in the neighbourhod. For a full list, see page 270.

Shops ★★★

The Pakuranga Town Centre shopping mall, which opened in 1965 to serve the new growing suburb, is now a much-improved Westfield Shopping Centre, with about 80 retailers. The retail competition around here is intense. Just a few minutes' drive from Westfield is The Hub on Ti Rakau Dr, with its emphasis on home décor retailers. And opposite The Hub is the inimitable Botany Town Centre. Highland Park has its own shopping centre, with some 30 shops and cafés including a newly spruced-up supermarket.

Leisure ★★★

Pakuranga residents are spoiled for choice when it comes to open recreational spaces. Lloyd Elsmore Park has everything from tennis courts and golf courses to horse riding and croquet, badminton and bowls. The Lloyd Elsmore Pool & Leisure Complex includes a 25-metre pool for lane swimming, a 15-metre teaching and water therapy pool, and a 25-metre leisure pool, which incorporates a toddlers' splash pool, complete with fun fountains. Entry to these pools is free. There is also a crèche, café, gym, spa pool, sauna and steam room. As if that weren't

enough, Pakuranga also has several gyms, a skate park, a beautiful golf course (the Pakuranga Country Club) on Cascades Rd, and a boat ramp at Tiraumea Drive reserve, which gives access to the Tamaki Estuary. Te Tuhi – The Mark on Reeves Rd is a friendly and diverse centre for community, cultural and arts events and exhibitions.

Real Estate

Trends

Pakuranga seemed completely developed by the 1980s, because all the empty sections had gone. After a lull of about 10 years, however, smaller sections became acceptable and in-fill housing really took off giving development another lease on life.

Extensive subdivision was still happening in Highland Park, Golflands and Edgewater until recently, but now there just isn't much development space left. The odd in-fill townhouse does occasionally still pop up, though.

Two-bedroom units within walking distance of Pakuranga Plaza are popular with downsizing retirees, and the well-renovated examples sell in the high $200,000s or low $300,000s.

This is still very much a family area, sought after both by those up-grading from South Auckland and coming from overseas – South Africa and Asia in particular – because of the pleasant surroundings and good schools.

Highland Park prices are consistently higher than Pakuranga prices, with three-bedroom homes fetching late $300,000s/early $400,000s. Properties near the Panmure Bridge are popular with businesspeople who need to work in the city and want to hone down their commute as much as possible without giving up their suburban lifestyle.

Best Streets

Desirable streets include Kentigern Cl, Browns Ave, Udys Rd, Portadown Ave and Chatsworth Cres. Ennis Ave has been transformed from a street full of shabby rentals into an attractive area for owner-occupiers.

At a Glance...

House Prices

Unit

Bedrooms	2
Price	$250,000 - $280,000

House

Bedrooms	3
Price	$350,000 - $450,000

Executive house

Bedrooms	4
Price	$450,000 - $550,000

Average Rents

Flat

Bedrooms	2
Price	$270/wk

House

Bedrooms	3
Price	$350/wk
Bedrooms	4
Price	$415/wk

Travel Times

From Pakuranga:

CBD	peak 60 min off peak 20 min
Southern motorway	5 min
Airport	30 min
Manukau City shopping centre	15 - 20 min

There are regular bus services to the CBD and to Manukau, but a ferry trip taking 30 minutes from nearby Half Moon Bay is a low-stress alternative for city commuters.

Whitford ★★★★★

including Brookby and Clevedon

Whitford, Brookby and Clevedon are to Auckland as Surrey is to London – a rural escape for the well-heeled, reasonably close to the city. With the endless stretches of wooden-rail fencing, mature trees and rolling fields, it's a very English-feeling place. And although the prices put it out of the reach of most Aucklanders, what you get for your money here would be astronomically expensive in most other countries. Development has been very tightly controlled, so most residents have plenty of room to swing a pony or two. The only downside to the sparseness of population is a lack of local amenities – there is no school in Whitford and there are no shops at Brookby. Still, there aren't many jobs out this way, either, so most people commute out of the area most days.

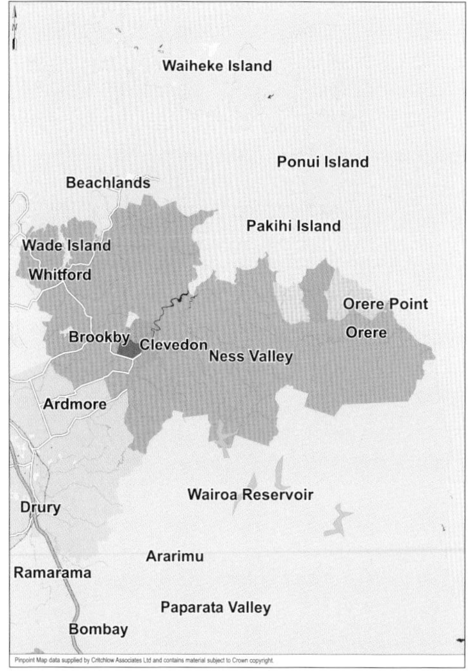

For colour key, see page 226

Population Profile

Population	5,121
% Aged Under 15 Years	23.73
% Aged Over 65 Years	9.26
% European	89.98
% Maori	7.03
% Pacific Peoples	1.11
% Asian	1.70

Who Lives There?

Community-minded people seem to gravitate to this area. It's been noted that people actually turn up to public meetings here! The vast majority of locals are white, some being recent immigrants taking advantage of the relative affordability of this lifestyle. A recent increase in the number of Asian buyers is possibly due to the advent of subdivisions, making smaller properties available on the market. And, of course, you have to love the land or love having lots of it around you to live here. It's a lifestyler's mecca.

Typical Homes

A typical home here is one you can't see from the road, because it's set far back, behind ıuge mature trees and vast expanses of ɔaddock. Lifestyle blocks and equestrian ɔroperties are very popular. In Brookby, a ȷroup of 1970s houses makes it obvious when hat farm was carved up for housing. Clevedon ıas some century-old villas and cottages. \part from having a certain graciousness and ›paciousness in common, the style of homes is ıctually very diverse.

Amenities

Schools ★★

Schooling options are limited. Brookby and Clevedon both have high-decile full primaries, ɔut Whitford children have to head elsewhere or schooling. Many of primary-age travel to Howick and its burgeoning surrounds - Point View School is a popular choice.

Jnsurprisingly, given the real estate prices ıround here, many opt to send their children o private high schools. In fact, there's a bus service to Pakuranga's co-ed St Kentigern College. Some parts of Whitford are zoned or Botany Downs College. For a full list, see page 270.

Shops ★★

Whitford retailers provide the basics for locals videos, petrol, groceries, saddlery) and the ıon-essentials for tourists (gift shops, an olde vorlde restaurant and a café/bakery). There ıre no shops at Brookby. At Clevedon, there ıre more horsey and touristy stores (including ıntiques), but also a wider range of shops, ncluding an organic food store.

Leisure ★★★★★

For many people out this way, life revolves around horses. Polo at Clevedon is a major event for a certain set and their big hats. There's also a pony club at Whitford, and an equestrian centre in Brookby. And whether you're on horse, foot or mountain bike, the numerous trails through the Whitford Forest are a great place to burn off some calories. Other sports are catered for too, with Clevedon having clubs for bowls, lawn tennis and cruising yachts. Whitford Park Golf Club has just upgraded its course, including new paths and bridges. It boasts 56ha of native trees and hosts many national golf tournaments. Formosa Country Club offers golfers fabulous harbour views and a real test of ability.

Duders Regional Park is an historic and beautiful seaside farm, with numerous tracks for walking and riding. It's a popular spot with bird watchers and picnickers, and the adjacent beach is a haven in summer – being a little further away it gets less crowded. There are cafés and restaurants at Whitford, Clevedon, Pine Harbour Marina and the Formosa Country Club.

Real Estate

Trends

There are no signs of money being tight in Whitford. For one real estate agency at the time of writing, the average price of their four most recent sales (all small- to medium-sized

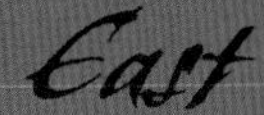

Why I Live There - Garden Owner Beverley McConnell

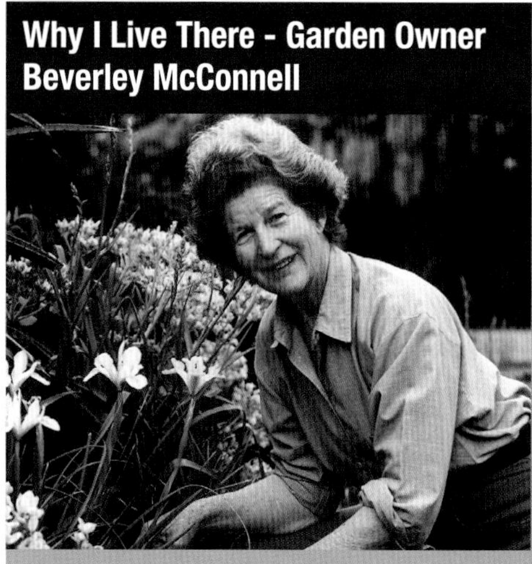

Beverley McConnell's magnificent 5ha country garden Ayrlies is well-known to green-thumbed Aucklanders. She and her husband moved to Whitford 40 years ago because he needed easy access to his newly established business in the city. They wanted their five children to grow up in the country, however, with the work (harvesting sweetcorn, milking cows) and the community spirit that it entails. In 2000 Beverley turned part of their farm into a wetland area, including a large lake, and she's been thrilled with the way that the project has been embraced by the local community. Ayrlies is open to visitors year-round, by appointment - ph (09) 530 8706.

lifestyle blocks) was almost $1.5 million. Forty hectares of bare land next to the old tip is currently being offered for $7 million.

You can still occasionally buy a property for a little over $600,000, but it would be a small cottage with an equally small section on the main road – perversely when these do come up, they take a long time to sell because they're not what people look for in Whitford.

It's hard to find a home of the sort of quality most Whitford residents expect without spending $1.5 million to $1.8 million. And that's without sea views!

The area is still extremely popular with English immigrants whose cashed-up pounds make great swathes through asking prices which many locals would choke on. There are also signs that Asian investors are buying up land for its future value, although they're not necessarily considering living in the area.

A canal development mooted for land by the Wairoa River north of Clevedon village has met with disfavour by the locals and the council.

Best Streets

Here they do things differently – you're looking at best peninsulas rather than best streets. Clifton or Broomfields Peninsulas are the places to be, no contest.

Local Hero: The Auckland Polo Club

The Auckland Polo Club has its home on the Clevedon-Kawakawa Bay Rd. Founded in 1899, it's the largest (with 40-plus members) in New Zealand, and one of the longest-established. Although New Zealand polo doesn't have quite the elitism that the sport is known for internationally, it's still a rich person's sport, and makes great sightseeing for lesser mortals.

There is polo at Clevedon every summer weekend from November to the end of March, but it's the New Zealand Open, held each February, which is the glamour event on the polo calendar.

At a Glance...

House Prices

Any house

If you're lucky	$800,000

1Ha lifestyle block with house

Bedrooms	4
Price	$1,000,000 +

Average Rents

As with sale prices, rental prices are difficult to gauge.

Small cottage

Bedrooms	2
Price	$270/wk

House

Bedrooms	4
Price	$800/wk
6ha land for horse grazing	$150/wk

Travel Times

From Whitford:

CBD	peak 55 min off peak 35 min
Motorway	12 min
Airport	25 min
Botany Town Centre	10 min

The Pine Harbour Ferry service from nearby Beachland is a boon for those who need to get to the CBD every day but don't want the stress of driving and parking. The ferry timetable is at www.pineharbour.co.nz. Howick & Eastern buses also serve this area.

South
vodafone
INSURANCE
INSURANCE

If you believed everything you heard in the media about south Auckland, you'd probably imagine it as an unsavoury cross between Harlem and Soweto, with all the poverty, crime and racial tension that entails.

But south Auckland is so much more than its shallow media image, and it has to be said that the Manukau City Council has done a great job during the years of raising local pride in cultural diversity.

Each March, for example, the Auckland Secondary Schools Maori and Pacific Island Cultural Festival – colloquially known as Polyfest – sees more than 13,000 students from some 50 Auckland secondary schools perform their unique traditional and contemporary dance styles.

For the rest of Auckland, there's a sense of improved attitude to the area, possibly helped along by the fact that east and south, once firmly separated by hectares of farmland, are now merging through the constant building of houses, roads, shops and offices.

Flat Bush is the most dramatic example of this: its population is predicted to go from 3,000 to around 40,000 by 2021, which would make it the country's largest new town. Funding has been announced for seven new Flat Bush schools over the next decade.

Flat Bush is home to the very impressive $30 million Fo Guang Shan Buddhist temple, built in the style of a traditional Chinese palace on a 4ha site. People come from as far away as Hamilton to worship, study and socialise; non-Buddhists visit out of curiosity and are welcomed.

multicultural & exciting colourful character-filled diverse easy-going

A different crowd is lured to Manurewa in south Auckland for the huge Ellerslie Flower Show, which draws almost 70,000 visitors from throughout New Zealand. That show takes place at the Auckland Regional Botanic Gardens, which is an impressive place in its own right. It's one of hundreds of reserves in south Auckland, many along the foreshore of the Manukau Harbour and along major streams.

South Auckland is the place where you can still buy waterfront property for prices that won't make you turn pale with shock.

The region also abuts the rich (as in, wealthy) semi-rural areas of Whitford and Karaka, where millionaire businessman Eric Watson established his enormous Westbury stud farm.

Manukau's visually striking flagship, the new TelstraClear Pacific Events Centre, had a very successful first year, with revenues almost double what was projected. Restaurants and shops opened in mid-2006 and a 140-bed hotel will open mid-2008.

And while Waitakere might be more famous for its bush, south Auckland has the Hunua Ranges, a reserve which covers some 16,000ha and contains the largest block of forest on the mainland of the Auckland region, as well as the only northern mainland habitat of the kokako.

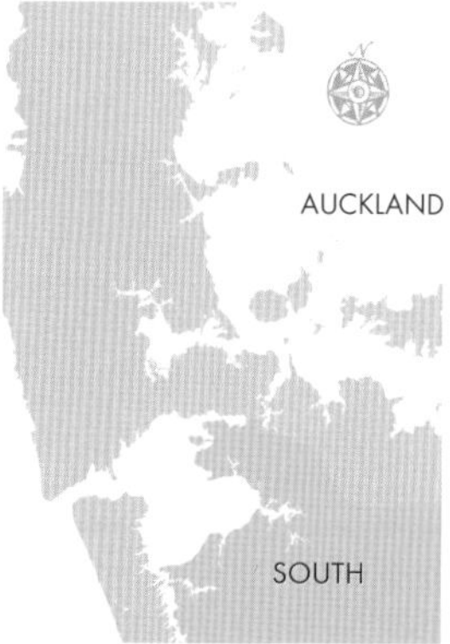

Mangere

including Mangere Bridge and Favona

The word Mangere strikes fear into the hearts of many people, albeit of those whose only experience of the place is the motorway trip to the airport. Sure, it's ominous when the shops have roller doors for night security and there are streets where ramshackle houses and unkempt lawns are the norm, but on the whole the area is looking at a brighter future. Former farms and market gardens are being developed and the new houses bring a look of relative respectability to the place. Also important is the fact that the Mangere sewage purification works no longer pong constantly, thanks to a $450 million overhaul. During the five-year project, 500ha of oxidation ponds were returned to the sea and 13km of shoreline returned to the Manukau Harbour. The wildlife has returned in droves, and it's a great place for walking and bird-watching.

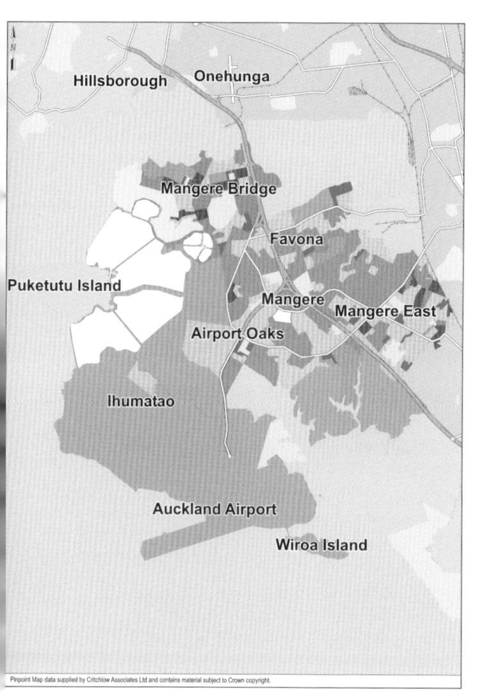

For colour key, see page 226

Population Profile

Population	53,304
% Aged Under 15 Years	31.61
% Aged Over 65 Years	6.61
% European	24.37
% Maori	19.01
% Pacific Peoples	53.83
% Asian	9.10

Who Lives There?

This is a very multicultural area, with Europeans, Maori, Pacific Islanders and Asians all having called Mangere home for a long time. Facing each other across Favona Rd are a Vietnamese Buddhist temple (a former state house, with a gold Buddha in the front yard) and a huge Tongan church (built in traditional style).

The newer subdivisions attract a lot of Indians, both from Fiji and from India. Mangere Bridge prices are higher than Favona or Mangere so it appeals to comparatively wealthier people.

Typical Homes

Being next to the sea, Mangere was one of the earliest parts of Auckland to be settled, so there is a smattering of villas and bungalows, often on the site of old farms or market gardens. Much of Mangere was developed by the state during the 1940s, 1950s and 1960s, with street after street of weatherboard homes. In Mangere Bridge, large brick-and-tile homes from the 1960s and 1970s dominate.

Amenities

Schools ★★★

Mangere is very family-oriented, and the families are often big, so you're never far from a school. Primary and intermediate options are plentiful. Several schools have religious affiliations, including the decile two co-ed Muslim school Al-Madinah, which delivers the New Zealand curriculum within an Islamic context.

The neighbourhood includes at least four other institutions catering for all levels including the recently established Southern Cross Campus, New Zealand's largest area school. A special feature is Te Kura Maori o Nga Tapuwae which provides a full curriculum in Maori.

At secondary level, choices include the Catholic De La Salle College, Auckland Seventh Day Adventist High School, and Mangere College.

For a full list, see page 270.

Shops ★★

Mangere Bridge has an established shopping centre. Tucked between the slopes of Mangere Mountain and the Kiwi Esplanade Reserve, it has an almost villagey atmosphere and offers most of the daily basics. Mangere Town Centre also sells just about everything, but it is run-down and rather depressing. Still, the shops of Otahuhu, Papatoetoe and Manukau are never far away.

Leisure ★★★

Mangere Mountain, once the site of one of the largest pa (fortified Maori village) in the region, is now a haven for recreation. It's a great place for walking (the view from the top is spectacular) and the sports fields are in regular use. Ambury Farm Park is a working farm where visitors are welcome. Located on the foreshore of the Manukau Harbour, more than 86 species of birds make their home. Ambury Park also has a horse-riding centre for people with disabilities.

The 100ha Otuataua Stonefields Historic Reserve near the tiny settlement of Ihumatao is fascinating, with remnants of early Maori and European occupation. There's a narrow strip of reserve along the pretty foreshore at Mangere Bridge. The abandoned bridge is now a popular spot for fishing and relaxing.

Moana-Nui-a-Kiwa Leisure Centre offers a full range of gym and swimming facilities, and there are regular exhibitions at the Mangere Community Arts Outreach Service. Dining out here generally means grabbing takeaways, although there are also casual ethnic cafes.

Real Estate

Trends

Mangere is a huge, sprawling and very diverse area, ranging from vast tracts of bland unkempt state housing to genteel waterfront residences in Mangere Bridge and new executive homes

in Mangere Heights (an affectation, given that Mangere is flat).

Most of the new subdivisions are on former farms or market gardens towards the airport. Three-bedroom homes in the subdivisions sell for around $350,000, compared with $250,000 to $280,000 in the older areas of Mangere.

With homeowners trying to get away with procuring as much room as they can for the lowest cost, authorised and unauthorised sleep-outs are a common sight.

This is still an affordable area for buyers who will never be able to contemplate buying a home in other parts of Auckland.

Best Streets

Kiwi Esplanade in Mangere Bridge has water views, nice houses, and a reserve running along its entire length. Nothing else can compete.

Why I Live There

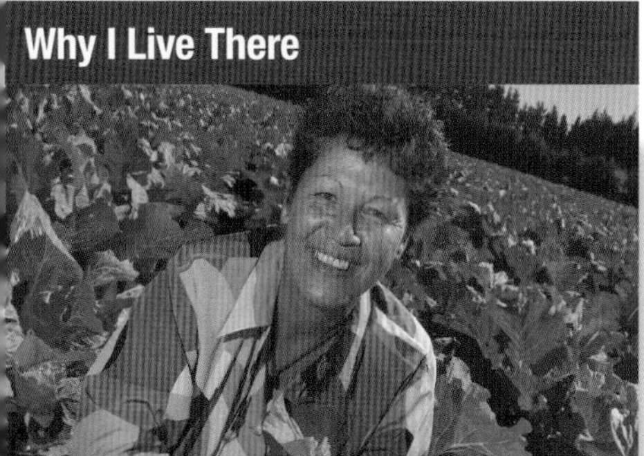

Organic Gardener Linda Lee

Linda Lee's grandfather was a Chinese market gardener in Mangere and her grandmother was Maori. Linda (Ngati Whatua, Te Arawa and Ngapuhi) grew up here and finds great sustenance for her soul in being back home. She established the Pukaki Worm Farm, a centre for educating the community about organic gardening and recycling, in 1999 as a way of giving back to the community that nurtured her. "This is a very historic and significant place," she says, "with an active volcano, the Manukau Harbour, fossilised kauri forests, good agricultural land, and two pa - Pukaki and Ihumatao. The people who live here are the remnants of Te Aakitai-Wai-o-Hua, the ancient tribe that was here before the great Maori migration."

At a Glance...

House Prices

Unit

Bedrooms	🛏 🛏
Price	$175,000 - $200,000

House

Bedrooms	🛏 🛏 🛏
Price	$250,000 - $350,000

Executive house

Bedrooms	🛏 🛏 🛏 🛏
Price	$375,000

Average Rents

Flat

Bedrooms	🛏 🛏
Price	$240/wk

House

Bedrooms	🛏 🛏
Price	$260/wk
Bedrooms	🛏 🛏 🛏
Price	$300/wk
Bedrooms	🛏 🛏 🛏 🛏
Price	$365/wk

There's high demand for rental properties here, but some landlords have problems with tenants not caring for properties, so be aware that this is not an investment for the faint-hearted.

Travel Times

From Mangere:

CBD	peak 60 min off peak 30 min
Southern motorway	2 min
Airport	5 min
Manukau city shops	10 min

Mangere is well-served by buses; the nearest train stations are Middlemore or Otahuhu.

Manukau/Clover Park ★★★★★

including Totara Heights, Flat Bush, East Tamaki Heights, Goodwood Heights, Chapel Downs, Wiri and Puhinui

Many people living in other parts of Auckland wouldn't give these suburbs a first look, let alone a second! But they are definitely worth considering if you like variety in geography, people and houses. You could even get a very good view at a very reasonable price. Most of this area has developed fairly quickly, which gives it a certain sameness. The newest subdivisions – where dairy cows crossing the road at milking time were a common sight a year or so ago – look very brash and man-made, but will soften in time. Large parts of East Tamaki, Wiri and Manukau are devoted to commercial and light industrial businesses. The juncture of Manukau/Wiri/Puhinui is dominated by the Manukau shopping centre and the endless streets of big retailers surrounding it, and by Rainbow's End amusement park.

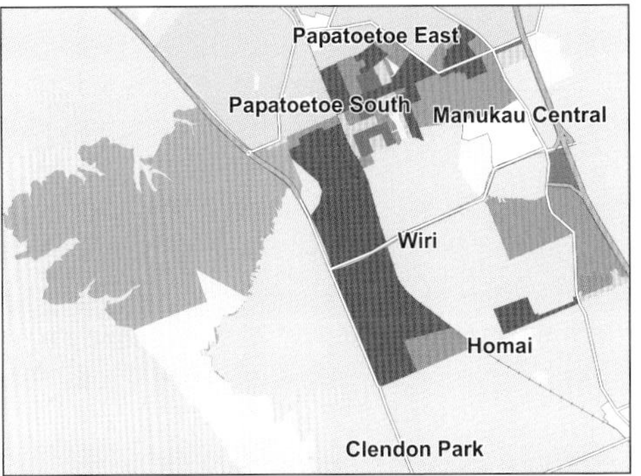

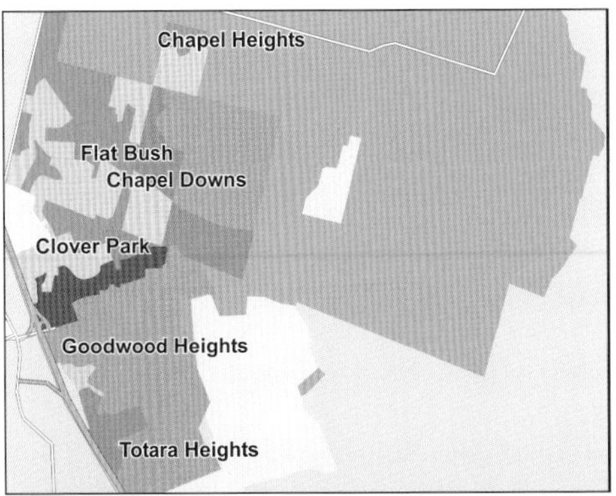

Population Profile

Population	31,632
% Aged Under 15 Years	29.47
% Aged Over 65 Years	5.73
% European	35.27
% Maori	17.61
% Pacific Peoples	36.47
% Asian	16.29

Who Lives There?

Auckland in the 21st century is ethnically a very diverse place, and you can see it al in these suburbs. Newer areas like Chape Downs are attracting young families who want a contemporary home at a good price. Totara Heights, with its views and leafy surroundings appeals to a more affluent and generally older demographic.

The area appeals to Asian immigrants too, with many moving here as renters, and then buying in the area once they're established.

Typical Homes

The standard Kiwi three-bedroom brick-and-tile house is everywhere, some meticulously maintained and some woefully neglected. With smaller sections and less time spent at home, townhouses are becoming very popular with developers and buyers. The majority of homes have been built as cheaply as possible.

But up at Manukau Heights and Totara Heights, it's a different story, with many multi-storey houses, often surrounded by mature gardens or tucked into patches of native bush.

Manukau and Wiri have extensive areas of fibrolite-clad state housing which, generally, has not aged well.

Amenities

Schools ★★

Hundreds of millions of dollars are to be spent on establishing schools in the Flat Bush area in the next decade, including a primary and a junior high school opening on Jeffs Rd between 2008 and 2011, and three schools – a primary, junior high and senior secondary school – on one Ormiston Rd site, each with its own principal.

These will join the already healthy number of primary and intermediate schools in the area. Much of Manukau/Wiri/Puhinui is in the highly-regarded Papatoetoe High School zone, and this has an impact on property prices. Others go to high schools in Manurewa or Otara.

For a full list, see page 270.

Shops ★★★★

Westfield Shoppingtown Manukau was one of the first shopping malls in Auckland, and it continues to go from strength to strength. It's a vibrant place with more than 120 stores, including Farmers and Foodtown.

In the past decade the streets surrounding the centre have become a vast ocean of retail and wholesale outlets, with the emphasis on bulk, bargain-style shopping. This is as far from main street shopping as you can get – without a car it would take you forever to get from one shop to another.

There is a shopping centre at Chapel Downs, and you're not far from The Hub and Botany Town Centre.

When the Flat Bush development is further down the track, residents should be able to buy most of what they need simply by strolling down the road.

New blocks of convenience shops – takeaways, greengrocers, video stores and bottle shops – continue to spring up near each of the new residential areas.

Leisure ★★★★

The $40 million TelstraClear Pacific Events Centre opened near Rainbow's End in April 2005. Its Pacific-themed structure includes a 700-seat theatre and a multi-purpose 3000-seat indoor arena.

Hayman Park next to the Manukau City Shopping Centre is a bonus for local families and for workers who want to take their lunch break outside. It is full of mature trees, and has a duck pond, a creek, and vast expanses of grass.

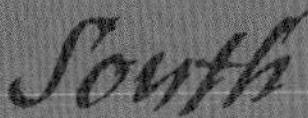

If you're travelling by car, the world of leisure activities is your oyster in this area. Totara Park is a haven of leafy tracks through native bush, with pleasant picnic spots and playgrounds, and a beautiful swimming pool. Some parts of the reserve are okay for mountain bikers.

Rainbow's End theme park entices families from all over Auckland, and is on the must-do list for many visitors to the city.

For eating out, there is ample choice in the shopping centre, as well as pubs and steak houses in the surrounding areas.

Real Estate

Trends

The property market is currently very buoyant in this area, and people are paying good prices in the expectation that it will keep on improving. There has been a lot of subdivision in the area. The arrival of Botany Downs further east has had a flow-on effect of improved image, and the promise of Flat Bush (New Zealand's most comprehensively planned new town and home to at least 40,000 people) being a high-quality development is also proving very beneficial. Agents report that buyers are confident about the area's future value.

One bedroom apartments are rare, but can be picked up occasionally for around $230,000. A new three-bedroom townhouse in Flat Bush will cost between $340,000 and $380,000.

Investors are still a key feature of the market in an area that has a large renting population.

Best Streets

For their elevation and views, Goodwood Dr in Goodwood Heights and Eugenia Rise in Totara Heights.

Smart Buy ✓

When development is well under way, Flat Bush should be a great place to live – the way all our suburbs ought to be, if only we'd thought about planning them properly.

At a Glance...

House Prices

Apartment

Bedrooms	
Price	$280,000

Unit

Bedrooms	
Price	$235,000 - $250,000

Family house

Bedrooms	
Price	$250,000 - $380,000

Executive house

Bedrooms	
Price	$550,000 - $700,000

Average Rents

Flat

Bedrooms	
Price	$245/wk

Apartment

Bedroom	
Price	$285/wk

House

Bedrooms	
Price	$315/wk

Travel Times

CBD	peak 60 min off peak 20 min
Motorway	5 min
Airport	15 min
Manukau city shopping centre	5 min
Botany Town Centre	10 min
Train to Britomart	20 min

Since the Wiri train station closed in 2005, the nearest station is Puhinui, but there are plans for a rail link to an underground station in Manukau's central business district.

Manurewa

Including Weymouth, Clendon Park, Homai, Hill Park, Manurewa East, Randwick Park, Wattle Downs and Conifer Grove

Manurewa demonstrates the breadth and depth of variety in Auckland real estate, by being made up of a hotch-potch of run-down state housing, luxurious contemporary homes, and some of the city's cheapest waterfront properties. There's a lot of coastline, thanks to three peninsulas jutting into the Manukau Harbour; it also has numerous reserves, many on the waterfront, and some glorious tracts of native bush. Manurewa is also home to the vast Auckland Regional Botanic Gardens, which are probably best known as the site of the Ellerslie Flower Show. The area is becoming very popular with families, and the new Alfriston College (which opened two years ago) is well regarded.

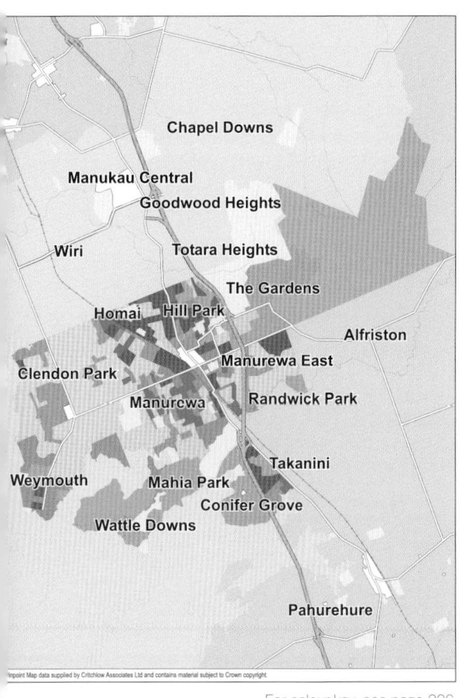

For colour key, see page 226

Population Profile

Population	61,434
% Aged Under 15 Years	28.84
% Aged Over 65 Years	7.04
% European	52.54
% Maori	26.99
% Pacific Peoples	19.99
% Asian	8.23

Who Lives There?

The availability of fairly cheap rental homes has made the area popular with those on low incomes, including refugees and other immigrants. Ethnicities represented include Iranians, Iraqis, Fijians, Indians (there is a Sikh temple on Great South Rd), Maori and Europeans. Blue collar workers who live in extended families and have a good community spirit make up the majority of residents.

To the east of the southern motorway around the botanic gardens, the homes are new and more upmarket, so the residents tend to be young professionals and families with more money. Further east, lifestylers live on the larger blocks of semi-rural land.

Typical Homes

Most Manurewa homes were built in the 1960s or later, so the most common materials are weatherboard and brick-and-tile and the sections are generously sized. There's some state and ex-state housing. The villas and bungalows seen in many other parts of Auckland are rare here. New and grander developments are typically of brick and plaster.

Amenities

Schools ★★★

With a large number of big families, this low-decile area has at least 18 primary schools (four include intermediate years), four dedicated intermediates and four secondary schools. A new primary school, Reremoana, opened in Wattle Downs in 2006. The Gardens School in Manurewa is also quite new (2002). Well resourced and highly regarded, it's the only decile 10 primary here.

At secondary level, Manurewa High School is the largest with a roll close to 2100 students. The two-year-old Alfriston College, which some parts of Manurewa are zoned for, is the most highly-regarded in the area.

For a full list, see page 270.

Shops ★★

Manurewa has mainstreet and mall shopping, but both are looking rather down at heel. It appears that those with discretionary income prefer to spend it elsewhere. There are a lot of $2-style shops, and a lot of Indian takeaways and Indian sweet shops. Most people go straight to Manukau City to do their shopping.

Leisure ★★★

Nathan Homestead, built in 1925 and still surrounded by 3.5ha of much-loved lawn and gardens, is an arts, community and function centre. The Manurewa Leisure Centre has full gymnasium facilities and a swimming pool.

For eating out, if you don't want takeaways then you'll need to head elsewhere.

Parks and reserves dotted all over the place make life more pleasant here. Totara Park and the Auckland Regional Botanic Gardens are the key places; other parks like Weymouth Domain which runs along more than three kilometres of coastline, are well used by locals.

The well regarded Manukau Golf Club is nestled between Wattle Downs and Conifer Grove.

Real Estate

Trends

Although the price you can expect to pay for a home here is as diverse as the area itself, with median monthly sales prices hovering around $250,000, it's still a bargain area. How long it can remain that way, given its proximity to the water and the rising values in other historically cheap areas such as Otahuhu, is another question.

For now, though, Manurewa has some of Auckland's cheapest waterfront property – harbourside homes in Mahia Park and

Nathan Homestead

Weymouth are being snapped up for $480,000 or even less.

Many sites in the area are large and, as prices rise, will be ripe for subdivision or complete redevelopment.

Hill Park and The Gardens are popular as well as anything near the reputable Alfriston College. However, in every one of these suburbs, prices are heading steadily up.

Best Streets

Any of the streets in Conifer Grove or next to the botanic gardens.

Local Hero: Auckland Regional Botanic Gardens

Every year more than 800,000 visitors enjoy the 65ha of gardens, first opened in 1982 – but there's no resting on laurels here. In March 2005 the new Potter Children's Garden and the much improved visitor's centre were officially opened. The children's garden includes a Coastal Garden, Sight and Sound area, Decay Garden, Vegetable Garden, Boardwalk and Creature Pool, surrounded by a grove of puriri trees. There is also a library with more than 2000 books on plants.

Every year in November, the gardens play host to the Ellerslie Flower Show. It's been going for 11 years, attracts around 70,000 people and features exhibition gardens, floral displays, garden art and entertainment.

At a Glance...

House Prices

Unit

Bedrooms

Price $220,000 - $230,000

House

Bedrooms

Price $230,000 - $270,000

Executive house

Bedrooms

Price $450,000 - $600,000

Average Rents

Flat

Bedrooms

Price $235/wk

House

Bedrooms

Price $250/wk

Bedrooms

Price $290/wk

Bedrooms

Price $370/wk

Travel Times

From Manurewa:

CBD	peak 60 min off peak 20 min by train 20 min
Southern motorway	2 min
Airport	10 min
Manukau city shopping centre	10 min
Botany Town Centre	15 min

There is a very good bus service, and three nearby train stations: Homai, Manurewa and Te Mahia. Traffic congestion in Manurewa should be eased by a new motorway link taking traffic from the Southern Motorway to the airport.

Otahuhu ★★½

including Middlemore and Papatoetoe

The narrowest part of the Auckland isthmus (a mere 1.3km across) is home to the staunchly working-class suburb of Otahuhu. It's an established area, as evidenced by the very English-looking, red-brick façade of Otahuhu College, which opened in 1931. It's also a very diverse area, with a great mix of cultures living side by side. Also side by side are the park-like grounds of King's College, one of the most expensive private schools in New Zealand, and Middlemore Hospital, which provides medical care to some of the poorest families in the country. Papatoetoe comes in two parts: "old" Papatoetoe and the newer Hunter's Corner. The area's about to get a huge injection of job opportunities with the massive developments at nearby Sylvia Park and on the Waiouru Peninsula. Otahuhu is one neighbourhood to watch, offering good value buying while being relatively close to central Auckland.

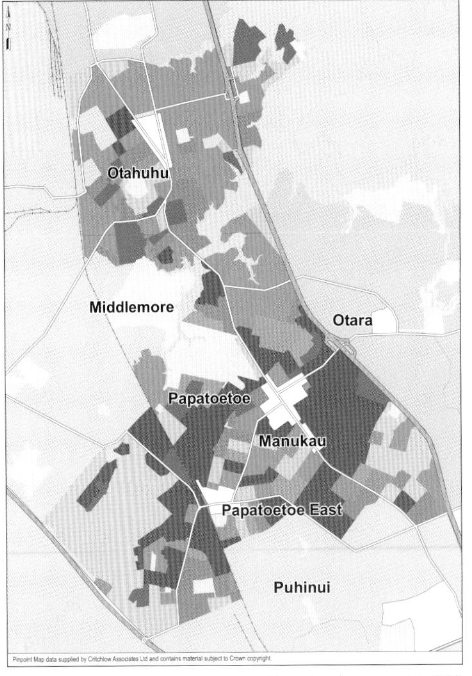

For colour key, see page 226

Population Profile

Population	39,006
% Aged Under 15 Years	25.78
% Aged Over 65 Years	10.41
% European	40.66
% Maori	17.05
% Pacific Peoples	27.81
% Asian	20.13

Who Lives There?

Otahuhu and Middlemore are definitely blue-collar suburbs – and proud of it. The affordability of these areas, as well as their proximity to the Mangere Immigration Hostel and the airport, has also made them attractive to immigrant families. Otahuhu is particularly popular with Chinese and Indians (there is a Sikh temple there), and Middlemore with Pacific Islanders. Papatoetoe High School is known in some quarters as "the grammar school of the south", attracting families who desire a private-school-style education but lack the financial resources.

Typical Homes

Some of the city's most affordable California bungalows and character villas are in Otahuhu.

but many are showing signs of neglect. Cheap housing has always been in demand here. In Papatoetoe, there are some 1930s bungalows, but the bulk of development occurred during the 1960s and 1970s. Those brick-and-tile homes were built well and have on the whole been consistently cared for.

Amenities

Schools ★★

While predominantly a low decile area, Otahuhu is home to one of the most exclusive private schools in New Zealand, Kings College. The fierce rivalry between the First XVs of Otahuhu College and King's College says it all – geographically, they're only divided by a fence, but in every other way they couldn't be further apart. One is a state school serving a poor community while the other is a select institution for the children of the privileged.

Primary and intermediate schools are plentiful and there are four local secondary schools. For a full list, see page 270.

Shops ★★★

Otahuhu's main street is a lively, pleasant place to be. Many of the big chain stores have deserted in favour of the malls, but most of what you need is here in some form or another. Middlemore has no shopping centre, but corner dairies and liquour stores aplenty.

Old Papatoetoe also offers good shopping; Hunter's Corner has a mall called Hunter's Plaza, and while its mainstreet has also been successfully spruced up, locals regularly voice their concern about the working girls, and boys, who come out at nightfall. As the vast new Sylvia Park development opens, it may pose a challenge to retailers in all of these areas.

Leisure ★★★

The adjacent Auckland Golf Club and Grange Golf Club attract mostly those from other suburbs: locals are more likely to play rugby, league, netball or kilikiti (a form of cricket). There are plenty of public reserves, many alongside the Tamaki River.

The new recreation and youth centre at Fairburn Reserve includes a sports stadium and youth drop-in centre. It's the first stage in a leisure precinct which will eventually have an aquatic centre and larger library.

Papatoetoe has the Centennial Pools and a roller skating rink. Otahuhu has rowing and badminton clubs, as well as a fantastic range of good, cheap, authentic Asian restaurants.

Real Estate

Trends

Prices have risen dramatically in Otahuhu in the past couple of years: with the declining affordability of areas closer to Auckland's CBD, buyers have been forced to cast their eyes in a wider arc. Many have been pleasantly surprised by what they can get here: traditional Kiwi-sized sections, good public transport and motorway access, old bungalows just begging to be improved.

In Otahuhu East (near the motorway), some large pieces of ex-glasshouse land have been subdivided. Three bedroom homes here (some on the water) are selling for up to $400,000 and

one architect-designed house on the Tamaki River recently sold for nearly $800,000.

The area is popular with investors – for the continuing good yields and for the capital gain some feel will certainly come.

Best Streets

Princes St East, Church St, Hutton St and Avenue Rd in Otahuhu. Fitzroy St, St George St and Omana Rd in Papatoetoe.

Smart Buy ✓

It might be a good idea to get in quick before word gets around that you can buy a spacious three-bedroom bungalow on 1000m² for $320,000. While you're at it, check out the houses along the estuary for affordable waterfront property.

Local Hero: Dawn Raid Entertainment

Since 1999, Brotha D and YDNA's Dawn Raid Entertainment has been discovering, recording and releasing undiscovered artists. In an industry heavily dominated by million-dollar marketing budgets and international influences, Dawn Raid wanted to show South Auckland and its talented musicians in a positive light. They did that: artists like Deceptikonz, Adeaze, Ill Semantics and Aaradhna are now well known.

The entrepreneurial crew also has spin-off businesses in streetwear, a digital recording studio which can be hired by the public, screenprinting, graphics and web design. No flies on these guys.

At a Glance...

House Prices

Flat

Bedroom	🛏
Price	$150,000 +

Unit

Bedrooms	🛏🛏
Price	$175,000 +

House

Bedrooms	🛏🛏🛏
Price	$260,000 - $400,000
Bedrooms	🛏🛏🛏🛏
Price	$360,000 - $500,000

Average Rents

Flat

Bedroom	🛏
Price	$170/wk
Bedrooms	🛏🛏
Price	$210/wk

House

Bedrooms	🛏🛏🛏
Price	$315/wk

Travel Times

From Otahuhu:

CBD	peak 45 min off peak 20 min
Southern motorway	5 min
Airport	10 min
Manukau city shopping centre	10 min
Train to Britomart	20 min

The area has a very good bus service, and Otahuhu has a train station (although it's a bit of a hike from the town centre). Otahuhu's motorway access and egress is being improved with the addition of a fourth lane either way between Water Street and Bairds Road, due for completion in March 2007.

What is that rumbling noise between Dannemora and Donegal Park? It's a bevy of bulldozers preparing for what is probably the most deliberately planned community in the history of Aotearoa. The new suburb of Flat Bush, in Manukau City, has been a concept since 1997 but is steadily blossoming toward reality and an eventual population of 40,000 by about 2020.

And the planners' vision may be pretty close to 20/20 on the new Flat Bush, since they seem determined to eliminate what they perceive to be the mistakes of suburbia, with its garage-dominated street-facings and the propensity of its inhabitants to drive five minutes to the dairy and back home again. Here residents will find amenities and services have been strategically placed, shops and eateries within a five- or 10-minute walk, and streams which look as though they had always been there, mainly because they have always been there. (The plan calls for enhancing, not eliminating or burying, the natural ditches and waterways, allowing eels and fish to get safely to the ocean.)

More than a quarter of the area will be left as open space. About 22km of roadway will have housing on only one side and no one will live more than a five-minute walk from one of the "green fingers". The greener surrounds are possible because housing will be dense: in the largest zone there will be 17 to 25 households per hectare, compared with 12 in older areas of the city.

The development of the 18ha town centre is in the hands of the city council, which owns the land. Future plans include a 20,000-capacity space for concerts and festivals and also an outdoor ampitheatre.

A Jeffs Rd primary/junior high school complex will be ready in 2010. An even more extensive complex, including a high school, is planned, as well as two more primary schools, and each of the four schools will have early-childhood centres attached.

The name Flat Bush, however, may not stick. It's already the name of a suburb east of Otara and west of the new development. "Ormiston" is being bandied about as a replacement. Historically, though, the entire region was called Flat Bush because there was no Maori name for it and the settling Europeans were amazed by the level conformity of the kahikatea bush.

Otara 

including East Tamaki

The name Otara is well-known outside of Auckland – and unfortunately not for gooc reasons. This place has come to symbolise poverty, and it's true that there are areas where unkempt, barefoot children roam the streets with malnourished dogs, and the gardens aren't as tidy as they might be (abandoned rusty cars can really ruin the look of a place). But Otara is also home to the industrious Manukau Institute of Technology, the unbeatable Saturday market, vibrant churches of myriad denominations and some of the country's best young musicians. East Tamaki, to the north of Otara, was primarily industria until a few years ago. Now subdivisions resembling those in the affluent eastern suburbs are springing up; some are terraced apartments with retail or office space on the grounc floor and living areas above.

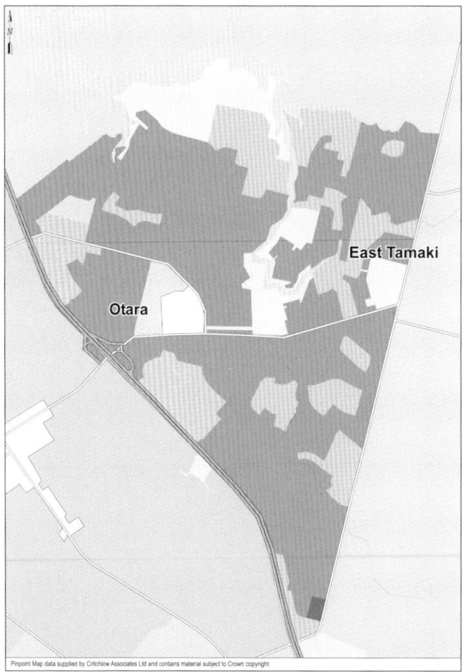

For colour key, see page 226

Population Profile

Population	16,371
% Aged Under 15 Years	35.55
% Aged Over 65 Years	5.24
% European	10.61
% Maori	21.26
% Pacific Peoples	71.49
% Asian	2.18

Who Lives There?

Otara is predominantly populated by Pacific Islanders and, to a lesser extent, Maori. The new subdivisions in East Tamaki have meant an influx of Indians into the area. There's a high percentage of blue-collar workers and unemployed. Huge numbers of Asians buy and sell at the Saturday morning market, but apparently they're not locals, coming from far and wide because it's such a great market.

Typical Homes

The classic mid-20th-century state house (three bedrooms, weatherboard-clad) is everywhere in Otara. There are stand-alones, duplexes and multi-unit townhouses. Over in East Tamaki, the homes (brick-and-tile with internal garaging) are slightly larger (with three or four bedrooms) and the sections slightly smaller.

Amenities

Schools ★★★

Otara has at least 12 primary schools, two intermediates and two secondary schools. Bairds Mainfreight Primary School, with a roll close to 400, gained national profile as the first school to win a business sponsorship and a recent ERO report described the teaching as consistent "and high quality."

Clover Park Middle School is a large, composite middle school for years 7-10 and in 2002 it was named the Goodman Fielder Composite School of the Year. Sir Edmund Hillary Collegiate has a primary, intermediate and high school (each with their own principals) on the same site.

The Manukau Institute of Technology is the biggest educational drawcard around here, offering 1500 full-time and part-time certificate, diploma, degree and post-graduate study programmes.

For a full list, see page 270

Shops ★★

You can get the basics at the Otara Town Centre... plus lavalava fabric by the truckload, tapa cloth by the kilometre and corned beef by the tonne. The weekend flea market is an Auckland-wide institution, but, given the choice, most people would travel to either Manukau or Botany Downs to do most of their shopping.

Leisure ★★

Otara is blessed with plentiful reserves, including an extensive one with a walkway along the foreshore of the Otara Creek. The basketball courts at O Tamariki Reserve, opposite the town centre, appear to be in constant use, day and night.

Manukau City Council runs a community centre with a difference in Otara: Takutai-a-kiwa, the Otara Music Arts Centre, has a recording studio, which is used by local amateur and professional musicians. Fresh Gallery opened in the Otara shopping centre in May 2006, to showcase the work of local artists. Next to the Otara town centre is a free swimming pool. The dining experience in Otara is largely fast food, with some exotic options at the Saturday market. East Tamaki has several large casual steak-and-chips-style restaurants, targeting families and the after-work crowd.

Real Estate

Trends

Prices are starting to rise, with other more desirable suburbs now out of reach of

many buyers. The development of the high-tech Highbrook business park on the Waiouru Peninsula just to the north of Otara is expected to at least maintain this momentum. It will provide 15,000 further jobs within the next decade and will have its own motorway interchange which will also be handy for Botany Downs, Flat Bush and Pakuranga. Its design makes the most of the site's green views and peninsula site, and has already won an award from an American professional body.

Otara is attracting more owner-occupiers, and there is a great increase in the amount of renovation going on. Four-bedroom homes are particularly popular for the larger and extended families that tend to live in South Auckland.

While the centre of East Tamaki is still primarily commercial and light industrial, the edges are developing very quickly into residential areas.

Best Streets

Anything near the Otara shopping centre or Manukau Institute of Technology.

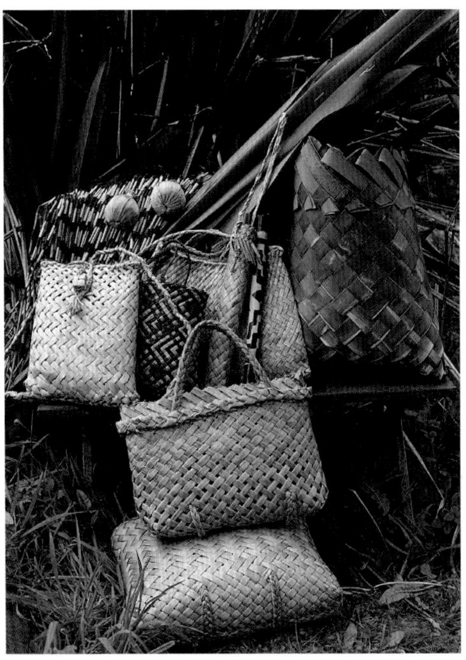

At a Glance...

House Prices

House

Bedrooms	🛏 🛏 🛏
Price	$220,000 - $260,000

Better house

Bedrooms	🛏 🛏 🛏 🛏
Price	$270,000 - $300,000

Average Rents

Flat

Bedrooms	🛏 🛏
Price	$275/wk

House

Bedrooms	🛏 🛏 🛏
Price	$310/wk
Bedrooms	🛏 🛏 🛏 🛏
Price	$425/wk

There's plenty of demand for rental properties in Otara but the area doesn't suit every investor. Many tenants don't come from a culture of home ownership and properties are not always cared for.

Travel Times

CBD	peak 80 min off peak 20 min
Southern motorway	3 min
Airport	15 min
Manukau city shopping centre	10 - 15 min

The area is well served by buses.

Papakura

including Takanini, Red Hill, Ardmore, Rosehill, Drury, Hingaia and Pahurehure

Papakura is where the city meets the country. Although it's less rural with every passing year and every new subdivision, it still feels like a country town and has its own council. As well as catering for its own population, townies and country folk, Papakura provides retail and other essential services to the lifestyle block crowd from Whitford, Clevedon and Brookby, which have few shops of their own. Although Papakura itself is considered a suburb of Auckland, it's big enough to have its own off-shoots – Red Hill and Pahurehure. Pahurehure is the most desirable area, with demand outstripping supply, especially for newer homes. However, the recently completed Addison residential development in Takanini is also considered highly desirable. New subdivisions on the Hingaia Peninsula, across the motorway, will have instant kudos just for having the horsey set at Karaka for neighbours.

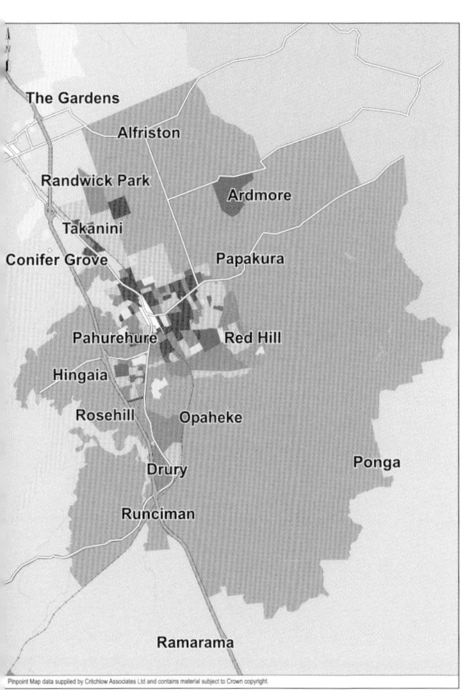

For colour key, see page 226

Population Profile

Population	36,135
% Aged Under 15 Years	25.58
% Aged Over 65 Years	9.95
% European	69.95
% Maori	24.43
% Pacific Peoples	7.83
% Asian	5.23

Who Lives There?

Although it has quite a diverse population, Papakura is still a fairly conservative town. The community is close-knit and largely working class. Papakura is considered a good place to raise a family - although bored teenagers who no longer see Calf Club Day as a social highlight might not agree!

When townie residents retire, they often buy a little block of land just outside town; when farmers retire, they do the opposite and move into town.

The area is earmarked to accommodate an extra 10,000 people over the next 40 years.

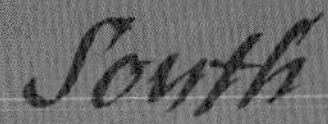

Typical Homes

Good solid standard Kiwi homes are the norm in central Papakura, which was mostly developed in the 1950s to 1970s. Red Hill and Pahurehure are newer developments, and the plaster homes which have sprung up around the substantial older farmhouses reflect that.

Amenities

Schools ★★★

The area is well-served with primary schools (both town-based and rural), most of which include intermediate years. The high decile Rosehill College is well regarded and the largest in the area with a roll close to 2000. Some parts of Papakura are in-zone for the increasingly popular Alfriston College in Manurewa. There are also three new schools planned for Takanini.

For a full list, see page 270.

Shops ★★★

While shops on the main street provide many necessities, luxuries had to be purchased elsewhere – but this is all changing, with bigger retailers moving in. Southgate shopping centre at Takanini including retailers like Hill & Stewart and Mitre 10, as well as some eateries.

Leisure ★★★★

There are ample parks and reserves in and around Papakura. There's also a golf course, and a pleasant drive in the countryside takes you to beaches as well as the country settlements of Whitford and Clevedon. Papakura is established enough to have a museum and an art gallery, and diverse enough to have many different ethnic eateries.

Real Estate

Trends

The diversity of the area is demonstrated by the price range for two-bedroom units, which start at $200,000 in Papakura itself and rocket to $325,000 in Pahurehure.

Lifestyle blocks are in high demand and very short supply, which keeps prices healthy.

Sections in the first stage of the new 450-lo Karaka Harbourside Estate on the Hingaia Peninsula start at $300,000 (for around 450m²) up to $600,000 (there are a few sections over 600m²).

Best Streets

In Pahurehure, Rushgreen Ave; in Papakura Opaheke Rd. Red Hill Rd (in Red Hill, of course is elevated and has beautiful views.

At a Glance...

House Prices

Unit

Bedrooms	2
Price	$200,000 - $325,000

House on full site

Bedrooms	3
Price	$290,000 - $400,000

Executive house

Bedrooms	4
Price	$550,000 - $650,000

Lifestyle block with modest house

Price	$550,000 – $750,000

Average Rents

Flat

Bedroom	1
Price	$150 – $220/wk

House

Bedrooms	3
Price	$260 – $290/wk
Bedrooms	4
Price	$360 – $410/wk

Travel Times

From Papakura:

CBD	peak 75 min off peak 25 min by train 50 min
Southern motorway	5 min
Airport	25 min
Manukau city shopping centre	15 min

There is a regular bus and train service.

ncluding Karaka

Gone are the days when Pukekohe was best known for its ability to grow great onions and potatoes – the word "onion" doesn't even appear on www.pukekohe.org.nz! 'oday most of the residents are more interested in motor sport or hanging out at the own's cafés, knowing that some day the town will succumb to Auckland's rampant urban prawl but enjoying the slightly hokey country town-ness of it all for now. The traditional ural businesses are still there, but they're no longer the essence of the place. Pukekohe, 2km south of the Auckland CBD, was settled by Europeans in the 1860s. Long a service own to the surrounding farmers and market gardeners, it is now the lively heart of ranklin District. A stroll down the main shopping street reveals Pukekohe as a pleasant, ncreasingly affluent, unpretentious and substantial country town.

For colour key, see page 226

Population Profile

Population	13,623
% Aged Under 15 Years	25.32
% Aged Over 65 Years	13.06
% European	69.68
% Maori	19.58
% Pacific Peoples	4.98
% Asian	7.66

Who Lives There?

The population is predominately European, but there are also Maori, Indian and Chinese. Pukekohe is attractive to those who need to be near Auckland but want a rural lifestyle with all the amenities of an established country town. People here are mostly middle-class, although there are a few seriously wealthy people too, especially in Karaka.

It's been noted that quite a few former All Blacks and high profile rugby players have moved to Pukekohe, because they don't get the unwanted attention they tend to attract in a more metropolitan area.

Typical Homes

Dwellings run the full spectrum, from old farmhouses, villas and bungalows, through to more modern brick-and-tile and weatherboard homes. The new developments tend to be brick-and-tile or have plastered finishes.

Amenities

Schools ★★★

Pukekohe has at least 11 primary schools (six include intermediate years), an intermediate school and two secondary schools. The private schools ACG Strathallan and Pukekohe Christian School are also in the area, catering for all levels.

The high decile Pukekohe East School continues to receive favourable ERO reports along with the equally well-regarded Pukekohe Hill School.

The semi-rural Pukekohe Intermediate has recently been renovated.

The decile six Pukekohe High School is the main state co-ed secondary school here, with a roll close to 1500. Wesley College (for girls) is also in the area.

For a full list, see page 270.

Shops ★★★★

Pukekohe has excellent main-street shopping. Overall it's a very pleasant place to be. The street was revamped in a pretty country-style a few years ago. The busy town centre has more than 200 businesses offering everything from tractors to fine wines.

There is also a booming retail area in Manukau Rd, with large car parks. Big retailers like Bunnings and Harvey Norman have arrived in town, but there's no room for them in the main street – and that will ensure that it keeps its much-loved character.

Leisure ★★★★

Locals are spoiled for choice, especially if they're keen on outdoor activities.

Pukekohe Park is the home of motorsport, and horse racing is getting bigger and bigger here.

There is a stadium, tennis and squash courts, gyms, an all-weather hockey ground, golf course, a recreation centre with a heated pool and courts. The fairly new Cosmopolitan Club sports complex has indoor and outdoor bowling greens, 10-pin bowling and more. There's a clay target-shooting club not far out of town, and the traditional A & P show still pulls the crowds.

Spookers is located in the former nurses' hostel in the old Kingseat Hospital grounds. Basically you pay for the pleasure of having freakily made-up actors frighten the bejeezus out of you in either the corn maze (summer only), the haunted forest or the haunted house.

Drive 40 minutes east or west and you're at the sea: many locals have baches on the Coromandel Peninsula.

And if you like the sophistication of city-style restaurants and cafés but hate the crowds, this is place for you – a relaxed weekend brunch can be just that, because you're not fighting 50 other people for a table.

Real Estate

Trends

Pukekohe has some very affordable properties, and is definitely worth a look: two-bedroom units start at around $230,000 and in the less desirable parts of town you can get a three-bedroom house on a full site for $250,000! This is a land of contrasts, so in a better area the same house might go for $450,000. Similarly, four bedrooms could set you back $700,000 or more in a very swanky part of town.

Little old family farms which are no longer economical are in great demand as lifestyle blocks, with the price being greatly influenced by location. For $1.5 million or thereabouts, you could be the proud owner of either 12ha at Pokeno, complete with established kiwifruit orchards for some income to support your lifestyle, or a whopping 27ha at less-desirable Ararimu, with a brand new house.

Best Streets

Sunset Dr and its off-shoot Cloverlea Pl are sought after because they back on to a pleasant reserve and are very close to Pukekohe Hill School.

Karaka

To the north of Pukekohe, Karaka is a lifestyle area of mainly 4ha blocks, popular with the same sort of people who flock to Whitford to live. Numbers are a good way to get a handle on the sort of place this is. Westbury, the 37ha Karaka stud farm of London-based Kiwi businessman Eric Watson, for example, is estimated to be worth about $60 million. A hectare of land in Karaka will cost anything upwards of $700,000, and that's without a view or a house. Mind you, they're rare. In Karaka Park, lifestyle properties sell for $1.5 million to $2 million.

Fees for senior students at local private school Strathallan are almost $12,000 a year. Strathallan is one of the largest independent school complexes in New Zealand, set on 14.5ha of gently rolling country with a tranquil tidal inlet winding round the property.

The Karaka Sales Centre is well-known as the home of the National Premier Yearling Sale, where each year tens of millions of dollars passes from one well-shod horse-lover to another.

Yes, this is a land of privileged beings, a world away from their neighbours across the Pahurehure Inlet: Weymouth, Wattle Downs and Conifer Grove. But when you're just passing through, Karaka could be any pretty part of rural New Zealand. Except, of course, that it's so close to urban amenities. Pukekohe is less than 10 minutes' drive south; Papakura about the same to the east.

Why I Live There

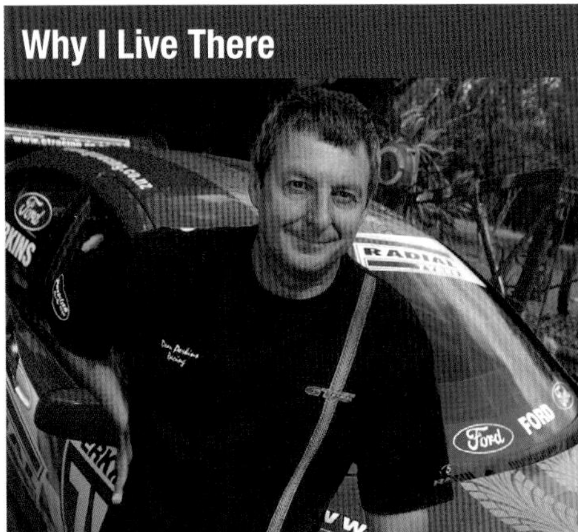

Racing Driver Dean Perkins

Racing driver Dean Perkins and his wife moved to Pukekohe 16 years ago because they wanted to raise their family in the country. For Dean, who says he's always been a petrol-head, the fact that New Zealand's top motor racing track was nearby was definitely a bonus. They bought a 3ha block and moved an old house on to it. The 200-pupil Buckland School was "brilliant" for their children.

Dean says Pukekohe's a very friendly place, and as a self-employed engineer it was easy for him to make good contacts and get to know everybody.

The "muscle car" his team built and ran about five years ago was always a crowd-pleaser at the track. Now Dean's involved in the New Zealand V8 Touring Car Championship, considered the pinnacle of local motor racing.

Smart Buy ✓

Smaller lifestyle blocks are taking a while to trade, because of the financial leap required up from a decent house. You might get a bargain and some serious capital gain: intensive development during the next few years is going to make those little rural oases more attractive than ever.

At a Glance...

House Prices

House

Bedrooms	
Price	$250,000 +
Bedrooms	
Price	$300,000 - $450,000

House on a big section

Bedrooms	
Price	$490,000 - $700,000

Large lifestyle block

Price	$600,000 - $1,000,000

Residential section, 500m²

Price	$300,000 +

Average Rents

Flat

Bedrooms	
Price	$215/wk

House

Bedrooms	
Price	$280/wk
Bedrooms	
Price	$330/wk

Travel Times

CBD	peak 75 min off peak 35 min
Southern motorway	10 min
Airport	30 min
Manukau city shopping centre	20 min

The area is served by buses and trains; the trains are not very frequent, as most don't currently go further south than Papakura.

where to live in AUCKLAND

Facts & Figures

Each neighbourhood in this book features a map colour-coded according to eleven population groups. This neighbourhood classification system, known as MOSAIC® is created by PMP MICROMARKETING, a division of PMP Limited.

MOSAIC® combines information on consumer demographics, households, lifestyles and attitudes so you can see who might live next door if you choose to buy in an area. The detailed descriptions on the following pages highlight characteristics such as what sports and activities people enjoy, typical occupations and even what they eat for dinner.

Information is gathered from the following sources:

- Property attribute data provided by Quotable Value NZ
- New Zealand Census data from Statistics NZ
- Motor vehicle data from Cadmus
- Market research data sourced from Roy Morgan Research

For more information on MOSAIC® and other segmentation and mapping solutions, contact PMP MICROMARKETING on 0800 938 555.

GROUP A

Elite Professionals

Elite Professionals are upper class mature families, located in affluent urban areas, though also increasingly on rural lifestyle blocks. They are typically between 45 and 54 years of age. Elite Professionals are successful, degree-qualified and work long hours in occupations that provide them with the highest median household incomes of all MOSAIC Groups, at over $78,000 per annum. The majority are employed as white-collar professionals and managers. Their houses are of the highest value, and consist mainly of large separate houses and apartments, with many of these being owned outright. These neighbourhoods revel in social interaction and their residents can often be seen sailing around the harbour, enjoying a game of tennis or golf, or at the beach. Keeping up with the cutting edge of fashion and technology at exclusive stores is considered a must. Fine dining at exclusive restaurants and cafes or hosting dinner parties is enjoyed regularly, especially over a premium bottle of wine. Elite Professionals like attending cultural activities such as ballet, opera and live theatre. Their occupations demand that they keep abreast of current affairs and the latest trends, so they are avid readers of newspapers and business, motoring and home lifestyle magazines.

GROUP B

Comfortable & Secure

Comfortable & Secure are typically middle-aged families with teenage children, or empty nesters. They are reasonably well qualified, and work as mid-level managers, professionals and technicians. Their household incomes are high, at over $60,000 the second highest of all MOSAIC Groups. They predominantly live in separate houses that they own outright. Busy with work and family commitments, these people generally don't have much time to spend cooking. When they do have a chance to relax, they like to spend it keeping up-to-date with ways to improve their homes. Given that home ownership is high this is not surprising, and many even admit to being more interested in their house than their career. Popular pastimes include jogging and going to the gym, as well as water sports such as sailing and power boating. Surfing the internet, shopping, frequenting cafes and weekends at the beach are other common ways to relax. Motor vehicle ownership is high across the group, with cars often purchased on looks - particularly by the teenaged members of the household. They keep up to date with current affairs through newspapers, television and the internet, and read major women's, home and lifestyle and business magazines.

Stylish Singles

Stylish Singles represent a mix of young professionals and students, and are typically aged between 20 and 34. The majority live in inner-suburban flats or close to tertiary campuses. Success-driven and with high qualification levels, most work in professional and technical occupations where they earn well above average household incomes - over $48,000 per annum. Stylish Singles live for the moment and will try anything once. They are extroverted and sociable, often letting their hair down at bars and clubs. Cars, clothes and accessories are seen as an extension of themselves. They wear stylish clothing with the right labels, and express themselves through conspicuous purchases. They were born to shop, and aren't afraid to use credit to buy the things they want. These people are technologically savvy - "early adopters" - and are into computers, DVD players and associated technical gadgets. They are heavy internet users and also cultured, generally appreciating art and fine food, but are just as comfortable with takeaways and a movie. Keeping fit is important, and exercise is often slotted into their busy schedules. Stylish Singles enjoy sporting activities such as aerobics, rugby, surfing and jet-skiing. On winter weekends, they can often be seen on the slopes of the nation's skifields.

GROUP C

Family Balance

Family Balance are usually middle-aged families with young school-aged children, located in the outer suburbs. A high proportion have two or more children. They predominantly live in separate houses in average condition, with slightly below average property values due to their location. Home ownership rates are high, and Family Balance take pride in their homes. Balancing family and career, they work hard to support their families in a variety of occupations, from trades to professional and technical occupations. Household incomes average just under $46,000. Shopping is completed after work or on weekends. Value for money is a key factor in the purchase decision process and Family Balance make a conscious effort to buy New Zealand-made products. Family Balance are not technically minded or particularly concerned with fashion. They prefer the familiar and simple things in life, such as motor sport, hunting and fishing. While not overly concerned with image, some are increasingly concerned with health issues, such as cholesterol. Increasing numbers are taking up physical activities such as walking, jogging, and working out at the gym.

GROUP D

Kiwiana

This group of classic Kiwis contains a mixture of ages and family groups - from young families to older retirees. Kiwiana live in a mixture of localities, including big city suburbs. Their houses are valued close to the national median, if not slightly below, and are in average condition. These tend to be rented privately, or owned with a mortgage. Occupations are more manual in nature or in trades, which bring home slightly below average household incomes of $38,000. Having to make their earnings stretch, Kiwiana look for bargains and are the most attracted to discounts, promotions and special offers. Although influenced by price, Kiwiana still only buy products they know and trust, including brands they have grown up with. This reluctance to try new things is highlighted by the fact they are likely to buy the same food from week to week. When it comes to fashion these people prefer function over style, and are somewhat hesitant when it comes to technology and the internet. Traditional Kiwi sports such as rugby, rugby league and cricket are popular with younger people, with pursuits such as darts popular with older people. Magazine readership is high within the Kiwiana types.

GROUP E

GROUP F

Local Pride

Local Pride contains a mixture of young families, and older 50-somethings, with a relatively high incidence of households containing more than one family. These people are proud of their close-knit local communities. Houses are generally separate dwellings, of average quality and below average capital value. However, their homes are built on above average sized sections, typically the classic quarter acre section. Homes are generally mortgaged. Education levels are among the lowest, and consequently some struggle to find employment. The most common jobs include trades, manual occupations and work in the primary sector, such as in agriculture and fishing. Household income levels of $37,000 are below average, but this doesn't necessarily mean they struggle, as the cost of living is significantly lower in their neighbourhoods. Local Pride live conservatively and are more likely to watch television at home than hold dinner parties or attend cultural events. They do not spend extravagantly and rarely eat at expensive restaurants. They can occasionally be found buying takeaways such as fish and chips. Local Prides don't welcome change, and are not particularly interested in technology.

GROUP G

Blue Collar Owners

Blue Collar Owners consist of families, generally aged between 20 and 34. These households contain a mixture of married and defacto couples, along with the occasional solo parent family. Home values are low and there is a mixture of government owned, privately rented and mortgaged houses. Tertiary qualifications are not common, and the average household income, at $35,000, is below average. Common occupations include agriculture and fisheries, trades and manual jobs. Unemployment is high. Blue Collar Owners are not interested in fashion, nor exercise such as aerobics and running. However, tough team sports such as rugby and rugby league are popular. Blue Collar Owners enjoy entering competitions and using coupons. One luxury is beer, particularly New Zealand beers, which are often consumed with mates. Wine is less popular than with other consumers. These people also enjoy fast food. Blue Collar Owners are sceptical about issues such as globalisation, believing they have yet to see any benefits from the so-called "global community". They are particularly wary of genetically modified food. New technology is not found particularly interesting or important, and internet usage is below average.

GROUP H

Grey Power

Grey Power are the oldest MOSAIC Group, with most aged over 55. Housing types consist of separate houses, flats and retirement homes. These properties have a capital value slightly below average and conditions vary from good to poor. Average household incomes are approximately $29,000. These people are proud of their country and try to buy the New Zealand-made products that they have grown up with, wherever possible. Set in their ways, they are not interested in trying new products often, even when discounted or on special. Grey Power rarely eat out. Instead they enjoy cooking and traditional meals at home. They don't often eat new, or foreign foods. Grey Power are indifferent to new technology, particularly the internet, and usage rates are some of the lowest of all New Zealanders. They enjoy reading magazines, however, and are particularly fond of women's lifestyle and home lifestyle magazines. When it comes to activities, slower games such as lawn bowls and darts are preferred, though they do enjoy watching active sports such as rugby and cricket on TV. They also watch horse racing which they occasionally flutter on. They spend more time watching TV than other consumer groups, though pay television subscriptions are low.

Cultural Diversity

These neighbourhoods are the most culturally diverse, with strong representations of Maori, Pacific Islanders and Asians. Households range from large young families to one-person retirees. Single parents are more commonly found in these neighbourhoods, making use of lower cost services and accommodation. Housing is low cost and below average quality, with the average home value being $139,000. A significant proportion of these people live in government-owned rental accommodation. Education levels are lower, and unemployment is higher, than all other MOSAIC Groups. Workers are usually employed in manual or service occupations, earning an average household income of just under $30,000 per annum. Bargain basement emporiums, factory outlets and traditional stores are favoured, with more expensive items frequently bought on credit. Takeaways and pre-prepared meals are regularly purchased to eat at home. They believe environmentally friendly products are overpriced. Betting on sport and racing is a popular pastime, albeit with minimal disposable income. Cultural Diversity also enjoy watching TV, recording the heaviest television viewing levels of all MOSAIC Groups. Tough sporting activities such as rugby and league appeal to this group.

GROUP I

Rural Lifestyle

Rural Lifestyle are located in country farming areas and rural service towns. This group includes school children with middle-aged parents, with grandparents, ranging in age from 25 to 64. Employment is generally on the farm, however there are lifestyle types within this group, such as Suits & Gumboots, who work in the city while living on lifestyle blocks or "toy farms". Rural Lifestyle types spend a disproportionate amount of time tending the land, and as most live at work, they find it difficult to switch off from their jobs. Average household income is approximately $48,000. Rural Lifestyle like to have traditional meals at home, often eating meat, and rarely buy frozen or ready prepared meals. New Zealand beer is popular, and preferred over wine. Self sufficient, they consider themselves as do-it-yourself kind of people, and are surprisingly adept at using computers and other technology. They are light internet users, however, as the technology is often not practical in remote areas. Rural Lifestyle don't trust the government, feeling the agricultural sector is increasingly neglected in favour of more "fashionable" industries. They enjoy a beer after a hard day and rarely eat at restaurants.

GROUP J

Brand New Houses

Brand New Houses are predominantly found in new subdivisions on the outskirts of the city. Many of these new subdivisions are being built on what was farmland. Some new houses are also found within established areas, where in-fill and higher density housing is occurring as vacant land runs out. These are typically homes built by executive families, but also include some lower cost first homes and retirement homes. Brand New Houses contain a cross section of age groups, and are mainly family households occupying larger than average sized homes. Although these homes are larger than average, mean prices are lower due to lower land prices further away from the central city. There are more Asian and fewer Maori and Pacific Islander new homeowners than elsewhere, and quite a few new homeowners are recent immigrants. Occupations are often managerial, technical or trades oriented. Brand New Houses are slightly more educated than the rest of the population, which results in an above average median household income of approximately $45,500. Internet access is high in these neighbourhoods. Motor vehicle ownership is high, with many households having three or more vehicles, and very few have only one car.

GROUP K

WHO LIVES WHERE?

Region	Suburb	2001 Population	% Change since 1996	% Aged Under 15 Years	% Aged Over 65 Years	% European	% Maori	% Pacific Peoples	% Asian
CENTRAL	Auckland City	11193	89.01	4.02	4.10	51.38	5.49	3.46	31.20
	Avondale	25206	11.61	22.80	10.08	45.11	10.93	24.57	20.02
	Blockhouse Bay	26283	6.12	22.44	12.24	50.43	5.95	14.67	29.06
	Eastern Bays	24801	3.35	17.54	14.47	83.41	4.68	2.03	9.19
	Epsom	9849	2.88	20.32	9.53	61.29	2.56	1.83	32.32
	Glen Innes/Pt England	16125	4.15	26.98	11.81	46.79	15.50	31.83	8.89
	Grey Lynn	23781	2.87	18.09	9.84	73.05	8.58	14.82	8.14
	Hauraki Gulf Islands	7242	12.33	20.05	13.84	86.12	11.10	3.15	2.03
	Kingsland	5421	10.59	13.61	3.98	65.52	8.36	15.05	9.96
	Meadowbank	24351	3.98	17.51	10.95	71.75	4.92	4.36	18.60
	Mt Albert	18591	5.12	19.40	9.29	62.27	6.99	11.46	18.28
	Mt Eden	36075	2.82	19.53	7.97	66.15	6.61	8.79	18.99
	Mt Roskill	21936	7.03	20.90	13.09	50.56	5.44	13.65	30.06
	One Tree Hill	11271	5.5	19.11	12.86	70.91	4.07	3.09	23.02
	Onehunga	25890	6.85	20.03	10.76	61.45	8.90	17.46	14.77
	Pamure	26049	5.57	23.62	8.81	45.02	16.01	24.42	18.93
	Parnell/New Market	7593	7.79	10.27	8.06	81.59	4.27	1.82	8.85
	Ponsonby	14415	0.38	14.19	7.62	82.39	6.66	8.14	4.79
	Remuera	18660	2.76	19.98	12.28	81.74	2.17	1.53	12.68
WEST	Helensville	6819	13.54	25.34	8.84	83.99	15.35	3.52	1.54
	Henderson	33156	15.21	23.96	10.54	63.32	13.83	15.08	12.54
	Kumeu/Huapai	14748	13.61	24.13	8.18	90.01	6.81	1.75	2.58
	New Lynn	42216	8.72	23.94	9.77	58.91	12.49	18.80	14.83
	Swanson	31485	8.53	27.59	6.03	64.70	15.46	18.11	7.37
	Te Atatu	16857	6.28	23.24	11.78	66.95	17.23	13.22	9.79
	Titirangi	24120	2.81	24.07	8.67	87.82	7.25	3.96	4.17
	West Coast Beaches	6894	6.54	24.76	5.87	88.99	8.96	2.61	1.65

NORTH	Albany	11634	60.58	24.29	5.65	84.01	7.14	1.88	8.38
	Beachhaven/Birkdale	18603	0.89	24.35	7.76	74.07	14.06	9.19	8.40
	Belmont/Bayswater	9015	-4.12	21.76	13.91	87.05	9.35	2.56	4.99
	Devonport	7374	-5.13	21.20	10.78	92.76	5.53	1.91	2.03
	Glenfield	30099	10.52	22.34	6.73	69.65	8.04	4.59	18.01
	Hibiscus Coast	31488	16.99	21.34	19.83	90.39	6.67	1.45	2.49
	Lower East Coast Bays	18456	0.92	19.64	11.64	87.29	2.57	0.75	9.56
	Northcote	32346	2.94	19.23	11.78	73.51	7.94	3.74	16.11
	Takapuna	12819	2.89	14.84	19.10	83.10	4.05	1.31	10.45
	Upper East Coast Bays	28626	14.84	21.21	10.68	86.08	4.37	1.36	8.79
	Warkworth	7836	14.01	20.52	20.75	91.42	7.27	1.34	1.91
	Westlake	20631	3.88	18.44	14.70	74.76	4.57	2.02	18.92
EAST	Beachlands-Maraetai	4419	8.39	25.19	10.39	89.61	7.60	1.97	1.70
	Botany	26064	65.96	22.43	7.38	62.43	3.36	1.55	31.64
	Bucklands Beach	10875	4.59	21.63	9.57	72.30	2.57	1.32	23.48
	Half Moon Bay	9150	-0.81	20.79	10.62	71.64	4.33	9.05	21.74
	Howick	18888	5.06	20.90	12.74	86.47	3.72	1.41	9.15
	Pakuranga	23451	2.9	20.21	13.06	66.18	6.95	4.35	24.36
	Whitford	5121	6.36	23.73	9.26	89.98	7.03	1.11	1.70
SOUTH	Mangere	53304	5.76	31.61	6.61	24.37	19.01	53.83	9.10
	Manukau/Clover Park	31632	16.71	29.47	5.73	35.27	17.61	36.47	16.29
	Manurewa	61434	12.37	28.84	7.04	52.54	26.99	19.99	8.23
	Otahuhu	39006	4.8	25.78	10.41	40.66	17.05	27.81	20.13
	Otara	16371	-1.36	35.55	5.24	10.61	21.26	71.49	2.18
	Papakura	36135	3.29	25.58	9.95	69.95	24.43	7.83	5.23
	Pukekohe	13623	13.55	25.32	13.06	69.68	19.58	4.98	7.66

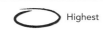

Highest Lowest

One of New Zealand's biggest attractions is not only it's clean, green image but its reputation for being a safe and secure place to live, with low crime and friendly people. Now, according to the New Zealand Police annual report for 2005, it is even safer, with a 24.4% drop in the recorded crime rate per head of population since 1995/96. The police also claim a favourable resolution rate of 44.2%.

Compared to the 2004 fiscal year, recorded crimes in Auckland City in 2005 have remained almost the same, although violent crime is up 11%. Kidnapping and abduction offences were down by 41% on 2004 figures. Burglaries were down 4% and resolved crimes were up 1.5%.

Recorded crime on the North Shore, West Auckland and Rodney continues to decline, due in part, to the continuing focus by police on burglary, theft and organised crime. Reported crime is down 4% on the North Shore and burglaries have dropped 6% in West Auckland.

It's not all good news though. Counties Manukau Police have reported an 11.8% rise in reported crime. Family violence in the region remains a high priority, accounting for 42% of all immediate calls for service.

The table below shows crime figures for the various regions of Auckland for the 2005 calendar year (Rodney includes the neighbourhoods of Hibiscus Coast, Helensville, Kumeu/Huapai and Warkworth.) The data was supplied by Statistics New Zealand and interpreted by Where to Live in Auckland editors.

Ultimately, Auckland is no different to any other major city in the world. Crime is a part of life, and it's important to take every precaution to protect yourself, your family and your property.

Sources:
NZ Police Releases 2363-2369.
NZ Police 2005 Annual Report.
Victim Support (crime referred to VS during June 2002-July 2003).
NZ National Survey of Victims and Crime (June 2003).
Statistics New Zealand 2005 Crime Data

CRIME IN AUCKLAND Recorded Crimes per 10,000 population

Location	City	Central	West	North	East	South	Rodney
Total Violent Crimes	**323**	**93**	**127**	**81**	**80**	**186**	**89**
Homicide	0.4	0.3	0.2	0.1	0.4	0.4	0.1
Kidnapping & Abduction	1	0.4	0.6	0.8	0.4	0.7	0.2
Robbery	21	9	6	3	8	10	3
Grievous Assaults	21	8	9	5	8	20	5
Sexual Crime	**18**	**7**	**6**	**5**	**6**	**10**	**5**
Drugs & Antisocial	**836**	**63**	**129**	**83**	**51**	**122**	**76**
Total Dishonesty Crimes	**2004**	**693**	**524**	**368**	**470**	**708**	**351**
Burglary	291	208	135	91	134	210	102
Car Theft (and related crimes)	314	118	84	42	91	140	38
Property Damage	**126**	**54**	**83**	**66**	**65**	**100**	**84**
Total Property Abuse Crimes	**168**	**34**	**45**	**34**	**27**	**60**	**41**
Trespass	135	23	32	20	18	41	26
Arms Act Offences	14	5	6	6	4	8	6
Administrative	**178**	**17**	**24**	**11**	**15**	**56**	**9**
Total Offences In 2005	**3654**	**961**	**938**	**649**	**715**	**1242**	**656**

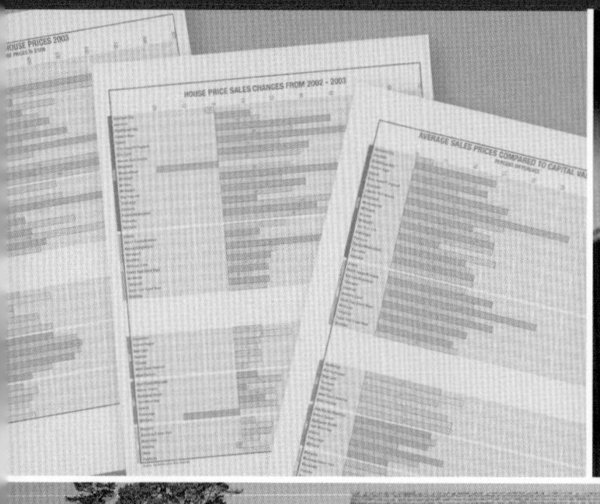

What are house prices doing?

A history of house sales is always a good yardstick on which to base your house-buying decisions. None of us wants to pay over the odds for a house but knowing what is reasonable, especially in a buoyant market, can be difficult to assess. While the information on the following pages is based on averages and is therefore broadbrush, it gives some useful guidelines, using three key measurements:

1. **Average house prices 2006**
   Check out the most expensive suburbs, and the cheapest. As with any figures based on averages, these can be skewed by particularly high or low sales prices in the area. If, for example, a large terraced housing development was launched and sold at very affordable rates during the year but located in an expensive suburb, it will bring the averages down.

2. **House price changes from 2005 to 2006**
   This shows the percentage increase in each suburb for the year ending March 2006 compared with March 2005. Again, certain sectors of the market, may appear to buck the trend in each area.

3. **Average 2006 house prices compared to capital values**
   Depending on when capital valuations for an area were last made, this can be a particularly good guide to market values. You can determine what premium property is attracting, say, 10% above capital valuation. This may then influence any offer you might make for a property in that area.

N.B. Average Sale Price: The average net sale price of the properties sold (excludes chattels).

Average Capital Value: The average capital value of the properties sold at the date of latest Rating Valuation.

Source: Quotable Value New Zealand
www.qv.co.nz

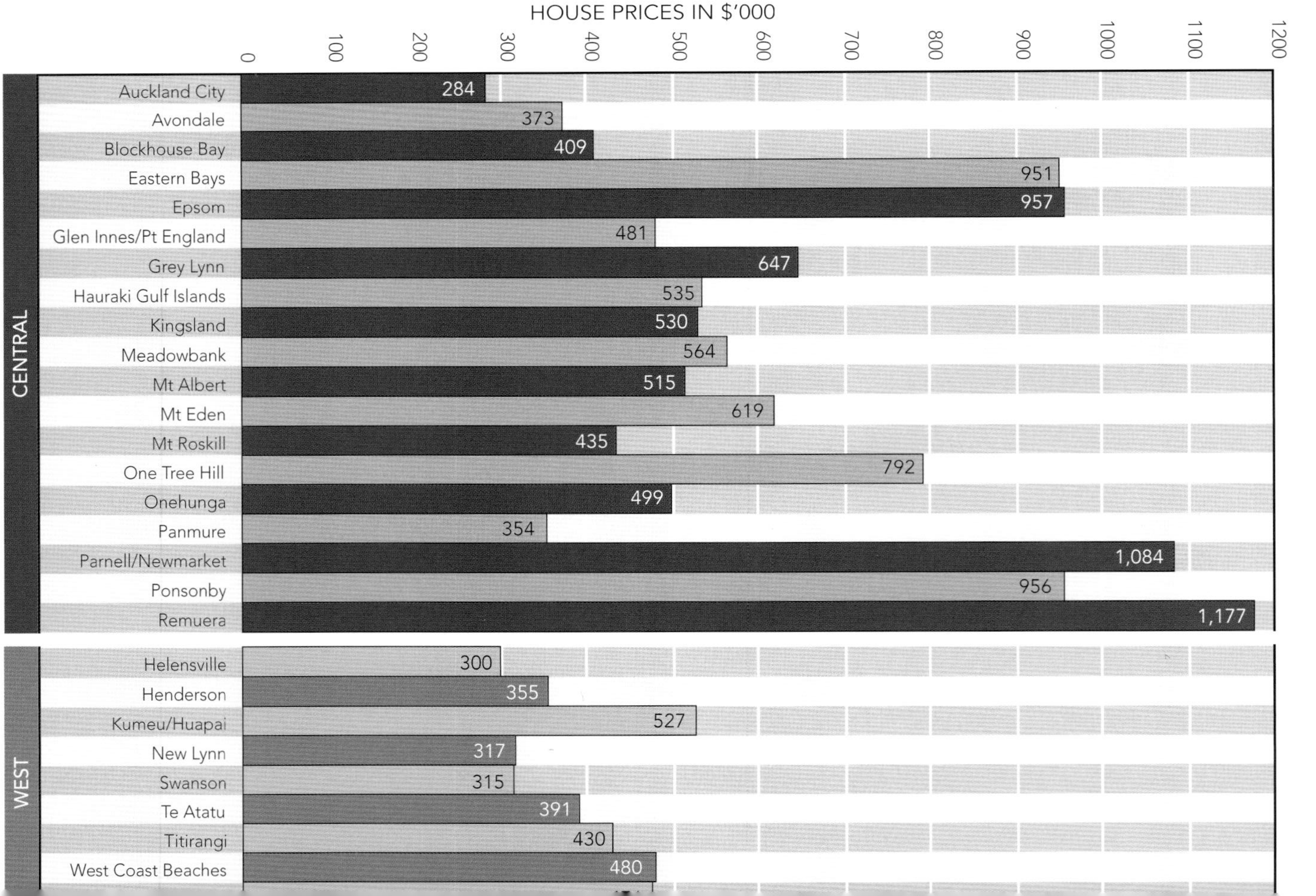
AVERAGE HOUSE PRICES 2006
HOUSE PRICES IN $'000
0
100
200
300
400
500
600
700
800
900
1000
1100
1200
CENTRAL
Auckland City 284
Avondale 373
Blockhouse Bay 409
Eastern Bays 951
Epsom 957
Glen Innes/Pt England 481
Grey Lynn 647
Hauraki Gulf Islands 535
Kingsland 530
Meadowbank 564
Mt Albert 515
Mt Eden 619
Mt Roskill 435
One Tree Hill 792
Onehunga 499
Panmure 354
Parnell/Newmarket 1,084
Ponsonby 956
Remuera 1,177
WEST
Helensville 300
Henderson 355
Kumeu/Huapai 527
New Lynn 317
Swanson 315
Te Atatu 391
Titirangi 430
West Coast Beaches 480

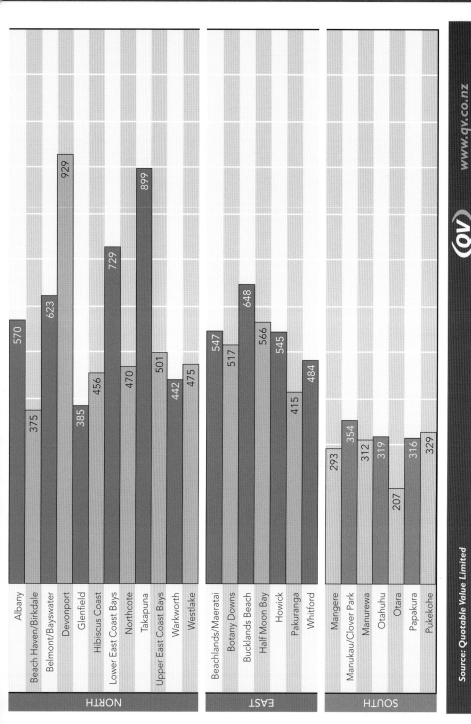

Region	Area	Value
NORTH	Albany	570
	Beach Haven/Birkdale	375
	Belmont/Bayswater	623
	Devonport	929
	Glenfield	385
	Hibiscus Coast	456
	Lower East Coast Bays	729
	Northcote	470
	Takapuna	899
	Upper East Coast Bays	501
	Warkworth	442
	Westlake	475
EAST	Beachlands/Maeratai	547
	Botany Downs	517
	Bucklands Beach	648
	Half Moon Bay	566
	Howick	545
	Pakuranga	415
	Whitford	484
SOUTH	Mangere	293
	Manukau/Clover Park	354
	Manurewa	312
	Otahuhu	319
	Otara	207
	Papakura	316
	Pukekohe	329

Source: Quotable Value Limited

www.qv.co.nz

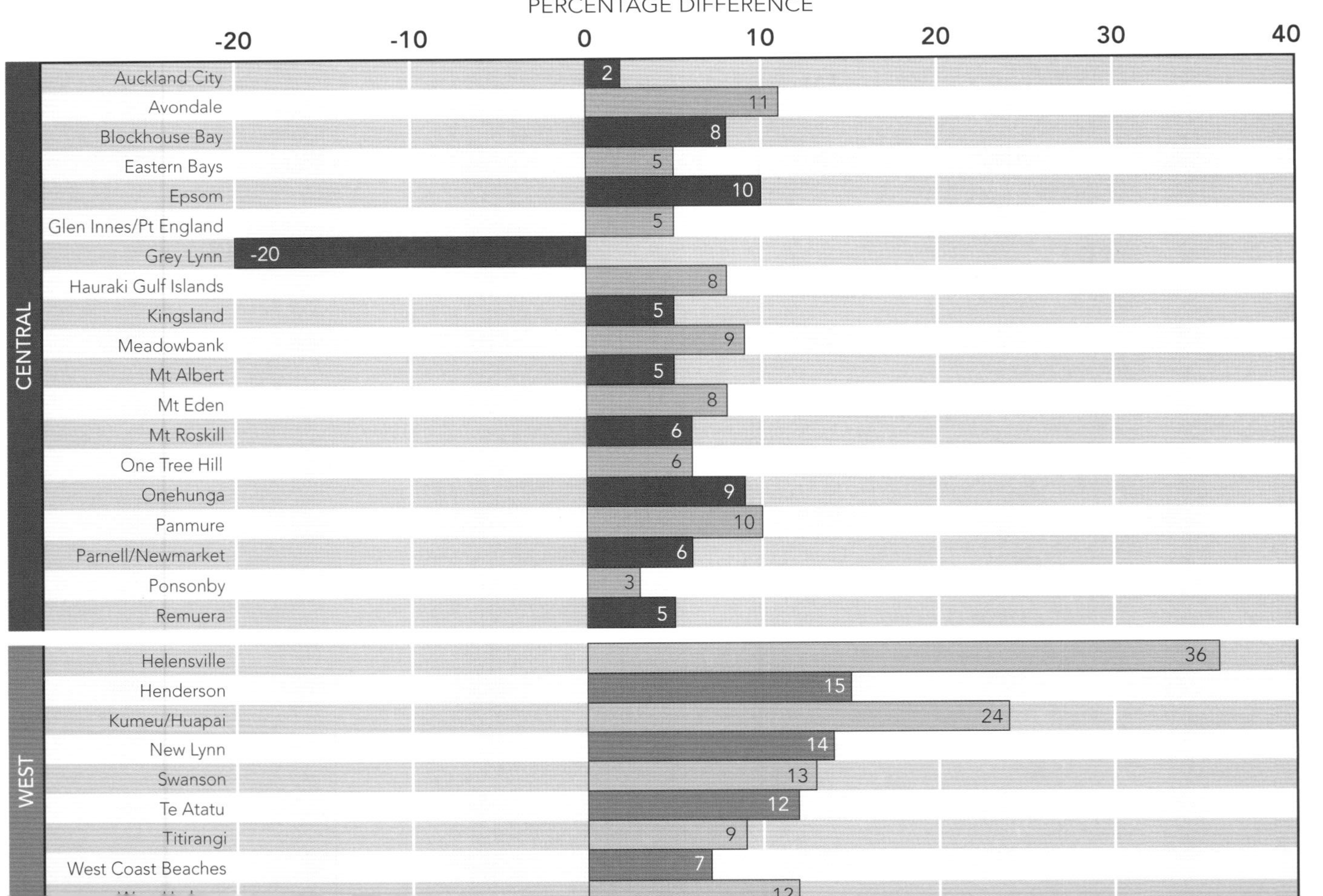
AVERAGE HOUSE PRICES CHANGES 2005-2006
PERCENTAGE DIFFERENCE
-20
-10
0
10
20
30
40
CENTRAL
Auckland City 2
Avondale 11
Blockhouse Bay 8
Eastern Bays 5
Epsom 10
Glen Innes/Pt England 5
Grey Lynn -20
Hauraki Gulf Islands 8
Kingsland 5
Meadowbank 9
Mt Albert 5
Mt Eden 8
Mt Roskill 6
One Tree Hill 6
Onehunga 9
Panmure 10
Parnell/Newmarket 6
Ponsonby 3
Remuera 5
WEST
Helensville 36
Henderson 15
Kumeu/Huapai 24
New Lynn 14
Swanson 13
Te Atatu 12
Titirangi 9
West Coast Beaches 7

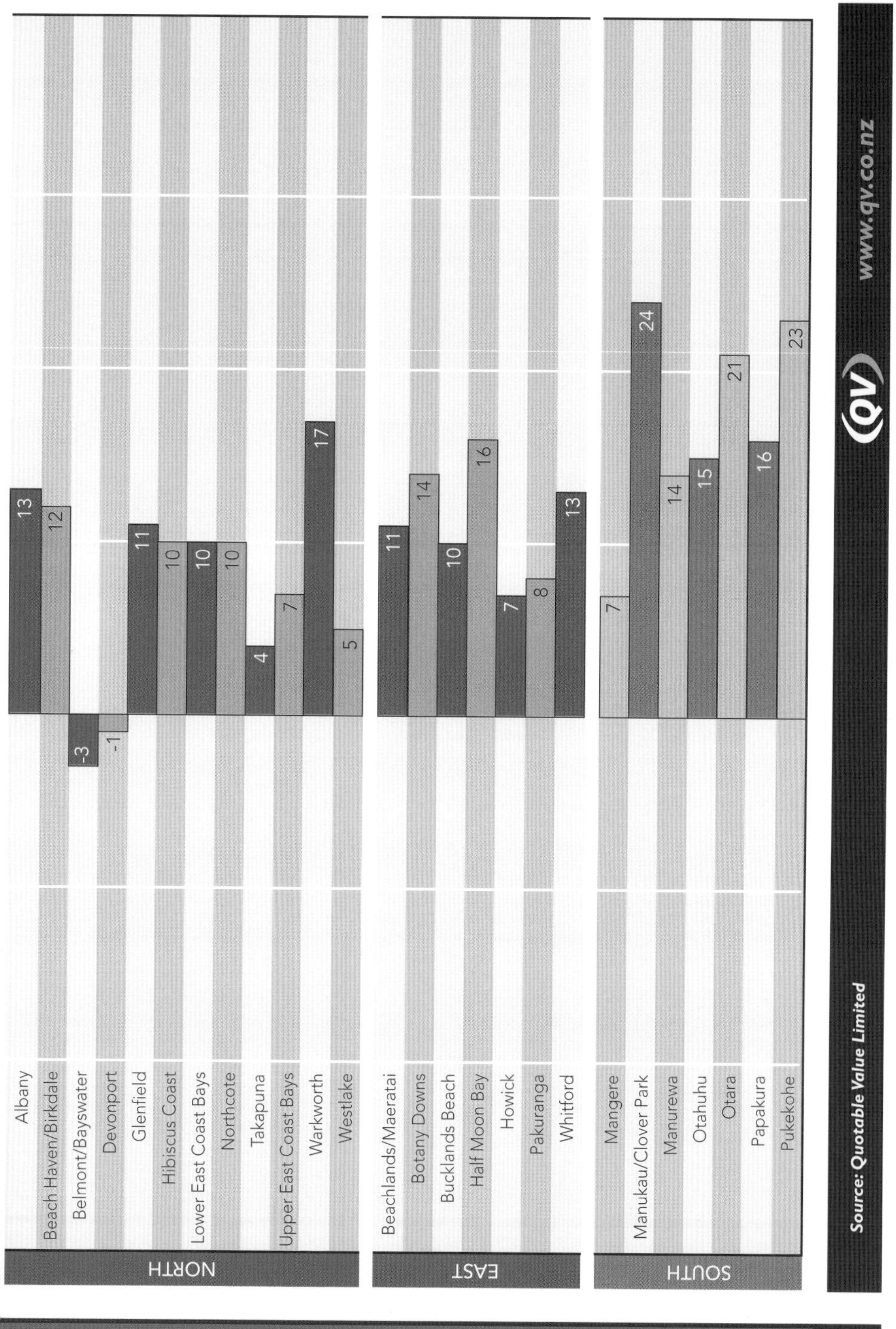

Region	Suburb	Value
NORTH	Albany	13
	Beach Haven/Birkdale	12
	Belmont/Bayswater	-3
	Devonport	-1
	Glenfield	11
	Hibiscus Coast	10
	Lower East Coast Bays	10
	Northcote	10
	Takapuna	4
	Upper East Coast Bays	7
	Warkworth	17
	Westlake	5
EAST	Beachlands/Maeratai	11
	Botany Downs	14
	Bucklands Beach	10
	Half Moon Bay	16
	Howick	7
	Pakuranga	8
	Whitford	13
SOUTH	Mangere	7
	Manukau/Clover Park	24
	Manurewa	14
	Otahuhu	15
	Otara	21
	Papakura	16
	Pukekohe	23

Source: Quotable Value Limited

www.qv.co.nz

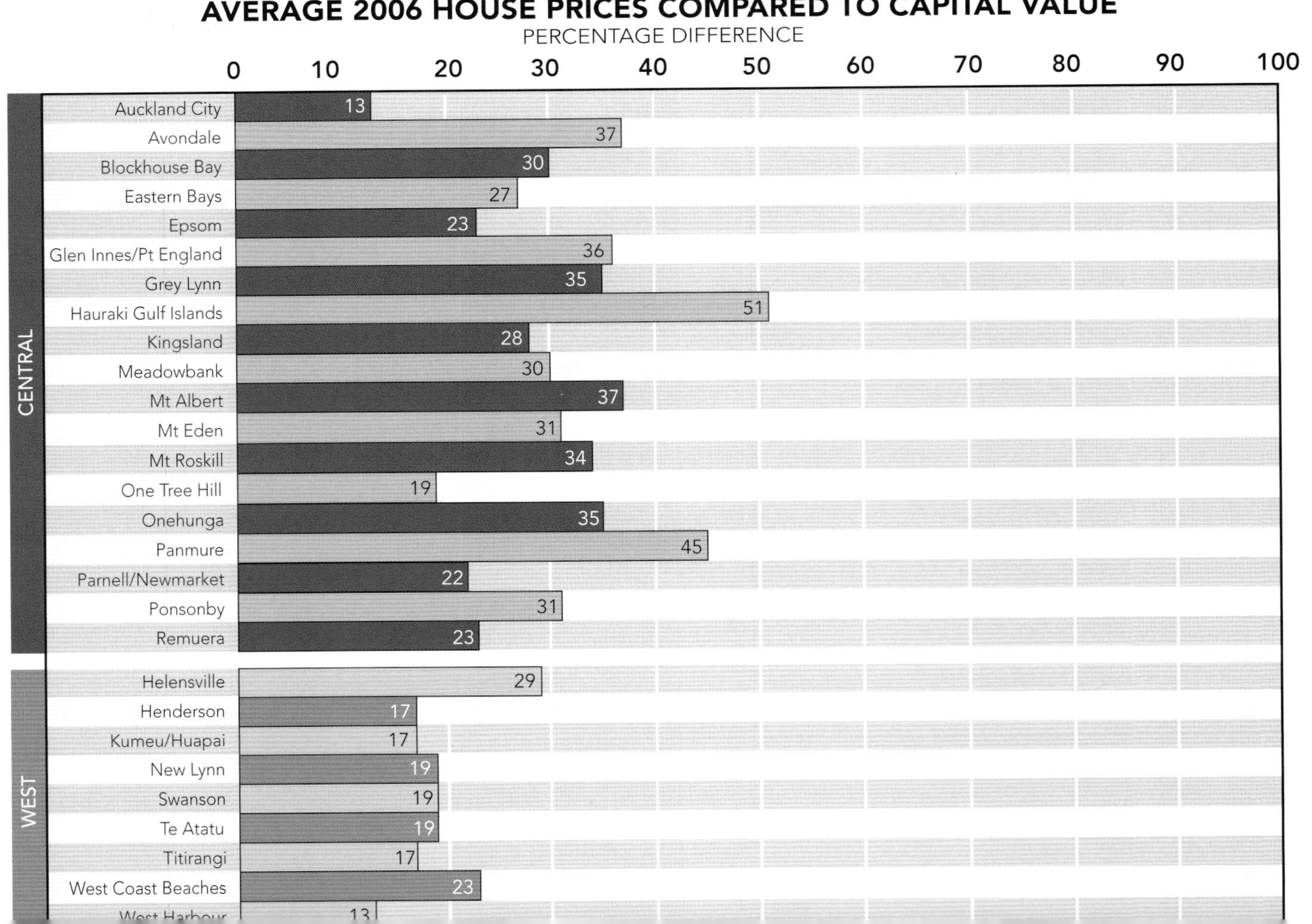
AVERAGE 2006 HOUSE PRICES COMPARED TO CAPITAL VALUE
PERCENTAGE DIFFERENCE
0
10
20
30
40
50
60
70
80
90
100
CENTRAL
Auckland City 13
Avondale 37
Blockhouse Bay 30
Eastern Bays 27
Epsom 23
Glen Innes/Pt England 36
Grey Lynn 35
Hauraki Gulf Islands 51
Kingsland 28
Meadowbank 30
Mt Albert 37
Mt Eden 31
Mt Roskill 34
One Tree Hill 19
Onehunga 35
Panmure 45
Parnell/Newmarket 22
Ponsonby 31
Remuera 23
WEST
Helensville 29
Henderson 17
Kumeu/Huapai 17
New Lynn 19
Swanson 19
Te Atatu 19
Titirangi 17
West Coast Beaches 23

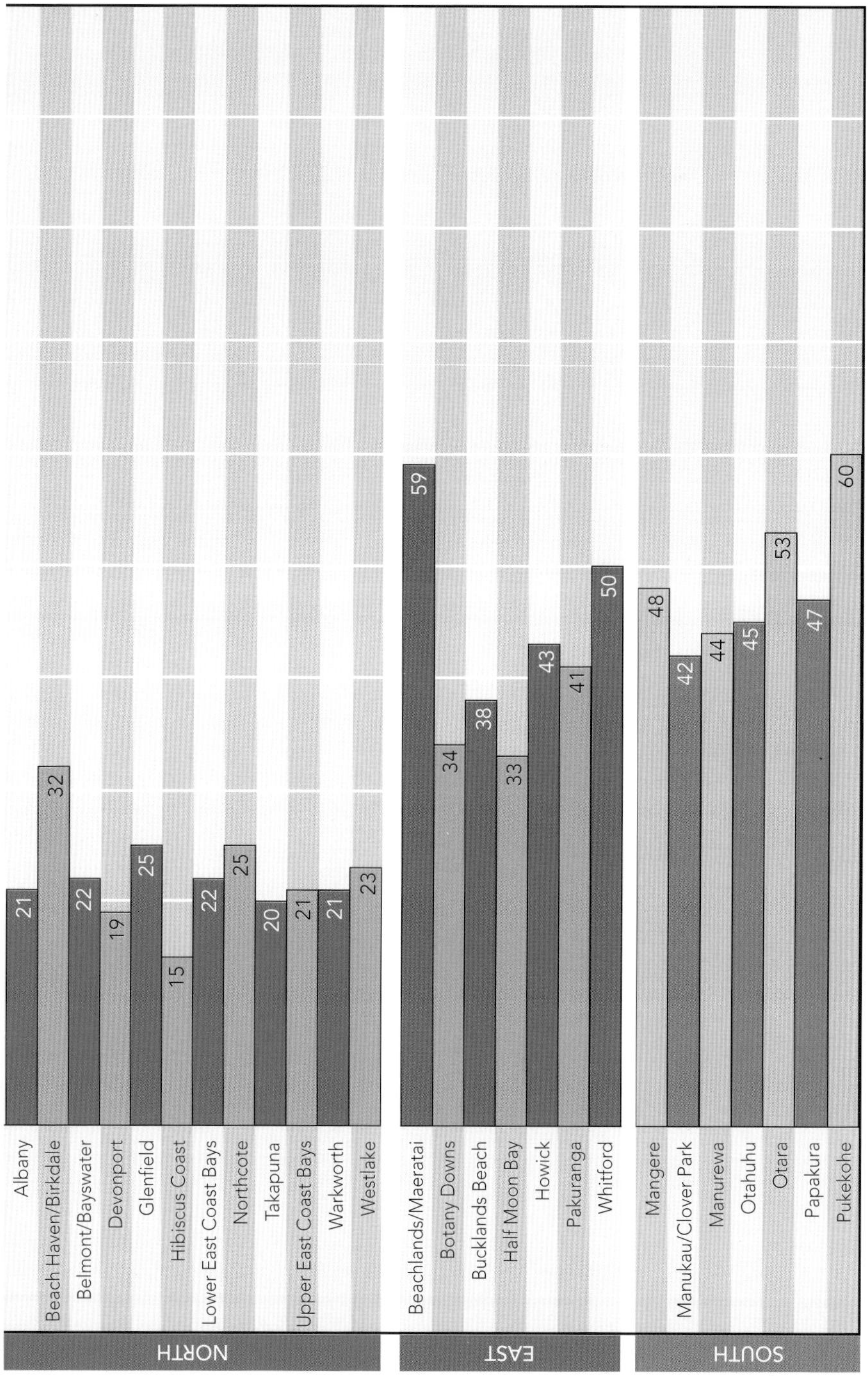

Region	Suburb	Value
NORTH	Albany	21
	Beach Haven/Birkdale	32
	Belmont/Bayswater	22
	Devonport	19
	Glenfield	25
	Hibiscus Coast	15
	Lower East Coast Bays	22
	Northcote	25
	Takapuna	20
	Upper East Coast Bays	21
	Warkworth	21
	Westlake	23
EAST	Beachlands/Maeratai	59
	Botany Downs	34
	Bucklands Beach	38
	Half Moon Bay	33
	Howick	43
	Pakuranga	41
	Whitford	50
SOUTH	Mangere	48
	Manukau/Clover Park	42
	Manurewa	44
	Otahuhu	45
	Otara	53
	Papakura	47
	Pukekohe	60

Source: Quotable Value Limited

www.qv.co.nz

The school zone maps on the following pages let you see which public secondary schools your children may be eligible to attend. We strongly recommend, however, that you contact the school to confirm the zone status of any particular street – or check the school's website. The star on each map shows the location of the school; roll numbers are as at 2006. If a public high school is not on these pages, it doesn't have a defined zone, so its roll is open to all-comers. Please contact your local school for more details. There is also a list of Auckland schools – primary, intermediate and secondary – grouped by region and neighbourhood. If you're considering a private school, we've compiled a list of Auckland's better-known private schools, including fees and other details.

If you have school-age children, good schools are high on the list of factors to take into account when choosing where to buy a home. Auckland has many excellent schools, but as the city's school-age population has mushroomed, access to the school of your choice can't be taken for granted.

In the past decade, student numbers at many of the city's most popular schools have rocketed, reflecting both a school's good reputation and the increased numbers of families living locally. To limit school size and prevent overcrowding, the Ministry of Education has a system of enrolment schemes, giving oversubscribed schools a home zone with clearly defined boundaries. If you live within the home zone, the school legally has to accept your child. Most schools have a few out-of-zone places available by ballot – applications close in September for the following year.

Currently around 25% of Auckland schools across all levels have enrolment schemes, including the four new secondary schools that opened in the past two years.

As a result, parents keen to send their children to prestigious state schools clamour to buy a family home in the right zone. They may not be paying private school fees, but they will certainly pay a premium for living in-zone. Real estate agents estimate, for example, that you can pay up to $150,000 more for a property in the Auckland Grammar School zone. The consolation is that these houses are seen as an investment. Once the kids are past school age, the house can be on-sold, with a heftier price tag – as long as the zone doesn't change! Some families opt out of the zoning problem by sending their children to private schools.

Don't presume a school is no good because it doesn't have a zone. There are a number of factors to take into account when assessing local schools. One source is the Education Review Office, which regularly reports on individual schools, and publishes its findings at www.ero.govt.nz. The ministry also publishes schools' academic results.

Each public school has a decile rating, which reflects the socio-economic level of the population from which the school draws its students – not academic results. Factors determining decile ratings are household income, occupation, crowding levels and tertiary educational qualifications.

Schools are rated from 1 to 10. A low decile rating reflects a low socio-economic group and a lower decile school gets more government funding than higher decile schools to help level the inequity among communities. Higher decile schools tend to have more successful parent-driven fundraising and will also charge higher school fees or "donations" – which aren't legally compulsory, but are important to a school's budget.

What is the NCEA?

The NCEA is New Zealand's rather controversial new senior high school assessment regime. It was phased into schools from 2002 and high school graduates of 2004 were the first to enter tertiary study with NCEA Level 3 (Year 13) university entrance grades.

NCEA stands for National Certificate of Educational Achievement, and it replaces the old system of School Certificate and Bursary exams and Sixth Form Certificate internal assessment. NCEA is a standards-based assessment – students are evaluated against a standard, not each other. Instead of marks or percentage ratings, students are given grades of Excellence, Merit, Credit or Incomplete gained through a combination of end-of-year exams run by the NZ Qualifications Authority and internal tests and assignments. Each NCEA subject breaks down into units so results comprehensively outline a student's strengths and weaknesses, eg units in English will include individual grades, such as Excellence for oral speech, Merit for formal writing and Achievement for comprehension.

There has been some disquiet about teething problems with the NCEA, particularly about huge discrepancies in the levels of difficulty among Level 4 Scholarship subject exams in 2004. As a result, ranking of students has been reintroduced at scholarship level and

To limit school size and prevent overcrowding, the Ministry of Education has a system of enrolment schemes, giving oversubscribed schools a home zone with clearly defined boundaries

scholarships will now be awarded to a set percentage of students.

So far, though, most practitioners at the coal face are keen to see NCEA continue. They feel the new system meets the needs of a wider range of students and recognises a wider range of achievement.

However, teachers and principals have identified a number of administrative aspects that need rectifying, including external moderation consistency and reliability. Some teachers are also concerned that the increased workload of assessment and moderation cuts into teaching time too much.

Those who oppose NCEA argue it is lowering standards and weakening our students' competitive edge. Some schools (including Auckland Grammar, King's College and Macleans College in Howick) offer the English-based Cambridge International Examinations alongside NCEA. The Cambridge exams are geared to the British school system, so there are concerns that while internationally recognised, they don't have any New Zealand content.

Despite talk from traditionalists about NCEA being easier, university entrance appears more stringent under NCEA. To enter degree level study with NCEA requires not only Level 3 (Year 13) passes but compulsory literacy levels at Level 2 (Year 12). Many students, especially international and new immigrants, have struggled to meet these requirements.

Albany Junior High School

Appleby Road, Albany, ph 09 415 5473
www.ajhs.school.nz

Roll 220; co-educational; years 7-10

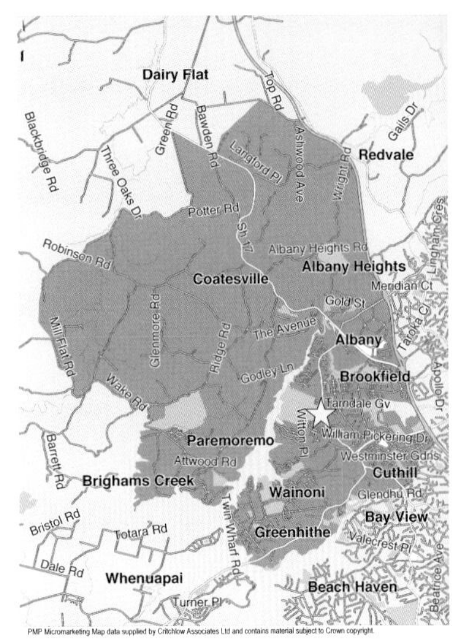

Albany Junior High School opened with 220 Year 7 students in 2005. The school roll will increase incrementally through 2006 and 2007. By 2008 all levels from Year 7 to Year 10 will be catered for. AJHS is a new model for middle years education in New Zealand. The school is a unique mix of models developed from middle schools in the UK and the American junior high schools. Students will have a four year transition from primary school through to high school. Year 7 students have a home room based teacher and over the course of three years gain increasingly specialised teaching. Year 10 students will have a largely secondary experience. There are plans to build a Senior High School in the Albany area in time for graduating Year 10 students to move into.

Zone boundary: The boundary starts on the Northern Motorway from the Upper Harbour Hwy on-ramp. It follows the Northern Motorway north until it turns west on Bawden Rd. At the start of Top Rd off Bawden Rd the boundary turns and continues in a straight line, south-west, to the end of Crossbridge Rd. It includes Crossbridge Rd and Hwy 17 until the western end of Bawden Rd. From this point it continues north along highway 17 to Green Rd. It does not include this portion of Highway 17. Top Rd and the greater portion of Bawden Rd are not included.

The boundary then follows Green Rd and continues west into Sunnyside Rd. It runs along Sunnyside Rd to the intersection with Robinson Rd where it continues along Robinson Rd across to the intersection of Sergeant Rd. It runs south along Sergeant Rd where it leaves the road and heads south across land to the top of Mill Flat Rd. From here it includes the end of Rangitopuni Rd and Croft Ln as it runs down Mill Flat Rd to the Coatsville-Riverhead Hwy. At this point it runs down the Coatsville-Riverhead Hwy to Wake Rd which it then follows to Ridge Rd. It turns east along Ridge Rd and then south into Brookdale Rd.

The Boundary follows Brookdale Rd to the nearest point to the Paremoremo Crk. From here it cuts across to the coast, including Iona Ave. It then follows the coast south and east all the way round Greenhithe to the Kereru Res.

At the eastern end of the Kereru Res the boundary continues again from the end of Kereru Grange. It follows Upper Harbour Drive, including Dene Court Ln, and then turns onto the Glenfield Hwy, which it runs along until Sunset Rd.

It then runs along sunset Road all the way to the Northern Motorway and then up to the start point.

Note: Both sides of all boundary roads are included in the zone, unless otherwise noted.

Alfriston College

550 Porchester Rd, Manurewa,
ph 09 269 0080
www.alfristoncollege.school.nz

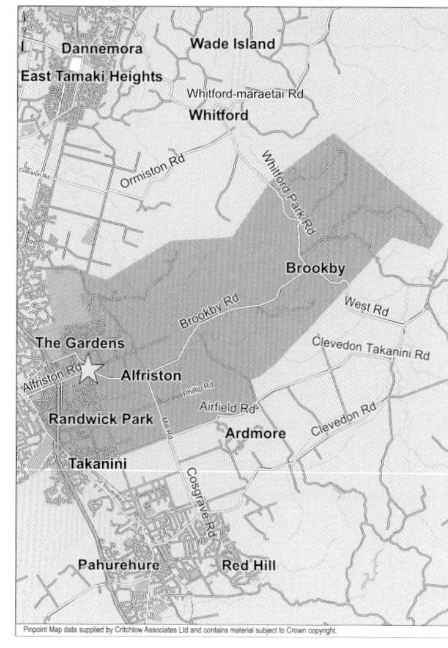

Roll 511 growing to 1500; co-educational; years 9-13

When Alfriston College opened its doors in 2004 it showcased outstanding 21st century architecture and an innovative approach. The first new school to be built in South Auckland for many years, it has an ethnically diverse roll. The school will grow its roll to Year 13 during the next three years and eventually cap at 1500 students.

Located on an enviable 11ha of land, Alfriston is now in its second construction phase with a gym being built this year. Rooms feature double glazed windows, controlled air temperature and full use of natural light. While there is currently no pool, there are playing fields, tennis courts, a sit-down cafeteria and state-of-the-art performing arts theatre. The school's architectural design strongly emphasises ICT with the whole school cabled so ICT can be accessed "anytime, anyplace". Alfriston has also taken an innovative approach to education up to Year 12. Students learn through blended courses such as Nature and Balance or Crime Scene and Investigation (combining social studies and science) that tie learning into real life. Three days each term are dedicated to specific challenges, such as an enterprise or community challenge or local event. Year 12 and 13 students learn traditional specialist subjects such as Physics, English etc.

Zone boundary: Starting at Gt South Rd / Hill Rd intersection the zone travels northeast up the centre of Hill Rd to the motorway bridge. Then north, following the boundaries of the botanic gardens and Totara Park (it does not include the suburbs of Totara Heights or Goodwood Heights). The northern boundary is the intersection of Totara Park, Redoubt Rd and Hilltop Rd. From here the zone moves east, including both sides of Redoubt Rd (and its side streets) and travels northeast (excluding Bownhill Rd) and intersects Whitford Park Rd at the bridge. It continues northeast until the end of Ara Kotinga is reached and then travels southeast until it reaches the Clevedon Scenic Reserve. From the Clevedon Scenic Reserve the zone travels southwest, intersecting Twilight Rd at the Quarry, and West Rd at their highest point, then continues southwest along the Watershed until the intersection of Alfriston-Ardmore Rd with Clevedon-Takanini Rd. From here, it travels south down the centre of Alfriston-Ardmore Rd until Airfield Rd. Then down the centre of Airfield Rd until Takanini School Rd and then down the centre of Taka St. From the Gt South Rd/Taka St intersection the zone moves northwards through the centre of Gt South Rd until Hill Rd is reached.

Auckland Grammar School

Mountain Rd, Epsom, ph 09 623 5400
www.ags.school.nz

Roll 2530; boys; years 9-13

Auckland Grammar is Auckland's highest-profile school in more ways than one. It's a state school with lots of status, carrying all the born-to-win authority of the best private school (and then some). The "grammar zone" takes in some of Auckland's top suburbs and the school's reputation is responsible for adding a substantial price premium to properties in these already desirable areas. Plenty of parents keen to make sure their sons get top education and sporting opportunities in a traditional all-male school think the investment is worth it. Auckland Grammar occupies a prominent chunk of real estate on the slopes of Mt Eden, with a historic Mission-style main building overlooking the motorway. (The school also has an outdoor education centre in Ohakune.) The school's students top the exam tables year after year and it offers the Cambridge International examinations as an adjunct.

Former students are a veritable Auckland old-boys' network of business leaders, doctors, lawyers, judges, rugby and cricket stars, including famed All Black captain Wilson Whineray, actor and Auckland Festival director Simon Prast, Maori leader Professor Sir Hugh Kawharu of Ngati Whatua, and Mt Everest conqueror, Sir Edmund Hillary.

Zone boundary: Northern boundary is the south side of Victoria St East from the Queen St intersection; Bowen St (south side), Waterloo Quadrant (south side) and Alten Rd (south side). Left into Stanley St (east side) and the Strand (south side), and north to Mechanics Bay. Western boundary is the east side of Queen St, Upper Queen St, Exmouth St, New North Rd to Dominion Rd. The east side of Dominion Rd to Grange Rd. Both sides of Grange Rd. South into Henley Rd (both sides) to Balmoral Rd. The north side of Balmoral Rd to Mt Eden Rd. The east side of Mt Eden Rd to Landscape Rd. Southern boundary is Landscape Rd, Selwyn Rd, Glenferrie Pl and Rostrevor Ave (both sides of all streets) to Pah Rd. Both sides of Pah Rd and Manukau Rd to Golf Rd (both sides) and Fern Rd (both sides). The western boundary of Cornwall Park to Claude Rd, and then in a direct line from the Cornwall Park end of Claude Rd to the intersection of Greenlane West and Pohutakawa Dr. The north side of Greenlane West to the intersection of Wheturangi Rd. Greenlane West (north side) from Wheturangi Rd to Great South Rd, and then Greenlane East (north side) to the intersection with Remuera Rd. Remuera Rd (north side) to Upland Rd. Eastern boundary is Upland Rd (west side) to the northern intersection with Orakei Rd to Hobson Bay, and the western foreshore of Hobson Bay to Judges Bay and Mechanics Bay.

Auckland Girls' Grammar School

Howe St, Newton, ph 09 307 4180
www.aggs.school.nz

Roll 1393; girls; years 9-13

Auckland Girls' Grammar School (AGGS) is a diverse multicultural inner city public girl's school. There are more than 50 ethnic groups, including 53 international students.

Academic standards are high with the school winning the Goodman Fielder School of the Year Award for 2000. This award acknowledges achievement in academic, sporting, cultural, social and environmental aspects of the school.

Zone boundary: From Waitemata Harbour via the Strand, Stanley St, Grafton Rd, Nugent St to Mt Eden Rd taking in Park Rd and Boston Rd and the streets between. Also Water, Kohutu, Enfield, Harold, Edwin, Mary and Kohekohe Sts. It runs along Mt Eden Rd to Landscape Rd, along Landscape Rd to Lambeth Rd to Sandringham Rd. Along Sandringham Rd to St Lukes Rd. Along St Lukes Rd to Great North Rd. Up China Man's Hill to Surrey Cres. Surrey Cres to Richmond Rd. Around Richmond Rd to Ponsonby Rd. Along Richmond Rd to Coxs Creek (Bayfield Park Side) to Marine Pde, along Marine Pde to the harbour. Both sides of all streets are included.

Avondale College

Victor St, Avondale, ph 09 828 7024
www.avcol.school.nz

Roll 2591; co-educational; years 9-13

Avondale College is one of the largest schools in Auckland. The roll reflects the multicultural mix of the surrounding suburbs with the largest groupings being Asian (23.5%), Pacific (21.5%) and NZ European (39%). It is a popular choice for secondary schooling in the area and is handily situated alongside Avondale Intermediate.

In recent years the college has developed strong business relationships with the local community and is known for its innovative approach to education.

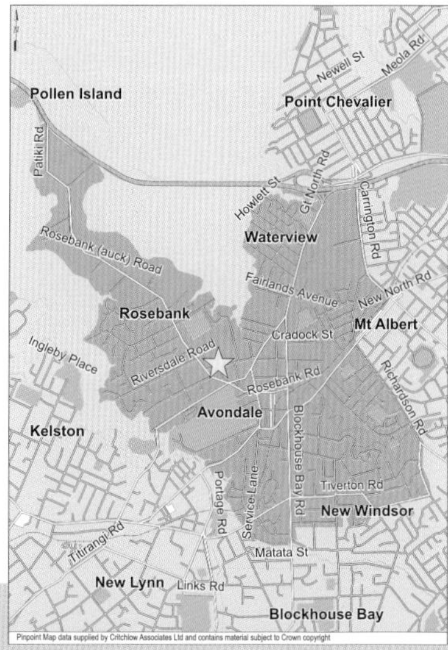

Zone boundary: From Oakley Creek to the junction of Great North Rd and Carrington Rd; the western side of Carrington Rd to the railway, along the railway to Woodward Rd. Both sides of Richardson Rd to the corner of Maioro St, across New Windsor Rd and Whitney St to both sides of Holbrook St. Across Blockhouse Bay Rd to both sides of Miranda St; across to the Whau Creek and Great North Rd; the rest of Rosebank Peninsula.

Botany Downs Secondary College

575 Chapel Rd, Botany Downs, ph 09 273 2310; www.bdsc.school.nz

Roll 642 growing to 1500; co-educational; years 9-13

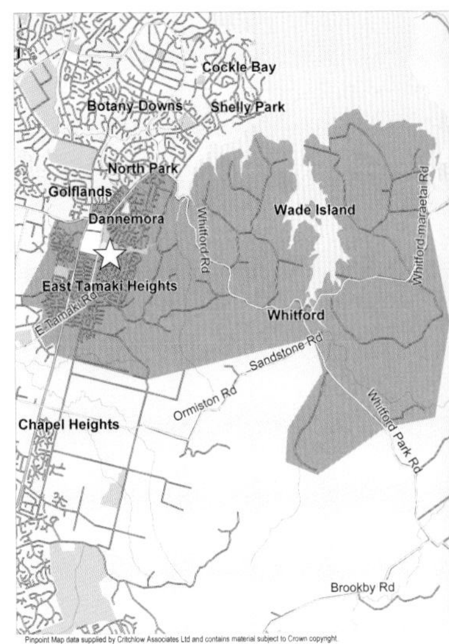

Opened in 2004, the groundbreaking design of east Auckland's newest school won it the New Zealand Institute of Architecture Resene Award for Architecture in Education 2004. The judges described it as "a spectacular learning environment". Environmentally sustainable features reduce the school's energy use. Classrooms have double-glazed windows, air conditioning and are designed to use plenty of natural light. Use of whanau and common space gives a 21st century twist to the old school house system. There are three two-storey Whanau House buildings with the ground floor teaching classrooms opening out onto a common space. Botany Downs has predominantly NZ European and Asian students.

Technology plays a major part and there are support programmes for high ability/gifted students and special needs students. The school is situated on pleasant grounds with plenty of room to expand. There are currently tennis courts, a gym and performing arts centre.

Zone boundary: From Mangemangeroa Bridge, west along Whitford Rd (both sides) until Chapel Rd; south down the centre of Chapel Rd to the right-hand intersection with Kilimanjaro Dr; west down the centre of Kilimanjaro Dr to the left-hand intersection with Tarnica Rd; south-west down the centre of Tarnica Rd (including Bampton, Ravensdale, Thirlmere and Caldbeck Rises, Ambleside Dr, Keswick Cl, Embleton Cl, Bowscale Pl and Fencote Pl) to the intersection with Botany Rd; south along Botany Rd (both sides) and all no-exit roads off it, to the intersection with Ti Rakau Dr; west down the centre of Ti Rakau Dr to the intersection with Huntington Dr; south across country until the intersection of Smales Rd and Sir Wlliam Ave (including Huntington Dr, Kelvin Hart Dr, Guys Rd and all streets directly off them). Following but excluding Sir William Ave, Lady Ruby Dr and all roads off them, along Accent Dr (excluded), excluding Reg Savoury Pl, until Chapel Rd (all roads north of Accent Dr included); north until the intersection of Chapel Rd (west side only) and Baverstock Rd; east along Baverstock Rd (both sides but no roads off southern side) and across country to Inchinamm Rd (both sides) to the intersection with Gracechurch Dr; east across country until the intersection of Sandstone Rd and Whitford Park Rd; south-east along Whitford Park Rd (both sides, including Brownhill Rd until Polo Lane, included); following the Whitford-Maraetai Rd (both sides) east including Trig Rd, until the northeast intersection with Henson Rd; east to the coast and west until the Mangemangeroa Bridge.

Edgewater College

Edgewater Dr, Pakuranga, ph 09 576 9039
www.edgewater.school.nz

Roll 1038; co-educational; years 9-13

There's a comprehensive range of subjects on offer. Sport, cultural and academic successes are encouraged. An English Language Foundation Programme is available for ESOL learners. The school has extensive landscaped grounds and well equipped classrooms, including upgraded science laboratories and computer facilities. The modern music rooms include recording studios. Golf, softball, touch rugby, volleyball and Waka Ama outrigger are just some of the sports on offer, along with cultural activities.

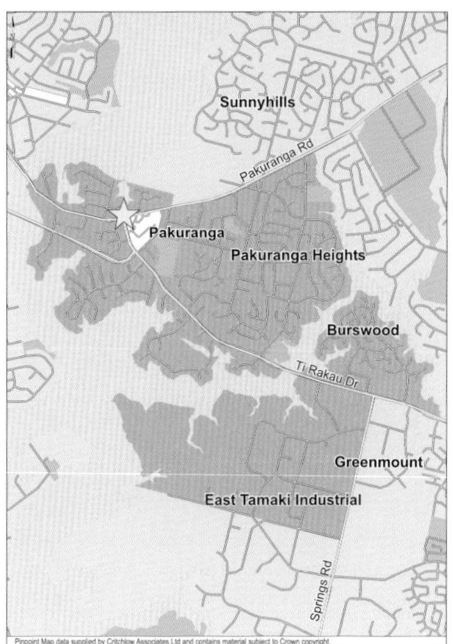

Pinpoint Map data supplied by Critchlow Associates Ltd and contains material subject to Crown copyright

Zone boundary: Left-hand side of the Pakuranga Highway. Gossamer Dr to Pakuranga Creek then Harris Rd. Crook Rd to Highbrook Dr. Tamaki River to the Panmure Bridge.

Epsom Girls' Grammar School

Silver Rd, Epsom, ph 09 630 5963
www.eggs.school.nz

Roll 1902; girls; years 9-13

Epsom Girls' Grammar is the girls' equivalent of Auckland Grammar – one of New Zealand's premier girls' schools, and also one of the largest. Like Auckland Grammar, the EGGS home zone takes in some of the city's most desirable suburbs. Epsom Girls' is on a pleasant 7.2ha campus between Gillies Ave and the Newmarket end of Manukau Rd. EGGS has long been respected for the high quality state education it delivers to young women, aiming for an ideal mix of traditional and modern. Its success is reflected in its exam results, and in the high performance of its students in tertiary education.

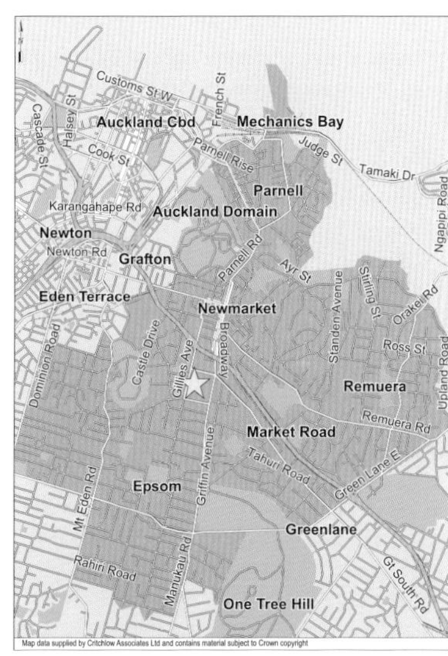

Map data supplied by Critchlow Associates Ltd and contains material subject to Crown copyright

Zone boundary: The area bounded by Upland Rd (from the harbour), Remuera Rd, Greenlane East, Greenlane West, around One Tree Hill as far south as Golf Rd, to Manukau Rd, to Pah Rd to Selwyn Rd via St Andrews Rd to Landscape Rd, to Mt Eden Rd to Balmoral Rd. Balmoral Rd to Dominion Rd, to Valley Rd to Horoeka Ave, to View Rd to Mt Eden Rd to Normanby Rd, Boston Rd to Khyber Pass to Park Rd to Carlton Gore Rd, George St and along the eastern side of the Auckland Domain, to Parnell Rd, The Strand to the harbour at Mechanics Bay. (Note: houses on both sides of the road on the boundaries plus any cul-de-sacs off an included road are in the zone.)

Glendowie College

Crossfield Rd, Glendowie, ph 09 575 9128
www.glendowie-college.school.nz

Roll 908; co-educational; years 9-13

Ethnic mix: 66% NZ European, 24% Asian, 6% Pacific, 3% Maori.

The college's main emphasis is on traditional academic subjects and NCEA assessment. It offers multi-level study options, accelerant learner programmes and comprehensive ESOL programmes. Students often perform above the national mean in external examinations.

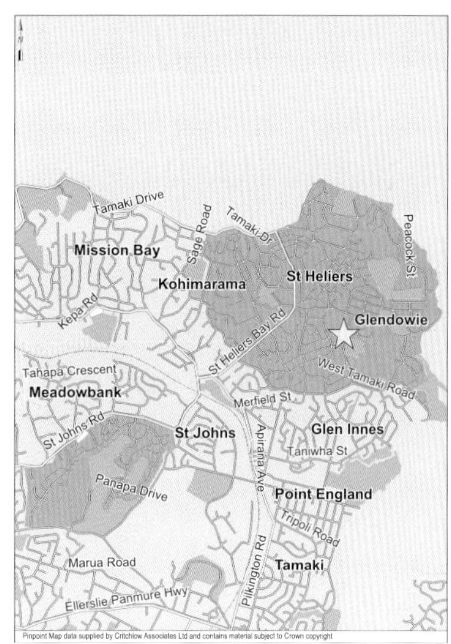

Zone boundary: In Glendowie and St Heliers, the area bounded by West Tamaki Rd, Grampian Rd, Allum St from Grampian Rd, Melanesia Rd from Allum St to Sage Rd, Sage Rd and the coastline from Sage Rd to West Tamaki Rd. Both sides of the boundary road are included. In St Johns Park, the area bounded by St Johns Rd, Remuera Rd, Koraha St, Abbotts Way and College Rd (boundary roads are excluded).

Howick College

Sandspit Rd, Howick, ph 09 534 4492
www.howickcollege.school.nz

Roll 2139; co-educational; years 9-13

Ethnic mix: NZ European 55%, Asian 29%, Maori 5%.

Howick College is well established in the neighbourhood and has a solid academic reputation. It provides a broad curriculum with more than 40 subjects for senior students. The college is recognised for cultural and sporting opportunities, with music groups including barbershop, chamber and rock. The Performing Arts Department is well known for technical and dramatic expertise.

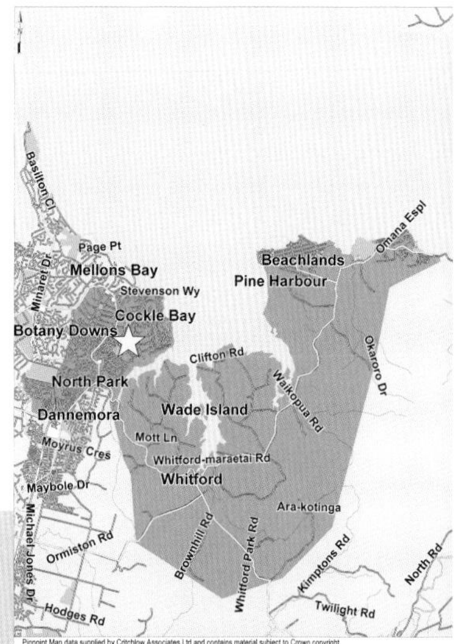

Note: A new zone was put in place for year 9 and 10 students in 2005 that will progressively replace the old zone for other levels from 2006 to 2008. For details of the old zone, contact the school direct.

New zone boundary: From Howick Beach via Uxbridge Rd (included), Picton St and Ridge Rd (both excluded). From Howick Intermediate School along Botany Rd (excluded) to Millhouse Dr; both sides of Botany Rd from Millhouse Dr to Ti Rakau Dr; Golflands Dr and all side streets (included). From the end of Botany Rd, east along Ti Rakau Dr until Chapel Rd; north along Chapel Rd until Whitford Rd (Kingsgate included); east along Whitford Rd to Whitford including all side roads (excluding Pt View Dr); Whitford Park Rd and all side roads (including Ara-Kotinga Rd, and Sandstone Rd and side roads and its extension into Ormiston Rd as far as the ridgeline of the Whitford watershed) and beyond Ara-Kotinga within walking distance of the school bus stop at Ara-Kotinga. From Whitford Rd, along Whitford-Maraetai Rd and Maraetai Beach Dr (including all roads leading off it) to the eastern end of Maraetai Beach.

Long Bay College

Ashley Avenue, Torbay, ph 09 473 2500
www.lbc.school.nz

Roll 1590; co-educational; years 9-15

Long Bay College is a well appointed decile 10 secondary school located on attractive grounds overlooking the Hauraki Gulf. According to recent ERO reports the college provides its students with high quality learning opportunities and enjoys national recognition in Technology and in the Creative and Performing Arts, consistently winning top New Zealand honours in these areas.

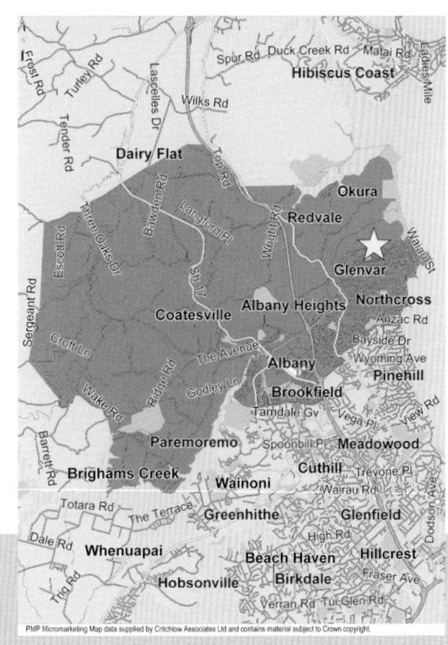

Zone boundary: The boundary starts at the intersection of Bawden Rd and State Hwy 1. It then travels west along Bawden Rd to Top Rd, including Top Rd and Oregon Pk to the intersection of Dairy Stream Rd (included). From the intersection of Dairy Stream Rd and Postman Rd (Postman Rd not included) across to Blackbridge Rd, along Blackbridge Rd to Drury Ln (not included). From this point, heading across country directly south to the intersection of Robinson Rd and Sergeant Rd. Continuing along Robinson Rd and into Sergeant Rd, it runs south along Sergeant Road where it leaves the road and heads south across land to the top of Mill Flat Rd. From here it includes the end of Croft Ln, Rangitopuni Rd and Bernice Ln as it runs down Mill Flat Rd to the Coatesville-Riverhead Hwy. At this point it runs down the Coatesville-Riverhead Hwy to Wake Rd then to Ridge Rd. From Ridge Rd to Brookdale Rd, from Brookdale Rd directly south to the coastline. Then following the coastline to the intersection of Kell Dr and Oteha Valley Rd Ext. Then, following the coastline south, down to the northern boundary of the North Shore City Golf Course then following Rosedale Rd east (northern side of Rosedale Rd only) to the motorway (SH1) then travel north along SH1 to Greville Rd. Travel east along Greville Rd (both sides included) to East Coast Road. Travel north along East Coast Road to Oaktree Ave and East along Oaktree Ave (both sides) including Palliser Ln, Squirrel Ln, Fallow St and Holly Hock Pl to Glencoe Rd. Travel along Glencoe Rd to the Glencoe Rd and Beach Rd intersection (south of this point not included) and north along Beach Rd to Anzac Rd. Travel east along Anzac Rd to the coastline including Many Esplanade. The boundary follows the coastline north around to the Okura Scenic Reserve and travels west back to Bawden Rd, crossing East Coast Rd (including Haigh Access Rd).

Lynfield College

White Swan Rd, Mt Roskill, ph 09 627 0600
www.lynfield.school.nz

Roll 1863; co-educational; years 9-13

Ethnic mix: NZ European 36.8%, Asian 38%, Pacific 6.6%, Other 6.6%, Maori 4.8%.

The college offers excellent broad-based education at junior level and flexible subject choices and multi level approaches at senior level. This includes many vocational options. Sport, cultural and academic successes are encouraged.

State of the art technology and computer systems are used in all learning areas. It has one of largest English as a Second Language Departments in Auckland schools and provides strong community education, refugee support and international student exchanges.

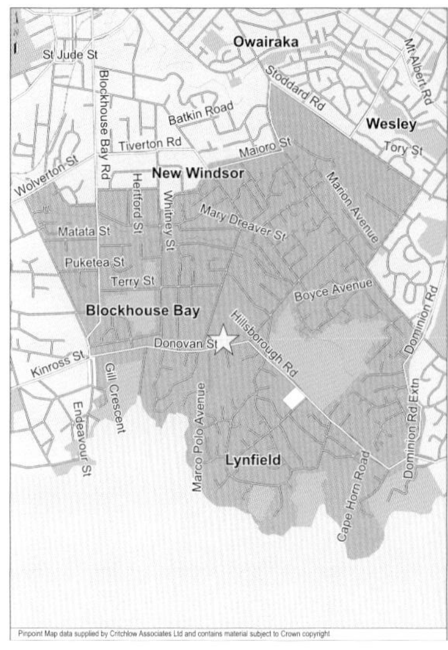

Zone boundary: Along Dominion Rd Extension, through Richardson Rd, May Rd (not included), Stoddard Rd (not included), Mairoro St (not included) through Trevola St, across Holbrook St (not included), Miranda St (not included), Wolverton St (not included) and down Taylor St (not included). For a full list of street names within the zone boundary please visit the Lynfield College website.

Macleans College

Macleans Rd, Bucklands Beach, ph 09 535 2620
www.macleans.school.nz

Roll 2298; co-educational; years 9-13

Opening its doors in 1980 to the affluent eastern suburbs, Macleans College is known for innovation and academic success and is now the largest co-educational Year 9-13 school in east Auckland. The school's ethnic mix reflects the suburbs: 35% NZ European, 21% Chinese, 17% Japanese and Korean, and 15.7% other European.

Macleans offers Cambridge International Examinations (CIE) as well as NCEA. Last year a Macleans College student was first in the world to gain a first year A level in French in CIE. Sporting and musical opportunities also abound.

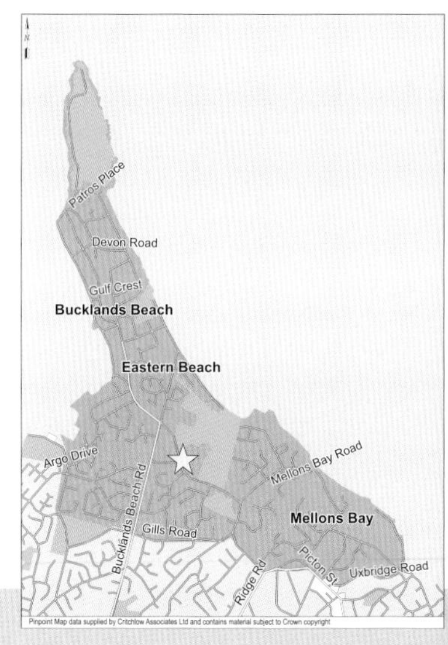

Zone boundary: A line from Howick Beach via Uxbridge Rd (both sides excluded), Picton St, Ridge Rd (1-47, 6-60 included) and Bleakhouse Rd (both sides included) to Gills Rd, then via Gills Rd (both sides excluded and with Udall Pl and other no exit streets off Gills Rd similarly excluded) to the junction of Pigeon Mountain Rd. Via Pigeon Mountain Rd (1-69, 2-60 included) and to the end of Ara Tai Pl (both sides included).

Manurewa High School

67 Browns Rd, Manurewa, ph 09 268 3888
www.manurewa.school.nz

Roll 2019; co-educational; years 9-13

The largest secondary school in south Auckland, Manurewa High School has a multi cultural population – 33% are NZ European, 26% Polynesian, 22% Maori and 15% Asian. The school opened in 1960 to accommodate growth in the area and has continued to be a favoured south Auckland school.

The Year 9-13 classes are streamed to allow students to work to their full potential and an advanced placement programme provides for gifted students. External examination results are consistently above the national average so the approach is working.

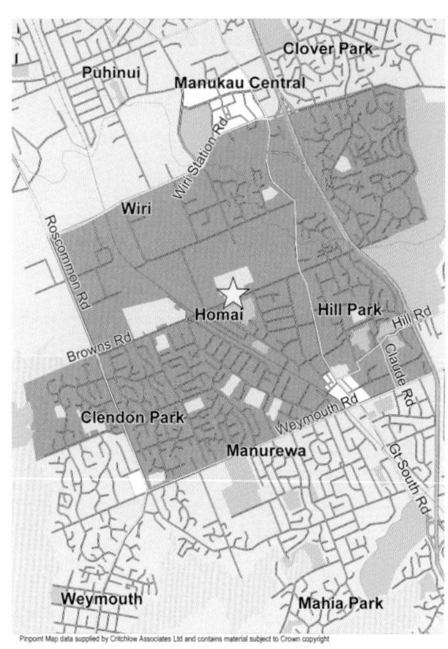

Pinpoint Map data supplied by Critchlow Associates Ltd and contains material subject to Crown copyright

This new home zone applies at the following year levels: 2006 – years 9-11; 2007 – years 9-12; 2008 – all year levels.

Zone boundary: Northern boundary is Redoubt Rd (west from the intersection with Hilltop Rd), Wiri Station Rd to Roscommon Rd. Western boundary is Cnr Wiri Station Rd along Roscommon Rd to Browns Rd. Manukau Harbour coastline from Browns Rd to Burundi Ave. Southern boundary is Burundi Ave to Weymouth Rd and east along Weymouth Rd. Alfriston Rd to motorway. Eastern boundary is Along motorway and across northern boundary of botanic gardens. Across Totara Park to the intersection of Redoubt Rd and Hilltop Rd. NB: On all boundary roads, the zone includes only those houses on the side of the road nearest the school.

Massey High School

274 Don Buck Rd, Massey, ph 09 831 0500
www.masseyhigh.school.nz

Roll 2359; co-educational; years 9-13

Situated on the northern boundary of West Auckland, Massey High School draws on a diverse mix of urban and rural families. The school's roll has grown significantly during the past few years, making it the second biggest in West Auckland.

The school has a strong Maori population at 20% alongside 43% NZ European, 23% Asian and 14% Pacific.

As well as having a strong academic record, Massey High School delivers outstanding sports people, musicians, artists, actors and Maori, Pacific and Asian cultural groups.

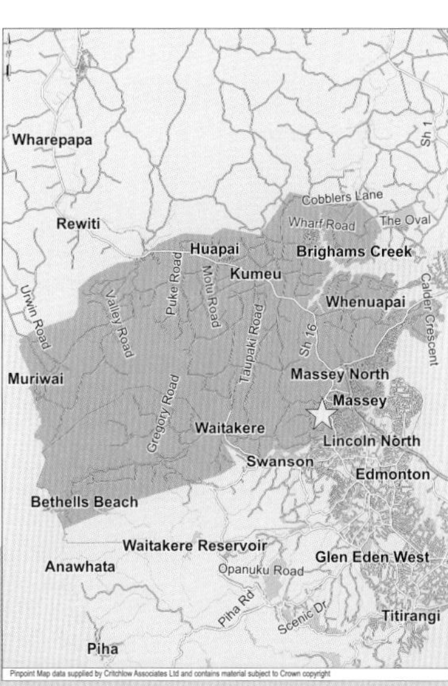

Pinpoint Map data supplied by Critchlow Associates Ltd and contains material subject to Crown copyright

Zone boundary: Northern boundary is Muriwai Beach, Muriwai Rd and side roads to Waimauku. Matua Rd, Deacon Rd, Cobblers Lane to Wake Rd. Eastern boundary is Waitemata Harbour. Southern boundary is the bottom of Don Buck Rd, Chamberlain Rd, Crows Rd, Kay Rd, Waitakere Rd, ANZAC Valley Rd and side roads, Te Henga Rd and side roads, Bethells Rd to Bethells Beach.

Mt Albert Grammar School

32 Alberton Ave, Mt Albert, ph 09 846 2044
www.mags.school.nz

Roll 2242; co-educational but single-sex classes; years 9-13

It's hard not to think sport when you hear the name Mt Albert Grammar School. The school has seven sporting academies, headed by noted sports people such as Kevin Fallon, Te Aroha Keenan and Bryan Williams. It is home to Philips Aquatic Centre's heated indoor swimming pool and wave pool, and has extensive sports grounds as well as a school farm and agricultural unit. The school also performs well academically and musically.

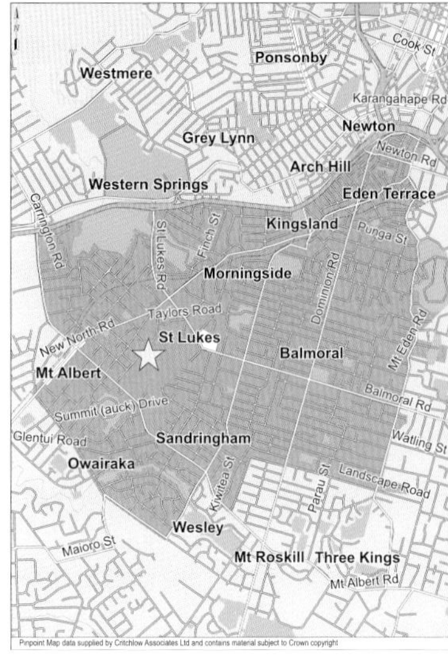

Pinpoint Map data supplied by Critchlow Associates Ltd and contains material subject to Crown copyright

Zone boundary: The northern boundary is the north-western motorway. Then all areas north of the junction of the north-western motorway and Carrington Rd, via Carrington Rd, to New North Rd, to Richardson Rd, to Stoddard Rd, to Sandringham Rd extension, to Mount Albert Rd, to Renfrew Rd, to Invermay Ave, to Landscape Rd, to Mount Eden Rd, to Symonds St, to the motorway. All no exit roads off the boundaries are included in the zone.

Mt Roskill Grammar

Frost Rd, Mt Roskill, ph 09 621 0050
www.mrgs.school.nz

Roll 2306; co-educational; years 9-13

In the past decade or so, Mt Roskill Grammar has grown from a relatively low-profile suburban co-ed to a school with a city-wide and even national reputation. In 2002 Mt Roskill Grammar was named Goodman Fielder Secondary School of the Year, reflecting the school's successes across the curriculum. It's now one of the most sought-after high schools on the Auckland isthmus.

The school offers a top-quality array of facilities, cultural and sporting activities to match its size, including 16 new science labs, six new computer rooms, a fully equipped music suite, floodlit artificial turf, fitness centre and two gyms.

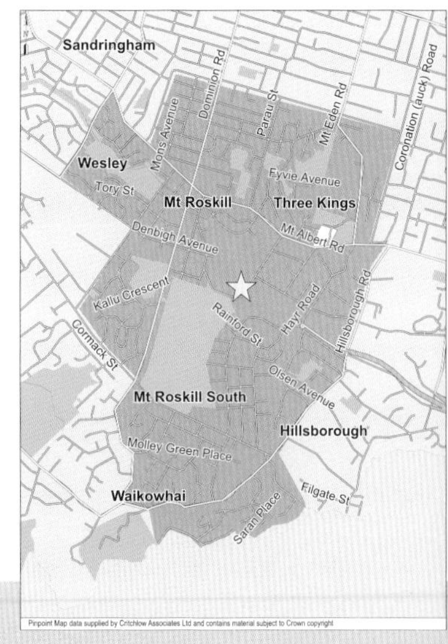

Pinpoint Map data supplied by Critchlow Associates Ltd and contains material subject to Crown copyright

Zone boundary: From the Manukau Harbour via Waikowhai Rd and Hillsborough Rd (both excluded) to Dominion Rd Extension; via Dominion Rd Extension (excluded) to Richardson Rd; then via Richardson Rd (excluded), May Rd and Stoddard Rd (both included) to Sandringham Rd; via Sandringham Rd (excluded) to Mt Albert Rd; via Mt Albert Rd (included), Renfrew Ave (excluded), Invermay Ave (included), Landscape Rd (excluded); via St Andrews Rd (excluded) to Mt Albert Rd (included); then via Hillsborough Rd (excluded) to Hillsborough Cemetery/Richardson Rd corner and the Manukau Harbour.

Northcote College

Kauri Glen Rd, Northcote, ph 09 481 0141
www.northcote.school.nz

Roll 1370; co-educational; years 9-13

The school is predominantly NZ European (58%) in make up, followed by 16% Asian and 9% Maori.

Established in 1877, Northcote College has expansive fields, established grounds and good facilities all within five minutes of Auckland City, North Shore City and the beaches of the North Shore.

The school is well known for its music, particularly its award winning jazz band.

Zone boundary: From Balmain Rd, Mokoia Rd, Roseberry Ave, Parkhill Rd, Glenfield Rd. Coronation Rd, Archers Rd, Sunnybrae Rd, Northcote Rd, the motorway to the harbour bridge and the harbour to Kauri Pt Domain and Balmain Rd.

Onehunga High School

Pleasant St, Onehunga, ph 09 636 6006
www.ohs.school.nz

Roll 1423; co-educational; years 9-13

Ethnic mix: 32% NZ European, 34% Pacific peoples, 16% Maori, 5% Asian and 13% Other. Business makes Onehunga High School unique! The school has established a first in New Zealand schools – a business school on site for secondary students where senior students study subjects such as entrepreneurship, starting and running a business, the global economy and strategic financial management. They undertake a cadetship/mentoring programme with a CEO and sit the internationally recognised Cambridge (CIE) AS Business Studies examination. Aside from the business school, there are a number of innovative learning programmes running in the school.

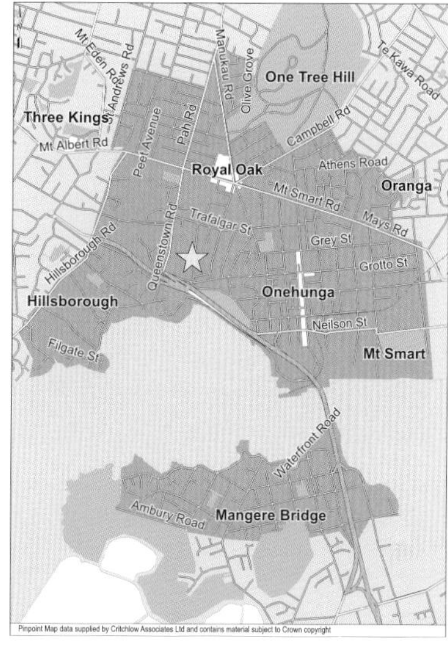

Zone boundary: On the northern side of the Manukau Harbour the boundary runs from Hillsborough Cemetery via Hillsborough Rd (including both sides), St Andrews Rd to Selwyn Rd, Pah Rd and Ngaroma Rd (included in each case) to One Tree Hill Domain. From the domain across Campbell Rd at its intersection with Moana Ave then via Moana Rd, Namata Rd, Curzon St, Mays Rd and Captain Springs Rd (included in each case) to the Manukau Harbour. South of the Manukau Harbour the boundary follows a line south of Ambury Rd, Taylor Rd, Domain Rd and Hastie Ave so that both sides of these streets, and the no exit streets leading off them, are included.

Orewa College

Riverside Rd, Orewa Ph 09 426 4075
www.oc.school.nz

Roll 1799; co-educational; years 7-13

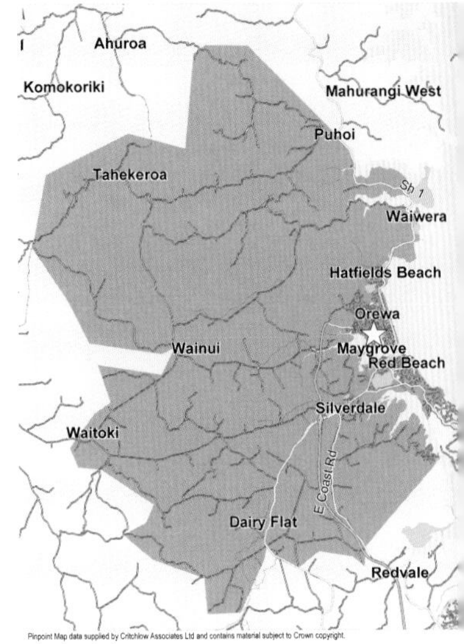

Ethnic mix: 78% NZ European, 8.7% Maori with more than 100 international students from South America, Asia, Europe and North America. Orewa College has an emphasis on languages from Year 8, including Spanish, Japanese and Maori. It has top-level social science and technology facilities, including a new automotive workshop. There are extensive grounds and sporting facilities.

Performing arts are important; prefects are appointed to this area of the curriculum.

Co curricular activities range from drama and musical theatre to community projects, charity work and clubs such as the Astronomy Club and Model United Nations Assembly. Gifted and talented students are catered for with Club 100.

Pupils from rural areas are serviced by a free school bus.

Zone boundary: On the Whangaparaoa Peninsula, it crosses Vipond Rd between Shadon Pl and Dobell Pl. Excludes house numbers greater than or equal to 400 Whangaparaoa Rd and 139 Vipond Rd. Includes Rivervale Grove, Blue Heron Rise, Brian Cres and John Rd but excludes Carento Way, Dobell Rd and Gledstanes Rd. North along the coast to include Wenderholm Regional Park. From the northern tip of the park, west in a line to the Puhoi/Ahuroa Rd turnoff from SH1 (excluding Hungry Creek Rd). From the Puhoi/Ahuroa Rd turnoff, it includes the roads south of, but not including, Moirs Hill Rd, then south to include J Tolhoph Rd. Then south-west to the intersection of Krippner Rd and Tahekeroa Rd, including Rauner Rd. Then west along Tahekeroa Rd to the intersection of Tahekeroa and Haruru Rds where it follows down Haruru Rd to its intersection with Monowai Rd, including Lee Anne Rd. Then west to include Pebble Brook Rd and then south to include Drinnan Rd where it turns south-east and cuts through the junction of Forestry Rd and Ireland Rd. It includes only the beginning of Forestry Rd, north of Ireland Rd, but does not include Ireland Rd. It then follows, but does not include, Ireland Rd to the intersection at the west end of Blackbridge Rd. Along the edge of Riverhead Forest, following Blackbridge Rd to SH17. It includes only Escott Rd, Three Oaks Rd and Jean Mackay Rd, off Blackbridge Rd. Then south down SH17 to the start of Bawden Rd, to include Jeffs Rd and Postmans Rd but not including Green Rd, Sunnyside or Robinson Rd. Then following Bawden Rd to its intersection with SH1 and Coast Rd, including all of Bawden Rd and the roads off it. Then in a straight line, north east, to Stillwater Heads where it includes Stillwater Rd and all the roads off it. Then up the coastline to the eastern boundary.

Otahuhu College

74-78 Mangere Rd, Otahuhu, ph 09 270 1170
www.otahuhucollege.school.nz

Roll 1463; co-educational; years 9-13

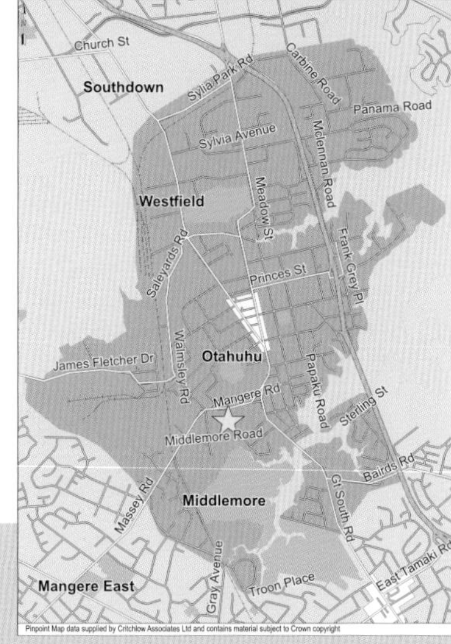

Otahuhu College has always been a working-class school in a working-class area – as evidenced by its Decile one ranking, but that doesn't stop it offering plenty of academic, sporting and cultural opportunities. Students are from the diverse ethnic community. Pacific students make up 71.3% (Samoan 34.5%, Tongan 16.2%, Cook Island 8.4%, Niuean 5.5%) with Maori 12.3% and NZ European 3.6%. There are also a number of Indian, Vietnamese and Chinese students.

Zone boundary: The northern boundary line goes from Anns Creek at Westfield, along the railway line through Sylvia Park on a direct line to the Tamaki River. The other boundary line begins at the Favona Bridge over Harania Creek to the junction of Massey Rd (up to and including 240 and 249) and Gray Ave, along Gray Ave (both sides included in the Otahuhu College zone up to and including 102 and 115A) to the railway line, along the railway line and across Swaffield Rd (62 and 41 and over) and the Grange Gold Course (so that Middlemore Cres is included), then to the motorway (Motatau Rd is excluded and Bairds Rd east until the motorway is included) and along the motorway to the Tamaki River.

Pakuranga College

Pigeon Mountain Rd, Bucklands Beach,
ph 09 534 7159 www.pakuranga.school.nz

Roll 2199; co-educational; years 9-13

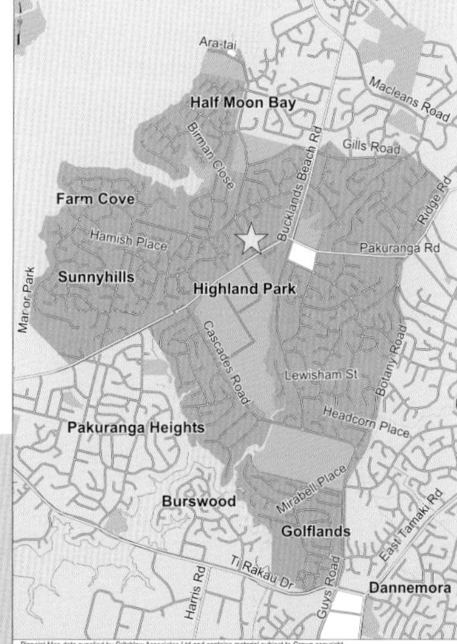

Ethnic mix: While 50% of the roll is NZ European and 34% Asian, students hail from over 48 countries. The college has a strong academic reputation and well resourced facilities, including the school's own television station! It has a new state-of-the-art library and information centre, science and English facilities, and new gymnasium.

Zone boundary: Western boundary is from the Tamaki River around the eastern boundary of St Kentigern College to the Pakuranga Main Highway so that Grammar School Rd is included, then along Pakuranga Rd to the Pakuranga Creek, with the northern side of the main highway included; along the line of the creek using Pakuranga Creek and its tributaries as the southern boundary as far as it can be taken, then taking a straight line to the intersection of Ti Rakau Dr with Botany Rd, including those streets coming west from Botany Rd and excluding Ti Rakau Dr and any streets coming from it. Northern boundary commences at Half Moon Bay then via Ara Tai and Pigeon Mountain Rds (both excluded) to the junction of Gills Rd, then via Gills Rd to Bleakhouse Rd, along Bleakhouse Rd (excluded) to Ridge Rd and along Ridge and Botany Rds (both included).

Papatoetoe High School

Nicholson Ave, Papatoetoe, ph 09 278 4086
www.papatoetoehigh.school.nz

Roll 1798; co-educational; years 9-13

Students represent more than 50 different nationalities (42% Asian, 21% NZ European, 16.8% Pacific, 15% Maori). The school has a solid reputation in academic and sporting activities. Ongoing roll growth has resulted in an extensive building and modernization programme. New facilities include grass hockey fields, new larger gym, sciences, technology and library blocks.

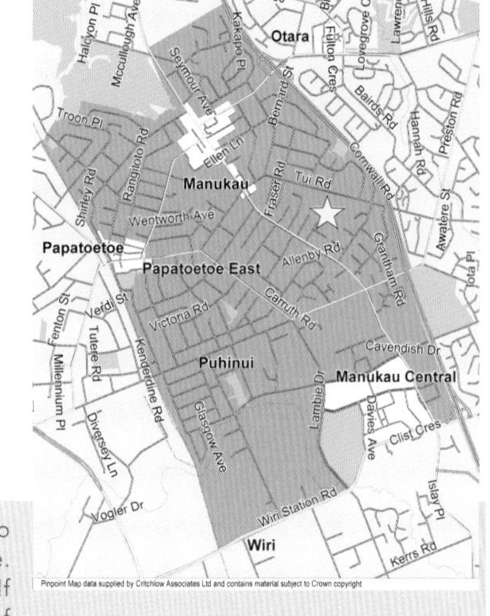

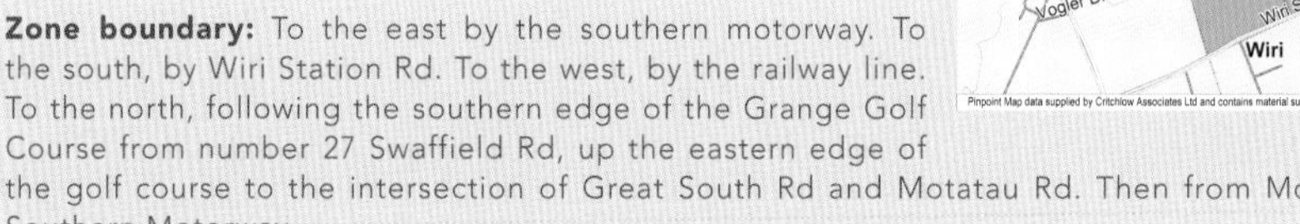

Zone boundary: To the east by the southern motorway. To the south, by Wiri Station Rd. To the west, by the railway line. To the north, following the southern edge of the Grange Golf Course from number 27 Swaffield Rd, up the eastern edge of the golf course to the intersection of Great South Rd and Motatau Rd. Then from Motatau Rd to the Southern Motorway.

Pukekohe High School

142 Harris St, Pukekohe, ph 09 238 6089
www.pukekohehigh.school.nz

Roll 1573; co-educational; years 9-13

Ethnic mix: Predominantly NZ European (70%).

This school has a broad curriculum across all levels with a strong emphasis on information technology. It has a tradition of academic, sporting and cultural endeavours. Alternative sporting codes include weightlifting, wrestling, orienteering and equestrian. Performing Arts activities include kapa haka, lip synch, Shakespeare competition and a range of music groups. New classrooms and other facilities are under development due to roll increases.

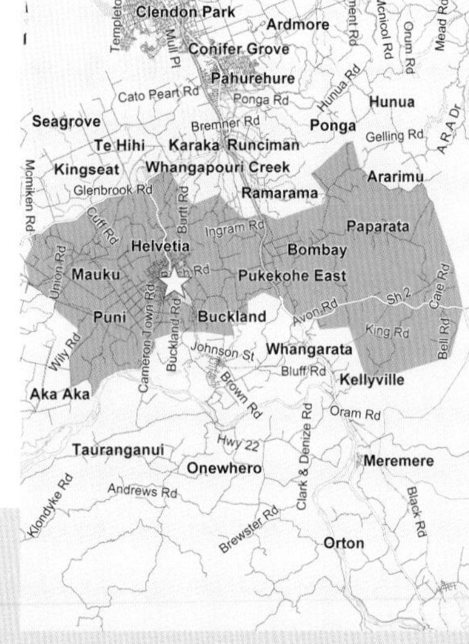

Zone boundary: SH22 north of Pukekohe to the edge of Rosehill College's zone; Sim Rd and Burtt Rd to Needham Rd; 2km north of Runcimann Rd and Tuhimata Rd intersection; Kern Rd and including Patrick Rd; Coulston Rd, Ambush Rd, Flay Rd, Great South Rd, north of Flay Rd; north of dogleg on Hillview Rd; Chamberlain Rd, Totara Rd, Dunn Rd; Ararimu Rd from Totara Rd to Paparimu Rd including all no exit roads off the northern side of Ararimu (Steel Rd, Sinclair Rd and Downs Rd) are included; Paparimu Rd, south of intersection with Matheson Rd; Matheson Rd; Lyons Rd, Caie Rd, Jeff Rd, McKenzie Rd; SH 2 to Mangatangi Rd intersection; Bell Rd, Homestead Rd, Chester Rd; Koheroa Rd east of no 341; SH2 to SH1(and including) Baird Rd, Dobson Rd, Serpell Rd, Irish Rd, Rimu Rd, McMillan Rd, O'Leary Rd;

Nikau Rd, Razorback Rd, Beaver Rd; Jericho Rd, Ruebe Rd; Harrisville Rd, Buckville Rd, Jamieson Rd; Buckland Rd to intersection of Tuakau Rd; Ray Wright Rd, Pukekohe; Upper Queen St, Camerontown Rd, Clifford Rd, Knight Lane; Tramway Rd, Settlement Rd, Fulton Rd, Puni; Aka Aka Rd (including Riverview Rd, Shipherd Rd and Massey Rd) until intersection with Eastern Drain Rd; Eastern Drain Rd and Wiley Rd; Waiuku Rd and including Waller Rd, up to 970; Baldhill Rd to top of hill (up to and including no 160); Farm Park Rd, Glenbrook Station Rd to Gearon Rd; Gearon Rd to Quinn Rd, Martyn Wright Rd; Glenbrook Rd east of Klipsch Rd (not included), to SH 22; Glenbrook Rd (both sides) and all roads south of it (Cuff Rd, Ostrich Rd, Pearson Rd, Kingseat Rd).

Rangitoto College

564 East Coast Rd, Browns Bay, ph 09 477 0150
www.rangitoto.school.nz

Roll 3074; co-educational; years 9-13

On a ridge overlooking the prosperous suburb of Mairangi Bay on Auckland's North Shore, Rangitoto College is not just the biggest school in Auckland, it's the biggest secondary school in the country. It's the most popular state school on the shore – a high-performing co-ed that's in big demand among shore families, longstanding residents and new migrants alike.

Rangitoto has a strong tradition of academic excellence, with outstanding results in national examinations. The school's size means it has superb international-class facilities (including a new auditorium and an Olympic-standard hockey turf).

Zone boundary: From Browns Bay via Anzac Rd (excluded) and Glencoe Rd (included) to the bridge over the Taiatoa Creek and then via John Downs Dr to East Coast Rd so that John Downs Dr and all no-exit streets off it are excluded. Then via Andersons Rd (excluded), the southern boundary of the sports fields to the junction of Masons Rd and Oteha Valley Rd, then via Oteha Valley Rd (excluded) to the motorway and south via the motorway to Sunset Rd (excluded to the junction of Juniper Rd), to East Coast Rd and then via East Coast Rd (included) to the southern boundary of Pupuke Golf Course, along the southern boundary of the golf course, excluding Aberdeen Rd and Rae Rd, to Beach Rd at the intersection of Red Bluff Rise (included) to the sea.

Rosehill College

Edinburgh Ave, Papakura, ph 09 295 0661
www.rosehill-college.co.nz

Roll: 1820; co-educational; years 9-13

Ethnic Mix. Predominantly: NZ European (63.5%), then Maori (16%) and Asian (10%).

On the rural edge of greater urban Auckland, sport, cultural and academic successes are encouraged. It is strong in languages, including German and Spanish. Co curricular activities include kapa haka, wearable arts, debating and talent quests. Traditional codes aside, Rosehill offers an eclectic sporting mix including canoe polo, cheerleading, equestrian, karate and lawn bowls.

Zone boundary: Western rural boundary Waiau Beach, Manukau Harbour, Pahurehure Inlet. Southern rural boundary (west of motorway): North bank of Taihiki River to Glenbrook Rd. Both sides of Glenbrook Rd. All areas between Glenbrook and Karaka Rds and Manukau Harbour, Gellert Rd, Sim Rd, Bycroft Rd, Woodlyn Rd, Snelgars Rd, Burtt Rd to intersection with Needham Rd (from 155 Burtt Rd onwards), Needham Rd, Solataire Rd, Cheriton Lane, Runciman Rd to the intersection with Coulston (from 377 Runciman Rd onwards, not 368 Runciman Rd). Tuhimata Rd to the first stream from the Runciman/Tuhimata intersection (includes 479 Tuhimata Rd), Ingram Rd. Southern rural boundary (east of motorway): Ararimu Rd to intersection with Dunn Rd includes Dale, Maxted, Fausett, Turner Rd, Steel Rd, Ponga Rd to intersection with McEntee Rd (includes all roads off Ponga Rd up to and including McEntee Rd, from the Opaheke Rd end). Urban boundary Manurewa/ Takanini motorway interchange, Manukau Harbour, Pahurehure Inlet, east of motorway, main trunk railway line.

Rutherford College

Kotuku St, Te Atatu Peninsula, ph 09 834 9790
www.rutherford.school.nz

Roll 1246; co-educational; years 9-13

Ethnic Mix: 47% NZ European, 18% Maori, 13.5% Asian, 9.8% Pacific.

Multi-level programmes are backed by a gifted and talented programme for those students requiring further extension, along with ESOL and special needs support. Performing arts such as music, drama and dance are offered as academic subjects right through to a senior level.

Rutherford's list of water based sports - water polo, underwater hockey, sailing, kayaking – reflect its peninsula location.

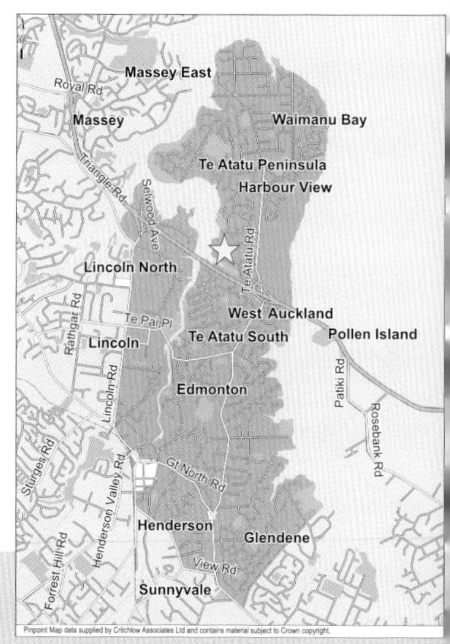

Zone boundary: The Rutherford College home zone starts at Lincoln Bridge (Triangle Rd), following a line down the centre of Lincoln Rd South until the railway line. Along the railway line south until View Rd. Along the centre of View Rd turning south into Great North Rd. Along the centre of Great North Rd turning east into Hepburn Rd. Along the centre of Hepburn Rd until the Whau River. Along the coast of the peninsula until reaching the Lincoln Bridge.

Sancta Maria College

Te Irirangi Dr, Manukau, ph 09 274 4081
www.sanctamaria.school.nz

Roll 469, growing to 1000; co educational; years 7-13

Ethnic mix: 44% NZ European, 25% Asian, 13% Pacific. Opening in 2004, the buildings of this new school are state of the art and include specialist science labs, art rooms, gym, auditorium and technology workshops. It's a state integrated school so 95% of the roll must be students with clear links to the Catholic Church. A chapel is an integral part of the attractively landscaped setting, including sports fields and walkways. Buses come from Howick, Pakuranga, Botany Downs, Maraetai, Beachlands and Whitford.

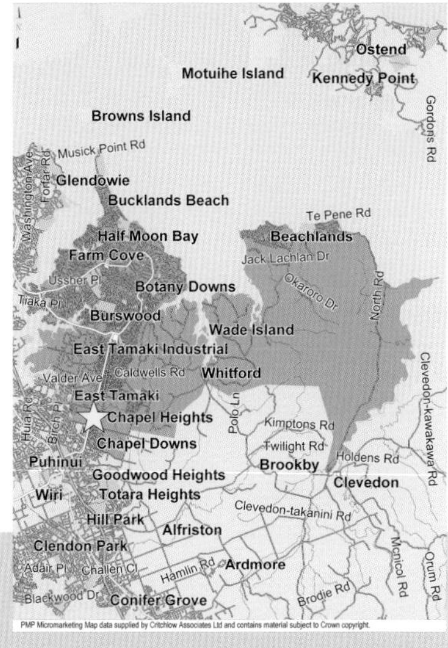

Zone boundary: From Otara Creek, following the Tamaki River north, around Musick Pt, around Whitford, Beachlands and Maraetai until the Wairoa River. Along the river and across to the intersection of North Rd, Twilight Rd and Papkura-Clevedon Rd. West until the intersection of Whitford Park Rd and Sandstone Rd, excluding Ara-Kotinga, Kimptons Rd and Polo Lane. Following Sandstone Rd until Ormiston Rd, including Regis and Shepherds Lanes. Following Ormiston Rd to the west, turning south into Murphy's Rd. Following Murphy's Rd until Thomas Rd. West down Thomas Rd and Dawson Rd (south sides excluded) until Te Irirangi Dr. North along Te Irirangi Dr (west side excluded) until Belinda Ave. Following Belinda Ave and Rongomai Rd (both excluded) until the intersection of Rongomai Rd and Dawson Rd. Along Dawson Rd (south side excluded) until Preston Rd. North along Preston Rd, East Tamaki Rd and Springs Rd (all west sides excluded) until Kerwyn Ave. West along Kerwyn Ave and south down Andromeda Cres until the Otara Creek. Note: Both sides of boundary roads included, unless otherwise noted.

Southern Cross Campus

253 Buckland Road West, Mangere, ph 09 255 0404
www.southerncross.school.nz

Roll 1706; co-educational; years 1-15

Ethnic mix: Maori 32%, European 2%, Samoan 23%, Tongan 21%, Cook Island Maori 14%, Niuean 6%, Other 2%.

Southern Cross Campus is New Zealand's largest and newest area school with over 1700 students. The student population is culturally diverse, the majority coming from Pacific backgrounds including Samoan, Tongan, Niuean and Cook Island Maori. A special feature of the Campus is Te Kura Maori o Nga Tapuwae which provides a full curriculum in the Maori language. Students move into a bi-lingual program at years 6 and 7 and continue their bilingual education through to year 13.

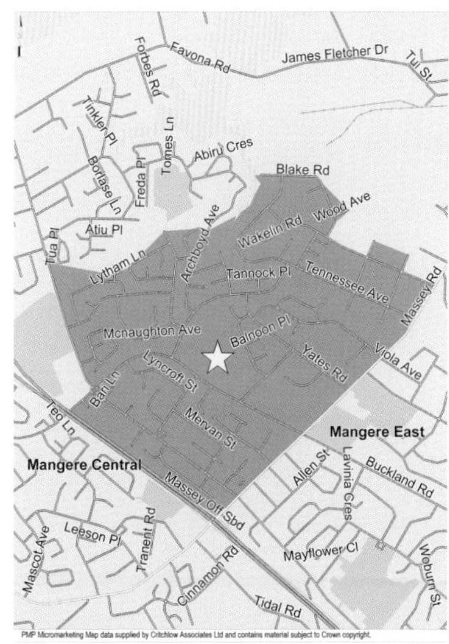

Zone boundary: The zone includes both sides of all boundary roads mentioned below, unless otherwise specified. Bader Dr from the motorway north-east until Robertson Rd. North along Robertson Rd until Calthorp Dr (excluded). Back along Robertson Rd until McKinstry Ave. East along McKinstry Ave turning north along Garus Ave and east along Archboyd Ave including all roads extending from these roads. Blake Ave (including Wood Ave) around until Vine St and along Vine St until Massey Rd (including all of Cleek Rd and Driver Rd). The western side of Massey Rd from Gray Ave to the motorway and along the motorway until Bader Dr. All of Lyncroft St (including Bellard Pl) to Buckland Rd and along Buckland Rd back to Robertson Rd (but excluding the southern side of Buckland Rd between Lyncroft St and Robertson Rd).

Tangaroa College

Haumia Way, East Tamaki, Manukau, ph 09 274 5764
www.tangaroa.school.nz

Roll 1076; co-educational; years 9-13

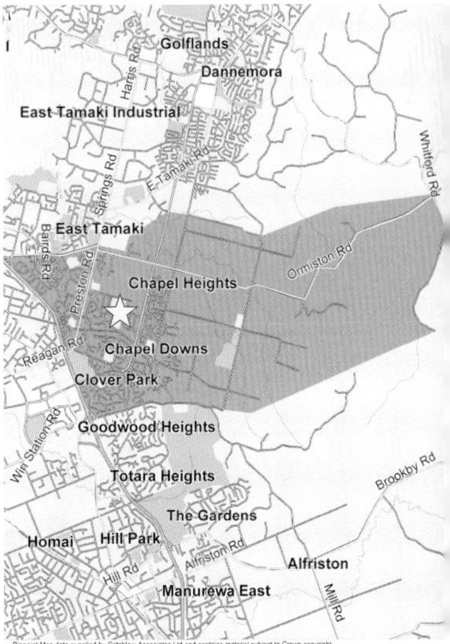

Tangaroa College has a very community-focused, team-oriented approach to education. Tutor teachers monitor attendance and behaviour and encourage learning; the health centre includes Home and Family Liaison; and Learning Support Teachers are available for students with learning difficulties. Students can study at multi-levels according to their abilities.

Nearly 95% of the school's students are of Pacific and Maori descent yet Tangaroa College was the surprise winner of an Auckland Indian high school dance competition in 2004, with a multicultural team of Maori, Samoan, Tongan and Nigerian students... but no Indians. The largely Indian crowd of 3000 loved the team's classical Indian dance and demanded an encore.

A state-of-the-art technology block was completed in 2004, complementing existing facilities such as the drama theatre, music studio, science laboratories and fitness centre.

Zone boundary: Western side of the Southern Motorway from East Tamaki Rd in the north to Redoubt Rd in the south. The northern side of Redoubt Rd. East Tamaki Rd from the Southern Motorway to East Tamaki War Memorial Park. Following a stream across to the corner of Te Irriangi Dr and Accent Rd. The southern side of Baverstock then across country to the intersection of Sandstone and Whitford Park Rd. The eastern side of Whitford Park Rd until Brownhill Rd and then the eastern side of Brownhill Rd and across country to Redoubt Rd.

Takapuna Grammar School

210 Lake Rd, Takapuna, ph 09 489 4167
www.takapuna.school.nz

Roll 1394; co-educational; years 9-13

The roll's ethnic make up reflects the surrounding neighbourhood. It is predominantly NZ European (70%) with only a small representation of Maori and Pacific Islanders. The next highest ethnic group is Asian at 14.3% and there are also 100 international students.

Takapuna claims its facilities are some of New Zealand's best. They include the Memorial Library, a weight-training room, a music suite (built in 1998) with a recording room and acoustically designed performance space, three computer classrooms, photographic facilities and pottery kilns.

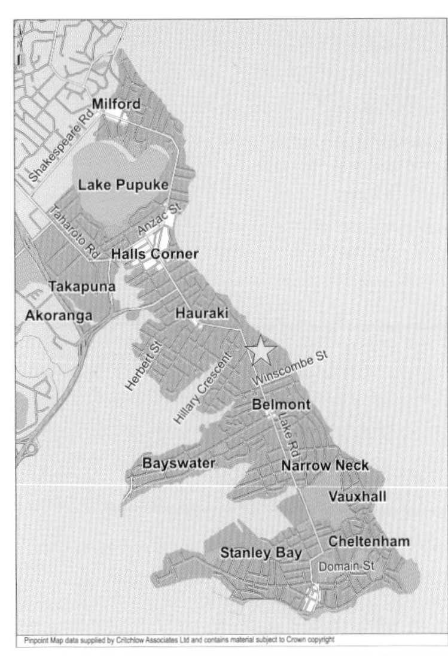

Pinpoint Map data supplied by Critchlow Associates Ltd and contains material subject to Crown copyright

Zone boundary: The Devonport peninsula from King Edward Pde and Jubilee Ave north to a boundary defined by and including Northcote Rd and its intersection with the northern motorway, Shea Tce and the southern shores of Lake Pupuke including Hurstmere Rd, Kitchener Rd and all side roads up to and including Fenwick Ave, Otakau Rd, Omana Rd and Craig Rd.

Waitakere College

42 Rathgar Rd, Henderson, ph 09 836 7890
www.waitakere.college.net.nz

Roll 1374; co-educational; years 9-13

Ethnic mix: NZ European 43%, Maori 22% , Pacific 20%, Asian 10%, other 5%.

The college offers a wide range of subjects including an enrichment programme and practical qualifications such as business administration and automotive engineering.

It runs special projects including the Maori Mainstream Pilot (to raise the achievement of Maori students) and the Gateway programme (a joint venture with Skill New Zealand to fund special work experience programmes for students).

Pinpoint Map data supplied by Critchlow Associates Ltd and contains material subject to Crown copyright

Zone boundary: Starts to the north of Bethells Beach at Te Waharoa Pt, then in a north-eastern line until it meets the Makoroa Stream, then east to the Wairere Stream. From the Wairere Stream the boundary joins Gregory Rd then to Wairere Rd (including Arrowsmith Rd). From Wairere Rd along Bethells Rd into Waitakere Township. The boundary crosses Waitakere Rd and the railway, including Township Rd and McEntee Rd. Then Sunnyvale Rd to Crows Rd. Where Crows Rd meets Birdwood Rd the boundary crosses directly to the Momutu Stream that runs through Te Rangi Hiroa Park. Momutu Stream joins the Swanson Stream and crosses Don Buck Rd at the point where Don Buck Rd meets the Huruhuru Creek. The Huruhuru Creek and Henderson Creek are the northeastern and eastern boundaries. Henderson Creek into the Opanuku Stream. The Opanuku Stream forms the southern boundary until a line from the headwaters of the Opanuku Stream crosses Scenic Dr and travels west to the coast at Wigmore Bay to the south of Bethells Beach.

Western Springs

100 Motions Rd, Western Springs, ph 09 846 8197
www.westernsprings.school.nz

Roll 855; co-educational; years 9-15

Ethnic mix: NZ European 69%, Maori 16%, Samoan 4%, Asian 4%, Niuean 3%, Cook Island 2%, Tongan 1%, Other 1%.

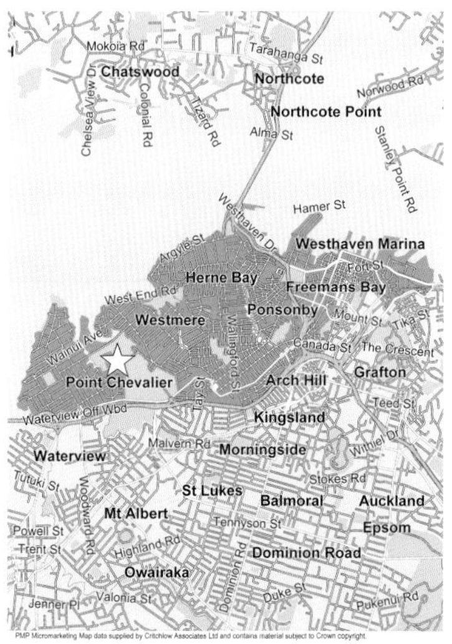

PMP Micromarketing Map data supplied by Critchlow Associates Ltd and contains material subject to Crown copyright.

Located close to Auckland City, the college caters for both its diverse local community, and for students prepared to travel to take advantage of its courses and special characteristics. According to recent ERO reports, the college provides a good variety of educational opportunities for students. Student achievement levels compare favourably with those of schools of a similar type, size and socio-economic status. The College has excelled in the high profile arts. In recent years students have won major regional and national competitions in drama and music.

Zone boundary: The boundary starts at: the North Western motorway/Pt Chevalier on ramp and travelling north following the coastline towards the container terminal to the inlet between Freyberg Wharf and Fergusson Wharf. Then travelling across to the intersection of Tamaki Drive and The Strand (Northern side only) and along The Strand (northern side only) to the intersection of Parnell Rise and Stanley Street (not including Stanley Street). From to the intersection of Parnell Rise and Stanley Street (west side only) to Alten Road (north side only) through to the intersection of Waterloo Quadrant (north side only) and Kitchener Street. Then travelling along Bowden Avenue (north side only) to Victoria Street (north side) and up along Queen Street to Upper Queen Street, then the boundary leaves Upper Queen Street and follows the Southern Motorway travelling north through to the North Western Motorway back to the Pt Chevalier on ramp.

Westlake Boys High School

30 Forrest Hill Rd, Forrest Hill, ph 09 410 8667
www.westlakebhs.school.nz

Roll 2100; boys; years 9-13

Westlake Boys High School prides itself in being both traditional and progressive in its outlook, with a proud record for academic, sporting and cultural achievement. Westlake Boys reflects the surrounding neighbourhood in its ethnic make up of predominantly NZ European (57%) and Asian (22%) students.

Cambridge International Exams are offered alongside NCEA. Sport is important. Last year Westlake Boys' won the national secondary schools' soccer championships. Boys are expected to participate in at least one team sport a year. Music is also encouraged through the curriculum and choir Voicemale, as well as concert, stage, rock and orchestral bands.

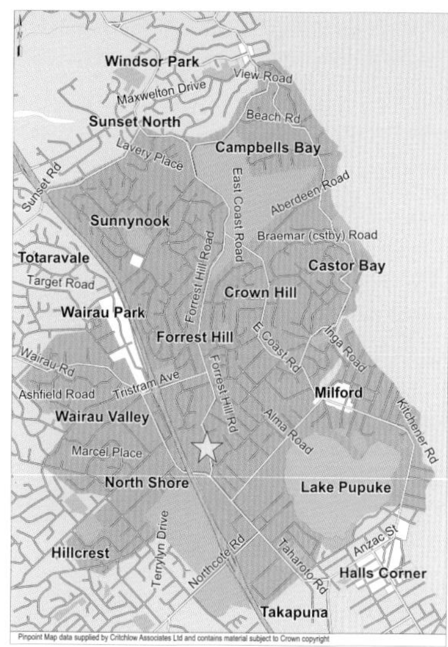

Pinpoint Map data supplied by Critchlow Associates Ltd and contains material subject to Crown copyright

Zone boundary: From the sea along Earnock (included), across Hurstmere Rd and along the edge of Lake Pupuke, excluding Killarney St and Manurere Ave to Taharoto Rd, but including Kowhai St and Pupuke Rd. It crosses Taharoto Rd at Killarney St and continues south of Dominion Rd (included) to Onewa Domain. Through the domain it crosses Northcote Rd and goes up by the golf course, excluding all streets to the west, to Benders Ave (included). Along Coronation Rd (included, also including Nicholson Pl) until Beatrice Ave (excluded). South of Archers Rd to Chivalry Rd, then north along Chivalry Rd (included, and including Edgeworth Rd) to Diana Dr. Along Diana Dr to Weldene Ave (excluded). North to Hogans Rd (excluded, Ngatoa Pl and Normanton Rd are also excluded). South of Hogans Rd and across Wairau Rd at Kathleen Pl, which is included. North of Ellice Rd (excluded), across Target Rd and south of Sunnynook Rd to the northern motorway. The northern boundary leaves the motorway at Sunset Rd and runs east along Sunset Rd (included) to East Coast Rd, along East Coast Rd (included) to Kowhai Rd (included). Along Kowhai Rd and across Beach Rd to the sea. Whitby Cres is included.

Westlake Girls High School

2 Wairau Rd, Takapuna, ph 09 489 4169
www.westlakegirls.school.nz

Roll 2174; girls; years 9-13

As the only public secondary single-sex girls school on the North Shore, Westlake Girls' High School is very popular. The roll reflects North Shore City's ethnicity, being 60% NZ European and 25% Asian.

The music suite includes a keyboard laboratory, classrooms and instrument practice rooms. The gymnasium, which opened in 2002, has a dance studio and fitness centre. There is also a swimming pool. The art rooms include a senior art area, design studio, photography and sculpture facilities. Students are exposed to a wide range of learning encounters, and leadership qualities are encouraged.

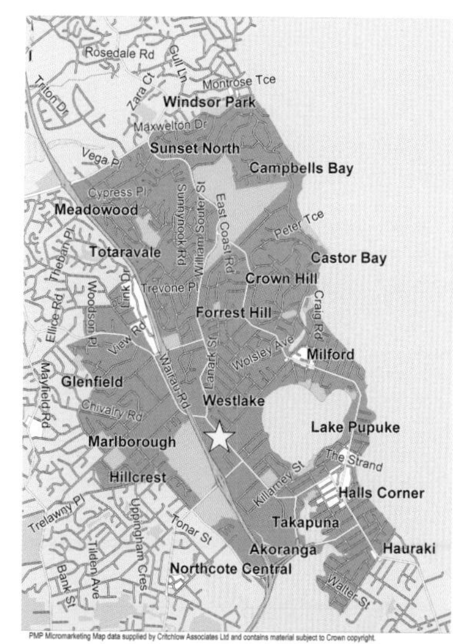

PMP Micromarketing Map data supplied by Critchlow Associates Ltd and contains material subject to Crown copyright

Sporting and cultural successes abound. Westlake Girls High School's Premier Cricket Team are the 2005 champs for the greater Auckland area; they go to the nationals in December.

Several Westlake Girls' musical groups, including their symphony orchestra and chamber orchestras, have won gold medals at regional and national music festivals. The school also recently won the North Island Inter-Secondary Schools Teams Dressage Championships for the fourth year in a row.

Zone boundary: Southern boundary is from Hauraki Rd, across Lake Rd and Jutland Rd, including all streets to the north, around Shoal Bay and to the western boundary of the Esmonde Rd interchange, along Akoranga Dr, crossing Northcote Rd, along Sunnybrae Rd to Coronation Rd, which is included, as is Nicholson Pl, until it reaches Beatrice Ave, which is excluded. It runs south of Archers Rd to the junction with Chartwell Ave, then up Chartwell Ave (included) to the junction with Diana Dr (included) and along Diana Dr until Weldene Ave (excluded). Ngatoa Pl and Normanton St are also excluded. The zone runs south of Hogans Rd and crosses Wairua Rd at Kathleen Pl, which is included. North to Ellice Rd (excluded), across Target Rd and south of Sunnynook Rd to the northern motorway. From the northern motorway down Constellation Dr to the junction at East Coast Rd, along East Coast Rd to Maxwelton Dr and down Maxwelton Dr to Ramsgate Tce and Sidmouth St to the sea.

Whangaparaoa College

15 Delshaw Ave, Whangaparaoa, ph 09 428 4724
www.wgpcollege.school.nz

Roll 854 growing to 2000; co-educational; years 9-13

The newest secondary school in Auckland, Whangaparaoa College opened its doors in 2005 with 865 Year 7 to 9 students. This makes it one of only a handful of New Zealand state schools that incorporate intermediate level students into the school.

Students in the junior level will be mainly taught by one teacher, but will move into different areas for specialist subjects. Approximately 85% of the roll is NZ European, the rest is mainly Maori and Asian. The school is to cap its roll at 2000.

Pinpoint Map data supplied by Critchlow Associates Ltd and contains material subject to Crown copyright.

Zone boundary: crosses Vipond Rd between Brian Cres and Ellenbury Pl, and includes house numbers greater than or equal to 139 Vipond Rd; and Whangaparaoa Rd between Shadon Place and Dobell, and include house numbers greater than or equal to 400 Whangaparaoa Rd.

If you're considering sending your child to private school, this information will provide an at-a-glance guide to what you'll pay and what you'll get for your money.
Different private schools have different fee structures for the four-term academic year and some of the fees quoted may include a discount for prompt payment. In most cases, the fees quoted don't include essential extras such as school trips, sports fees, uniforms, laptop computers etc. Boarding fees are in addition to tuition fees. Some schools (*) quote a per term rate which we have converted to an annual fee for easy comparison.

Auckland International College

Auckland City; ph 09 309 4480

www.aic.ac.nz; years 11-13; co-ed; roll 170; established 2003. A three-year senior secondary school for international and New Zealand students who wish to gain entry to universities in New Zealand as well as in other countries. Fees: year 11 $11,450; years 12-13 $11,950.

Carey College

Panmure; ph 09 570 5873

www.carey.school.nz; years 1-13; co-ed; roll 50; established 1988. "A friendly and nurturing family-based school, uncompromising in its commitment to biblical schooling, to the building of Christ-like character, and to teaching of the highest standards." Fees: years 1-8 $5000; years 9-10 $5840; years 11-13 $7080.

Corran School

Remuera; ph 09 520 1400

www.corran.school.nz; years 1-13; girls only; roll 500; established 1954; Christian. "A small school which allows individual attention, where the uniqueness of every student is fully acknowledged, and where pastoral care really works." Fees: years 1-6 $10,782; years 7-8 $13,168; years 9-13 $12,993.

Diocesan School *

Epsom; ph 09 520 0221

www.diocesan.school.nz; girls only; years 1-13 1522 students including 35 boarders; Anglican; founded 1903. Fees: years 1-6 $11,612; years 7-13 $13,356.

ACG Parnell College

Parnell (alongside the domain); ph 09 308 1666

www.acg.ac.nz; co-ed; 375 students; years 7-10.

Established 1998. Special features: junior high school; high-interest academic programme. Fees: $11,250.

Kadimah College

Auckland City; ph 09 373 3072

www.kadimah.co.nz; preschool to year 8; co-ed; roll 165; established 1971. Jewish – although children from all backgrounds are welcome. "Small classes and children learning in ability rather than age groups for subjects such as maths and reading ensure individual attention and promote the joy of learning."

Fees: preschool $7421; years 1-6 $9569; years 7-8 $10,013.

King's College

Otahuhu; ph 09 276 0600

www.kingscollege.school.nz; 948 students; years 9-13; boys only up to year 11; accepts girls in year 12 and 13. Boarders and day students. Established 1896; Christian (Anglican) ethos. Offers Cambridge International examinations. Fees: years 9-11 $16,132; years 12-13 $16,776.

The closest thing Auckland has to the traditional public schools of Great Britain.

King's School (primary)

Remuera; ph 09 520 7770

www.kings.school.nz; boys only; 656 students; years 1-8. Established 1922; Christian (Anglican). Fees: years 1-3 $9800; years 4-6 $10,520; years 7-8 $11,280.

Kristin*

Albany, ph 09 415 9566

www.kristin.school.nz; co-ed; 1586 students from kindergarten to year 13. Established 1972; non-denominational Christian ethos; second language teaching; International Baccalaureat syllabus and exams. Fees: years 0-6 $10,100; years 7-10 $12,520; years 11-13 $12,788.

Established 30 years ago by a group of parents who wanted a high-quality independent school for the North Shore. It has a strong international focus, aiming to prepare students to be "responsible world citizens". Kristin provides all-round education that's "vibrant, innovative, yet rigorous".

Pinehurst School

Albany, ph 09 414 0960

www.pinehurst.school.nz; co-ed; 800 from year 0 to year 13. A non-denominational independent school established in 1991. Offers Cambridge International exams. Fees: years 0-6 $7600; years 7-8 $8480; years 10-13 $9840. The schools vision - "Children should be proud of who they are, what they know and what they can achieve." Pinehurst's goal is to raise children who are not only able to succeed academically, but also succeed at life; be secure, happy, confident individuals who understand the importance of community,respect and caring.

Senior College

Auckland; ph 09 307 4477

www.acg.ac.nz; co-ed; 466 students; years 11-13. Established 1995. Special features: Senior students only; "challenging schooling for students to reach their potential" in a pre-university environment; specialist teaching;

Cambridge International Examinations. Fees $13,200. A school for year 11, 12 and 13 students aiming to be a "specialist pre-university centre", meeting the special needs of senior secondary students.

The school's stated intention is "educating young men and women who will make a difference", and there's a focus on giving students the freedom to make choices and take responsibility for their learning.

St Cuthbert's College *

Epsom; ph 09 520 4159

www.stcuthberts.school.nz; years 1-13; girls only;1409 students; including 130 boarders. Established 1915; Presbyterian; very strong academically – in 2002 top school in country for scholarships, second for A bursary, top for School Certificate. Fees: years 1-6 $11,304; years 7-8 $13,020; years 9-10 $13,200; years 11-13 $13,415.

St Kentigern College

Pakuranga; ph 09 576 9019

www.saintkentigern.com; years 7-13; fully co-ed (since 2003); 1598 students; established 1953. Presbyterian; "broad, sound, innovative education"; strong in academics, IT and extra-curricular activities; sports academy. Fees: $12,279.

St Kentigern School (primary)

Remuera; ph 09 520 7682

www.saintkentigern.com; years 1-8; boys only; 493 students. Established 1959; Presbyterian. Fees: years 1-3 $9924; years 4-6 $10,830; years 7-8 $12,279.

Strathallan College

Hingaia Peninsula, ph 09 295 0830

www.acg.ac.nz; years 1-13, plus kindergarten; co-ed; 875 students; established 2001. Part of AGC private education group (which also includes Junior and Senior Colleges), the school offers Cambridge International exams. It's one of largest independent school complexes in New Zealand and offers a complete pathway from kindergarten to year 13. Fees: years 0-6 $9100; years 7-10 $10,800; years 11-13 $11,400.

Wentworth College

Whangaparaoa; ph 09 358 0676

www.wentworthcollege.school.nz; years 7-13; co-ed; roll 156; established 2003; secular.

"Wentworth College provides a high quality, comprehensive and challenging education in a positive, caring school environment. Traditional values of respect, courtesy and consideration are clearly articulated and students respond positively to the expectations of their teachers." Fees: $11,000.

Auckland Schools are listed only under the suburb in which they are physically located. Many will have wider catchment areas or zones.
A decile rating is given to each state or state integrated school, of between one and 10. The decile rating is based on census information and reflects the socio-economic level of the population from which the school draws its students – not academic results. A lower socio-economic area will have schools with lower ratings. Decile ratings are not applicable to private schools. A state integrated school is a school with a special (religious or philosophical) character, which has been integrated into the state system. It has state funding but the school owns the land and buildings.

CENTRAL

Name	Addresss	Phone	Level	Funding	Gender	Decile	Roll
AUCKLAND CITY							
MindAlive	68a Nelson St	849 4780	all levels	private	co-ed	n/a	35
Kadimah College	108 Greys Ave	373 3072	primary	private	co-ed	10	165
ACG New Zealand International College	Cnr Rutland & Lorne St	307 5399	secondary	private	co-ed	7	447
ACG Senior College	Cnr Rutland & Lorne St	307 4477	secondary	state	co-ed	n/a	466
Auckland Girls' Grammar School	Howe St	307 4180	secondary	state	girls	5	1393
Auckland International College	85 Airedale St	309 4480	secondary	private	co-ed	n/a	88
AVONDALE							
Immanuel Christian School	63 St Georges Rd	828 4545	all levels	private	co-ed	n/a	165
Avondale Primary School	Crayford St West	828 8929	primary	state	co-ed	3	370
New Windsor School	New Windsor Rd	626 6356	primary	state	co-ed	5	505
Waterview School	Oakley Ave	828 7227	primary	state	co-ed	1	157
Rosebank School	217 Rosebank Rd	828 6319	primary	state	co-ed	2	659
St Mary's School	2140 Great North Rd	828 5599	prim+interm	state integrated	co-ed	2	294
Avondale Intermediate	Holly St	828 7883	Intermediate	state	co-ed	3	541
Avondale College	Victor St	828 7024	secondary	state	co-ed	5	2591
Odyssey House School	56 Bollard Ave	374 4556	secondary	private	co-ed	n/a	18
BLOCKHOUSE BAY							
Hill Top School	37 Heaphy St	627 9295	all levels	private	co-ed	7	110
Blockhouse Bay School	584 Blockhouse Bay Rd	627 9940	primary	state	co-ed	8	606
Chaucer School	Chaucer Place	626 6699	primary	state	co-ed	4	213
Halsey Drive School	106 Halsey Drive	627 9106	primary	state	co-ed	8	507
Glenavon School	340 Blockhouse Bay Rd	828 7029	prim+interm	state	co-ed	2	276
St Dominic's School	32 Bolton St	626 5391	prim+interm	state	co-ed	7	259
Blockhouse Bay Intermediate	Bolton St	626 6414	Intermediate	state	co-ed	6	611
EASTERN BAYS							
St Ignatius School	72 Speight Rd	575 7081	primary	state integrated	co-ed	10	200
St Joseph's School	16 Brenton Place	521 0866	primary	state integrated	co-ed	6	84
Churchill Park School	Riddell Rd	575 8156	prim+interm	state	co-ed	10	481
Glen Taylor School	172 West Tamaki Rd	528 6325	prim+interm	state	co-ed	1	267
Glendowie School	217 Riddell Rd	575 7374	prim+interm	state	co-ed	7	554
Kohimarama School	112 Kohimarama Rd	528 5306	prim+interm	state	co-ed	10	442
Orakei School	Grace St	521 0657	prim+interm	state	co-ed	4	157
St Heliers School	126-160 St Heliers Bay Rd	575 8311	prim+interm	state	co-ed	6	480
St Thomas School	Allum St	528 3938	prim+interm	state	co-ed	9	607

CENTRAL

		Phone	Level	Funding	Gender	Decile	Roll
Glendowie College	Crossfield Rd	575 9128	secondary	state	co-ed	9	908
Sacred Heart College	West Tamaki Rd	529 3660	secondary	state integrated	boys	8	1011
Selwyn College	Kohimarama Rd	521 9610	secondary	state	co-ed	5	1043
EPSOM							
Diocesan School For Girls	Clyde St	520 0221	all levels	private	girls	n/a	1522
St Cuthbert's College	Market Rd	520 4159	all levels	state	girls	n/a	1409
Epsom Normal School	41 The Drive	630 5144	primary	state	co-ed	10	605
Kohia Terrace School	3 Kohia Terrace	630 4525	prim+interm	state	co-ed	10	345
Our Lady Sacred Heart School	19 Banff Ave	638 6200	prim+interm	state integrated	co-ed	10	223
Auckland Grammar	Mountain Rd	623 5400	secondary	state	boys	10	2530
Epsom Girls' Grammar School	Silver Rd	630 5963	secondary	state	girls	10	1902
Marcellin College	617 Mt Albert Rd	625 6509	secondary	state integrated	co-ed	3	782
St Peter's College	Mountain Rd	524 8108	secondary	state integrated	boys	7	1129
GLEN INNES/PT ENGLAND							
Glen Innes School	Eastview Rd	528 3507	primary	state	co-ed	1	202
Glenbrae School	Leybourne Circle	528 5025	primary	state	co-ed	1	178
St Pius X School	103 Castledine Crescent	528 7257	prim+interm	state integrated	co-ed	1	142
Te Kura Kaupapa Puau Te Moana-Nui-A-Kiwa	26a Farringdon St	528 0210	prim+interm	state	co-ed	1	32
Tamaki College	Elstree Ave	521 1104	secondary	state	co-ed	1	636
GREY LYNN							
Grey Lynn School	Surrey Crescent	376 3255	primary	state	co-ed	5	251
Newton Central School	Monmouth St	378 6883	primary	state	co-ed	6	222
Pt Chevalier School	Te Ra Rd	846 1359	primary	state	co-ed	7	576
St Francis School	Montrose St	846 4696	primary	state integrated	co-ed	6	197
Westmere School	Larchwood Ave	361 0014	primary	state	co-ed	9	422
St Joseph's School	456 Great North Rd	376 5456	prim+interm	state integrated	co-ed	3	146
Pasadena Intermediate	Moray Place	846 2169	Intermediate	state	co-ed	5	275
Western Springs College	Motions Rd	846 8197	secondary	state	co-ed	7	855
HAURAKI GULF ISLANDS							
Te Huruhi School	7 Donald Bruce Rd	372 0200	primary	state	co-ed	5	472
Kaitoke School	Kaitoke Lane	429 0273	prim+interm	state	co-ed	2	71
Mulberry Grove School	Shoal Bay Rd	429 0475	prim+interm	state	co-ed	3	17
Okiwi School	Great Barrier Island	429 0138	prim+interm	state	co-ed	3	22
Waiheke Primary School	26 Sea View Rd	372 2372	prim+interm	state	co-ed	6	113
Waiheke High School	11 Donald Bruce Rd	372 8938	secondary	state	co-ed	4	464
KINGSLAND							
Kowhai Intermediate	26 Onslow Rd	846 7534	Intermediate	state	co-ed	6	370
MEADOWBANK							
Michael Park School	55 Amy St	579 3083	all levels	state integrated	co-ed	9	391
Mt Carmel School	6 Mt Carmel Place	521 5161	primary	state integrated	co-ed	9	190

CENTRAL

Name	Addresss	Phone	Level	Funding	Gender	Decile	Roll
Ellerslie School	12 Kalmia St	579 5477	prim+interm	state	co-ed	7	487
St Mary's School	58 Main Highway	579 8937	prim+interm	state integrated	co-ed	5	226
MT ALBERT							
Hebron Christian College	1 McLean St	846 2159	all levels	private	co-ed	9	272
Edendale School	419 Sandringham Rd	846 6340	primary	state	co-ed	5	550
Gladstone School	8 Seaview Terrace	846 9744	primary	state	co-ed	7	810
Marist School	14 Kitenui Ave	846 7408	primary	state integrated	co-ed	7	292
Mt Albert School	Sainsbury Rd	846 9288	primary	state	co-ed	5	159
Owairaka District School	113-115 Richardson Rd	846 5091	primary	state	co-ed	2	357
Te Kura Kaupapa Maori O Nga Maungarongo	140 Haverstock Rd	815 6349	prim+interm	state	co-ed	4	88
Marist College	31 Alberton Ave	846 8311	secondary	state integrated	girls	6	749
Mt Albert Grammar School	Alberton Ave	846 2044	secondary	state	co-ed	5	2242
MT EDEN							
Good Shepherd School	30 Telford Ave	620 4962	primary	state integrated	co-ed	7	177
Maungawhau School	Ellerton Rd	638 8829	primary	state	co-ed	10	650
Mt Eden Normal School	Valley Rd	630 0009	primary	state	co-ed	9	599
Balmoral S D A School	10 a Wiremu St	638 7903	prim+interm	state integrated	co-ed	5	130
Balmoral School	19 Brixton Rd	638 7960	prim+interm	state	co-ed	8	700
Ficino School	27 Esplanade Rd	623 3385	prim+interm	private	co-ed	10	103
St Therese School	463 Mt Albert Rd	620 9441	prim+interm	state integrated	co-ed	2	123
Auckland Normal Intermediate	Poronui St	630 1109	Intermediate	state	co-ed	10	644
MT ROSKILL							
Sunnydene Special School	48 Smallfield Ave	620 7680	special	state	co-ed	3	61
Dominion Rd School	Quest Terrace	620 9483	primary	state	co-ed	3	376
Hay Park School	670 Richardson Rd	625 9531	primary	state	co-ed	1	204
Hillsborough School	Belfast St	625 7307	primary	state	co-ed	9	404
Marshall Laing School	Marshall Laing Ave	626 5103	primary	state	co-ed	7	452
May Rd School	504 Richardson Rd	626 8021	primary	state	co-ed	2	245
Mt Roskill Primary School	Frost Rd	620 5050	primary	state	co-ed	5	766
Three Kings School	944 Mt Eden Rd	625 7208	primary	state	co-ed	7	433
Waikowhai School	381 Hillsborough Rd	627 9665	primary	state	co-ed	3	197
Wesley School	Potter Ave	620 9261	primary	state	co-ed	1	236
Christ The King School	288 Richardson Rd	626 7123	prim+interm	state integrated	co-ed	4	158
Monte Cecilia School	72 Hillsborough Rd	625 5018	prim+interm	state integrated	co-ed	8	196
Mt Roskill Intermediate	Denbigh Ave	620 8508	intermediate	state	co-ed	4	818
Waikowhai Intermediate	Richardson Rd	620 1600	intermediate	state	co-ed	5	393
Wesley Intermediate	Sandringham Rd Extension	620 9367	intermediate	state	co-ed	1	154
Lynfield College	White Swan Rd	627 0600	secondary	state	co-ed	7	1863
Mt Roskill Grammar	Frost Rd	621 0050	secondary	state	co-ed	4	2306

CENTRAL

Name	Addresss	Phone	Level	Funding	Gender	Decile	Roll
ONEHUNGA							
Onehunga Primary School	122 Arthur St	636 6256	primary	state	co-ed	3	324
Te Papapa School	219 Mt Smart Rd	634 5252	primary	state	co-ed	1	205
St Joseph's School	125 Church St	636 8102	prim+interm	state integrated	co-ed	3	296
Onehunga High School	Pleasant St	636 6006	secondary	state	co-ed	3	1423
Penrose High School	421 - 451 Great South Rd	579 5049	secondary	state	co-ed	3	830
ONE TREE HILL							
Cornwall Park School	193 Greenlane West	524 6574	primary	state	co-ed	9	640
Oranga School	21 Rangipawa Rd	579 4189	primary	state	co-ed	2	330
Royal Oak School	Chandler Ave	624 2800	primary	state	co-ed	7	596
Royal Oak Intermediate School	74 Symonds St	636 5667	Intermediate	state	co-ed	3	588
PANMURE							
Sommerville School	7a Bengazi Rd	570 9787	special	state	co-ed	5	136
Carey College	21 Domain Rd	570 5873	all levels	private	co-ed	8	39
Panmure Bridge School	76 Kings Rd	527 6462	primary	state	co-ed	1	167
Pt England School	130 Pt England Rd	527 6247	primary	state	co-ed	1	449
Ruapotaka School	10 a Taratoa S	527 6244	primary	state	co-ed	1	238
Tamaki School	Alamein Rd	527 6345	primary	state	co-ed	1	171
Bailey Rd School	19 Bailey Rd	579 4619	prim+interm	state	co-ed	3	446
Destiny School	18 Allright Place	570 7150	prim+interm	private	co-ed	n/a	45
Panmure District School	87 Mount Wellington Highway	527 7659	prim+interm	state	co-ed	2	177
St Patrick's School	5 Church Crescent	527 7016	prim+interm	state integrated	co-ed	1	132
Stanhope Rd School	2 b Harris Rd	579 6434	prim+interm	state	co-ed	4	502
Sylvia Park School	Longford St	527 6526	prim+interm	state	co-ed	2	248
Tamaki Intermediate	80 a Tripoli Rd	527 6525	Intermediate	state	co-ed	1	359
PARNELL/NEWMARKET							
ACG Parnell College	39 George St	308 1666	all levels	private	co-ed	n/a	368
Newmarket School	7 Gillies Ave	520 2959	primary	state	co-ed	9	225
Parnell School	St Stephens Ave	379 3008	prim+interm	state	co-ed	10	404
PONSONBY							
Bayfield School	2 - 12 Clifton Rd	376 5703	primary	state	co-ed	10	332
Freemans Bay School	Wellington St	378 6904	primary	state	co-ed	8	340
Ponsonby Primary School	Curran St	376 3568	primary	state	co-ed	10	340
Richmond Rd School	Richmond Rd	376 1091	primary	state	co-ed	8	326
Ponsonby Intermediate	50 Clarence St	376 0096	intermediate	state	co-ed	9	462
St Mary's College	11 New St	376 6568	secondary	state integrated	girls	5	729
St Paul's College	183 Richmond Rd	376 1287	secondary	state integrated	boys	3	259
REMUERA							
Corran School	514 Remuera Rd	520 1400	all levels	private	girls	n/a	394
Dilworth School	2 Erin St	523 1060	all levels	private	boys	5	495

Name	Addresss	Phone	Level	Funding	Gender	Decile	Roll
Mt Hobson Middle School	131 Remuera Rd	523 1241	all levels	private	co-ed	n/a	54
Meadowbank School	Waiatarua Rd	520 3739	primary	state	co-ed	10	630
Remuera School	25-33 Dromorne Rd	520 2458	primary	state	co-ed	10	584
St Michael's School	6 Beatrice Rd	520 0933	primary	state	co-ed	10	233
Victoria Ave School	282 Victoria Ave	520 0602	primary	state	co-ed	10	485
Kings School	258 Remuera Rd	520 7770	prim+interm	private	boys	10	656
St Kentigern Primary School	82 Shore Rd	520 7682	prim+interm	private	boys	10	493
Remuera Intermediate	Ascot Ave	522 9890	intermediate	state	co-ed	9	783
Baradene College	237 Victoria Ave	524 6019	secondary	state integrated	girls	10	936
HELENSVILLE							
Westbridge Residential School	488e Don Buck Rd	832 4918	special	state	co-ed	2	51
Tau Te Arohanoa Akoranga	162 Awaroa Rd	420 9300	all levels	private	co-ed	n/a	43
Helensville School	Rata St	420 8005	prim+interm	state	co-ed	5	382
Kaukapakapa School	Kaipara Coast Highway	420 5477	prim+interm	state	co-ed	7	255
Parakai School	Fordyce Rd	420 8494	prim+interm	state	co-ed	4	165
Wainui School	492 Waitoki Rd	420 5127	prim+interm	state	co-ed	9	239
Waioneke School	South Head Rd	420 2884	prim+interm	state	co-ed	7	66
Waitoki School	1119 Kahikatea Flat Rd	420 5244	prim+interm	state	co-ed	10	130
Woodhill School	State Highway 16	420 8108	prim+interm	state	co-ed	7	132
Kaipara College	Rautawhiri Rd	420 8640	secondary	state	co-ed	7	652
HENDERSON							
Arohanui Special School	Tirimoana Rd	838 6696	special	state	co-ed	4	143
Nga Kakano Christian Reo Rua Kura	333 Great North Rd	835 3626	all levels	state	co-ed	3	49
Edmonton School	Edmonton Rd	838 9318	primary	state	co-ed	5	255
Flanshaw Rd School	Flanshaw Rd	834 7224	primary	state	co-ed	5	328
Freyberg Community School	Roberts Rd	838 9664	primary	state	co-ed	6	349
Henderson North School	Norval Rd	838 8229	primary	state	co-ed	2	421
Henderson School	Montel Ave	838 9667	primary	state	co-ed	3	195
Henderson South School	Garelja Rd	838 8766	primary	state	co-ed	2	222
Henderson Valley School	389 Henderson Valley Rd	837 0545	primary	state	co-ed	6	407
Matipo Rd School	Matipo Rd	834 6909	primary	state	co-ed	6	387
Peninsula Primary School	Waipani Rd	834 6711	primary	state	co-ed	4	366
Pomaria Rd School	Pomaria Rd	836 4919	primary	state	co-ed	3	469
Rutherford School	7 Toru St	834 5467	primary	state	co-ed	5	253
Summerland Primary	62 Summerland Dr	836 7460	primary	state	co-ed	8	481
Sunnyvale School	Ribblesdale Rd	838 9248	primary	state	co-ed	4	428
Tirimoana School	Kokiri St	838 9737	primary	state	co-ed	6	571
Western Heights School	Sturges Rd	836 1213	primary	state	co-ed	8	553
Holy Cross School	8 Lavelle Rd	838 8802	prim+interm	state integrated	co-ed	4	486
Taupaki School	Cottle Rd	810 9855	prim+interm	state	co-ed	10	246

WEST

WEST

Name	Address	Phone	Level	Funding	Gender	Decile	Roll
Waitakere S D A School	26 Corban Ave	836 6330	prim+interm	state integrated	co-ed	3	41
Bruce McLaren Intermediate	Bruce McLaren Rd	836 3175	intermediate	state	co-ed	4	530
Henderson Intermediate	70 Lincoln Rd	838 8529	intermediate	state	co-ed	3	511
Rangeview Intermediate	Keru Pl	838 9468	intermediate	state	co-ed	6	830
Te Atatu Intermediate	Harbour View Rd	834 5371	intermediate	state	co-ed	4	255
Henderson High School	Henderson Valley Rd	838 9085	secondary	state	co-ed	3	848
Liston College	16 Edwards Ave	838 9350	secondary	state integrated	boys	6	648
Rutherford College	Kotuku St	834 9790	secondary	state	co-ed	5	1246
St Dominic's College	29 Rathgar Rd	839 0380	secondary	state integrated	girls	6	837
Waitakere College	Rathgar Rd	836 7890	secondary	state	co-ed	4	1374
KUMEU/HUAPAI							
Hare Krishna School	Highway 28	412 6325	prim+interm	state integrated	co-ed	4	71
Huapai District School	40 Station Rd	412 5042	prim+interm	state	co-ed	9	365
Jireh School	Access Rd	412 6386	prim+interm	private	co-ed	n/a	18
Riverhead School	21 School Rdl	412 9105	prim+interm	state	co-ed	8	245
Waimauku School	Muriwai Rd	411 8222	prim+interm	state	co-ed	9	664
NEW LYNN							
Kelston Deaf Education Centre	Archibald Rd	827 4859	special	state	co-ed	3	151
Oaklynn Special School	20 Mayville Ave	827 4748	special	state	co-ed	4	105
Te Kura Kaupapa Maori O Hoani Waititi	441 West Coast Rd	818 2317	all levels	state	co-ed	3	259
West City Christian College	4341 Great North Rd	838 7710	all levels	private	co-ed	6	96
Arahoe School	Arahoe Rd	827 2710	primary	state	co-ed	5	592
Fruitvale Rd	Croydon Rd School	827 2752	primary	state	co-ed	3	296
Glen Eden School	3 Glenview Rd	818 6686	primary	state	co-ed	4	301
Glendene School	Barrys Rd	838 8603	primary	state	co-ed	3	163
Kelston School	5 Archibald Rd	827 2187	primary	state	co-ed	3	404
New Lynn School	Hutchinson Ave	827 4382	primary	state	co-ed	3	242
Prospect School	Rosier Rd	818 5219	primary	state	co-ed	3	488
St Leonards Rd School	15 St Leonards Rd	818 7717	primary	state	co-ed	3	427
TKKM Pumau Ki Te Reo O Ngapuhi	3 Archibald Rd	827 0937	prim+interm	state	co-ed	3	36
Kelston Intermediate	Vanguard Rd	818 5544	intermediate	state	co-ed	3	324
Kelston Boys' High School	Archibald Rd	818 6185	secondary	state	boys	4	1103
Kelston Girls' High School	Great North Rd	827 6063	secondary	state	girls	4	953
SWANSON							
Ranui School	Ranui Station Rd	833 6286	primary	state	co-ed	2	530
St Paul's School	498 Don Buck Rd	832 7200	primary	state integrated	co-ed	6	324
Birdwood School	Karepo Cres	833 8479	prim+interm	state	co-ed	1	299
Colwill School	Kintara Dr	833 6081	prim+interm	state	co-ed	4	394
Don Buck School	124 Don Buck Rd	833 6005	prim+interm	state	co-ed	3	254
Lincoln Heights School	Keegan Dr	833 7480	prim+interm	state	co-ed	4	579

Region	Name	Addresss	Phone	Level	Funding	Gender	Decile	Roll
WEST	Massey Primary School	326 Don Buck Rd	833 7232	prim+interm	state	co-ed	5	419
	Royal Rd School	Royal Rd	833 7675	prim+interm	state	co-ed	3	396
	Swanson School	703 Swanson Rd	833 3500	prim+interm	state	co-ed	5	601
	Waitakere School	10 Bethells Rd	810 9607	prim+interm	state	co-ed	8	387
	Massey High School	274 Don Buck Rd	831 0500	secondary	state	co-ed	6	2359
	TITIRANGI							
	Kaurilands School	Atkinson Rd	817 5645	primary	state	co-ed	7	754
	Konini School	Withers Rd	818 5005	primary	state	co-ed	7	377
	Laingholm School	Victory Rd	817 8874	primary	state	co-ed	8	355
	Oratia School	Cnr Shaw & West Coast Rds	818 6216	primary	state	co-ed	8	517
	Titirangi School	Atkinson Rd	817 8346	primary	state	co-ed	10	499
	Woodlands Park School	Woodlands Park Rd	817 5140	primary	state	co-ed	9	177
	Green Bay Primary School	Godley Rd	817 6666	prim+interm	state	co-ed	8	472
	Titirangi Rudolf Steiner School	5 Helios Pl	817 4386	prim+interm	private	co-ed	9	193
	Glen Eden Intermediate	Kaurilands Rd	817 0032	intermediate	state	co-ed	8	1050
	Green Bay High School	Godley Rd	817 8173	secondary	state	co-ed	7	892
	WEST HARBOUR							
	Hobsonville School	Hobsonville Rd	416 8619	prim+interm	state	co-ed	10	616
	Marina View School	97-99 Marina View Dr	416 7524	prim+interm	state	co-ed	10	680
	Timatanga Community School	9 Mamari Rd	416 6000	prim+interm	state integrated	co-ed	6	20
	West Harbour School	Oriel Ave	416 7105	prim+interm	state	co-ed	3	481
	Whenuapai School	14 Airport Rd	416 8779	prim+interm	state	co-ed	10	379
NORTH	**ALBANY**							
	Kristin School	360 Albany Highway	415 9566	all levels	private	co-ed	10	1586
	Pinehurst School	75 Bush Rd	414 0960	all levels	private	co-ed	n/a	724
	Albany School	6 Bass Rd	415 9668	primary	state	co-ed	10	598
	Coatesville School	Mahoenui Valley Rd	415 9218	primary	state	co-ed	10	283
	Greenhithe School	Isobel Rd	413 9838	primary	state	co-ed	10	452
	Upper Harbour Primary School	140 Kyle Rd	413 7065	primary	state	co-ed	10	n/a
	Oteha Valley School	Medallion D	477 0033	primary	state	co-ed	10	115
	Ridgeview School	Cutts Cres	413 9808	primary	state	co-ed	10	96
	Dairy Flat School	State Highway 17	415 9071	prim+interm	state	co-ed	10	272
	Albany Junior High School	Appleby Rd	415 5473	interm+sec	state	co-ed	10	220
	BEACH HAVEN/BIRKDALE							
	Beach Haven School	Tramway Rd	483 7615	primary	state	co-ed	3	368
	Birkdale North School	213 Birkdale Rd	483 8674	primary	state	co-ed	4	220
	Birkdale Primary School	Salisbury Rd	483 7767	primary	state	co-ed	5	332
	Kauri Park School	McGlashen Pl	483 6539	primary	state	co-ed	6	349
	BELMONT/BAYSWATER							
	Bayswater School	Bayswater Ave	445 6226	primary	state	co-ed	9	147

NORTH

Name	Addresss	Phone	Level	Funding	Gender	Decile	Roll
Belmont School	3a Harrison Ave	445 6605	primary	state	co-ed	9	284
Belmont Intermediate	188 Lake Rd	489 4878	intermediate	state	co-ed	10	525
DEVONPORT							
Devonport School	Kerr St	445 0183	primary	state	co-ed	10	284
St Leos School	4 Owens Rd	445 9339	primary	state integrated	co-ed	10	129
Stanley Bay School	15 Russell St	445 2510	primary	state	co-ed	10	301
Vauxhall School	Morrison Ave	445 0052	primary	state	co-ed	10	249
GLENFIELD							
Wairau Valley School	102 Hillside Rd	444 5552	special	state	co-ed	8	84
Bayview School	Bayview Rd	444 2222	primary	state	co-ed	7	365
Glenfield Primary School	101 Chivalry Rd	441 8730	primary	state	co-ed	7	422
Manuka Primary School	Manuka Rd	444 8775	primary	state	co-ed	8	343
Marlborough School	Wykeham Pl	481 0365	primary	state	co-ed	7	276
Target Rd School	Target Rd	444 8493	primary	state	co-ed	7	378
Windy Ridge School	Seaview Rd	444 3105	primary	state	co-ed	7	242
Westminster Christian School	31 Westminster Gardens	444 1983	prim+interm	state integrated	co-ed	10	160
Glenfield Intermediate	Chivalry Rd	444 6582	intermediate	state	co-ed	8	665
Glenfield College	Kaipatiki Rd	444 9066	secondary	state	co-ed	8	1243
HIBISCUS COAST							
Kingsway School	100 Jelas Rd	427 0900	all levels	state integrated	co-ed	10	798
Orewa North School	Centreway Rd	426 4849	primary	state	co-ed	7	279
Orewa School	Riverside Rd	426 5548	primary	state	co-ed	9	274
Red Beach School	20 Albert Hall Dr	426 8915	primary	state	co-ed	8	554
Stanmore Bay School	Waiora Rd	424 5540	primary	state	co-ed	7	546
Whangaparaoa School	39 Ladies Mile	424 9029	primary	state	co-ed	9	646
Gulf Harbour School	65 Alec Craig Way	428 0202	prim+interm	state	co-ed	9	541
Silverdale School	Foundry Rd	426 5510	primary	state	co-ed	9	129
Stella Maris Primary School	51 Siverdale Pkwy	427 9189	prim+interm	state	co-ed	8	225
The Happy Rainbow Primary School	293 Wainui Rd	426 4411	primary	state	co-ed	9	38
Orewa College	Riverside Rd	426 4075	secondary	state	co-ed	9	1799
Wentworth College	65 Gulf Harbour Dr	424 3273	secondary	state	co-ed	n/a	156
Whangaparaoa College	15 Delshaw Ave	428 4724	secondary	state	co-ed	8	854
LOWER EAST COAST BAYS							
Campbells Bay School	Aberdeen Rd	410 7444	primary	state	co-ed	10	651
Mairangi Bay School	Agathis Ave	478 8424	primary	state	co-ed	10	392
Murrays Bay School	Clematis Ave	478 6239	primary	state	co-ed	10	579
St John's School	87 a Penzance Rd	478 7734	primary	state integrated	co-ed	10	286
Murrays Bay Intermediate	Sunrise Ave	477 2121	intermediate	state	co-ed	10	894
Rangitoto College	564 East Coast Rd	477 0150	secondary	state	co-ed	10	3074

NORTH

Name	Addresss	Phone	Level	Funding	Gender	Decile	Roll
NORTHCOTE							
Birkenhead School	Mokoia Rd	480 7365	primary	state	co-ed	10	357
Chelsea School	Onetaunga Rd	418 0082	primary	state	co-ed	10	333
Northcote School	2 Lake Rd	480 7376	primary	state	co-ed	9	376
Onepoto School	Fraser Ave	480 7469	primary	state	co-ed	1	109
Verran Primary School	Verran Rd	483 7052	primary	state	co-ed	6	209
Willowpark School	Compton St	480 9236	primary	state	co-ed	9	593
St Mary's School	115 Onewa Rd	418 4333	prim+interm	state integrated	co-ed	7	419
Birkdale Intermediate	200 Birkdale Rd	483 9168	intermediate	state	co-ed	6	574
Northcote Intermediate	Lake Rd	419 4700	intermediate	state	co-ed	7	266
Birkenhead College	140 Birkdale Rd	483 9039	secondary	state	co-ed	6	986
Hato Petera College	103 College Rd	480 7784	secondary	state integrated	co-ed	3	133
Northcote College	Kauri Glen Rd	481 0141	secondary	state	co-ed	9	1370
TAKAPUNA							
Wilson School	1 St Leonards Rd	489 5648	special	state	co-ed	8	58
Hauraki School	Jutland Rd	489 4568	primary	state	co-ed	10	343
Milford School	34 Shakespeare Rd	489 7216	primary	state	co-ed	10	479
St Joseph's School	2 Taharoto Rd	489 4994	primary	state integrated	co-ed	9	361
Sunnybrae Normal School	36 Sunnybrae Rd	443 5058	primary	state	co-ed	7	370
Sunnynook School	Lyford Cres	410 6534	primary	state	co-ed	8	488
Takapuna School	23 Auburn St	489 6339	primary	state	co-ed	9	289
Takapuna Normal Intermediate	54b Taharoto Rd	489 3940	intermediate	state	co-ed	10	624
Carmel College	114 Shakespeare Rd	486 1132	secondary	state integrated	girls	10	944
Rosmini College	36 Dominion St	489 5417	secondary	state integrated	boys	10	950
Takapuna Grammar School	210 Lake Rd	489 4167	secondary	state	co-ed	10	1394
UPPER EAST COAST BAYS							
The Corelli School	50 Anzac Rd	476 5043	all levels	private	co-ed	10	66
Browns Bay School	Masterton Rd	479 4301	primary	state	co-ed	10	574
Glamorgan School	Glamorgan Dr	473 6453	primary	state	co-ed	10	562
Long Bay School	Ralph Eagles Pl	473 6077	primary	state	co-ed	10	333
Pinehill School	Hugh Green Dr	478 0301	primary	state	co-ed	10	542
Sherwood School	Sartors Ave	478 3024	primary	state	co-ed	10	449
Torbay School	Deep Creek Rd	473 8603	primary	state	co-ed	10	431
Northcross Intermediate	10 Sartors Ave	477 0167	intermediate	state	co-ed	10	1121
Long Bay College	Ashley Ave	473 2500	secondary	state	co-ed	10	1590
WESTLAKE							
Forrest Hill School	50 Forrest Hill Rd	410 8939	primary	state	co-ed	8	376
Wairau Intermediate	Becroft Dr	410 7805	intermediate	state	co-ed	8	409
Westlake Boys' High School	Forrest Hill Rd	410 8667	secondary	state	boys	10	2100
Westlake Girls' High School	2 Wairau Rd	489 4169	secondary	state	girls	10	2174

EAST

Name	Addresss	Phone	Level	Funding	Gender	Decile	Roll
WARKWORTH							
Kaipara Flats School	School Rd	422 5819	primary	state	co-ed	7	80
Leigh School	Hauraki Rd	422 6031	primary	state	co-ed	6	50
Matakana School	Main Rd	422 7309	primary	state	co-ed	7	378
Warkworth School	35 Hill St	425 8300	primary	state	co-ed	8	551
Ahuroa School	Ahuroa Rd	422 5898	prim+interm	state	co-ed	2	9
Mahurangi Christian School	406-410 Mahurangi East Rd	425 6878	prim+interm	state integrated	co-ed	7	109
Tauhoa School	Naumai Rd	422 5722	prim+interm	state	co-ed	7	41
Mahurangi College	Woodcocks Rd	425 8039	secondary	state	co-ed	7	1185
BEACHLANDS/MARAETAI							
Beachlands School	18 Bell Rd	536 6757	prim+interm	state	co-ed	9	396
Maraetai Beach School	154 Maraetai Dr	536 6570	prim+interm	state	co-ed	9	241
BOTANY DOWNS							
Botany Downs School	Mirrabooka Ave	534 9848	primary	state	co-ed	9	468
Botany Downs College	575 Chapel Rd	273 2310	secondary	state	co-ed	10	642
BUCKLANDS BEACH							
Waimokoia Residential School	Thurston Place	538 0036	special	state	co-ed	2	41
Bucklands Beach Primary School	107 Clovelly Rd	534 6543	primary	state	co-ed	10	291
Macleans Primary School	Wycherley Drive	534 5191	primary	state	co-ed	9	344
Pigeon Mountain School	22 Wells Rd	534 9765	primary	state	co-ed	10	463
Bucklands Beach Intermediate	247 Bucklands Beach Rd	534 2896	intermediate	state	co-ed	10	761
Macleans College	Macleans Rd	535 2620	secondary	state	co-ed	10	2298
HALF MOON BAY							
Wakaaranga School	18 Butley Dr	576 8205	primary	state	co-ed	9	610
HOWICK							
Elim Christian College	159 Botany Rd	538 0368	all levels	state integrated	co-ed	9	526
Cockle Bay School	Sandspit Rd	534 8333	primary	state	co-ed	10	696
Howick Primary School	Willoughby Ave	534 6082	primary	state	co-ed	8	358
Mellons Bay School	140 Mellons Bay Rd	534 4363	primary	state	co-ed	10	520
Owairoa School	Nelson St	534 6107	primary	state	co-ed	9	794
Point View School	Kilkenny Dr	274 0637	primary	state	co-ed	10	761
Shelly Park School	Sunnyviews Ave	535 8784	primary	state	co-ed	10	413
Star of the Sea School	14 Oakridge Way	534 6766	primary	state integrated	co-ed	10	508
Willowbank School	Gracechurch Dr	271 1077	primary	state	co-ed	10	757
Howick Intermediate	Botany Rd	534 3922	intermediate	state	co-ed	6	744
Somerville Intermediate School	39 Somerville Rd	535 1070	intermediate	state	co-ed	10	915
Howick College	Sandspit Rd	534 4492	secondary	state	co-ed	10	2139
Sancta Maria College	319 Te Irirangi Dr	274 4081	secondary	state integrated	co-ed	7	469
PAKURANGA							
Anchorage Park School	Swan Cres	576 9175	primary	state	co-ed	4	201

Region	Name	Addresss	Phone	Level	Funding	Gender	Decile	Roll
EAST	Elm Park School	46 Gossamer Dr	577 0070	primary	state	co-ed	7	562
EAST	Pakuranga College	Pigeon Mountain Rd	534 7159	secondary	state	co-ed	9	2199
EAST	Pakuranga Heights School	77 Udys Rd	576 9209	primary	state	co-ed	7	479
EAST	Riverhills School	13 Waikaremoana Place	576 8105	primary	state	co-ed	7	111
EAST	Riverina School	30 Millen Ave	527 7377	primary	state	co-ed	4	295
EAST	St Mark's School	334 Pakuranga Rd	576 5296	primary	state integrated	co-ed	8	279
EAST	Sunny Hills School	17 The Crest	576 8031	prim+interm	state	co-ed	10	556
EAST	Farm Cove Intermediate	Butley Dr	576 6624	intermediate	state	co-ed	9	589
EAST	Pakuranga Intermediate	43-49 Reeves Rd	576 1860	intermediate	state	co-ed	4	411
EAST	Edgewater College	Edgewater Dr	576 9039	secondary	state	co-ed	4	1038
EAST	St Kentigern College	130 Pakuranga Rd	576 9019	secondary	private	co-ed	n/a	1598
EAST	**WHITFORD**							
EAST	Brookby School	West Rd	530 8569	prim+interm	state	co-ed	7	85
EAST	Clevedon School	13 North Rd	292 8654	prim+interm	state	co-ed	10	386
SOUTH	**MANGERE**							
SOUTH	Sir Keith Park School	33 Robertson Rd	275 4455	special	state	co-ed	1	108
SOUTH	Al-Madinah School	8 Westney Rd	275 5195	all levels	state integrated	co-ed	2	334
SOUTH	Southern Cross Campus	Buckland Rd West	255 0404	all levels	state	co-ed	1	1701
SOUTH	Te Kura Kaupapa Maori O Mangere	7 Comet Crescent	275 1821	all levels	state	co-ed	2	263
SOUTH	Westmount School	47 Rennie Rd	256 2266	all levels	private	co-ed	7	941
SOUTH	Zayed College for Girls	44 Westney Rd	255 0904	all levels	private	girls	4	57
SOUTH	Favona School	Wakefield Rd	275 8449	primary	state	co-ed	1	411
SOUTH	Jean Batten School	6 Imrie Ave	275 5733	primary	state	co-ed	1	507
SOUTH	Kingsford School	54 Raglan St	275 9447	primary	state	co-ed	1	440
SOUTH	Mangere Bridge School	Coronation Rd	636 7304	primary	state	co-ed	3	394
SOUTH	Mangere East School	Yates Rd	276 4689	primary	state	co-ed	1	587
SOUTH	Mountain View School	81 Mountain Rd	636 5410	primary	state	co-ed	1	259
SOUTH	Nga Iwi School	60 Mascot Ave	275 4921	primary	state	co-ed	1	513
SOUTH	Papatoetoe North School	Graeme Ave	278 6153	primary	state	co-ed	2	666
SOUTH	Waterlea Public School	House Ave	636 4233	primary	state	co-ed	5	409
SOUTH	Calvin Christian School	22 Rosella Rd	276 7272	prim+interm	private	co-ed	4	33
SOUTH	Koru School	71 Robertson Rd	275 9194	prim+interm	state	co-ed	1	593
SOUTH	Mangere Central School	254 Kirkbride Rd	275 9979	prim+interm	state	co-ed	1	408
SOUTH	Mary MacKillop School	12 McNaughton Ave	257 1435	prim+interm	state integrated	co-ed	1	323
SOUTH	Robertson Rd School	205 Robertson Rd	275 6224	prim+interm	state	co-ed	1	488
SOUTH	Sutton Park School	89 Vine St	276 4560	prim+interm	state	co-ed	1	545
SOUTH	Viscount School	Viscount St	275 4699	prim+interm	state	co-ed	1	767
SOUTH	Sir Douglas Bader Intermediate School	Court Town Close	275 4332	intermediate	state	co-ed	1	292
SOUTH	Ambury Park Centre for Riding Therapy	66 Wellesley Rd	634 0763	secondary	private	co-ed	n/a	31
SOUTH	Auckland Seventh-Day Adventist HS	119 Mountain Rd	275 9640	secondary	state integrated	co-ed	2	312

Name	Addresss	Phone	Level	Funding	Gender	Decile	Roll
De La Salle College	81 Gray Ave	276 4319	secondary	state integrated	boys	1	881
Mangere College	Bader Drive	275 4029	secondary	state	co-ed	1	715
MANUKAU/CLOVER PARK							
The Bridge Academy	Cnr Murphys & Flat Bush School Rd	535 0574	all levels	private	co-ed	n/a	17
Everglade School	64 Everglade Dr	262 0244	primary	state	co-ed	7	526
Redoubt North School	Diorella Dr	263 9060	primary	state	co-ed	2	528
Weymouth School	23 Evans Rd	267 3569	primary	state	co-ed	3	490
Baverstock Oaks School	Baverstock Rd	278 6741	prim+interm	state	co-ed	10	113
Wiri Central School	Inverell Ave	262 0594	prim+interm	state	co-ed	1	499
Tangaroa College	Haumia Way	274 5764	secondary	state	co-ed	1	1076
MANUREWA							
Homai National School for the Blind	Browns Rd	266 7109	special	state	co-ed	3	48
Manukau Christian School	150 Great South Rd	266 4444	all levels	private	co-ed	n/a	126
Clayton Park School	Coxhead Rd	267 0077	primary	state	co-ed	3	482
Clendon Park School	145 Rowandale Ave	267 6671	primary	state	co-ed	1	413
Finlayson Park School	85 John Walker Dr	266 5558	primary	state	co-ed	1	850
Hillpark School	57 Grand Vue Rd	267 6252	primary	state	co-ed	8	499
Homai School	89 Browns Rd	266 8918	primary	state	co-ed	2	359
Leabank School	Dr Pickering Ave	267 6939	primary	state	co-ed	2	471
Manurewa Central School	Hill Rd	266 8782	primary	state	co-ed	4	563
Manurewa East School	Scotts Rd	266 9487	primary	state	co-ed	2	305
Manurewa South School	Tawa Crescent	266 8341	primary	state	co-ed	2	384
Manurewa West School	McKean Ave	266 8631	primary	state	co-ed	2	382
Roscommon School	Burundi Ave	266 5731	primary	state	co-ed	1	533
Rowandale School	73 Rowandale Ave	267 6663	primary	state	co-ed	1	465
Te Matauranga	206 Finlayson Ave	266 9493	primary	state	co-ed	1	478
Randwick Park School	Riverton Dr	267 0112	prim+interm	state	co-ed	2	733
Reremoana Primary School	Scotsmoor Sr	269 0069	prim+interm	state	co-ed	8	n/a
St Anne's School	124 Russell Rd	269 0023	prim+interm	state integrated	co-ed	2	521
Te Kura A aori O Manurewa	17 Trounsson Ave	268 2031	prim+interm	state integrated	co-ed	1	87
The Gardens School	101 Charles Prevost Dr	269 0041	prim+interm	state	co-ed	10	418
Greenmeadows Intermediate	Greenmeadows Ave	267 6255	intermediate	state	co-ed	3	560
Manurewa Intermediate	Russell Rd	266 8268	intermediate	state	co-ed	2	746
Weymouth Intermediate	Palmers Rd	266 7455	intermediate	state	co-ed	1	568
Alfriston College	550 Porchester Rd	269 0080	secondary	state	co-ed	4	511
James Cook High School	Dr Pickering Ave	268 3950	secondary	state	co-ed	2	1372
Manurewa High School	67 Browns Rd	268 3888	secondary	state	co-ed	3	2019
Te Wharekura o Manurewa	81 Finlayson Ave	266 0158	secondary	state	co-ed	1	44
OTAHUHU							
Mt Richmond School	30 Albion Rd	259 1425	special	state	co-ed	2	141

SOUTH

Name	Addresss	Phone	Level	Funding	Gender	Decile	Roll
Dingwall Trust School	8 Dingwall Place	278 3675	all levels	private	co-ed	2	13
Tyndale Park Christian School	206 Murphys Rd	274 9771	all levels	private	co-ed	n/a	110
Fairburn School	Pukeora St	270 1130	primary	state	co-ed	1	746
Otahuhu School	41 Station Rd	259 0109	primary	state	co-ed	1	482
Panama Rd School	Panama Rd	276 8508	primary	state	co-ed	1	279
Papatoetoe Central School	Great South Rd	278 7557	primary	state	co-ed	4	694
Papatoetoe East School	Tui Rd	278 5446	primary	state	co-ed	3	533
Papatoetoe South School	Milan Rd	278 5231	primary	state	co-ed	3	533
Papatoetoe West School	Hillcrest Rd	278 6274	primary	state	co-ed	2	742
Puhinui School	116 Puhinui Rd	278 8703	primary	state	co-ed	3	598
Holy Cross School	Carruth Rd	278 8224	prim+interm	state integrated	co-ed	3	372
South Auckland S D A School	42a Puhinui Rd	278 6055	prim+interm	state integrated	co-ed	2	302
St Joseph's School	29 High St	276 4563	prim+interm	state integrated	co-ed	1	317
Kedgley Intermediate	Portage Rd	278 4202	intermediate	state	co-ed	2	687
Otahuhu Intermediate	22-24 Luke St	276 6421	intermediate	state	co-ed	1	434
Papatoetoe Intermediate	Motatau Rd	278 9763	intermediate	state	co-ed	3	896
Aorere College	Portage Rd	278 5608	secondary	state	co-ed	2	1309
Kings College	Golf Ave	276 0600	secondary	private	boys	10	948
McAuley High School	26 High St	276 8715	secondary	state integrated	girls	1	636
Otahuhu College	Mangere Rd	270 1170	secondary	state	co-ed	1	1463
Papatoetoe High School	Nicholson Ave	278 4086	secondary	state	co-ed	4	1798
OTARA							
Bairds Mainfreight Primary School	Edward Ave	274 8271	primary	state	co-ed	1	344
Chapel Downs School	Cnr Chapel & Dawson Rds	274 8002	primary	state	co-ed	2	661
Dawson School	Haumia Way	274 5390	primary	state	co-ed	1	460
East Tamaki School	Preston Rd	274 9246	primary	state	co-ed	1	282
Flat Bush School	Flat Bush Rd	274 8279	primary	state	co-ed	1	415
Mayfield School	Pearl Baker Dr	274 9374	primary	state	co-ed	1	503
Rongomai School	20 Rongomai Rd	274 6055	primary	state	co-ed	1	146
Sir Edmund Hillary Collegiate Junior School	2 Franklyne Rd	274 8269	primary	state	co-ed	1	448
Wymondley Rd School	Wymondley Rd	276 7241	primary	state	co-ed	1	189
Yendarra School	Bairds Rd	274 7431	primary	state	co-ed	1	378
St John The Evangelist School	14 b Otara Rd	274 7558	prim+interm	state integrated	co-ed	1	342
Te Kura Kaupapa Maori O Otara	52 Alexander Crescent	274 6687	prim+interm	state	co-ed	1	100
Ferguson Intermediate	Ferguson Rd	274 8471	intermediate	state	co-ed	1	513
Sir Edmund Hillary Collegiate Middle Sch	2 Franklyne Rd	274 5782	intermediate	state	co-ed	1	245
Sir Edmund Hillary Collegiate Senior Sch	2 Franklyne Rd	274 5782	secondary	state	co-ed	1	541
Clover Park Middle School	51 Othello Dr	274 5807	secondary	state	co-ed	1	320
PAPAKURA							
Rosehill School	50 Rosehill Dr	298 4569	special	state	co-ed	2	94

SOUTH

Name	Addresss	Phone	Level	Funding	Gender	Decile	Roll
Cosgrove School	10 Cosgrove Rd	298 8365	primary	state	co-ed	2	555
Kelvin Rd School	Kelvin Rd	298 8417	primary	state	co-ed	1	432
Papakura Central School	23 Ray Small Dr	299 6009	primary	state	co-ed	5	420
Park Estate School	Park Estate Rd	298 4139	primary	state	co-ed	1	130
Ararimu School	7 Steel Rd	294 8372	prim+interm	state	co-ed	9	133
Ardmore School	Clevedon Rd	299 6228	prim+interm	state	co-ed	6	308
Conifer Grove School	Evanda Crescent	299 7490	prim+interm	state	co-ed	8	498
Edmund Hillary School	Hunua Rd	298 9132	prim+interm	state	co-ed	1	152
Hunua School	Lockwood Rd	292 4889	prim+interm	state	co-ed	9	132
Karaka School	Blackbridge Rd	294 8166	prim+interm	state	co-ed	8	179
Opaheke School	Tasman Dr	298 5410	prim+interm	state	co-ed	7	581
Orere School	Orere Point Rd	292 2736	prim+interm	state	co-ed	3	33
Papakura Normal School	143 Porchester Rd	298 7524	prim+interm	state	co-ed	3	581
Papakura South School	58 Beach Rd	296 9040	prim+interm	state	co-ed	1	160
Paparimu School	7 Matheson Rd	292 5861	prim+interm	state	co-ed	10	56
Ramarama School	126 Ararimu Rd	294 8795	prim+interm	state	co-ed	10	172
Redhill School	Redcrest Ave	298 4377	prim+interm	state	co-ed	1	232
St Mary's School	Clark Rd	298 4450	prim+interm	state integrated	co-ed	6	374
Takanini School	School Rd	299 9349	prim+interm	state	co-ed	2	344
Te Hihi School	Linwood Rd	292 7706	prim+interm	state	co-ed	10	229
Mansell Senior School	Settlement Rd	298 8737	intermediate	state	co-ed	1	304
Rosehill Intermediate	Jupiter St	298 5827	intermediate	state	co-ed	5	306
Papakura High School	Willis Rd	296 4400	secondary	state	co-ed	2	1302
Rosehill College	5 Edinburgh Ave	295 0661	secondary	state	co-ed	7	1820
PUKEKOHE							
Parkside School	184 Wellington St	238 9689	special	state	co-ed	4	101
ACG Strathallan	Hayfield Way Karaka	295 0830	all levels	private	co-ed	n/a	875
Pukekohe Christian School	82 Yates Rd	238 6449	all levels	private	co-ed	7	60
Mauku School	Union Rd	236 3654	primary	state	co-ed	8	78
Pukekohe East School	137 Runciman Rd	238 8708	primary	state	co-ed	9	146
Pukekohe Hill School	Green Lane	238 6374	primary	state	co-ed	5	551
Puni School	Waiuku Rd	238 7403	primary	state	co-ed	4	188
Valley School	East St	238 8774	primary	state	co-ed	5	350
Buckland School	72 George Crescent	238 9419	prim+interm	state	co-ed	7	198
Kings Gate Primary School	53 Victoria St	239 0297	prim+interm	private	co-ed	n/a	26
Paerata School	Tuhimata Rd	238 7050	prim+interm	state	co-ed	4	120
Pukekohe North School	Princes St	238 8552	prim+interm	state	co-ed	1	294
St Joseph's School	94 Seddon St	238 7745	prim+interm	state	co-ed	6	347
Waiau Pa School	Waiau Pa Rd	232 1753	prim+interm	state	co-ed	8	347
Pukekohe Intermediate	Queen St	238 6568	Intermediate	state	co-ed	5	582
Pukekohe High School	Harris St	238 6089	secondary	state	co-ed	6	1513
Wesley College	State Highway 22	238 7014	secondary	state	girls	2	373

Notes

Notes